FIRE FORCE

05

ATSUSHI
OHKUBO

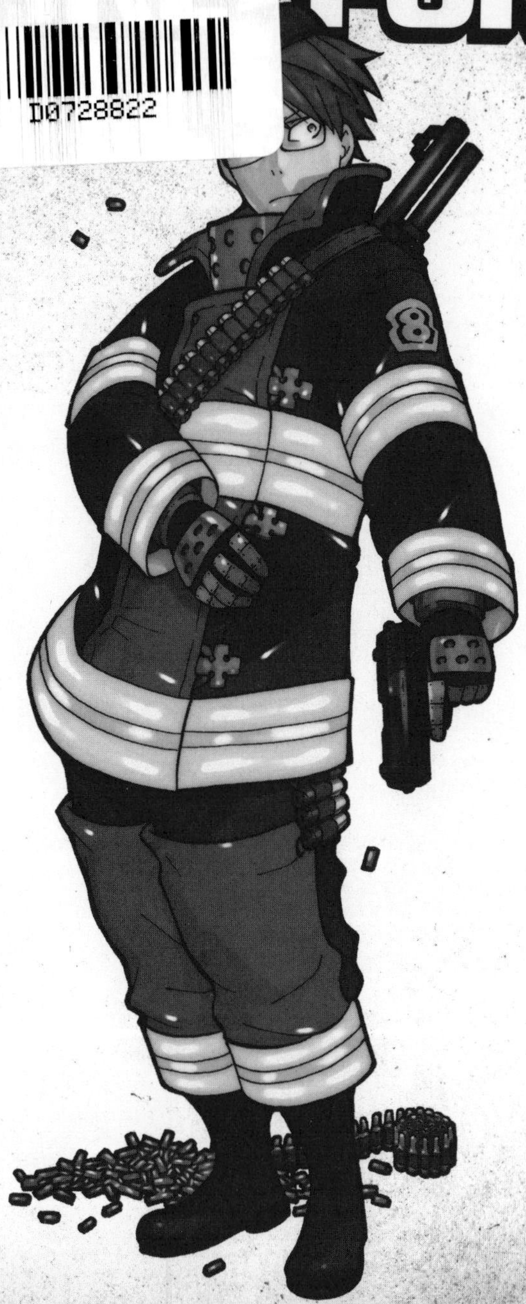

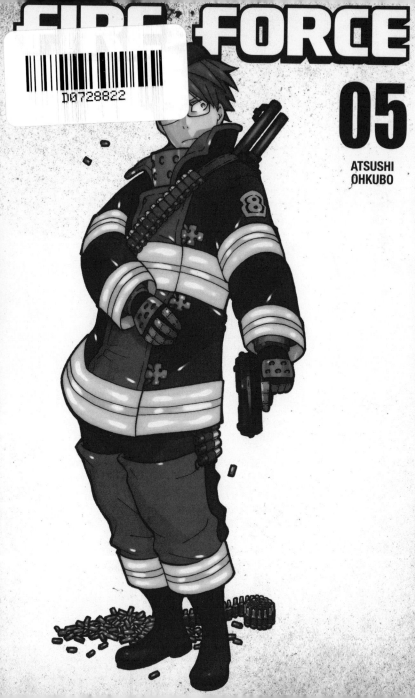

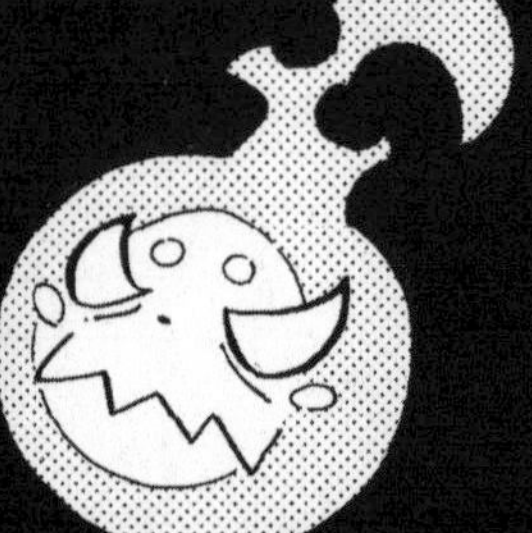

life the inferno.

VOL.5

ATSUSHI OHKUBO

Risking your to calm

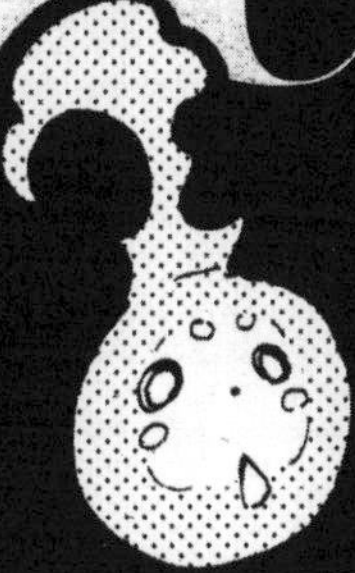

FIRE FORCE

SPECIAL FIRE FORCE COMPANY 8

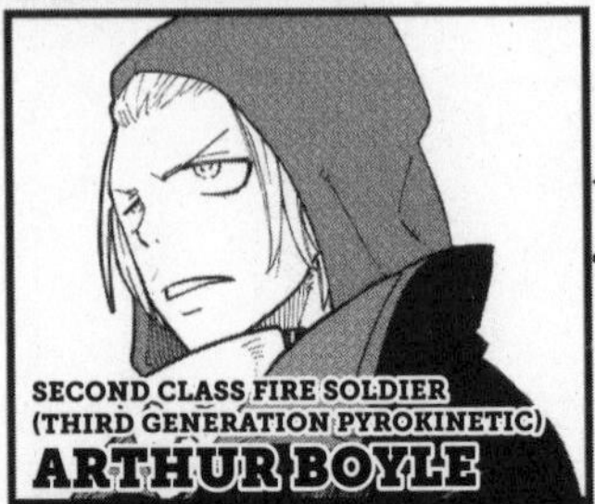

SECOND CLASS FIRE SOLDIER
(THIRD GENERATION PYROKINETIC)

ARTHUR BOYLE

Trained at the academy with Shinra. Although he follows his own personal code of chivalry as the self-proclaimed Knight King, he is so incredibly stupid that he will forget which hand is his dominant one. But girls love him. He creates a fire sword with a blade that can cut through most anything.

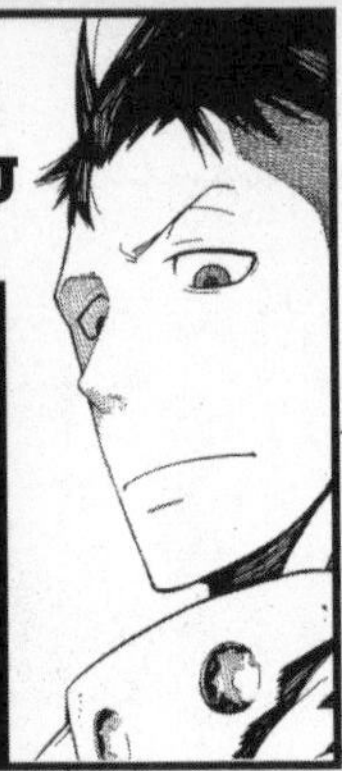

CAPTAIN
(NON-POWERED)

AKITARU ŌBI

The popular and charismatic leader of the newly established Company 8. His goal is to investigate the other companies and uncover the truth about spontaneous human combustion. He has no powers, but uses his finely honed muscles as a weapon to accomplish at least as much as the pyrokinetics. Loves bodybuilding to an almost creepy extent.

WATCHES OUT FOR

TRUSTS

IDIOT!!

WATCHES OUT FOR

TRUSTS

STRONG BOND

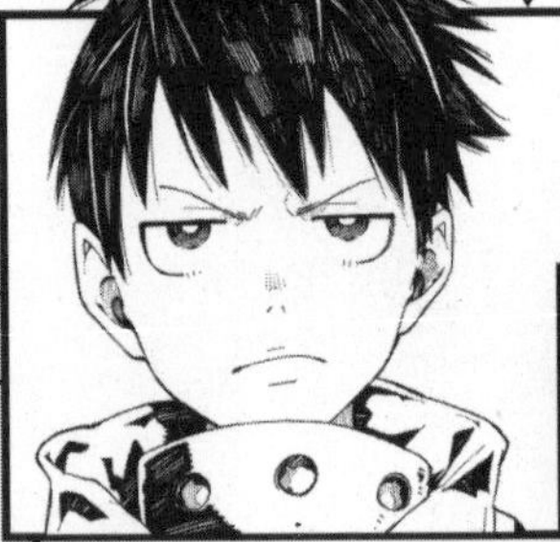

SECOND CLASS FIRE SOLDIER
(THIRD GENERATION PYROKINETIC)

SHINRA KUSAKABE

Since being accused of using his powers to cause the fire that took his family, his face's habit of tensing up into a bizarre smile when he gets nervous has earned him the derisive nickname of "devil." He is searching for his long-lost brother. He dreams of solving the mystery of spontaneous human combustion (SHC) and becoming a life-saving hero!

A NICE GIRL

LOOKS AWESOME ON THE JOB

A TOUGH BUT WEIRD LADY

HANG IN THERE, ROOKIE!

TERRIFIED

STRICT DISCIPLINARIAN

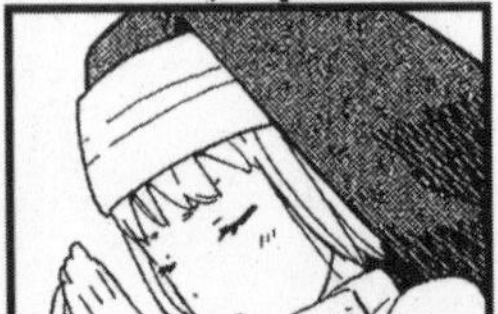

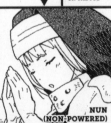

NUN
(NON-POWERED)

IRIS

A sister of the Holy Sol Temple, her prayers are an indispensable part of extinguishing Infernals. Personality-wise, she is no less than an angel. Her boobs are big. Very big. When enjoying girl talk with Maki, she is, surprisingly, the voice of reason.

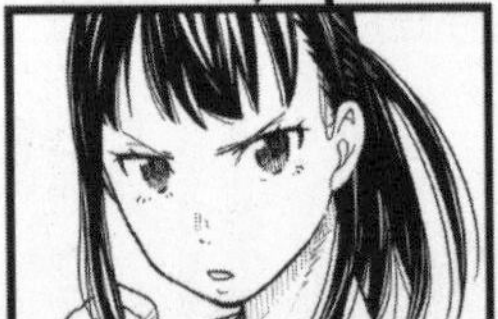

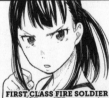

FIRST CLASS FIRE SOLDIER
(SECOND GENERATION PYROKINETIC)

MAKI OZE

A former member of the military, she is an excellent fighter who controls fire. She's a cool lady, but is mad about love stories, and her beauty is overshadowed by her "head full of flowers and wedding bells." She's friendly, but when anyone comments on her muscles she goes into gorilla cyclops mode.

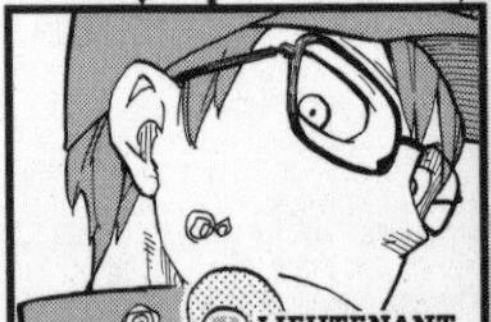

LIEUTENANT
(SECOND GENERATION PYROKINETIC)

TAKEHISA HINAWA

A dry, unemotional ex-military man. His stern discipline is feared among the new recruits, and he will even shoot them in response to their nonsense. He never allows the soldiers to play with fire. Has odd taste in hats. Is a good cook.

THE GIRLS' CLUB

RESPECTS

● SPECIAL FIRE FORCE COMPANY 7

An unorthodox company made up of former vigilante corps members?!

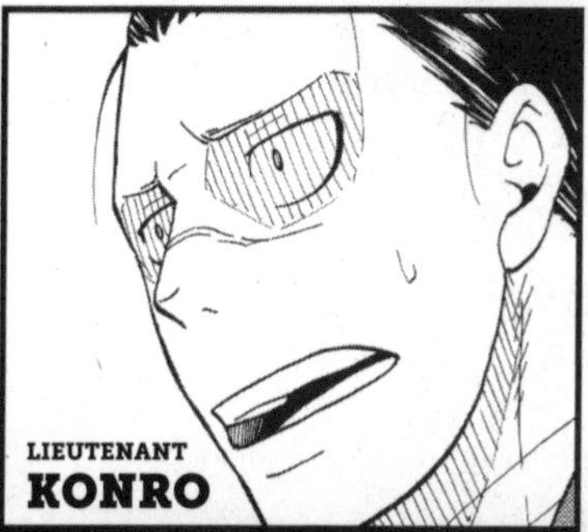

LIEUTENANT
KONRO

The man who is always found at Benimaru's side, addressing him as "Waka." One of Konro's duties is to rein in the combative Benimaru.

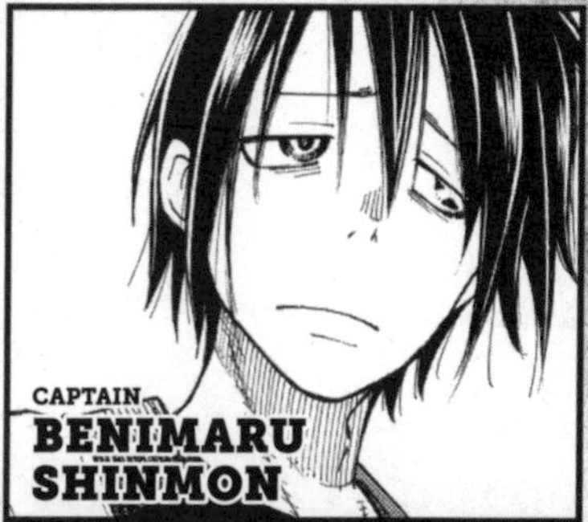

CAPTAIN
BENIMARU SHINMON

The leader of the rough-and-tumble Company 7. There are whispered rumors that he is the toughest soldier on the force. He has little faith in the Great Sun God, and is a proto-nationalist opposed to the reign of the Holy Sol Temple.

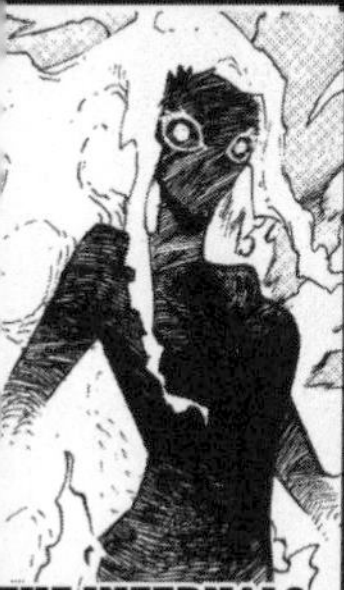

THE INFERNALS

Born from the cryptogenic phenomenon of spontaneous human combustion (SHC), they have no self-awareness, and only wreak havoc until their lives burn out.

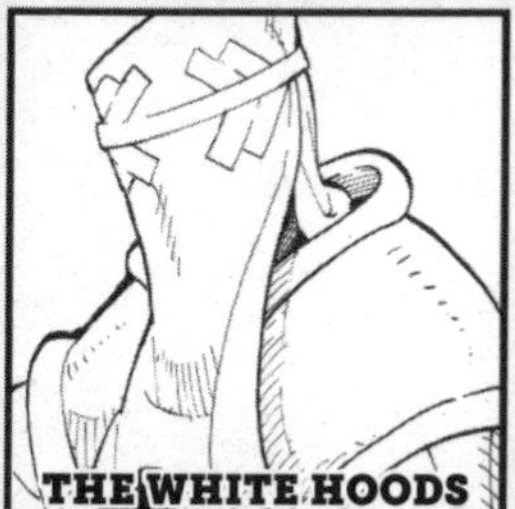

THE WHITE HOODS

An esoteric group that uses bugs to artificially ignite Infernals in their mission to carry out the Evangelist's precepts. They appear to have high-level fighting powers, but there are many aspects of their objective that remain unclear.

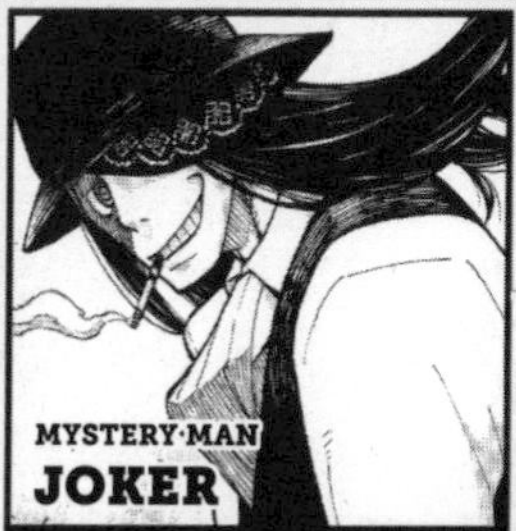

MYSTERY MAN
JOKER

A mysterious man who once crashed the Fire Force's Rookie Games and attacked fire soldiers. He seems to know something about the fire that took Shinra's family 12 years ago, but...?

SUMMARY...

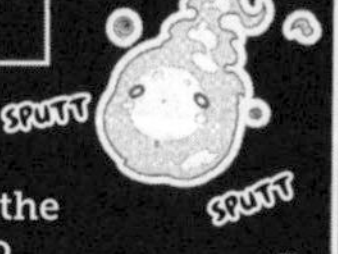
SPUTT
SPUTT

Fire Force Company 1's Lieutenant Rekka Hoshimiya turned out to be a sympathizer of the Evangelist. They finally manage to detain him, but the "white hoods" kill him to keep him from talking. Seeing this as a very serious incident, Raffles III, Sovereign of the Tokyo Empire, assembles the company captains and gives them strict orders to track down the Evangelist. Soon thereafter, the Joker suddenly appears before Shinra, and tells him that if he finds the Evangelist, he'll find his brother, Shō!!

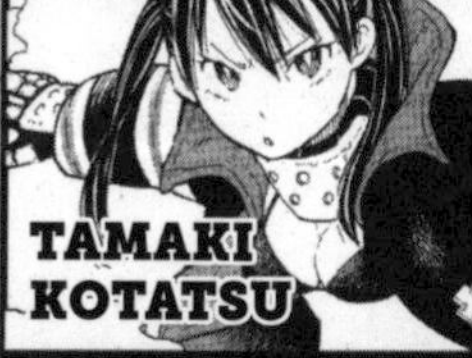

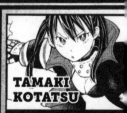

TAMAKI KOTATSU

Originally a rookie member of Company 1, she was caught up in the treasonous plot of her superior officer Hoshimiya, and is currently being disciplined. Ōbi arranged for her to stay with Company 8. A girl with an unfortunate "lucky lecher lure" condition.

FIRE FORCE 05

CONTENTS

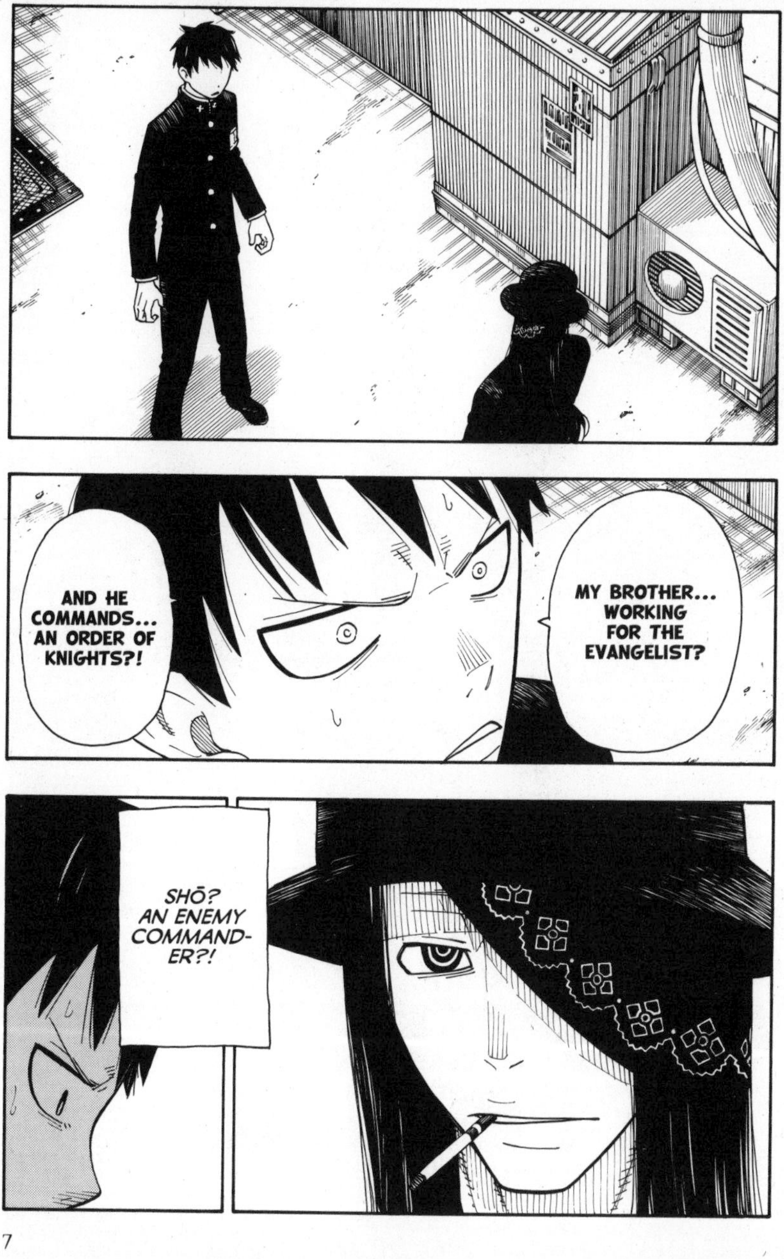
MY BROTHER... WORKING FOR THE EVANGELIST?
AND HE COMMANDS... AN ORDER OF KNIGHTS?!
SHŌ? AN ENEMY COMMANDER?!

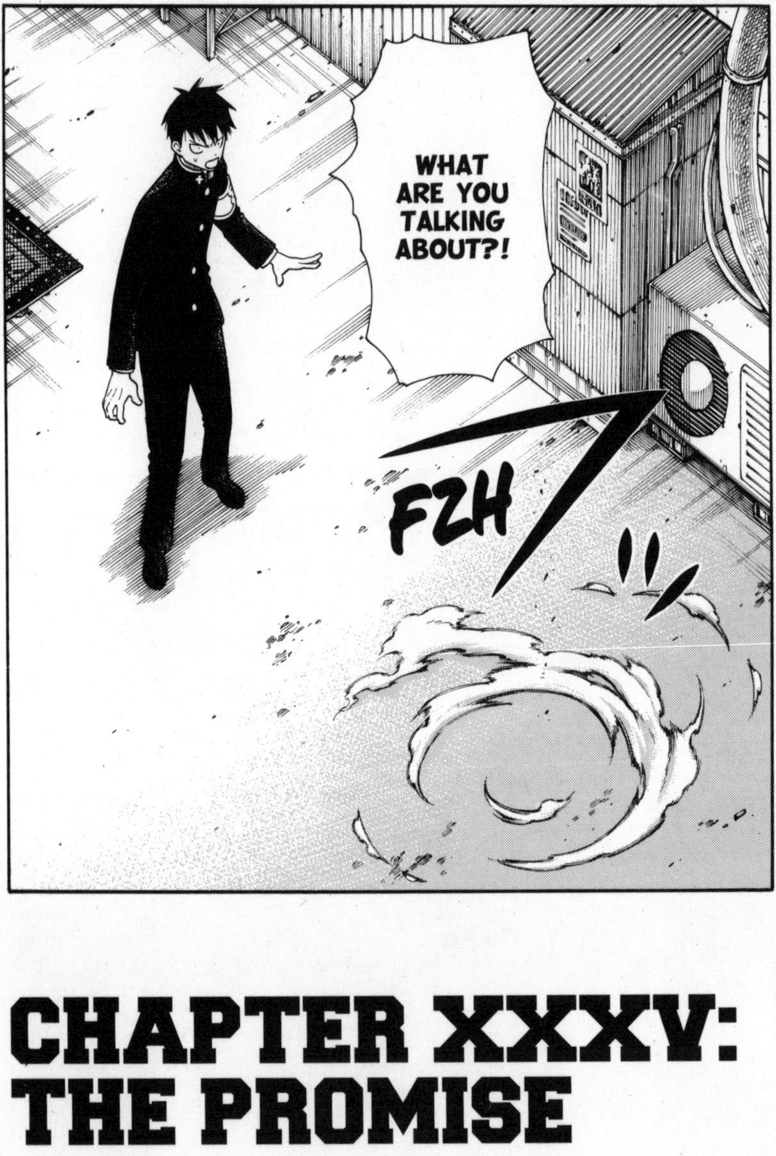
WHAT ARE YOU TALKING ABOUT?!
FZH

CHAPTER XXXV: THE PROMISE

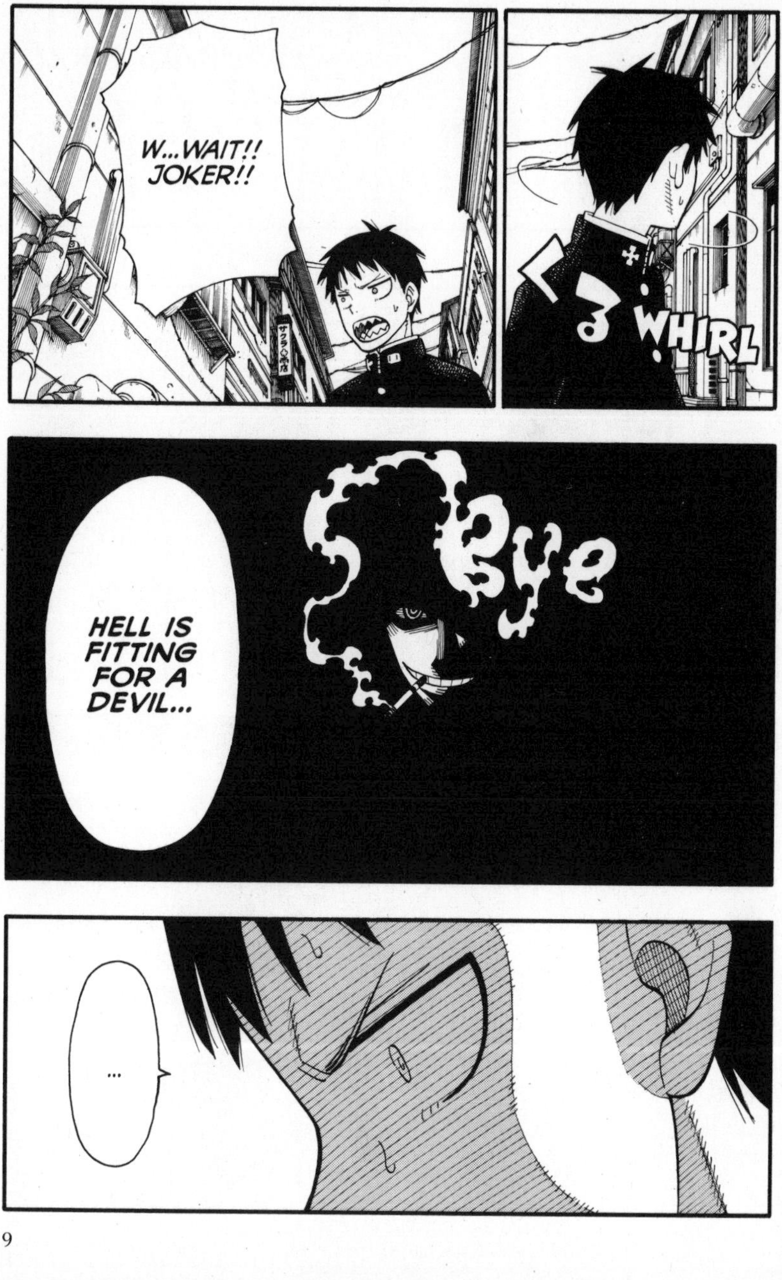
WHIRL
W...WAIT!! JOKER!!
Bye
HELL IS FITTING FOR A DEVIL...
...

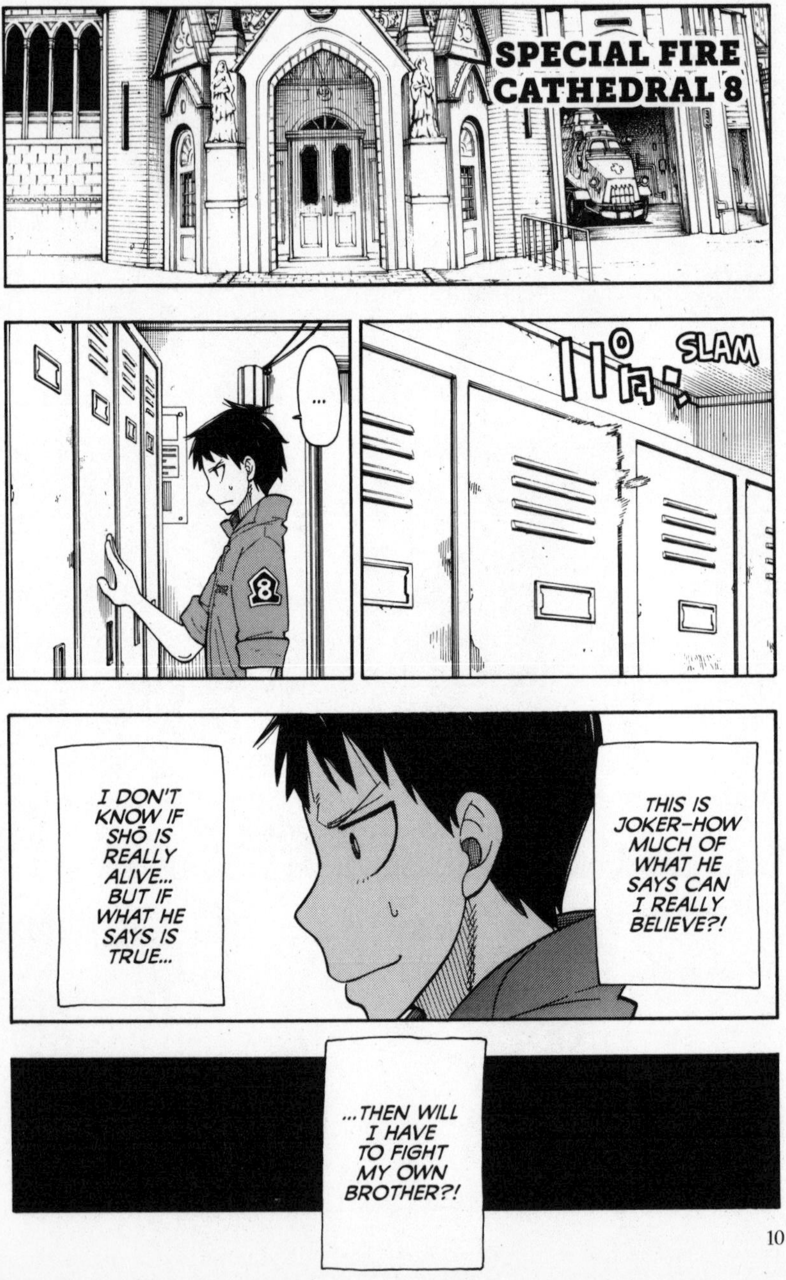
SPECIAL FIRE CATHEDRAL 8
SLAM
...
THIS IS JOKER—HOW MUCH OF WHAT HE SAYS CAN I REALLY BELIEVE?!
I DON'T KNOW IF SHŌ IS REALLY ALIVE... BUT IF WHAT HE SAYS IS TRUE...
...THEN WILL I HAVE TO FIGHT MY OWN BROTHER?!

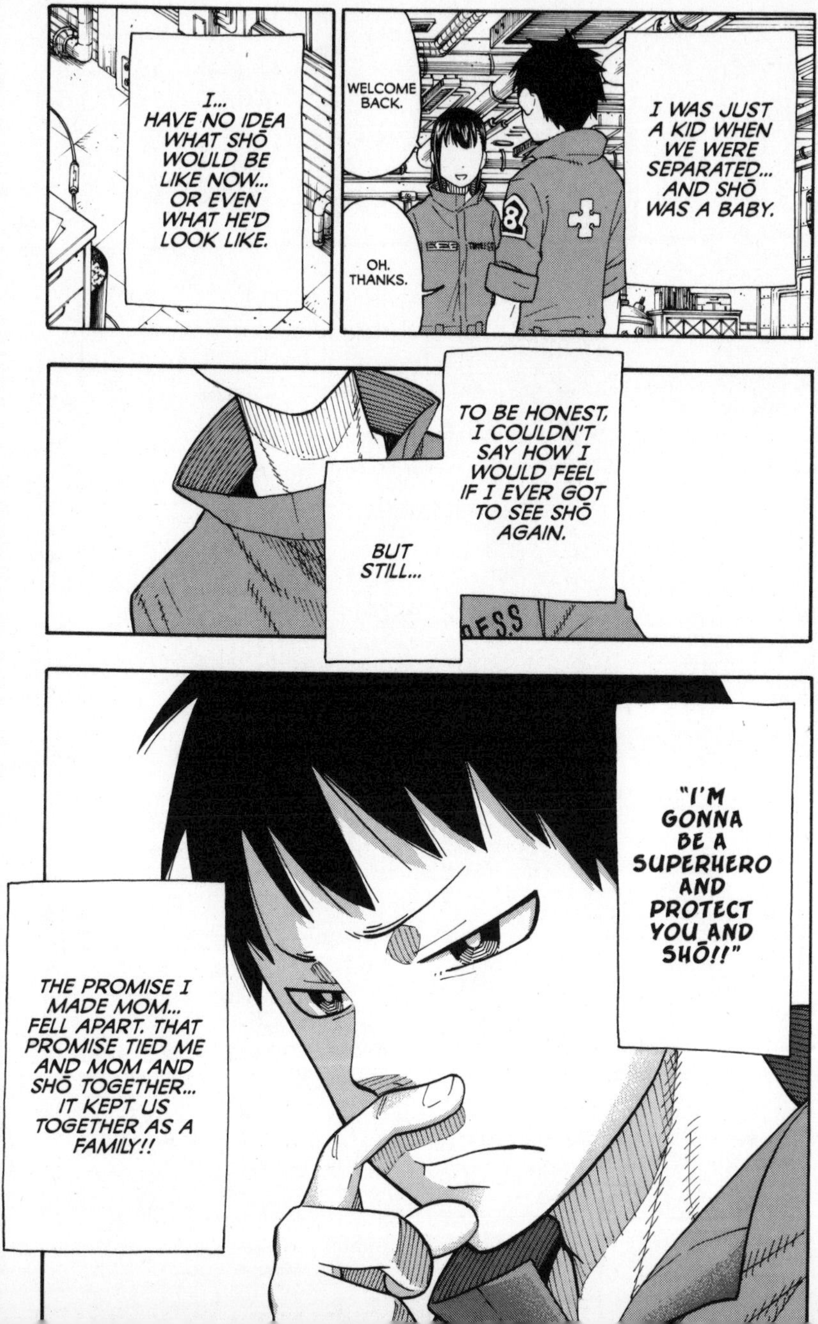
I WAS JUST A KID WHEN WE WERE SEPARATED... AND SHŌ WAS A BABY.
WELCOME BACK.
OH. THANKS.
I... HAVE NO IDEA WHAT SHŌ WOULD BE LIKE NOW... OR EVEN WHAT HE'D LOOK LIKE.
TO BE HONEST, I COULDN'T SAY HOW I WOULD FEEL IF I EVER GOT TO SEE SHŌ AGAIN.
BUT STILL...
"I'M GONNA BE A SUPERHERO AND PROTECT YOU AND SHŌ!!"
THE PROMISE I MADE MOM... FELL APART. THAT PROMISE TIED ME AND MOM AND SHŌ TOGETHER... IT KEPT US TOGETHER AS A FAMILY!!

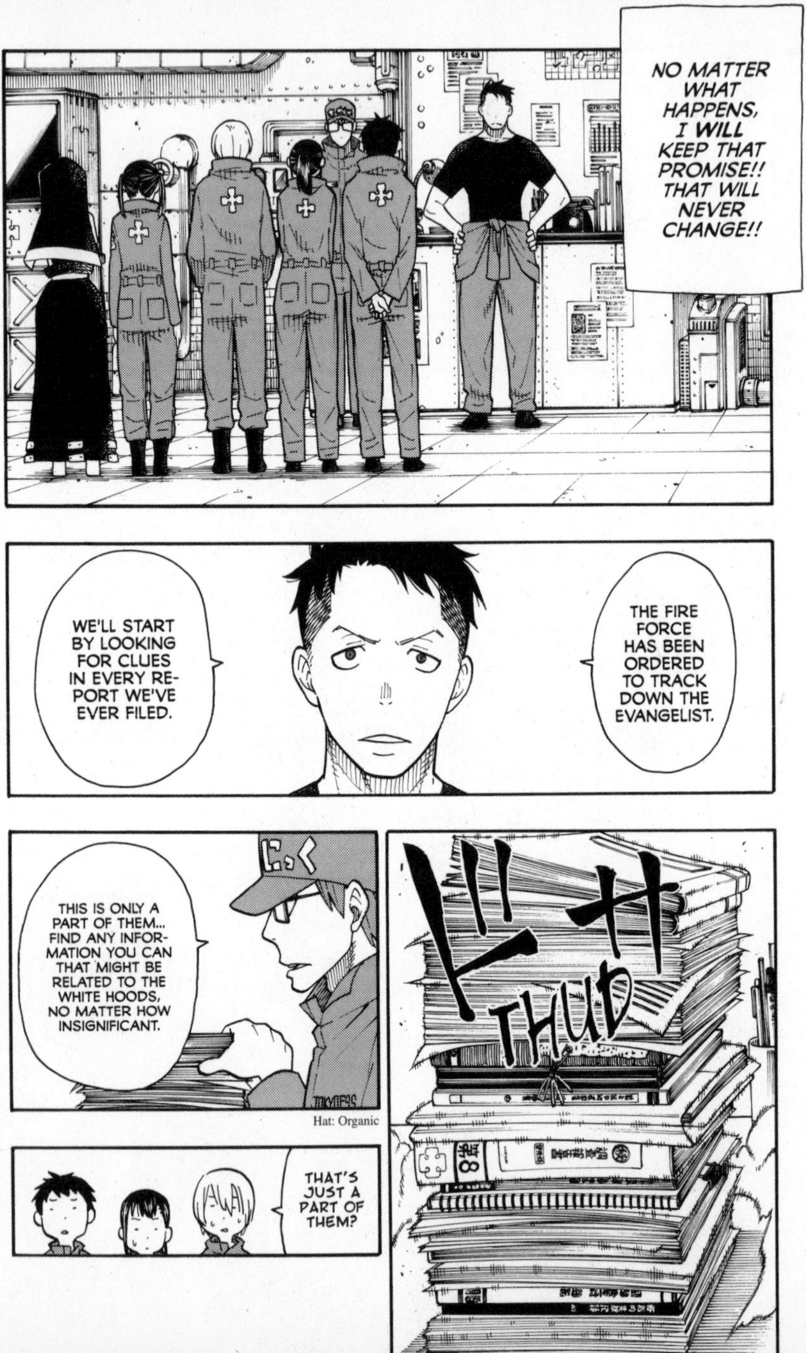
NO MATTER WHAT HAPPENS, I **WILL** KEEP THAT PROMISE!! THAT WILL NEVER CHANGE!!
THE FIRE FORCE HAS BEEN ORDERED TO TRACK DOWN THE EVANGELIST.
WE'LL START BY LOOKING FOR CLUES IN EVERY RE-PORT WE'VE EVER FILED.
THUD
THIS IS ONLY A PART OF THEM... FIND ANY INFOR-MATION YOU CAN THAT MIGHT BE RELATED TO THE WHITE HOODS, NO MATTER HOW INSIGNIFICANT.
Hat: Organic
THAT'S JUST A PART OF THEM?

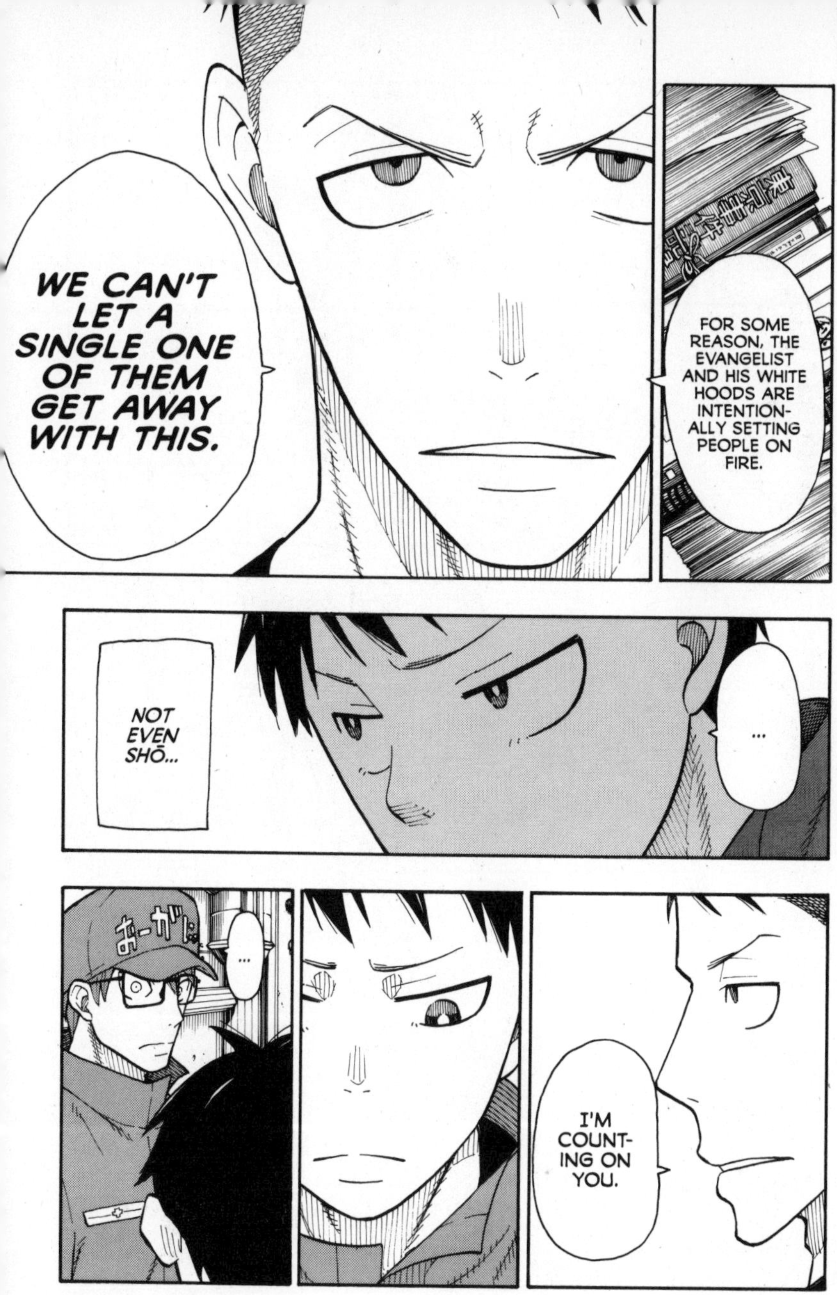
FOR SOME REASON, THE EVANGELIST AND HIS WHITE HOODS ARE INTENTIONALLY SETTING PEOPLE ON FIRE.
WE CAN'T LET A SINGLE ONE OF THEM GET AWAY WITH THIS.
...
NOT EVEN SHŌ...
I'M COUNTING ON YOU.
...

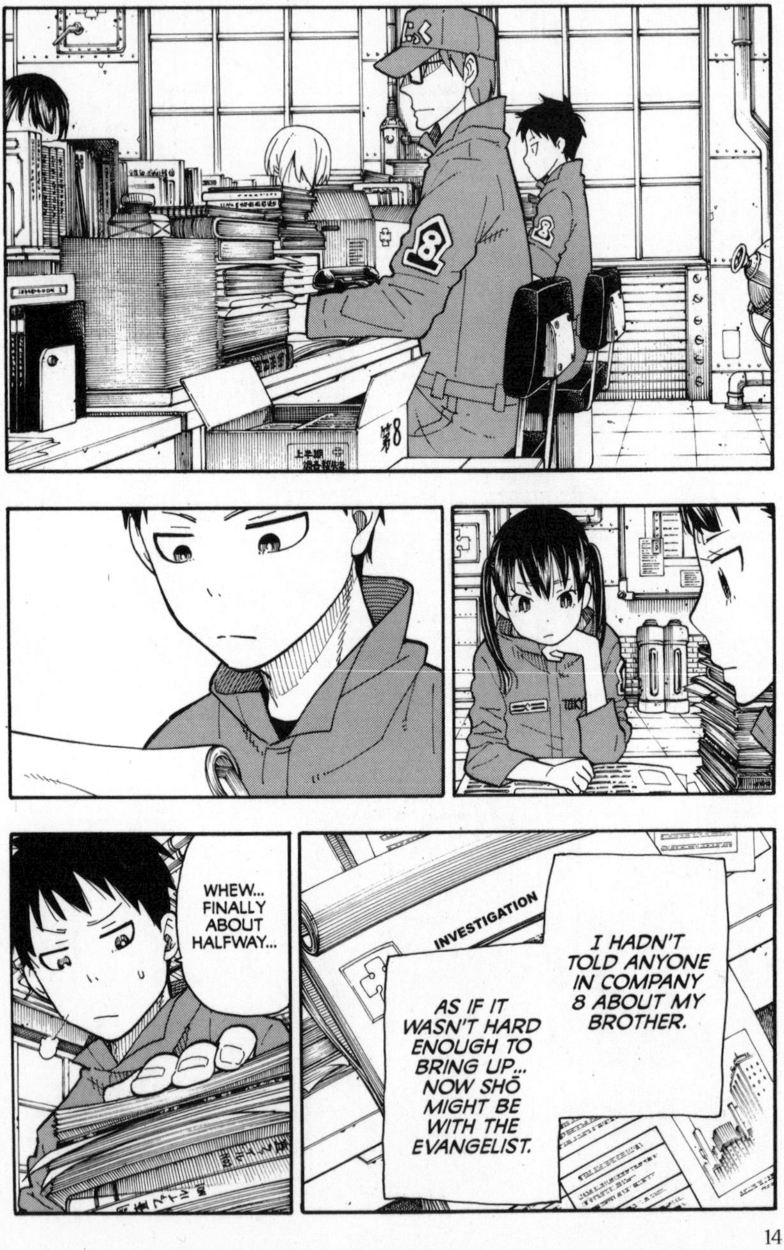
I HADN'T TOLD ANYONE IN COMPANY 8 ABOUT MY BROTHER.
INVESTIGATION
AS IF IT WASN'T HARD ENOUGH TO BRING UP... NOW SHŌ MIGHT BE WITH THE EVANGELIST.
WHEW... FINALLY ABOUT HALFWAY...

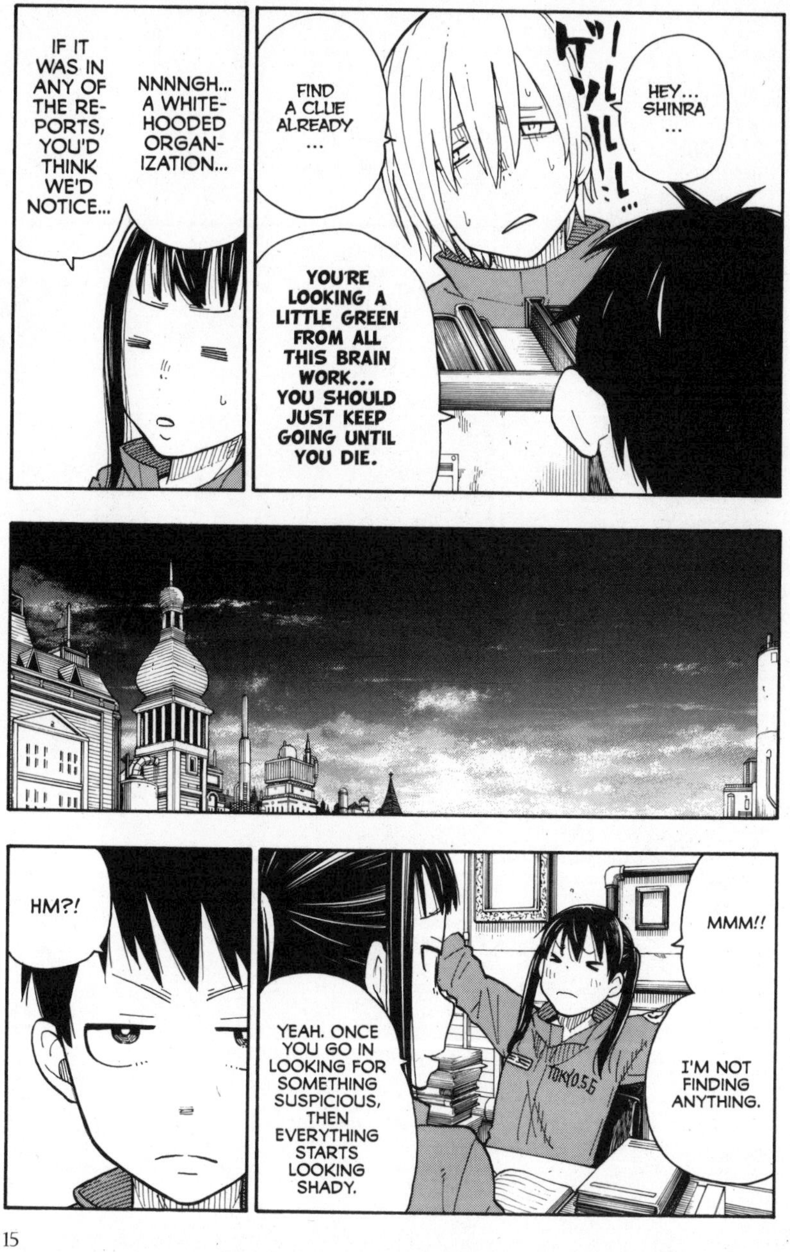
HEY... SHINRA ...
FIND A CLUE ALREADY ...
YOU'RE LOOKING A LITTLE GREEN FROM ALL THIS BRAIN WORK... YOU SHOULD JUST KEEP GOING UNTIL YOU DIE.
NNNNGH... A WHITE-HOODED ORGANIZATION...
IF IT WAS IN ANY OF THE REPORTS, YOU'D THINK WE'D NOTICE...
MMM!!
I'M NOT FINDING ANYTHING.
TOKYO.5.5
YEAH. ONCE YOU GO IN LOOKING FOR SOMETHING SUSPICIOUS, THEN EVERYTHING STARTS LOOKING SHADY.
HM?!

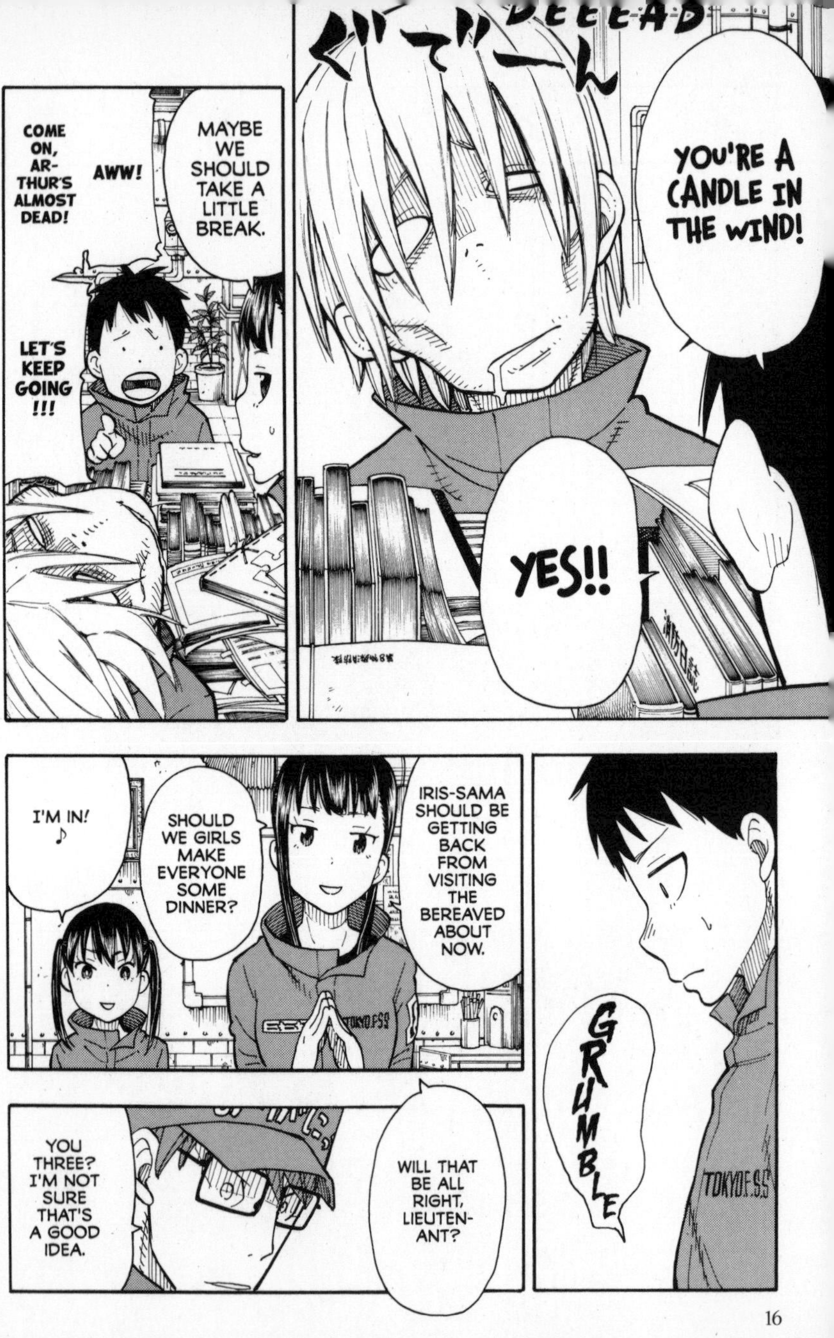
DEEEAD
ぐでーん
YOU'RE A CANDLE IN THE WIND!
YES!!
MAYBE WE SHOULD TAKE A LITTLE BREAK.
AWW!
COME ON, AR-THUR'S ALMOST DEAD!
LET'S KEEP GOING!!!
GRUMBLE
IRIS-SAMA SHOULD BE GETTING BACK FROM VISITING THE BEREAVED ABOUT NOW.
SHOULD WE GIRLS MAKE EVERYONE SOME DINNER?
I'M IN! ♪
WILL THAT BE ALL RIGHT, LIEUTEN-ANT?
YOU THREE? I'M NOT SURE THAT'S A GOOD IDEA.

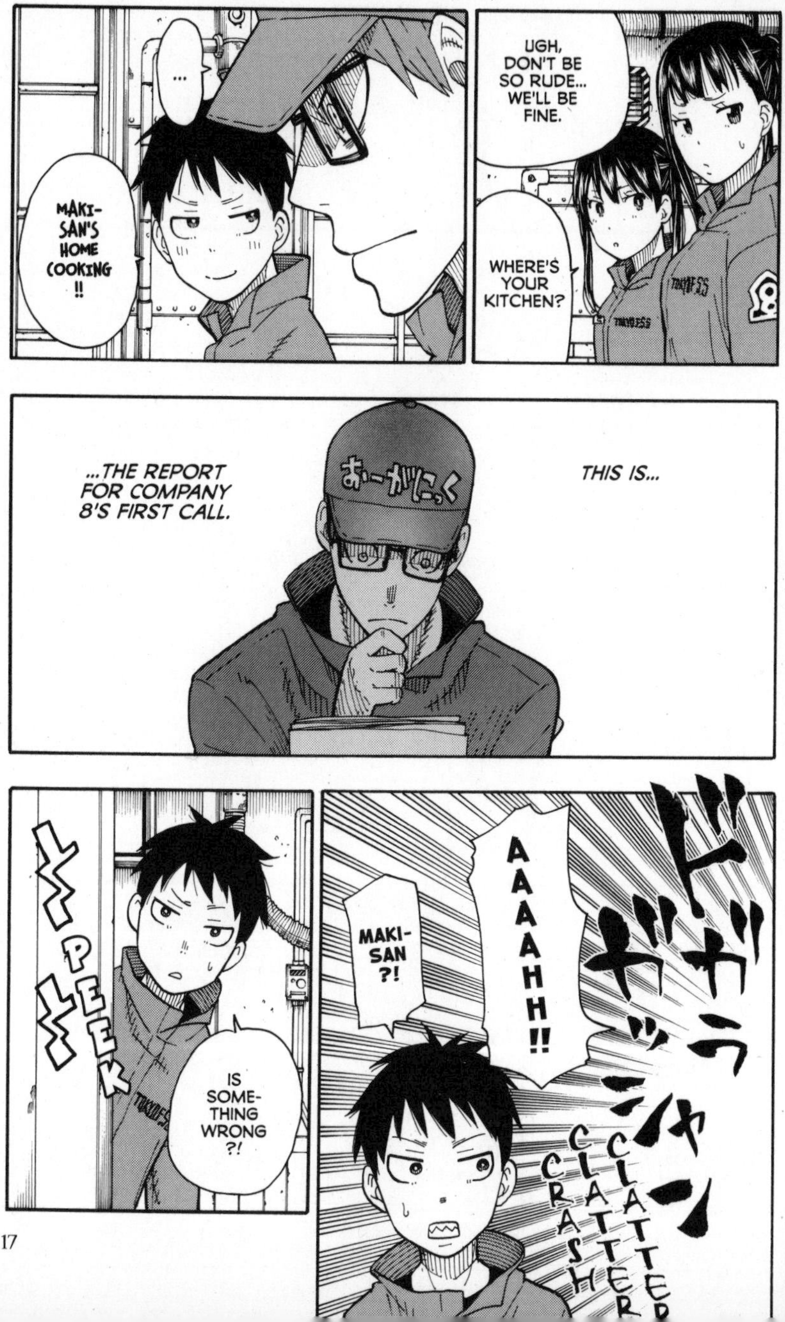
UGH, DON'T BE SO RUDE... WE'LL BE FINE.
WHERE'S YOUR KITCHEN?
...
MAKI-SAN'S HOME COOKING !!
THIS IS...
...THE REPORT FOR COMPANY 8'S FIRST CALL.
AAAAAHH!!
MAKI-SAN ?!
CLATTER
CLATTER
CRASH
PEEK
IS SOMETHING WRONG ?!

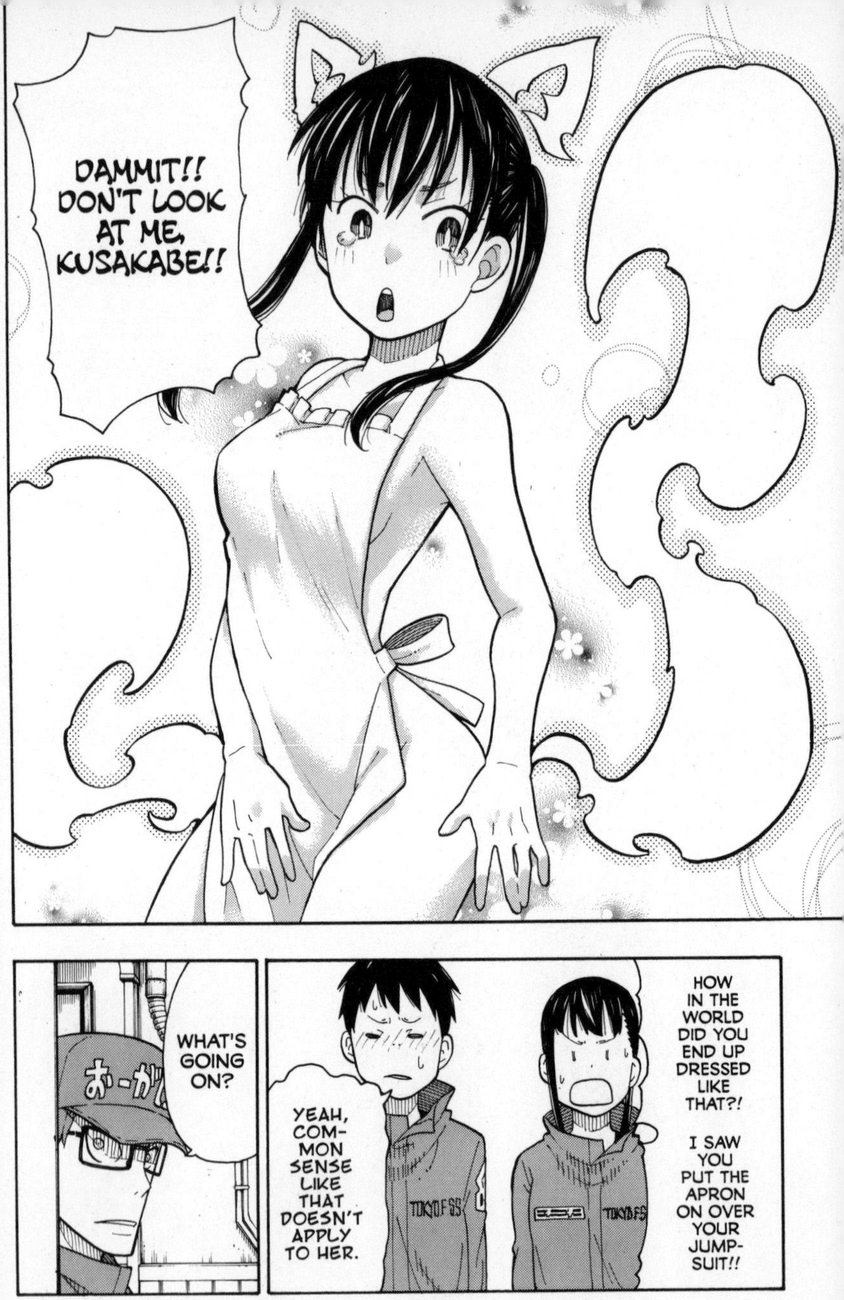
DAMMIT!! DON'T LOOK AT ME, KUSAKABE!!
HOW IN THE WORLD DID YOU END UP DRESSED LIKE THAT?!
I SAW YOU PUT THE APRON ON OVER YOUR JUMP-SUIT!!
YEAH, COM-MON SENSE LIKE THAT DOESN'T APPLY TO HER.
WHAT'S GOING ON?

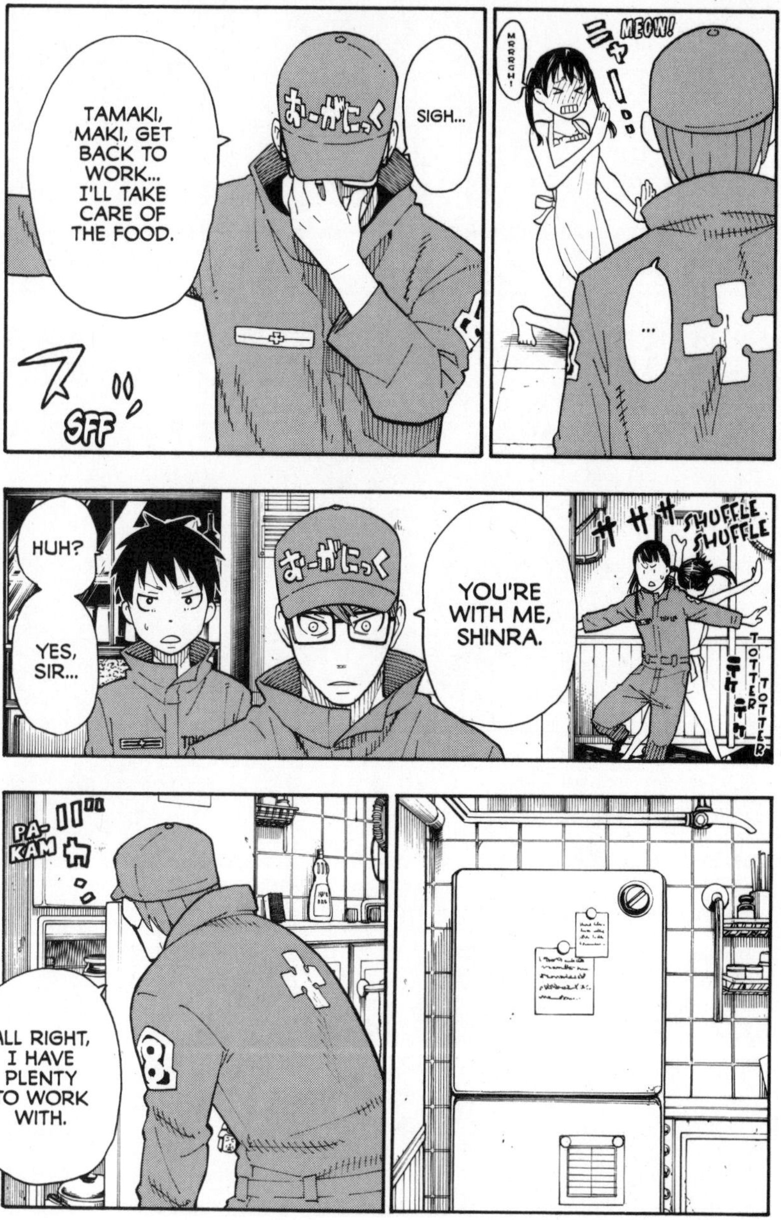
MEOW!
MRRRGH!
...
SIGH...
TAMAKI, MAKI, GET BACK TO WORK... I'LL TAKE CARE OF THE FOOD.
SFF
SHUFFLE SHUFFLE
TOTTER TOTTER
YOU'RE WITH ME, SHINRA.
HUH?
YES, SIR...
PA-KAM
ALL RIGHT, I HAVE PLENTY TO WORK WITH.

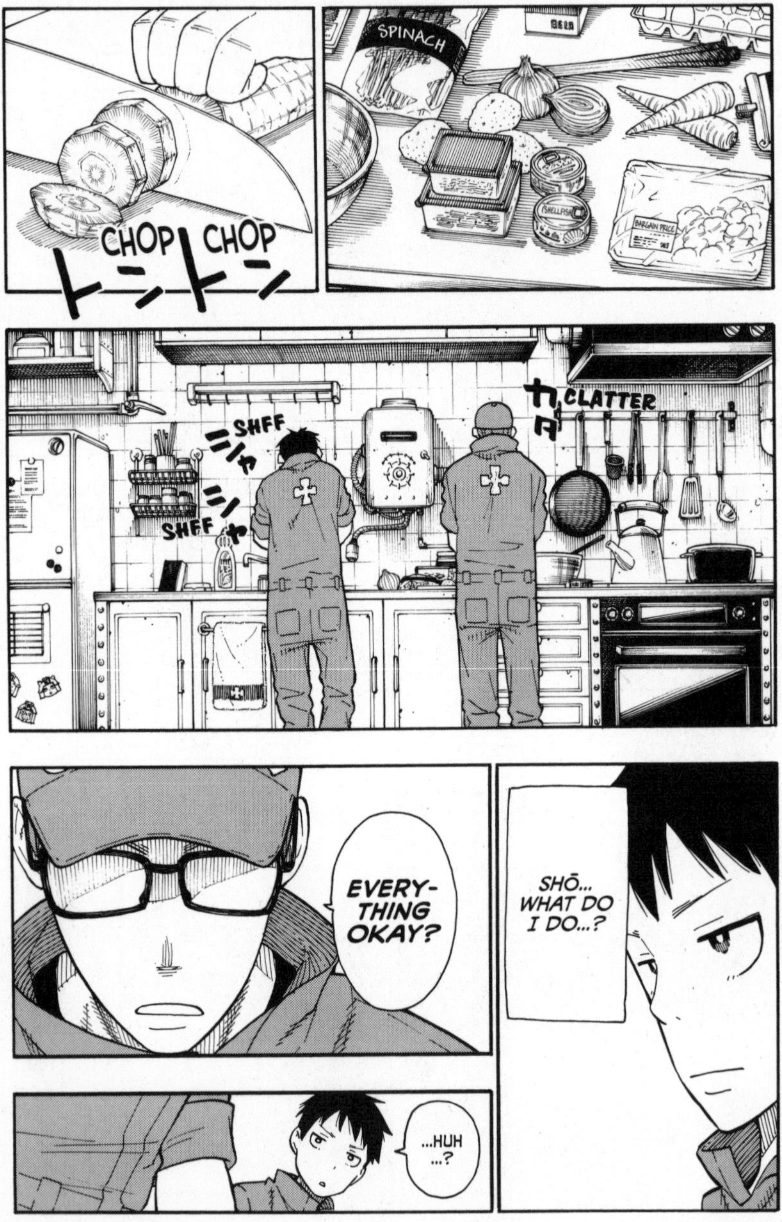
SPINACH
SHELLFISH
BARGAIN PRICE
CHOP CHOP
トントン
CLATTER
カタ
SHFF
シャ
SHFF
シャ
SHŌ... WHAT DO I DO...?
EVERY-THING OKAY?
...HUH ...?

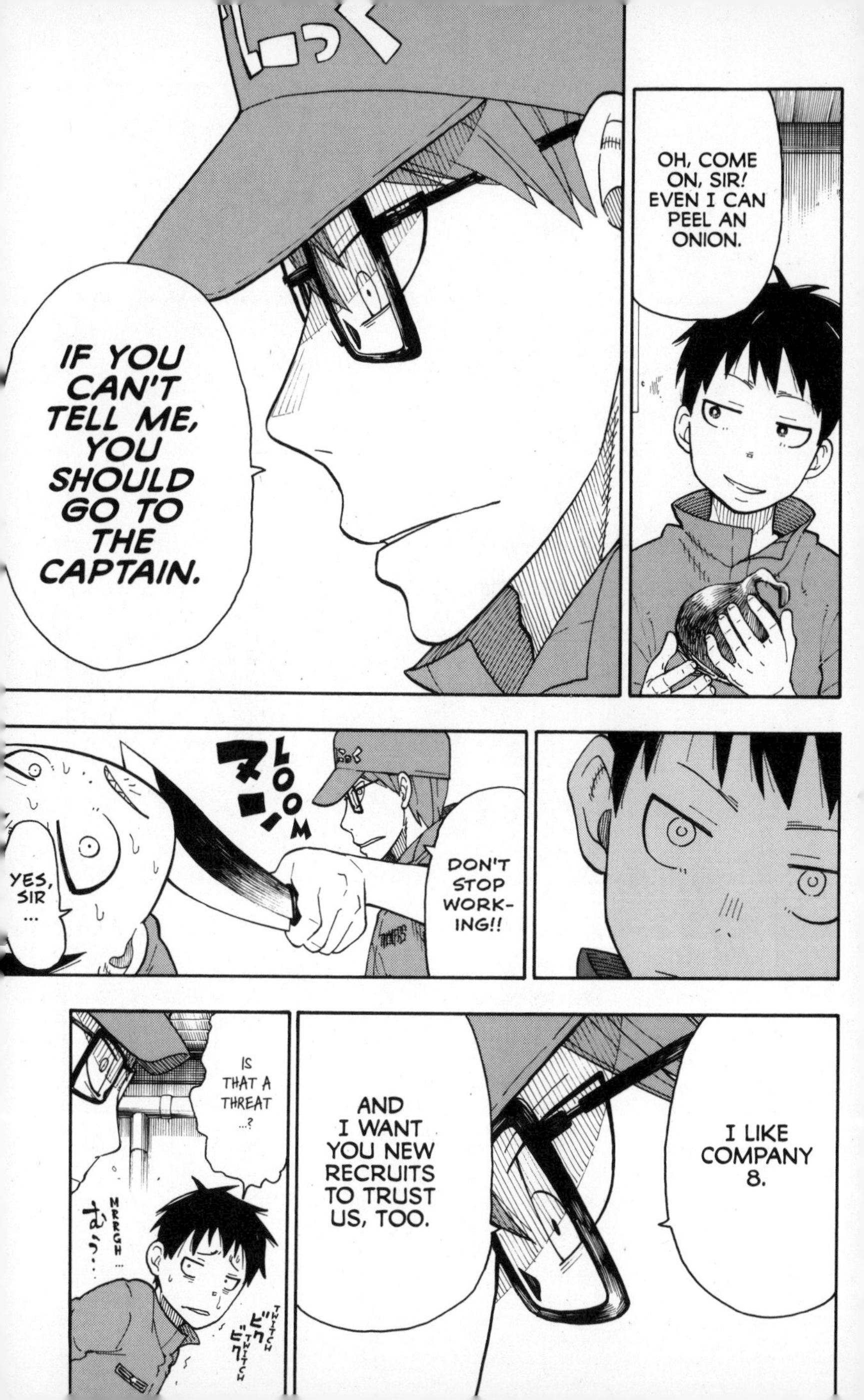
OH, COME ON, SIR! EVEN I CAN PEEL AN ONION.
IF YOU CAN'T TELL ME, YOU SHOULD GO TO THE CAPTAIN.
DON'T STOP WORKING!!
YES, SIR ...
I LIKE COMPANY 8.
AND I WANT YOU NEW RECRUITS TO TRUST US, TOO.
IS THAT A THREAT ...?
MRRGH ...
TWITCH
TWITCH

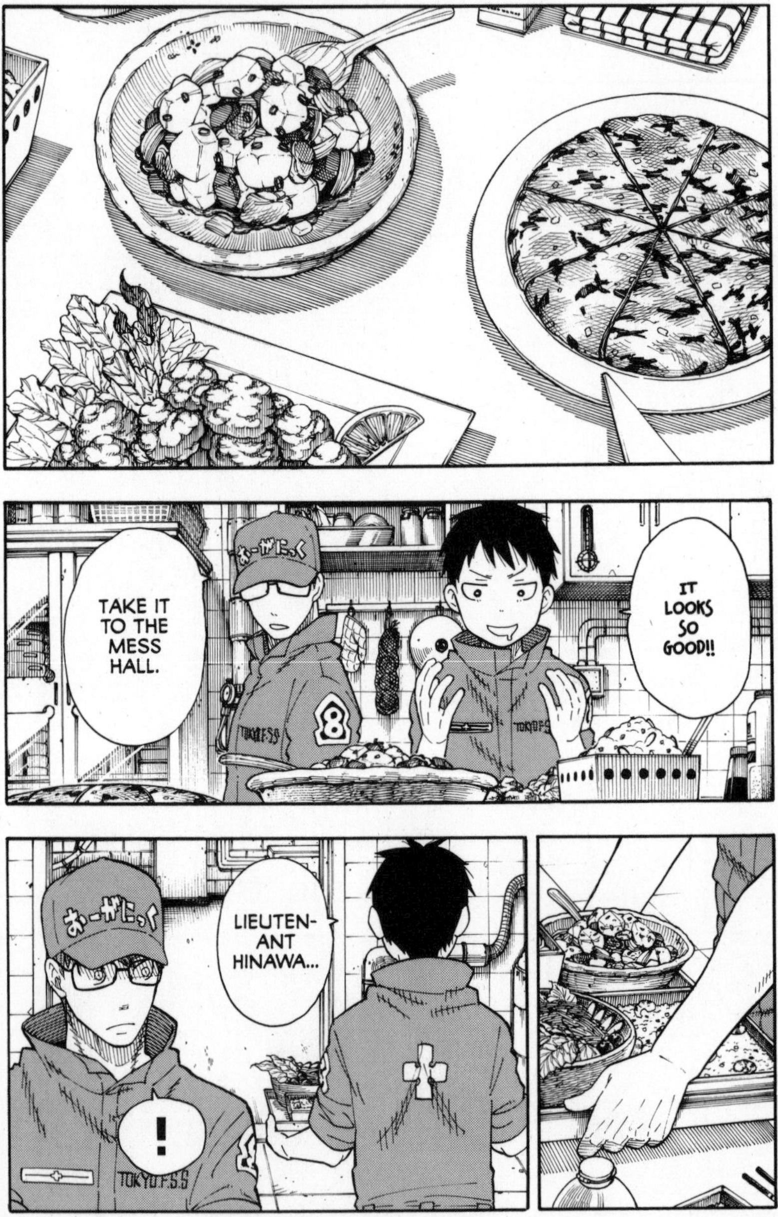
IT LOOKS SO GOOD!!
TAKE IT TO THE MESS HALL.
LIEUTEN-ANT HINAWA...
!

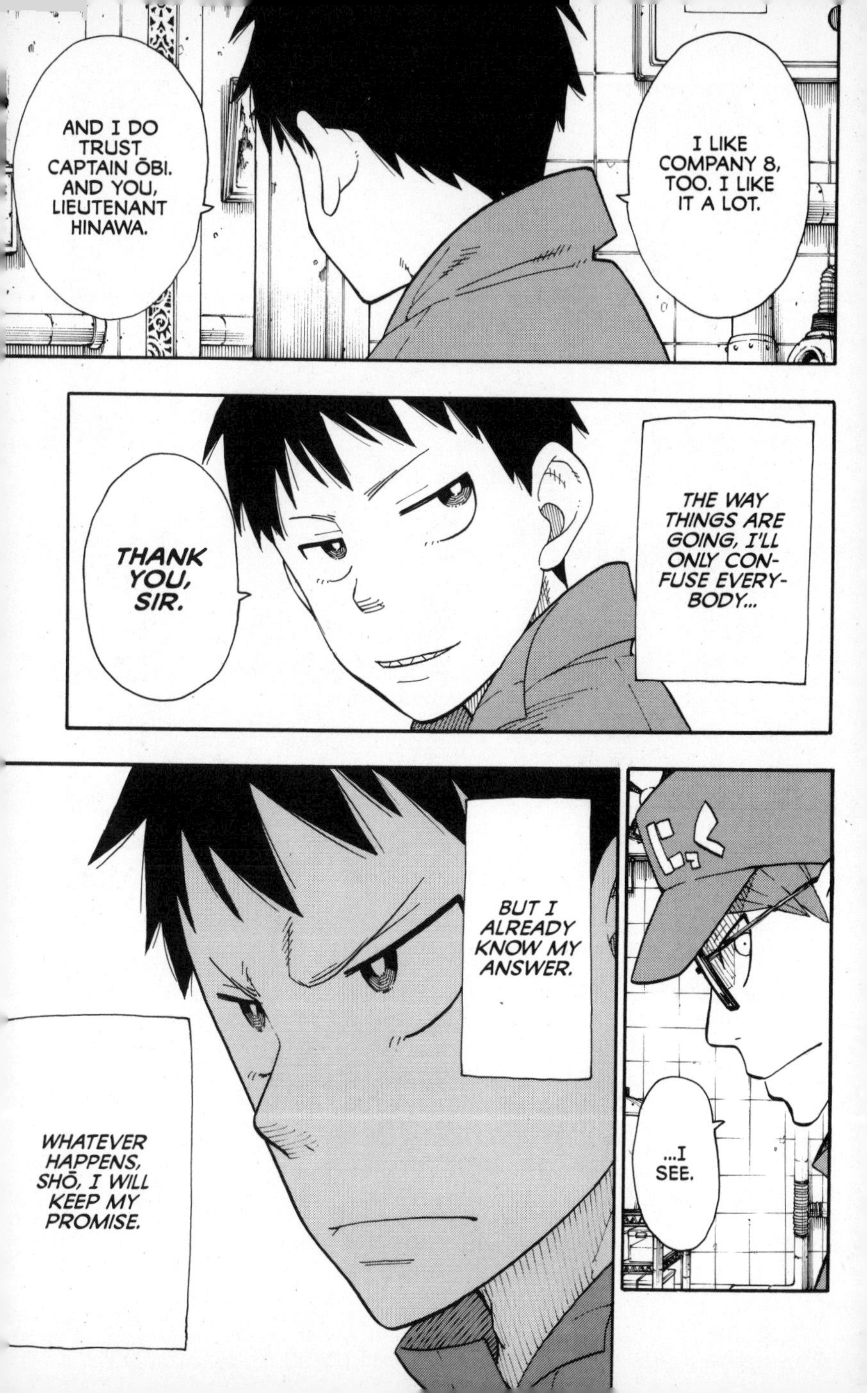
I LIKE COMPANY 8, TOO. I LIKE IT A LOT.
AND I DO TRUST CAPTAIN ŌBI. AND YOU, LIEUTENANT HINAWA.
THE WAY THINGS ARE GOING, I'LL ONLY CONFUSE EVERYBODY...
THANK YOU, SIR.
...I SEE.
BUT I ALREADY KNOW MY ANSWER.
WHATEVER HAPPENS, SHŌ, I WILL KEEP MY PROMISE.

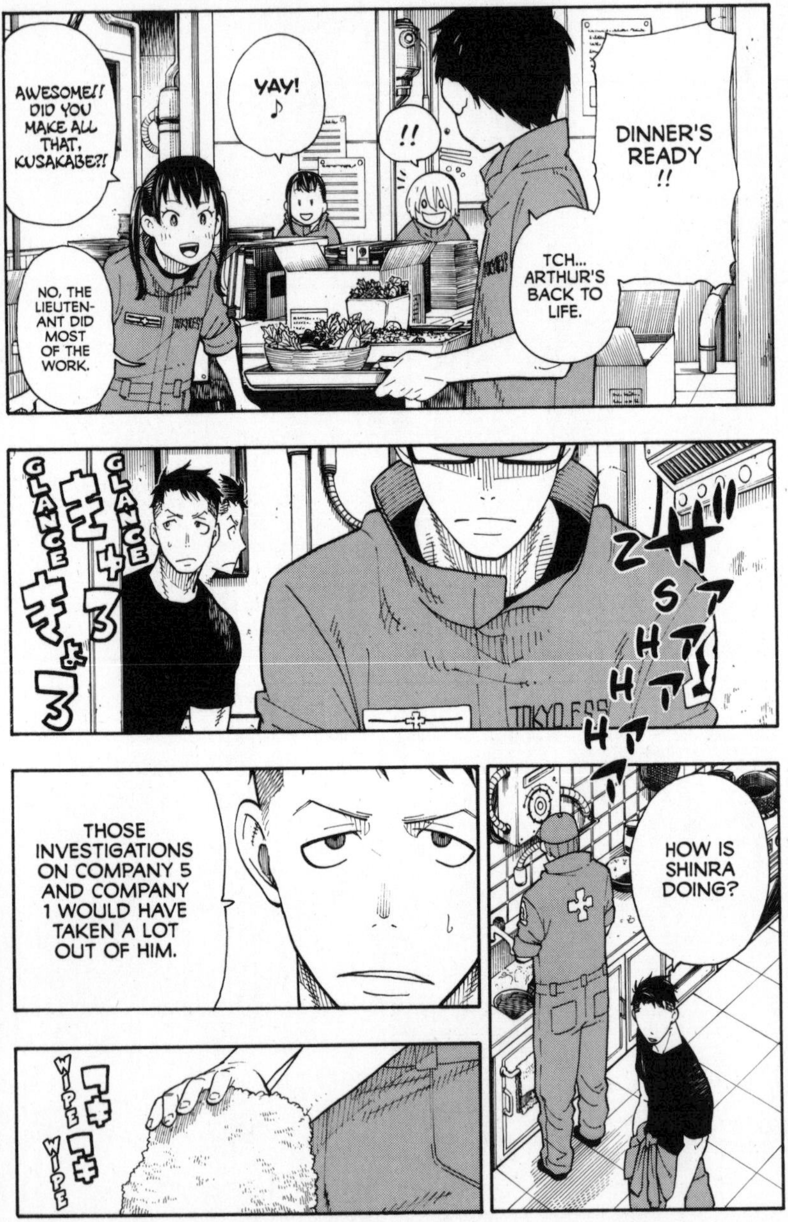
DINNER'S READY!!
TCH... ARTHUR'S BACK TO LIFE.
!!
YAY! ♪
AWESOME!! DID YOU MAKE ALL THAT, KUSAKABE?!
NO, THE LIEUTENANT DID MOST OF THE WORK.
ZSHHH
GLANCE GLANCE
HOW IS SHINRA DOING?
THOSE INVESTIGATIONS ON COMPANY 5 AND COMPANY 1 WOULD HAVE TAKEN A LOT OUT OF HIM.
WIPE WIPE

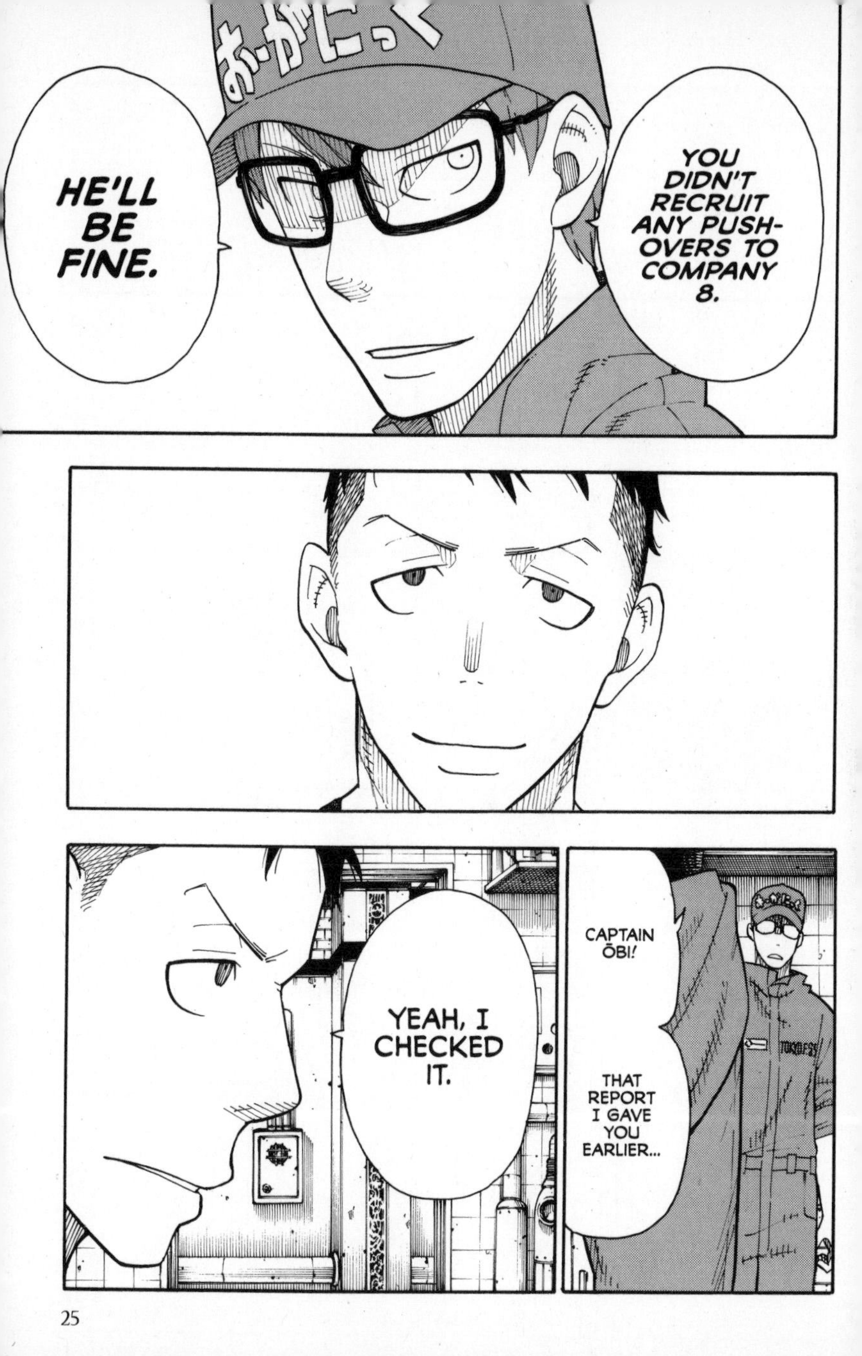
YOU DIDN'T RECRUIT ANY PUSH-OVERS TO COMPANY 8.
HE'LL BE FINE.
CAPTAIN ŌBI!
THAT REPORT I GAVE YOU EARLIER...
YEAH, I CHECKED IT.

Stamp: Company 8

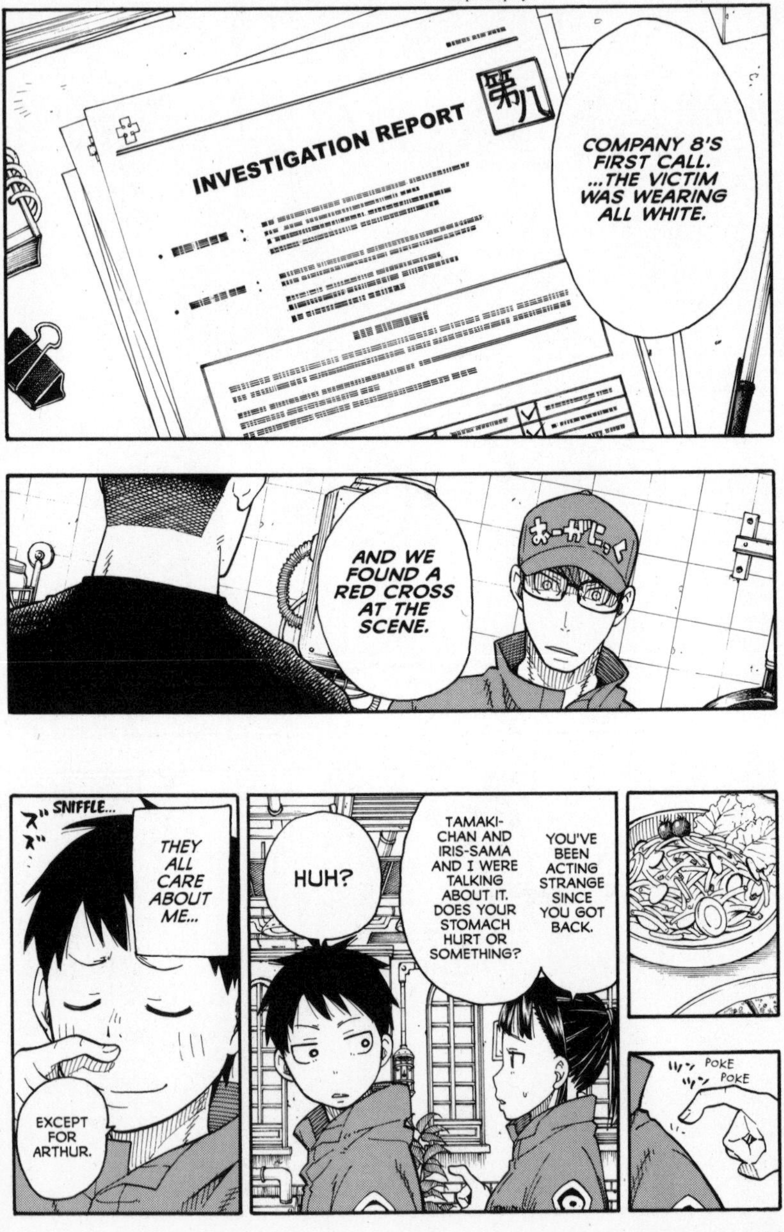

第八
INVESTIGATION REPORT
COMPANY 8'S FIRST CALL. ...THE VICTIM WAS WEARING ALL WHITE.
AND WE FOUND A RED CROSS AT THE SCENE.
POKE POKE
YOU'VE BEEN ACTING STRANGE SINCE YOU GOT BACK.
TAMAKI-CHAN AND IRIS-SAMA AND I WERE TALKING ABOUT IT. DOES YOUR STOMACH HURT OR SOMETHING?
HUH?
SNIFFLE...
THEY ALL CARE ABOUT ME...
EXCEPT FOR ARTHUR.

FIRE FORCE

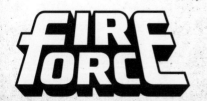

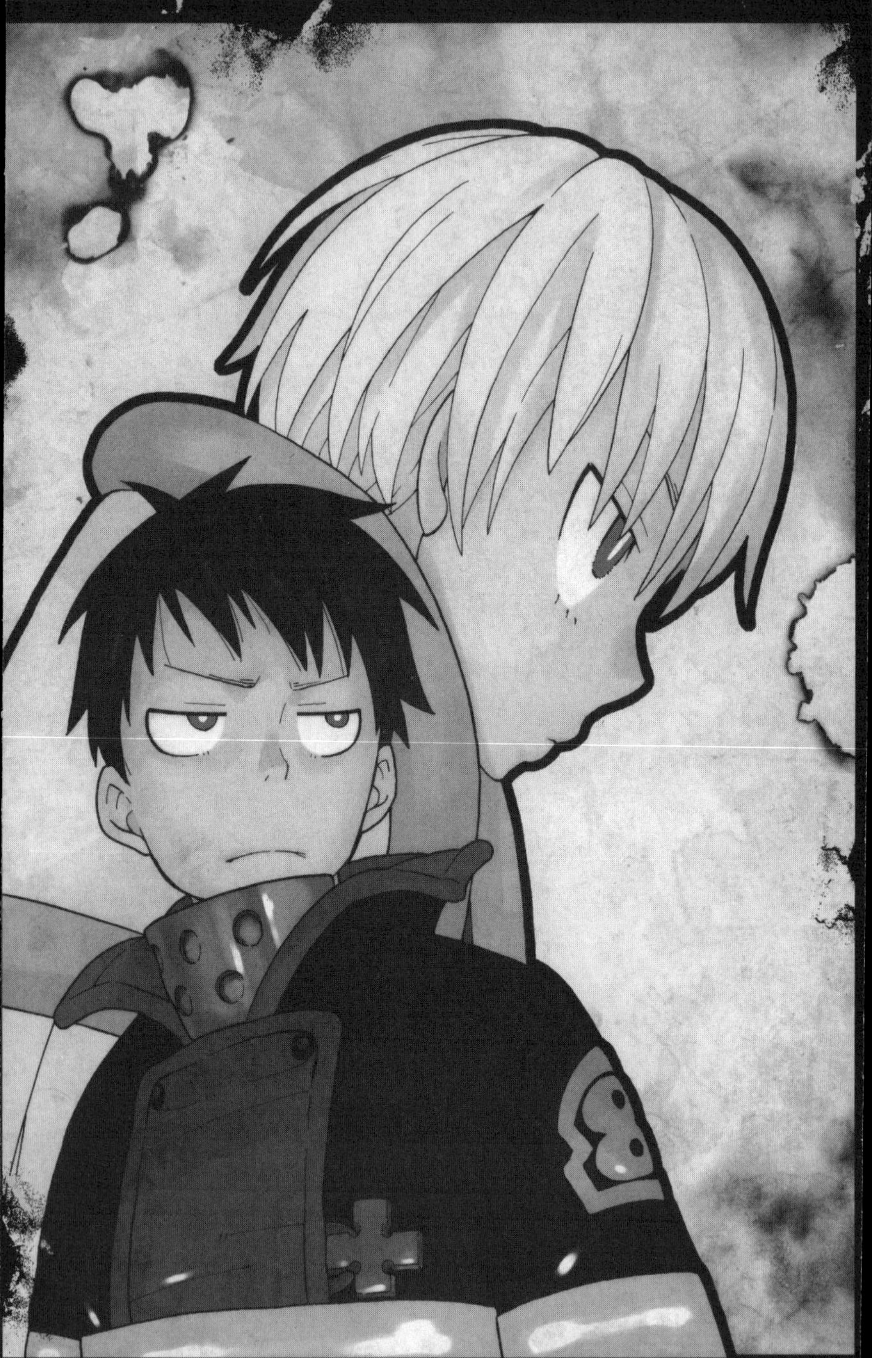

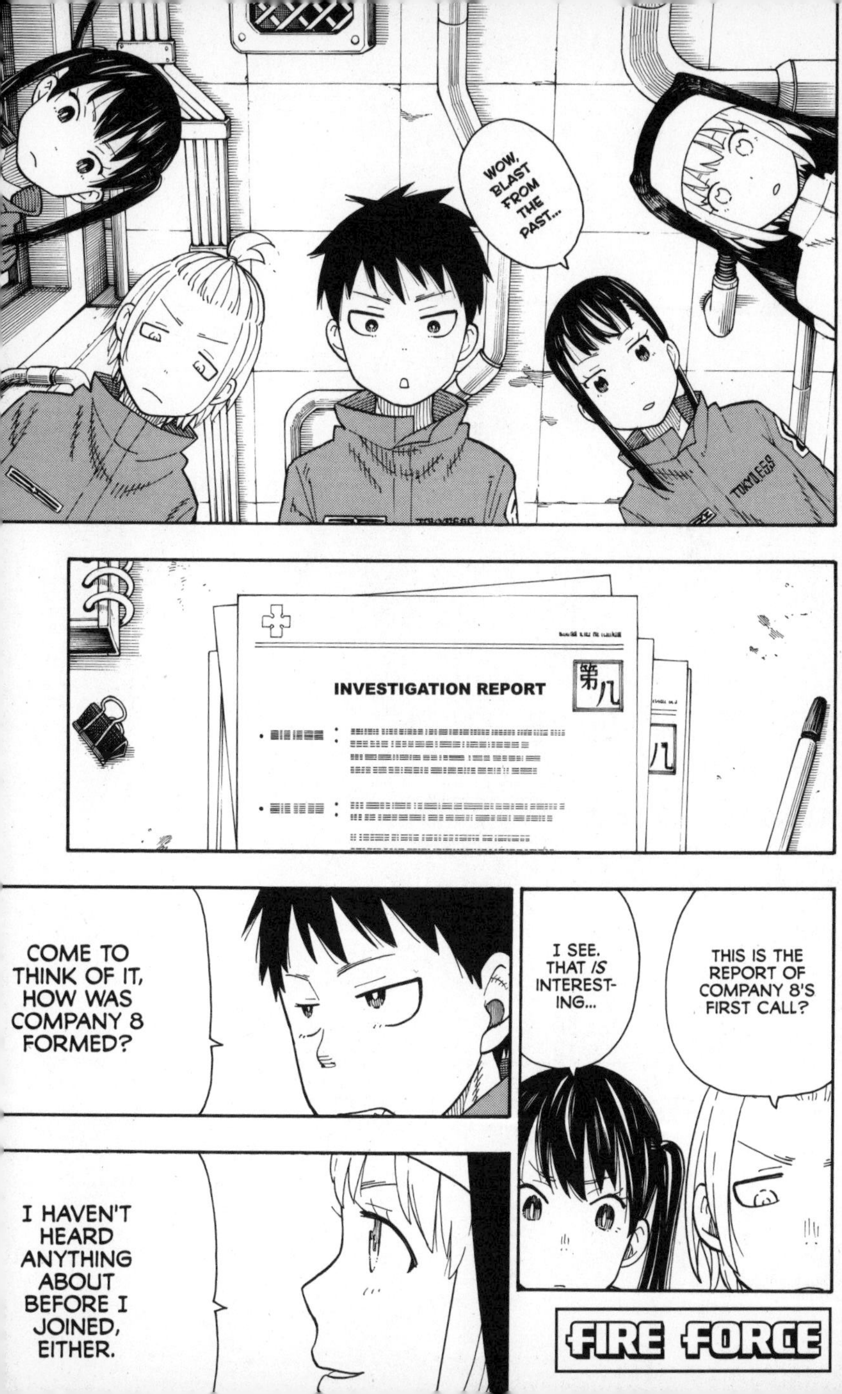
WOW, BLAST FROM THE PAST...
INVESTIGATION REPORT
第八
THIS IS THE REPORT OF COMPANY 8'S FIRST CALL?
I SEE. THAT *IS* INTERESTING...
COME TO THINK OF IT, HOW WAS COMPANY 8 FORMED?
I HAVEN'T HEARD ANYTHING ABOUT BEFORE I JOINED, EITHER.
FIRE FORCE

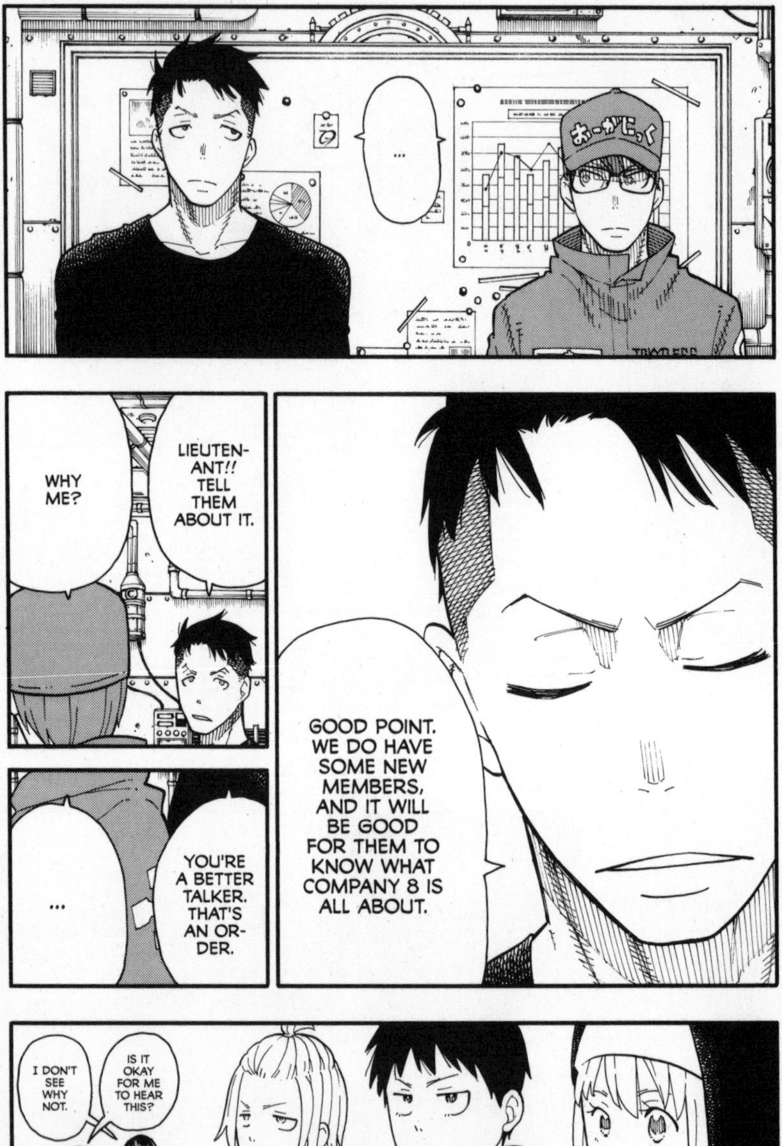
...
GOOD POINT. WE DO HAVE SOME NEW MEMBERS, AND IT WILL BE GOOD FOR THEM TO KNOW WHAT COMPANY 8 IS ALL ABOUT.
LIEUTEN-ANT!! TELL THEM ABOUT IT.
WHY ME?
YOU'RE A BETTER TALKER. THAT'S AN OR-DER.
...
IS IT OKAY FOR ME TO HEAR THIS?
I DON'T SEE WHY NOT.

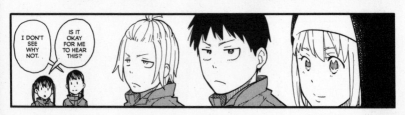

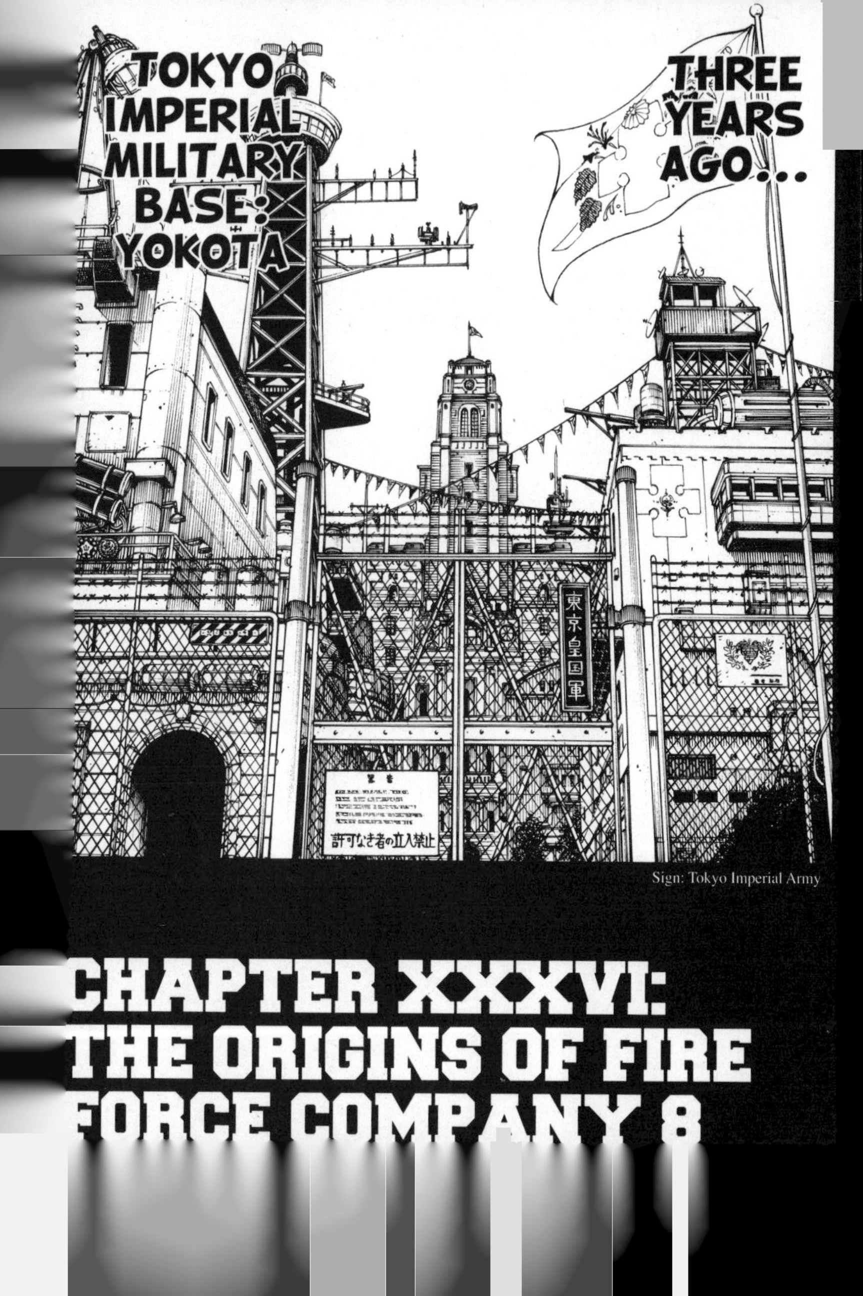
THREE YEARS AGO...
TOKYO IMPERIAL MILITARY BASE: YOKOTA
東京皇国軍
許可なき者の立入禁止
Sign: Tokyo Imperial Army

CHAPTER XXXVI: THE ORIGINS OF FIRE FORCE COMPANY 8

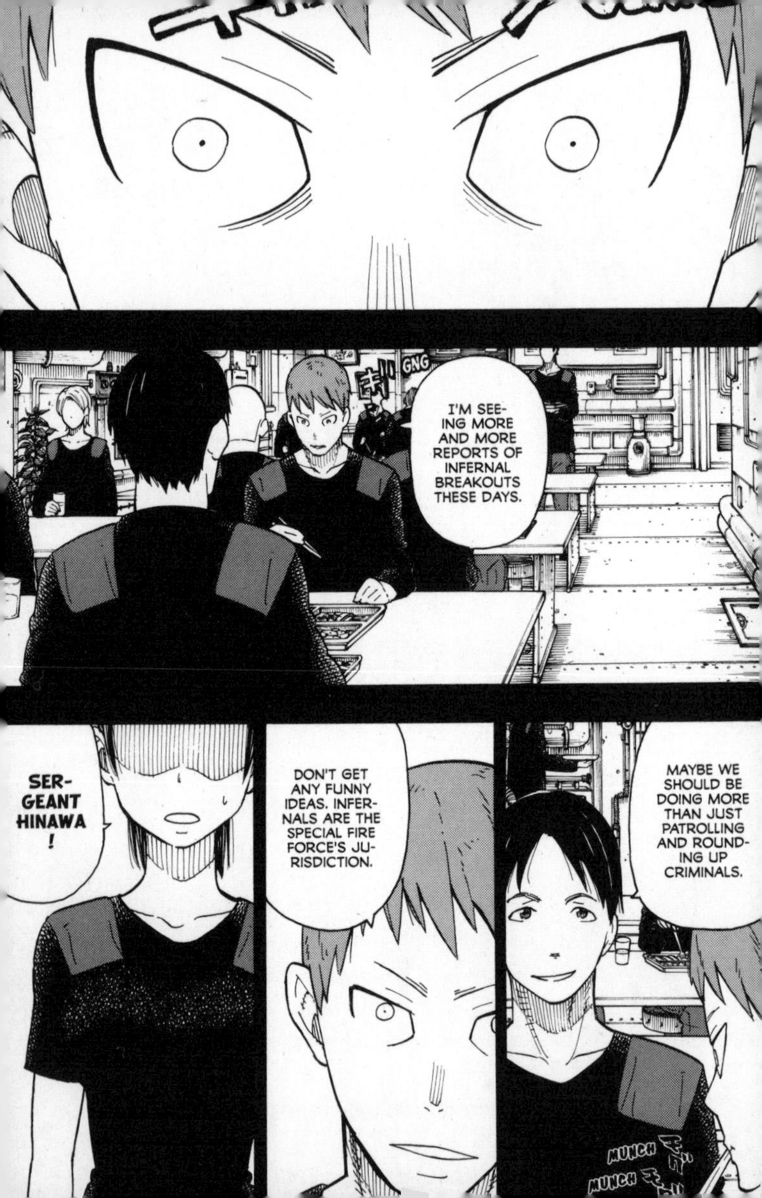
GNG
I'M SEE-ING MORE AND MORE REPORTS OF INFERNAL BREAKOUTS THESE DAYS.
MAYBE WE SHOULD BE DOING MORE THAN JUST PATROLLING AND ROUND-ING UP CRIMINALS.
MUNCH
MUNCH
DON'T GET ANY FUNNY IDEAS. INFER-NALS ARE THE SPECIAL FIRE FORCE'S JU-RISDICTION.
SER-GEANT HINAWA!

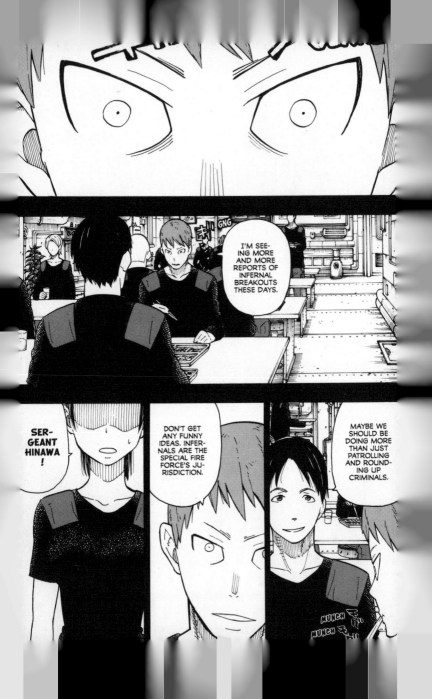

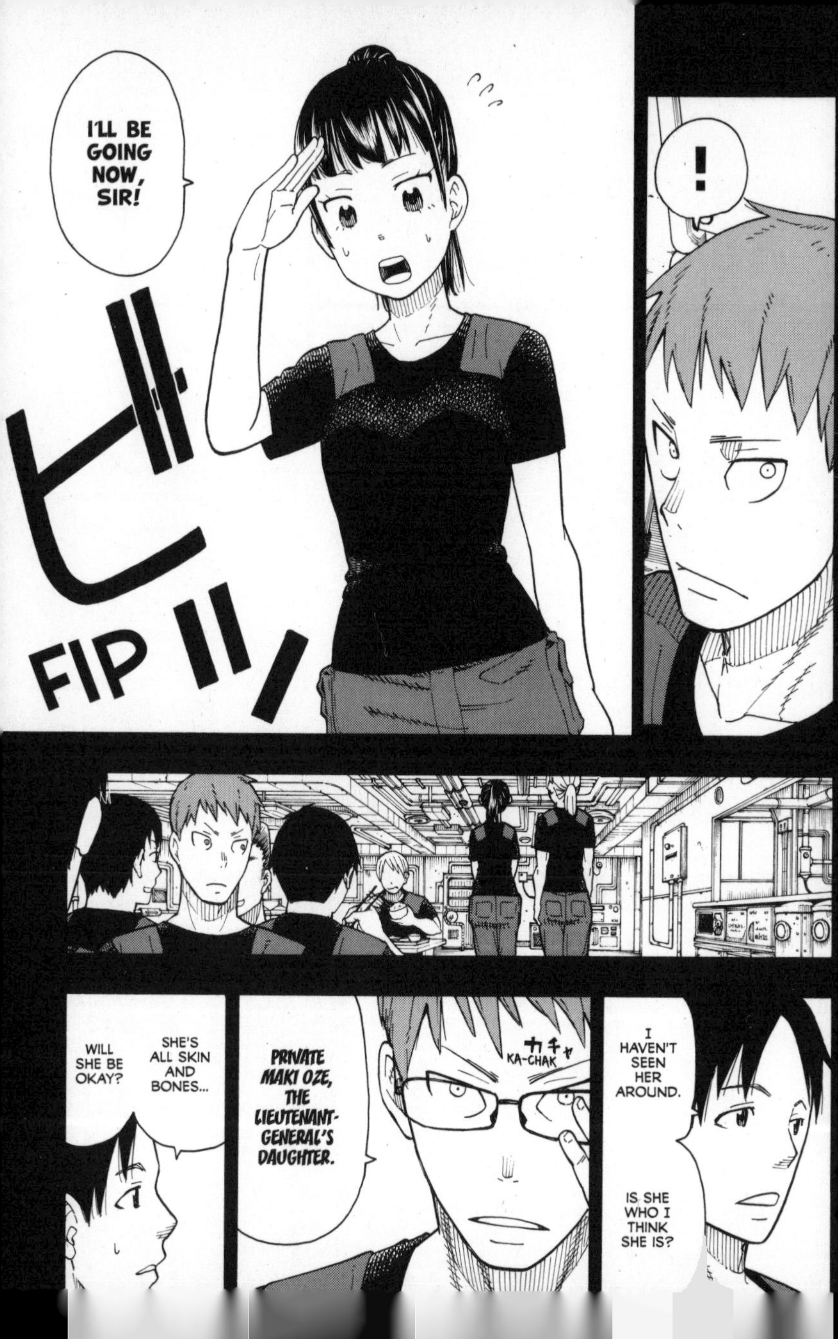
!
I'LL BE GOING NOW, SIR!
FIP
I HAVEN'T SEEN HER AROUND.
IS SHE WHO I THINK SHE IS?
カチャ
KA-CHAK
PRIVATE MAKI OZE, THE LIEUTENANT-GENERAL'S DAUGHTER.
SHE'S ALL SKIN AND BONES...
WILL SHE BE OKAY?

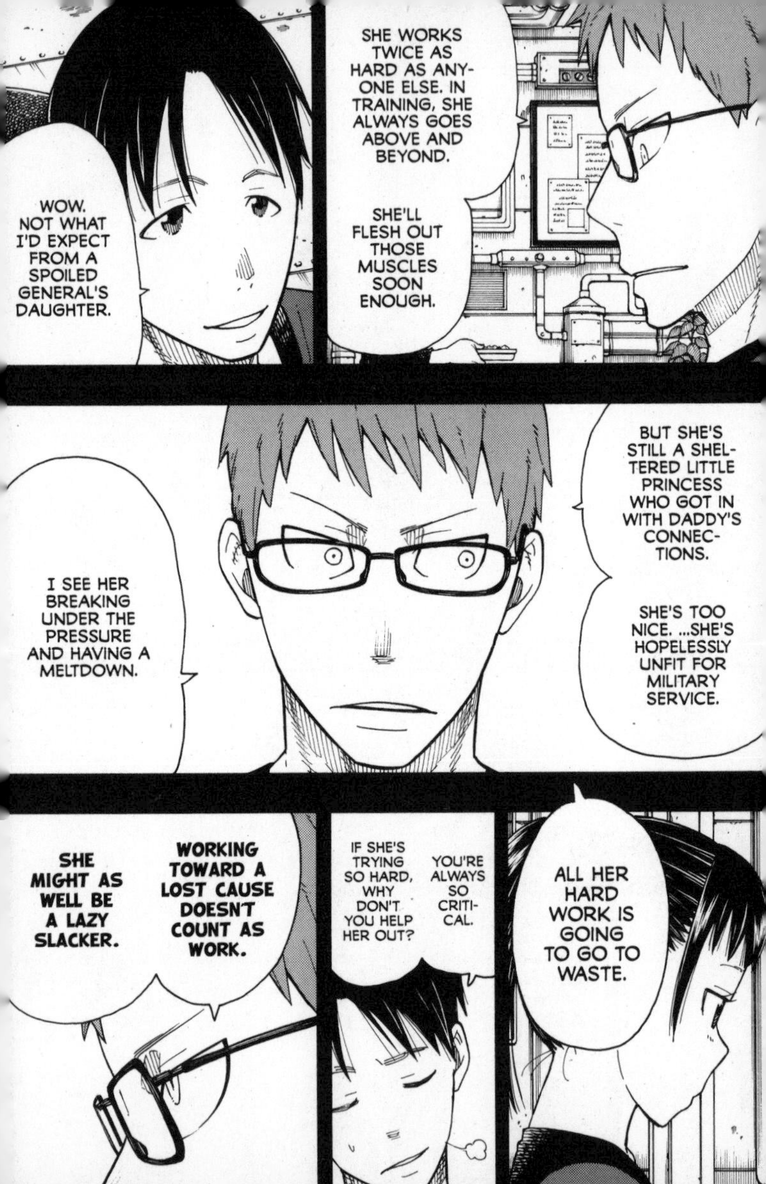
SHE WORKS TWICE AS HARD AS ANYONE ELSE. IN TRAINING, SHE ALWAYS GOES ABOVE AND BEYOND.
SHE'LL FLESH OUT THOSE MUSCLES SOON ENOUGH.
WOW. NOT WHAT I'D EXPECT FROM A SPOILED GENERAL'S DAUGHTER.
BUT SHE'S STILL A SHELTERED LITTLE PRINCESS WHO GOT IN WITH DADDY'S CONNECTIONS.
SHE'S TOO NICE. ...SHE'S HOPELESSLY UNFIT FOR MILITARY SERVICE.
I SEE HER BREAKING UNDER THE PRESSURE AND HAVING A MELTDOWN.
ALL HER HARD WORK IS GOING TO GO TO WASTE.
YOU'RE ALWAYS SO CRITICAL.
IF SHE'S TRYING SO HARD, WHY DON'T YOU HELP HER OUT?
WORKING TOWARD A LOST CAUSE DOESN'T COUNT AS WORK.
SHE MIGHT AS WELL BE A LAZY SLACKER.

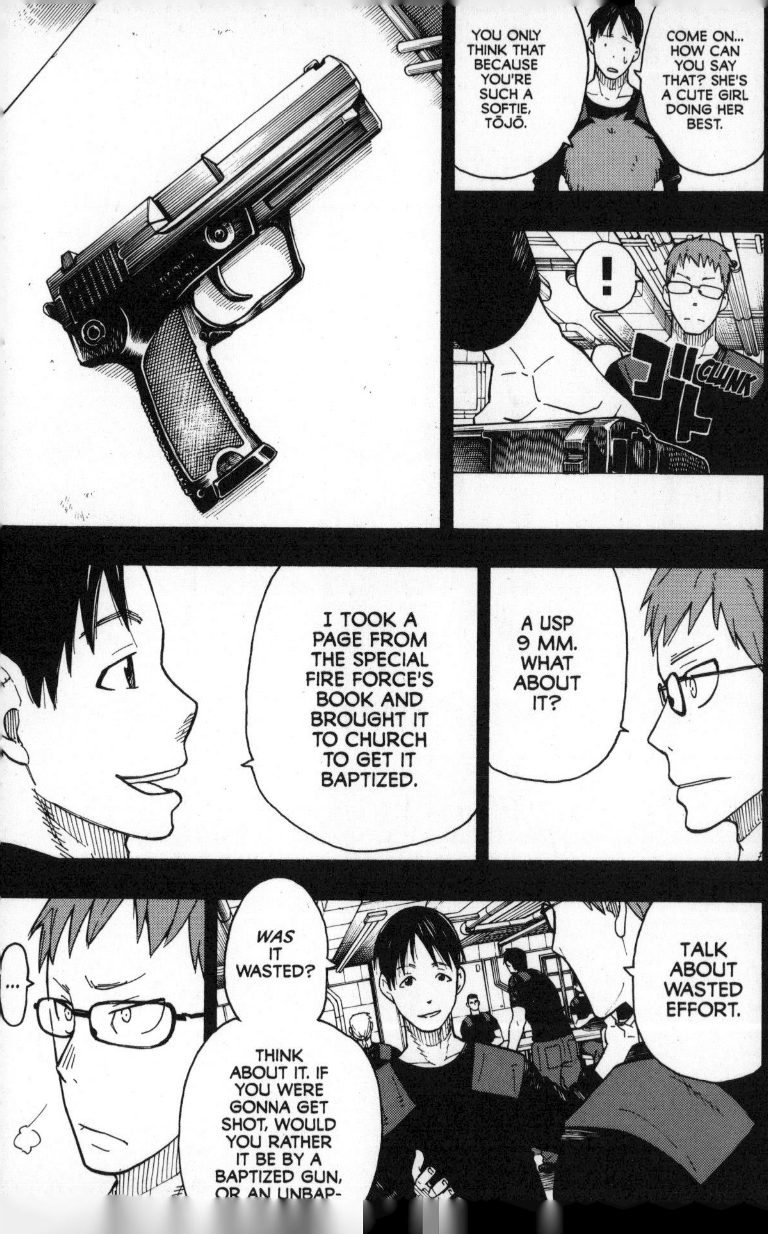
COME ON... HOW CAN YOU SAY THAT? SHE'S A CUTE GIRL DOING HER BEST.
YOU ONLY THINK THAT BECAUSE YOU'RE SUCH A SOFTIE, TŌJŌ.
!
CLUNK
A USP 9 MM. WHAT ABOUT IT?
I TOOK A PAGE FROM THE SPECIAL FIRE FORCE'S BOOK AND BROUGHT IT TO CHURCH TO GET IT BAPTIZED.
TALK ABOUT WASTED EFFORT.
WAS IT WASTED?
THINK ABOUT IT. IF YOU WERE GONNA GET SHOT, WOULD YOU RATHER IT BE BY A BAPTIZED GUN, OR AN UNBAP-
...

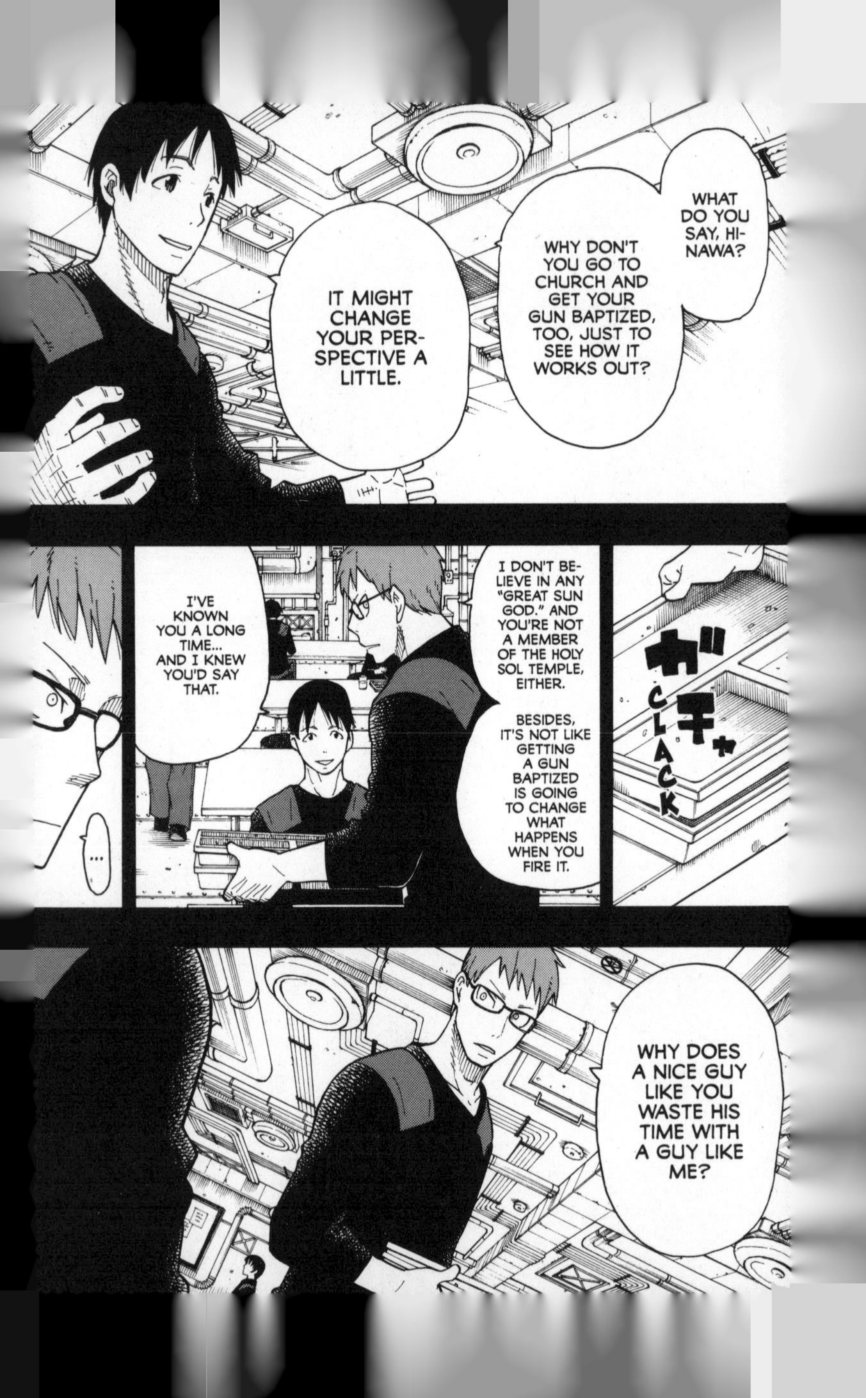
WHAT DO YOU SAY, HI-NAWA?
WHY DON'T YOU GO TO CHURCH AND GET YOUR GUN BAPTIZED, TOO, JUST TO SEE HOW IT WORKS OUT?
IT MIGHT CHANGE YOUR PER-SPECTIVE A LITTLE.
ガチャ
CLACK
I DON'T BE-LIEVE IN ANY "GREAT SUN GOD." AND YOU'RE NOT A MEMBER OF THE HOLY SOL TEMPLE, EITHER.
BESIDES, IT'S NOT LIKE GETTING A GUN BAPTIZED IS GOING TO CHANGE WHAT HAPPENS WHEN YOU FIRE IT.
I'VE KNOWN YOU A LONG TIME... AND I KNEW YOU'D SAY THAT.
...
WHY DOES A NICE GUY LIKE YOU WASTE HIS TIME WITH A GUY LIKE ME?

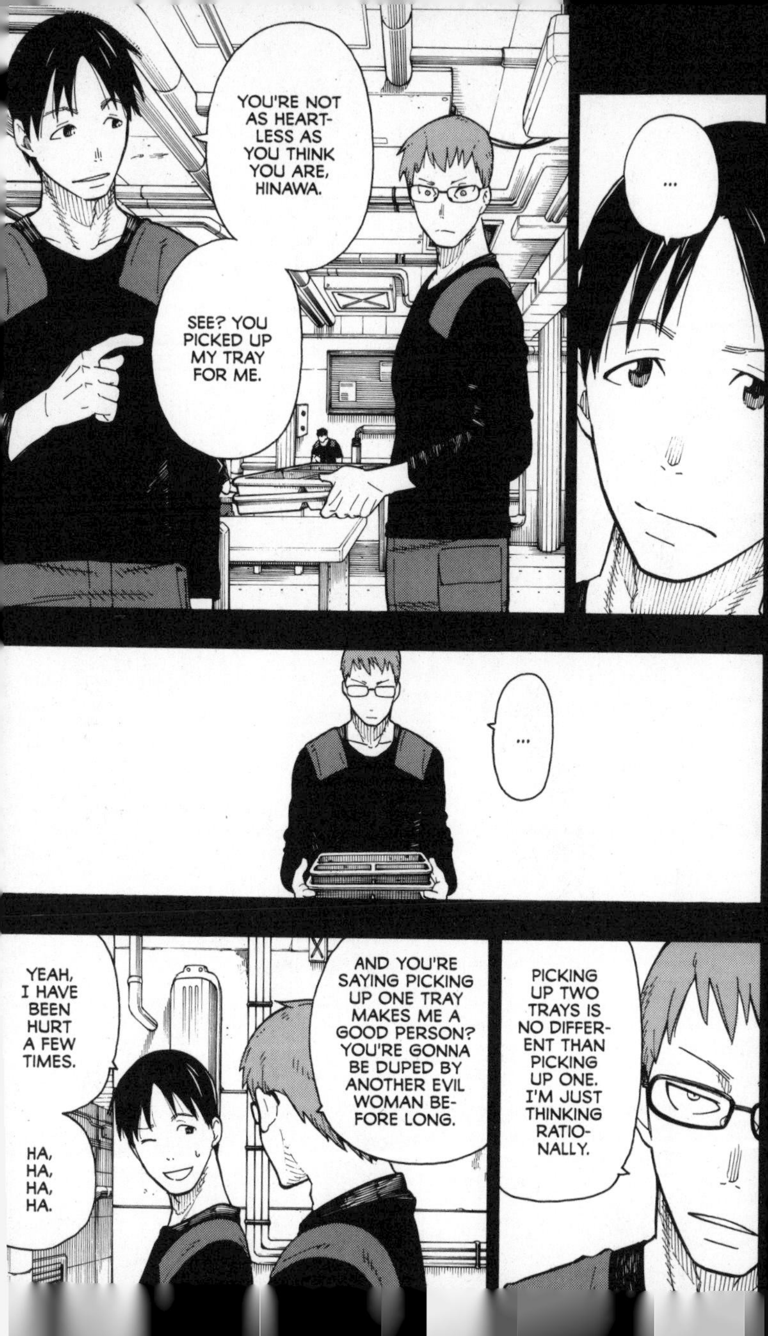
...
YOU'RE NOT AS HEART-LESS AS YOU THINK YOU ARE, HINAWA.
SEE? YOU PICKED UP MY TRAY FOR ME.
...
PICKING UP TWO TRAYS IS NO DIFFER-ENT THAN PICKING UP ONE. I'M JUST THINKING RATIO-NALLY.
AND YOU'RE SAYING PICKING UP ONE TRAY MAKES ME A GOOD PERSON? YOU'RE GONNA BE DUPED BY ANOTHER EVIL WOMAN BE-FORE LONG.
YEAH, I HAVE BEEN HURT A FEW TIMES.
HA, HA, HA, HA.

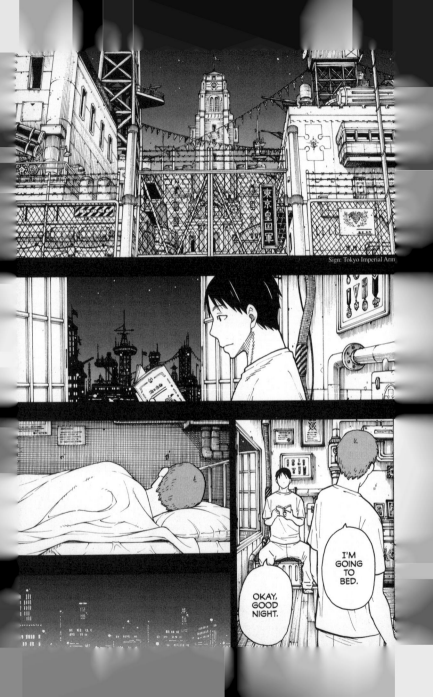

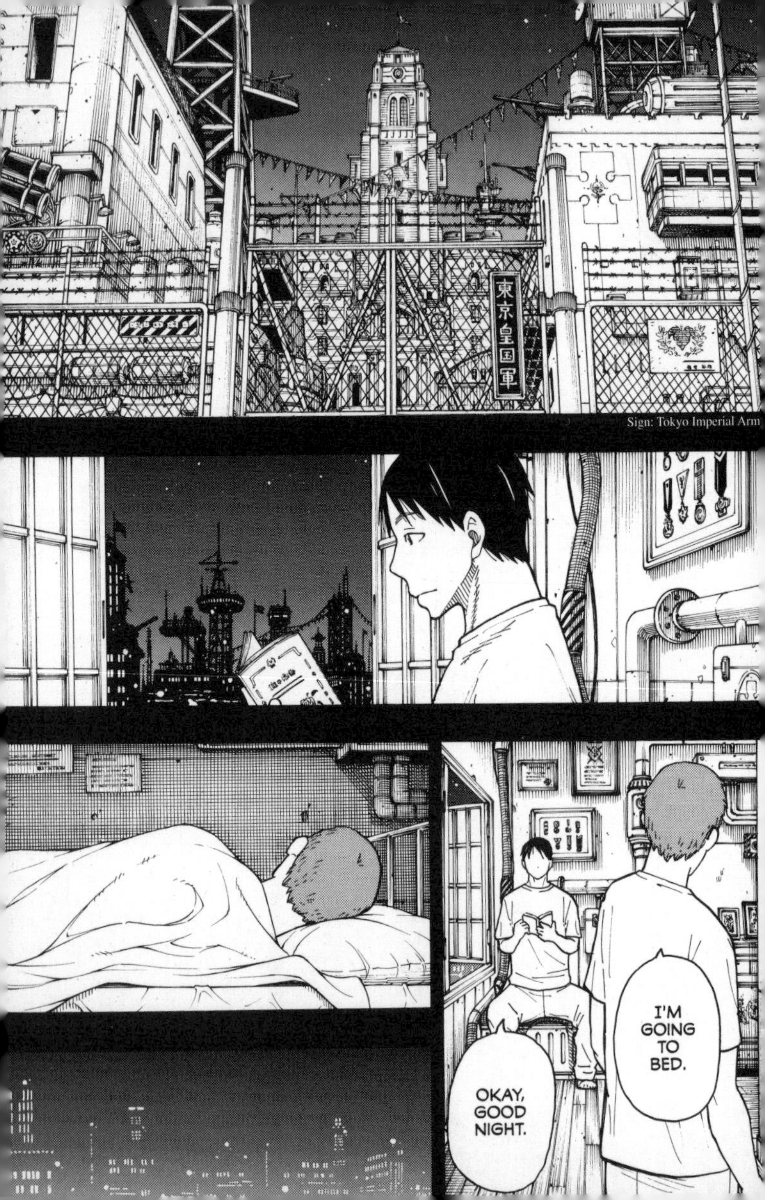
東京皇国軍
Sign: Tokyo Imperial Arm
I'M GOING TO BED.
OKAY, GOOD NIGHT.

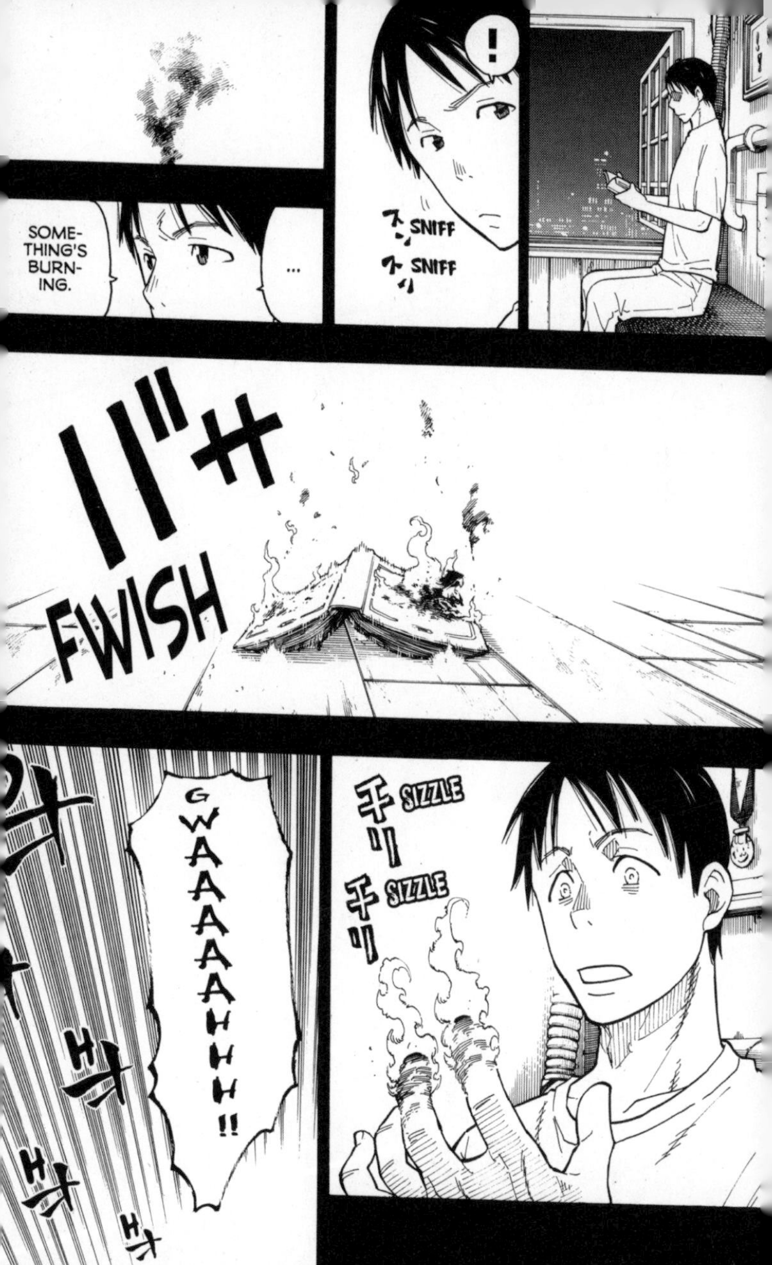
!
SNIFF
SNIFF
...
SOME-
THING'S
BURN-
ING.
FWISH
SIZZLE
SIZZLE
GWAAAAAHHH!!
H
H
H

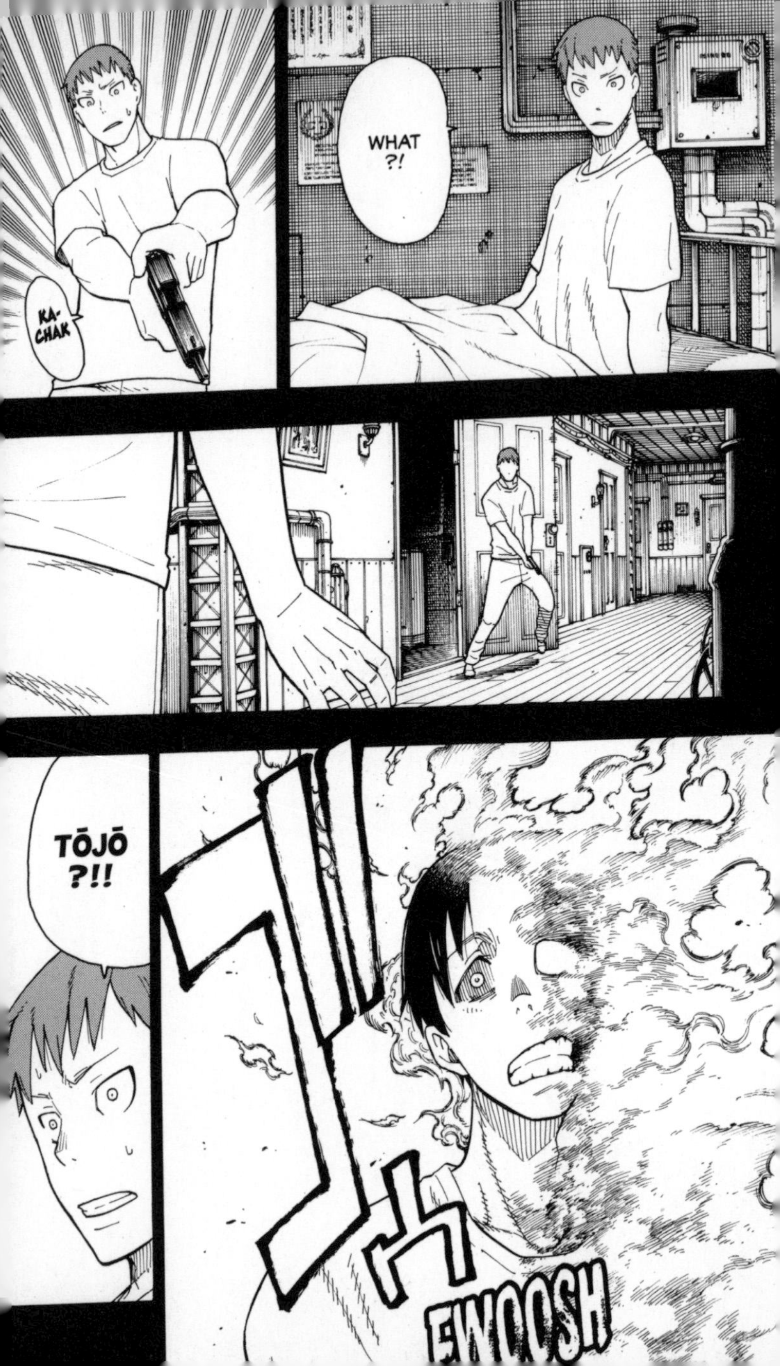
WHAT ?!
KA-CHAK
FWOOSH
TŌJŌ ?!!

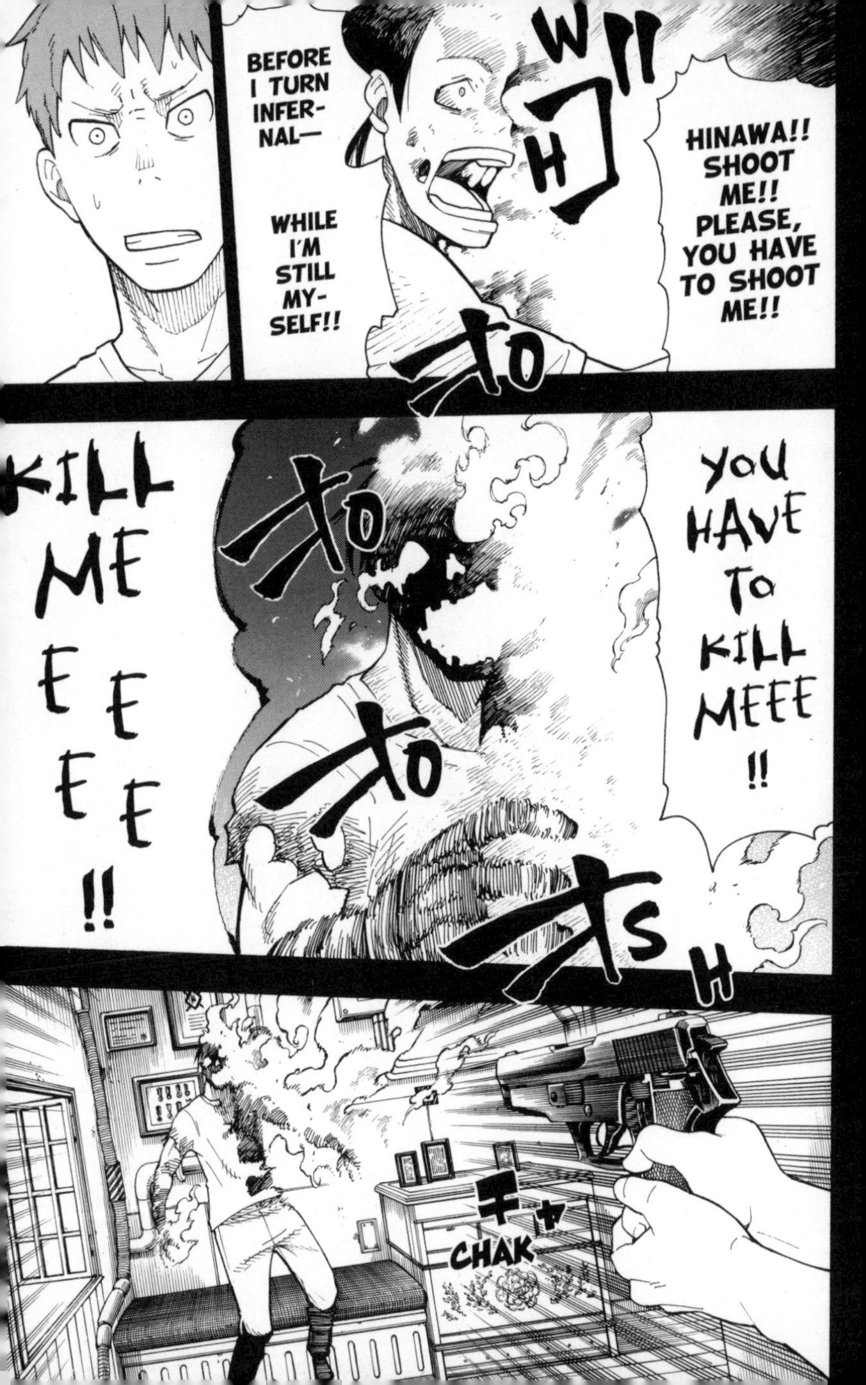
HINAWA!! SHOOT ME!! PLEASE, YOU HAVE TO SHOOT ME!!
BEFORE I TURN INFER-NAL—
WHILE I'M STILL MY-SELF!!
YOU HAVE TO KILL MEEE!!
KILL MEEEEEE!!
CHAK

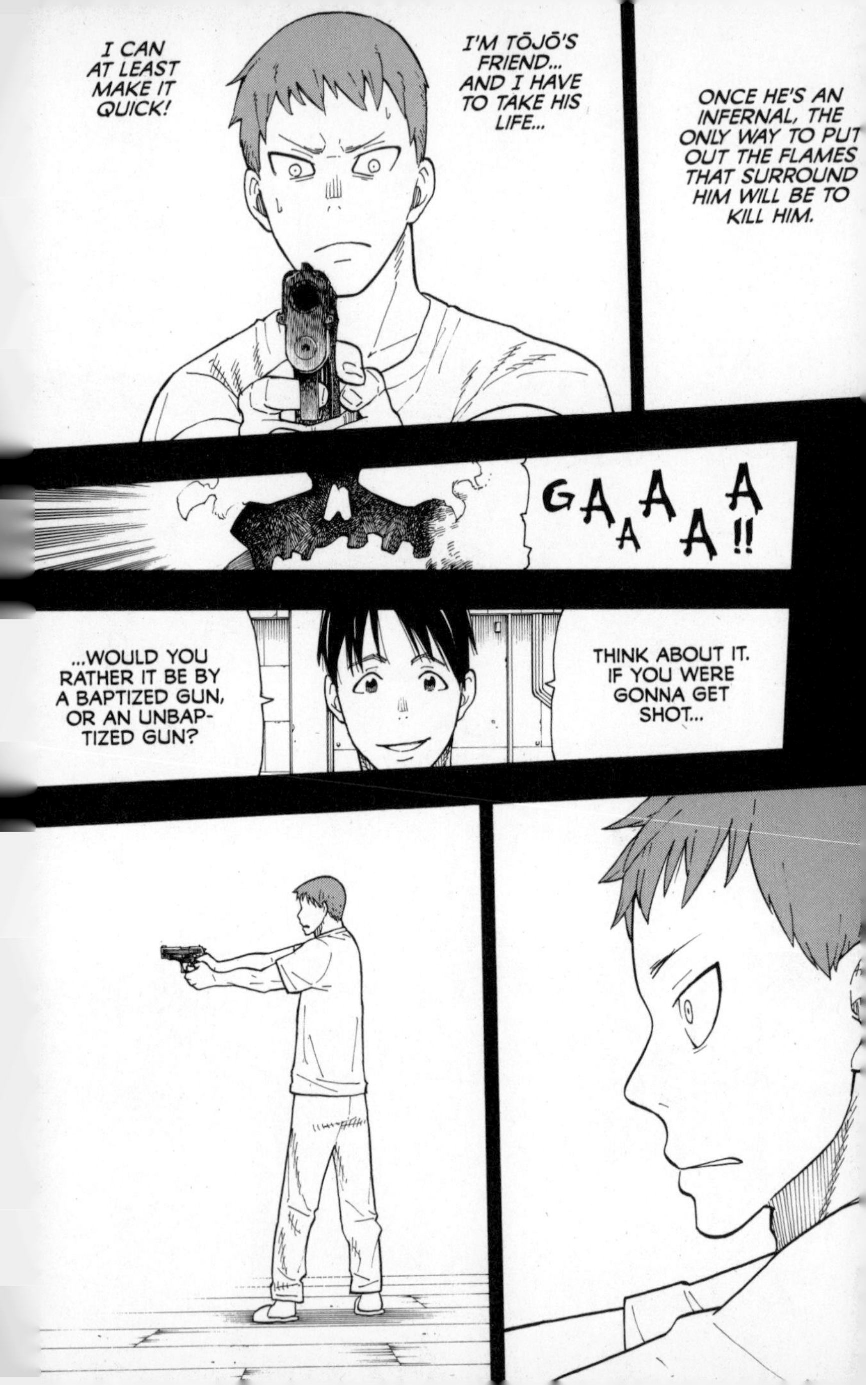
ONCE HE'S AN INFERNAL, THE ONLY WAY TO PUT OUT THE FLAMES THAT SURROUND HIM WILL BE TO KILL HIM.
I'M TŌJŌ'S FRIEND... AND I HAVE TO TAKE HIS LIFE...
I CAN AT LEAST MAKE IT QUICK!
GAAAAA!!
THINK ABOUT IT. IF YOU WERE GONNA GET SHOT...
...WOULD YOU RATHER IT BE BY A BAPTIZED GUN, OR AN UNBAP-TIZED GUN?

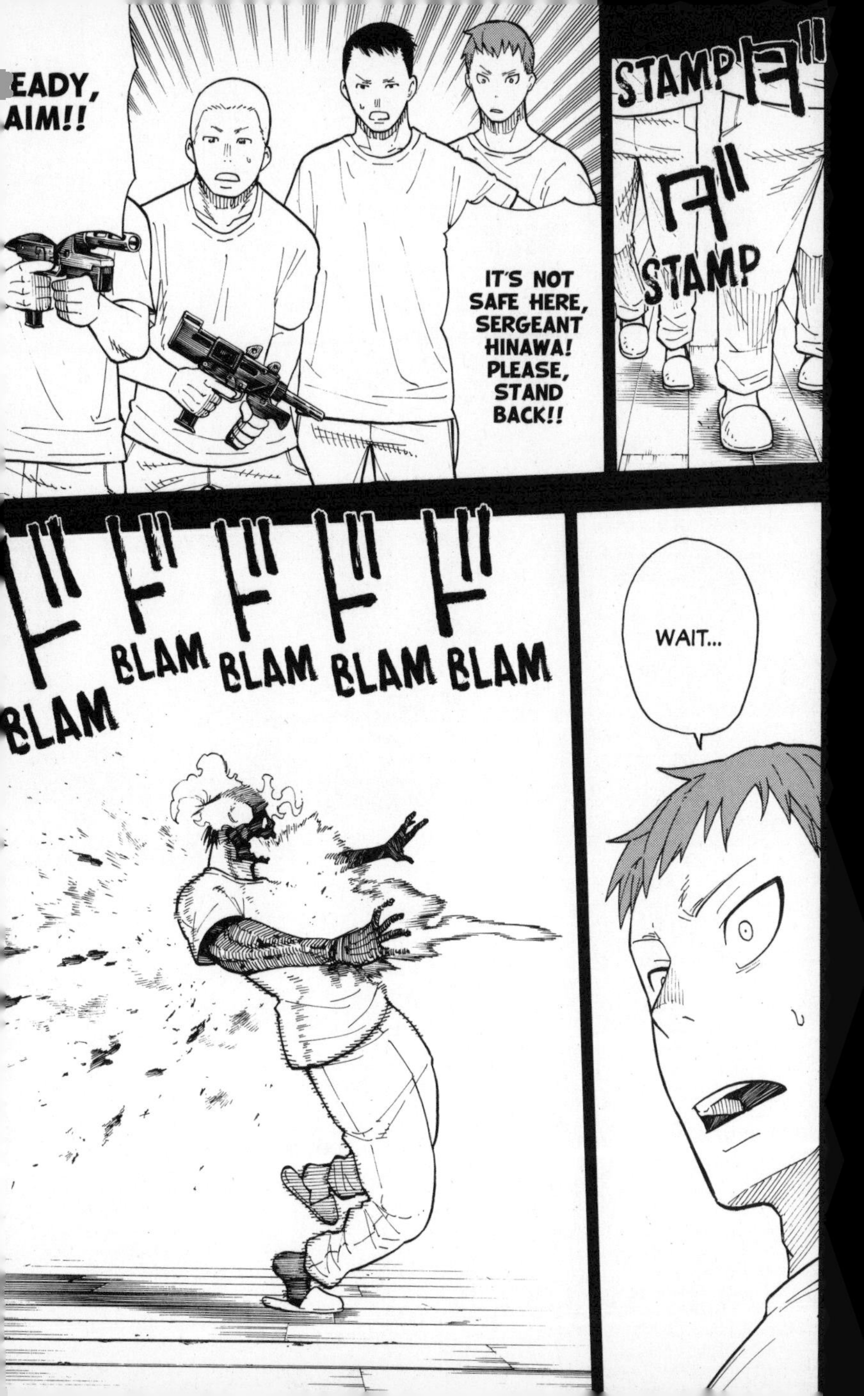
STAMP ダ
ダ STAMP
IT'S NOT SAFE HERE, SERGEANT HINAWA! PLEASE, STAND BACK!!
EADY, AIM!!
WAIT...
ドドドドド
BLAM BLAM BLAM BLAM BLAM

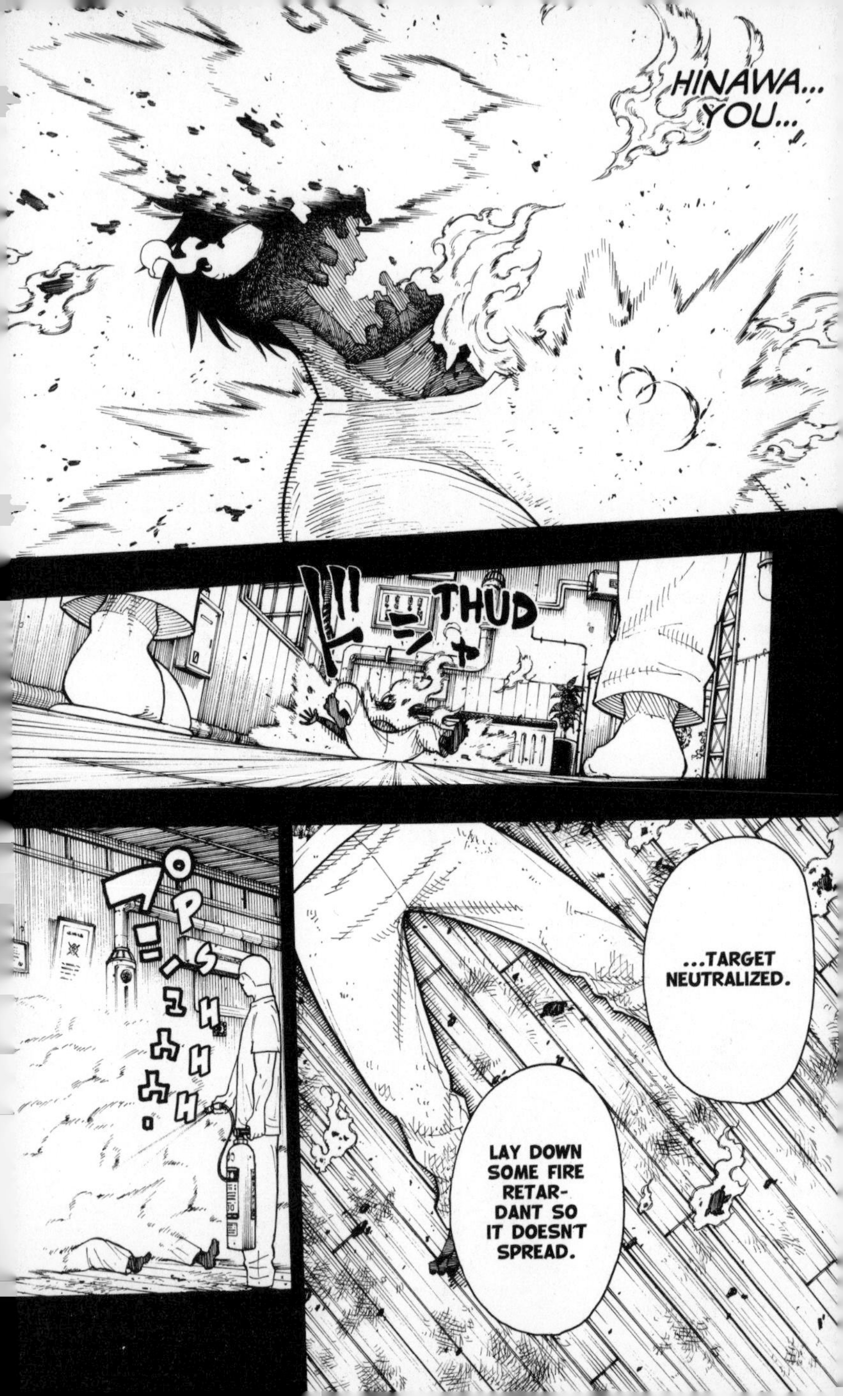
HINAWA... YOU...
THUD
...TARGET NEUTRALIZED.
LAY DOWN SOME FIRE RETAR-DANT SO IT DOESN'T SPREAD.
PSHHH

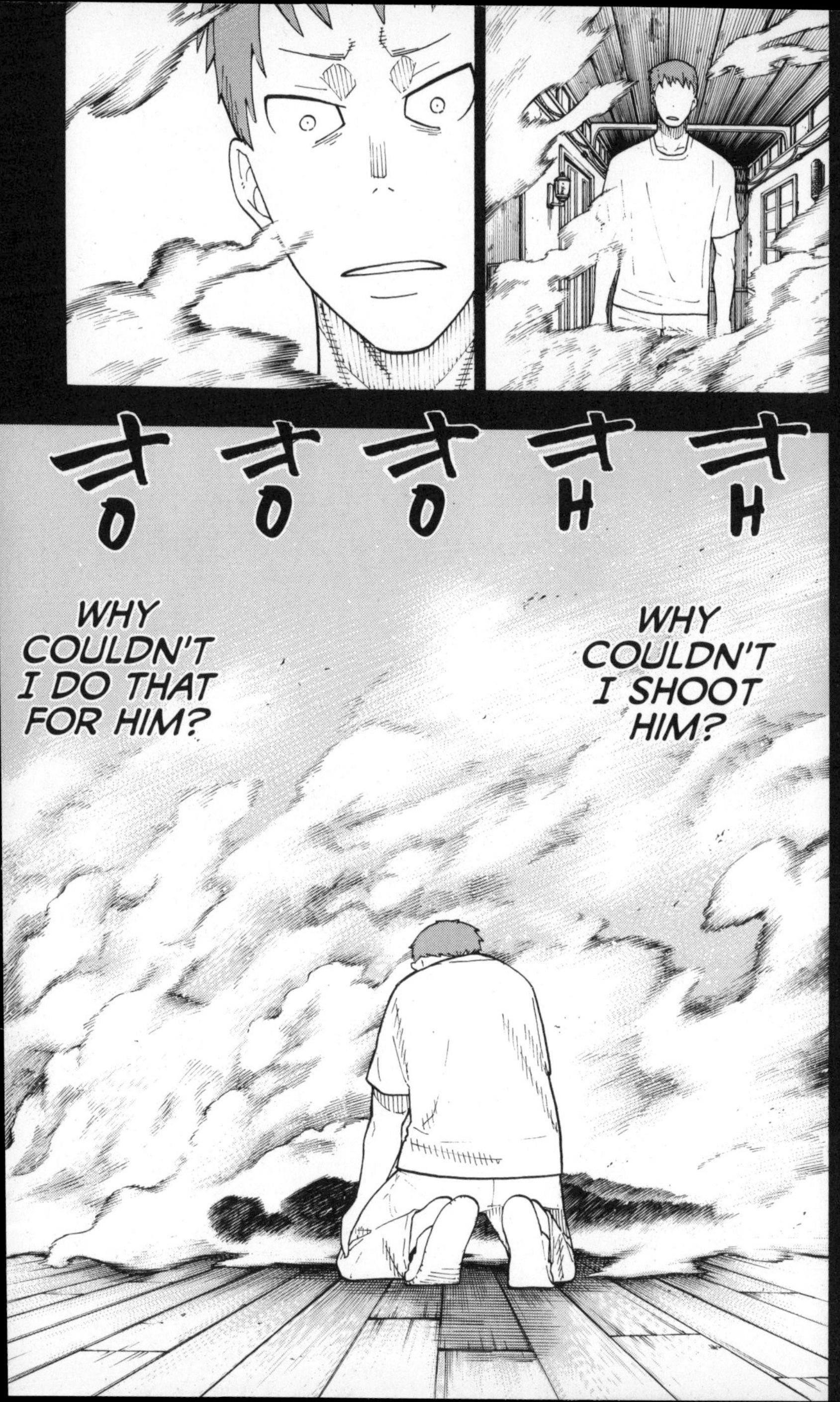
オオオオオ
OOOHH
WHY COULDN'T I SHOOT HIM?
WHY COULDN'T I DO THAT FOR HIM?

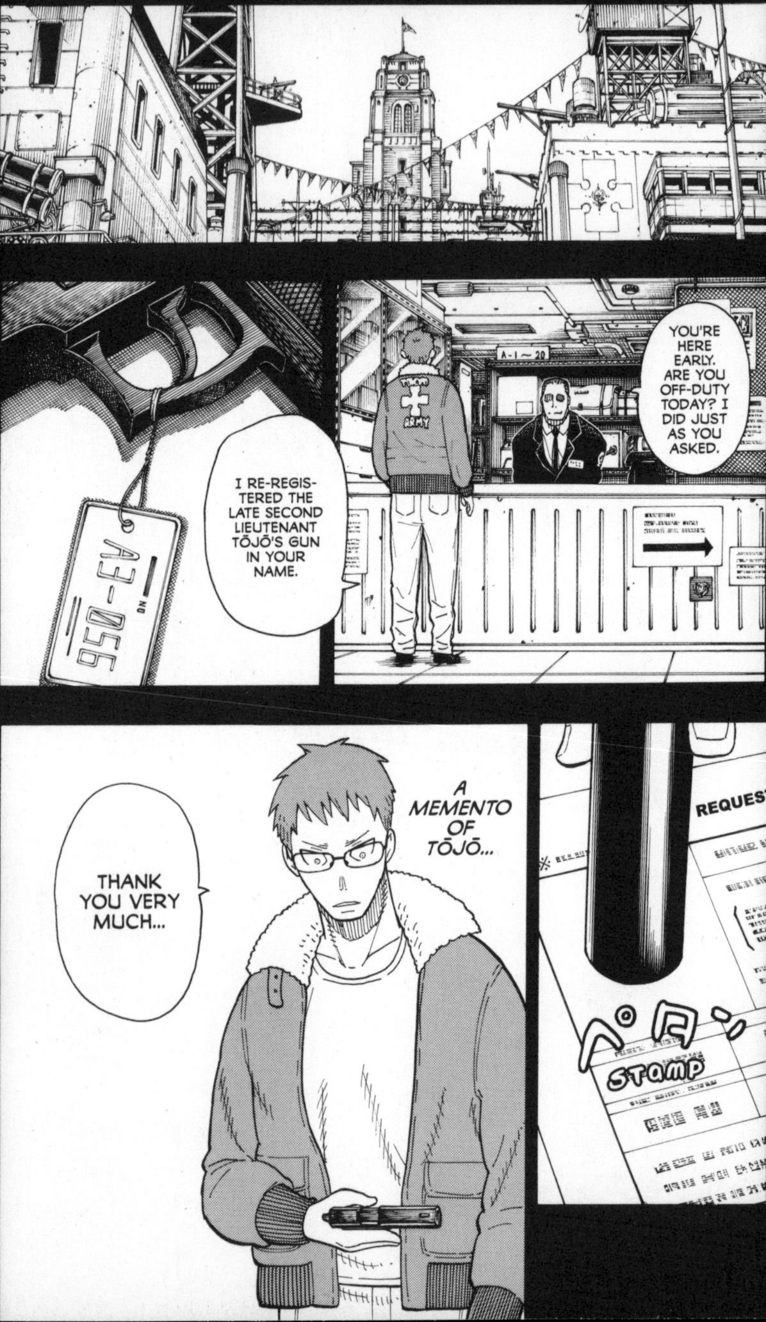

A-1～20
ARMY
YOU'RE HERE EARLY. ARE YOU OFF-DUTY TODAY? I DID JUST AS YOU ASKED.
I RE-REGISTERED THE LATE SECOND LIEUTENANT TŌJŌ'S GUN IN YOUR NAME.
REQUEST
STAMP
A MEMENTO OF TŌJŌ...
THANK YOU VERY MUCH...

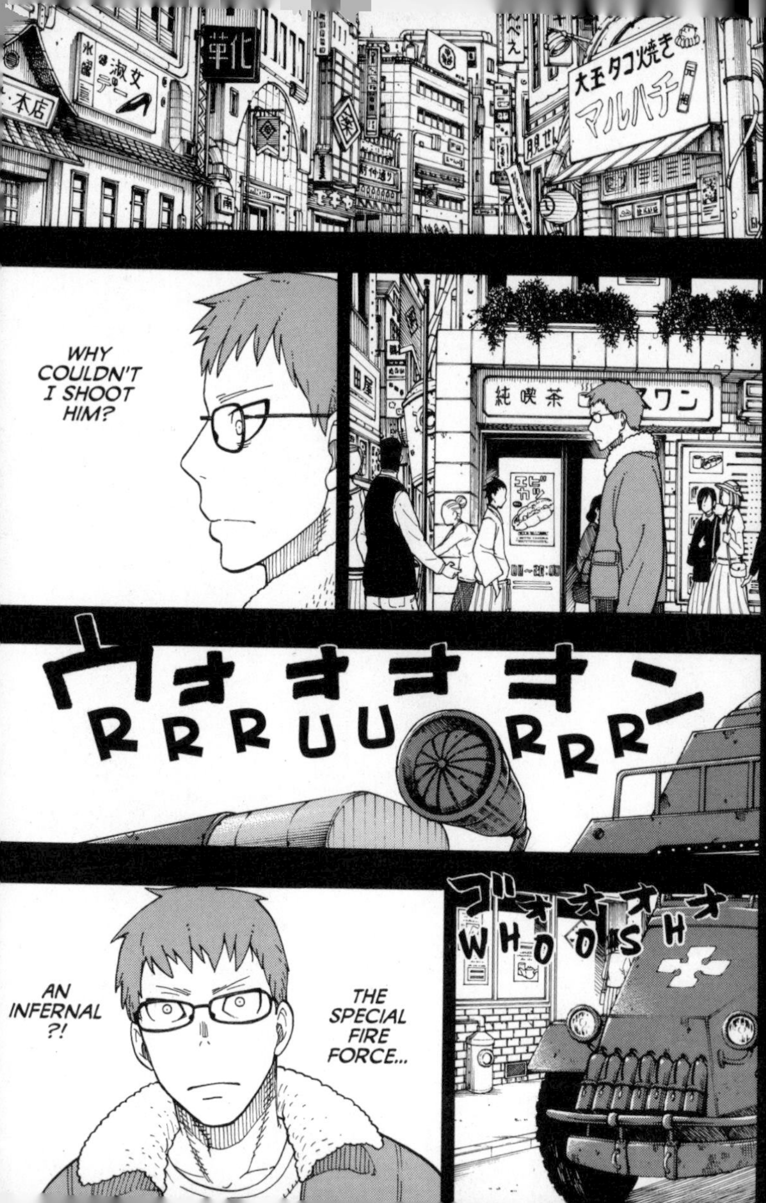

大玉タコ焼き
マルハチ
本店
WHY COULDN'T I SHOOT HIM?
純喫茶 スワン
ウォォォォン
RRRUURRR
ゴォォォォ
WHOOSH
THE SPECIAL FIRE FORCE...
AN INFERNAL ?!

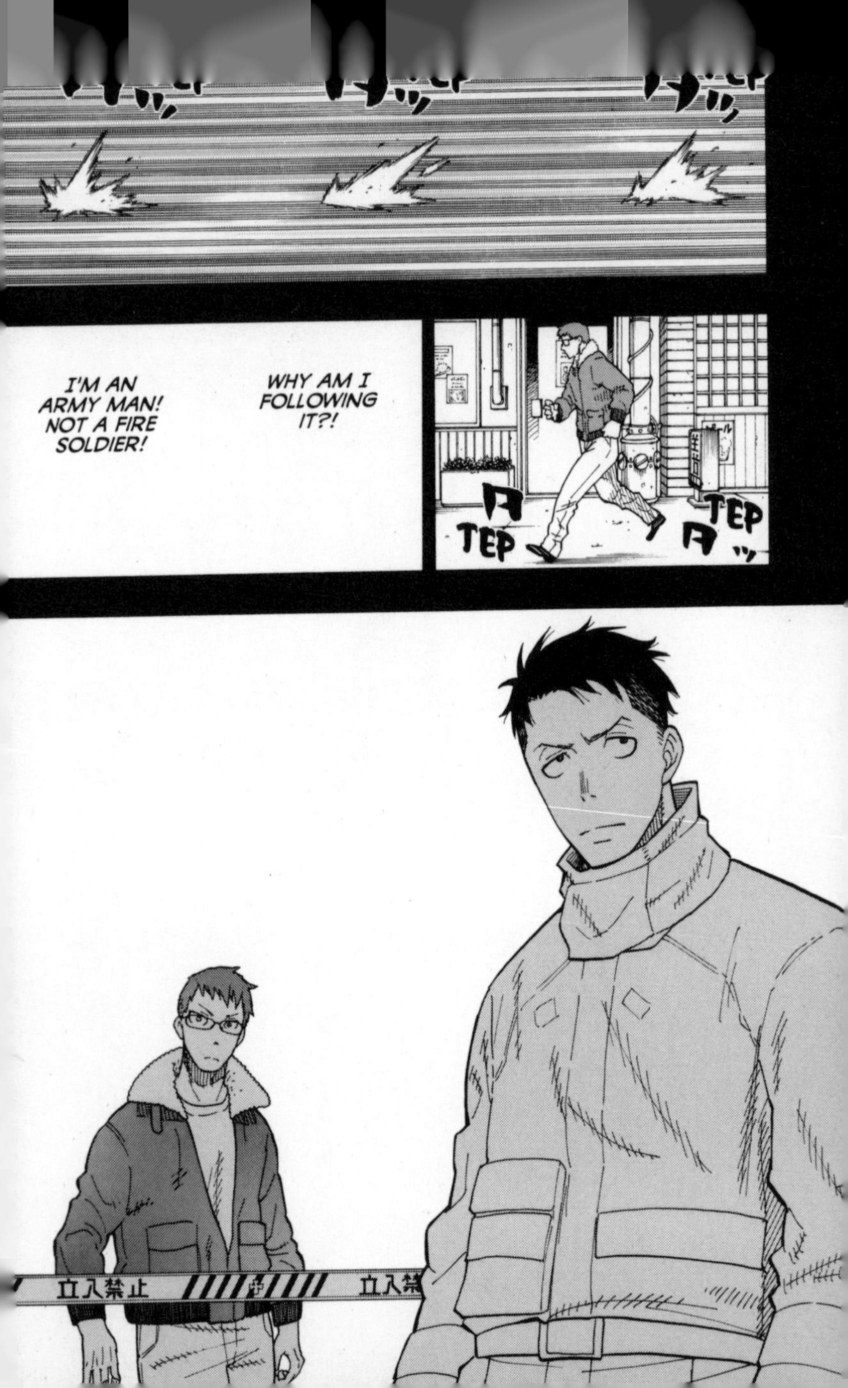
TEP
TEP
WHY AM I FOLLOWING IT?!
I'M AN ARMY MAN! NOT A FIRE SOLDIER!
立入禁止
立入禁

FIRE FORCE

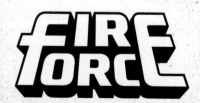

FIRE FORCE

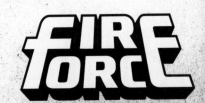

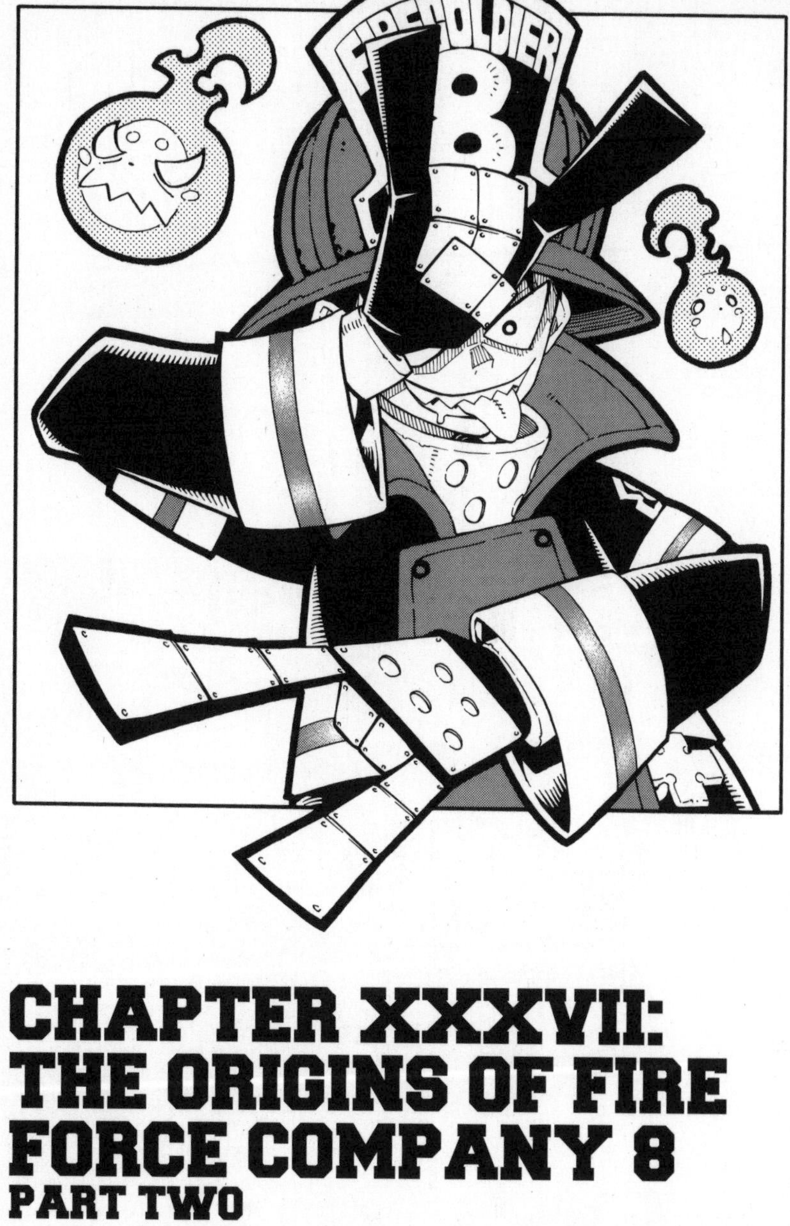
FIRE SOLDIER
8

CHAPTER XXXVII: THE ORIGINS OF FIRE FORCE COMPANY 8

PART TWO

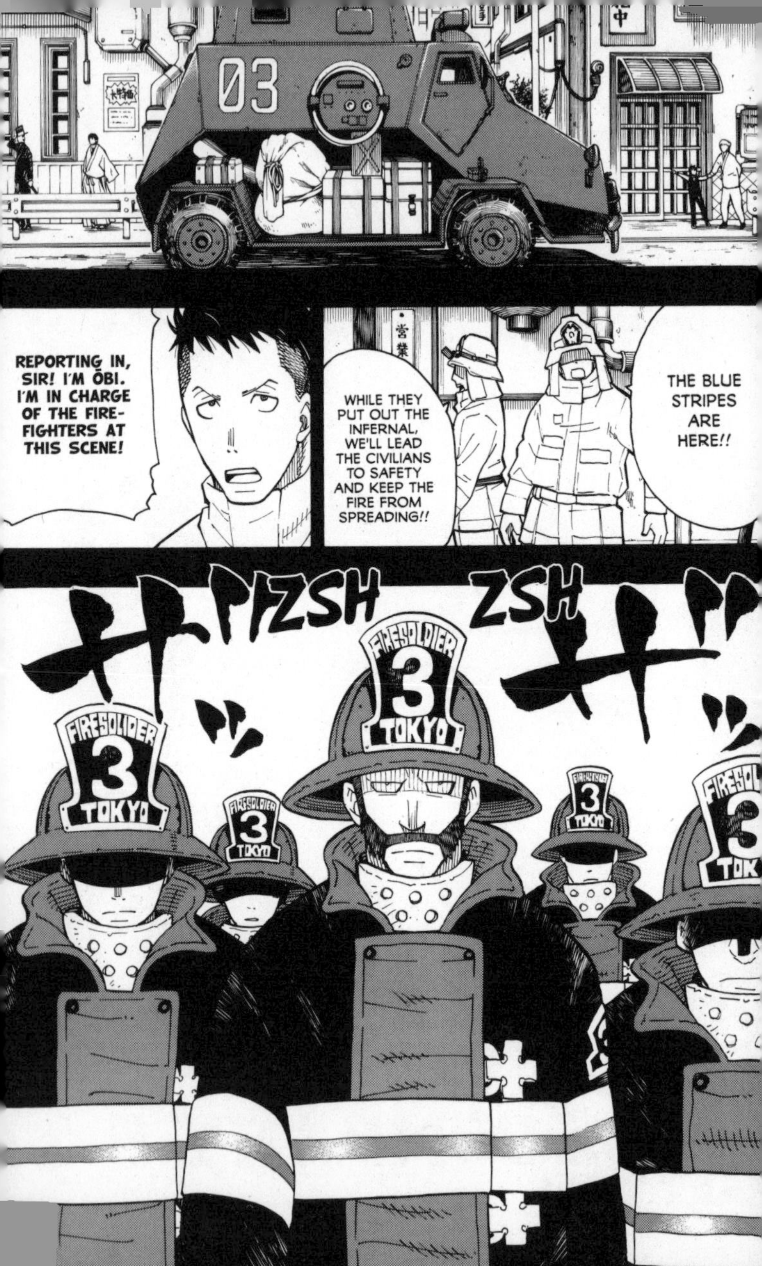

THE BLUE STRIPES ARE HERE!!
WHILE THEY PUT OUT THE INFERNAL, WE'LL LEAD THE CIVILIANS TO SAFETY AND KEEP THE FIRE FROM SPREADING!!
REPORTING IN, SIR! I'M ŌBI. I'M IN CHARGE OF THE FIRE-FIGHTERS AT THIS SCENE!
ZSH
ZSH

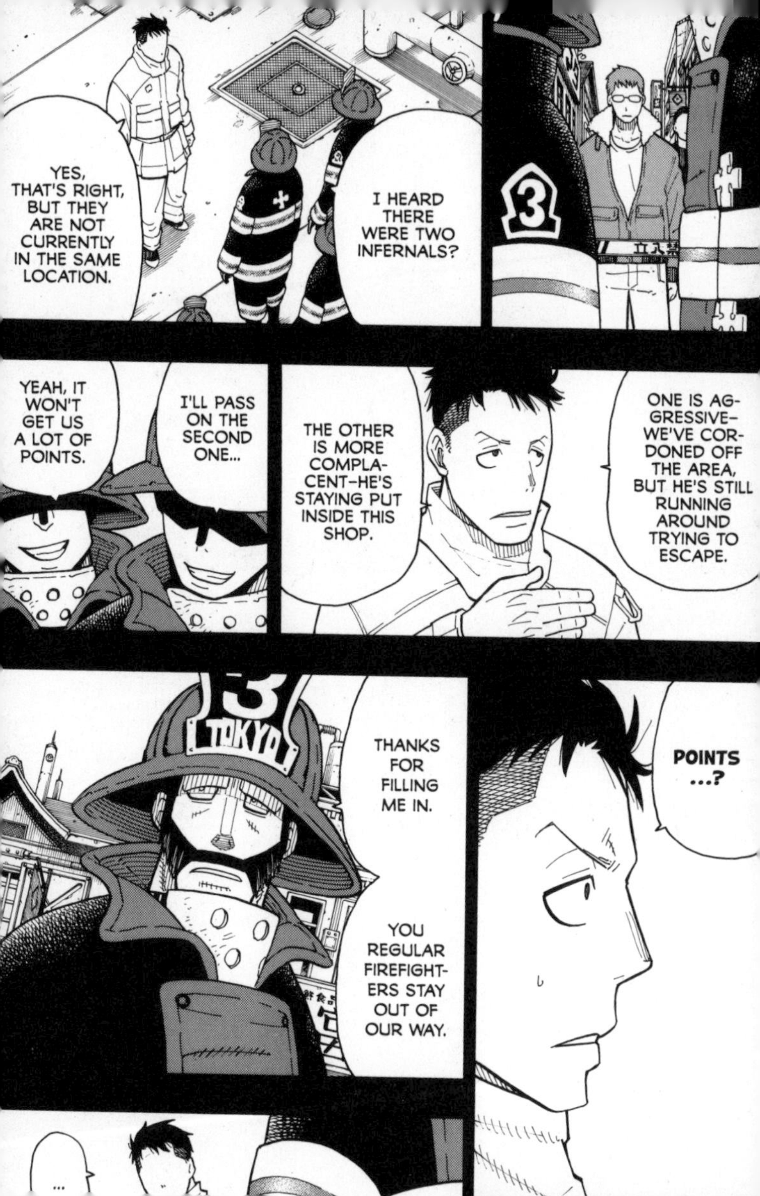
I HEARD THERE WERE TWO INFERNALS?
YES, THAT'S RIGHT, BUT THEY ARE NOT CURRENTLY IN THE SAME LOCATION.
ONE IS AG-GRESSIVE—WE'VE COR-DONED OFF THE AREA, BUT HE'S STILL RUNNING AROUND TRYING TO ESCAPE.
THE OTHER IS MORE COMPLA-CENT—HE'S STAYING PUT INSIDE THIS SHOP.
I'LL PASS ON THE SECOND ONE...
YEAH, IT WON'T GET US A LOT OF POINTS.
POINTS ...?
THANKS FOR FILLING ME IN.
YOU REGULAR FIREFIGHT-ERS STAY OUT OF OUR WAY.
...

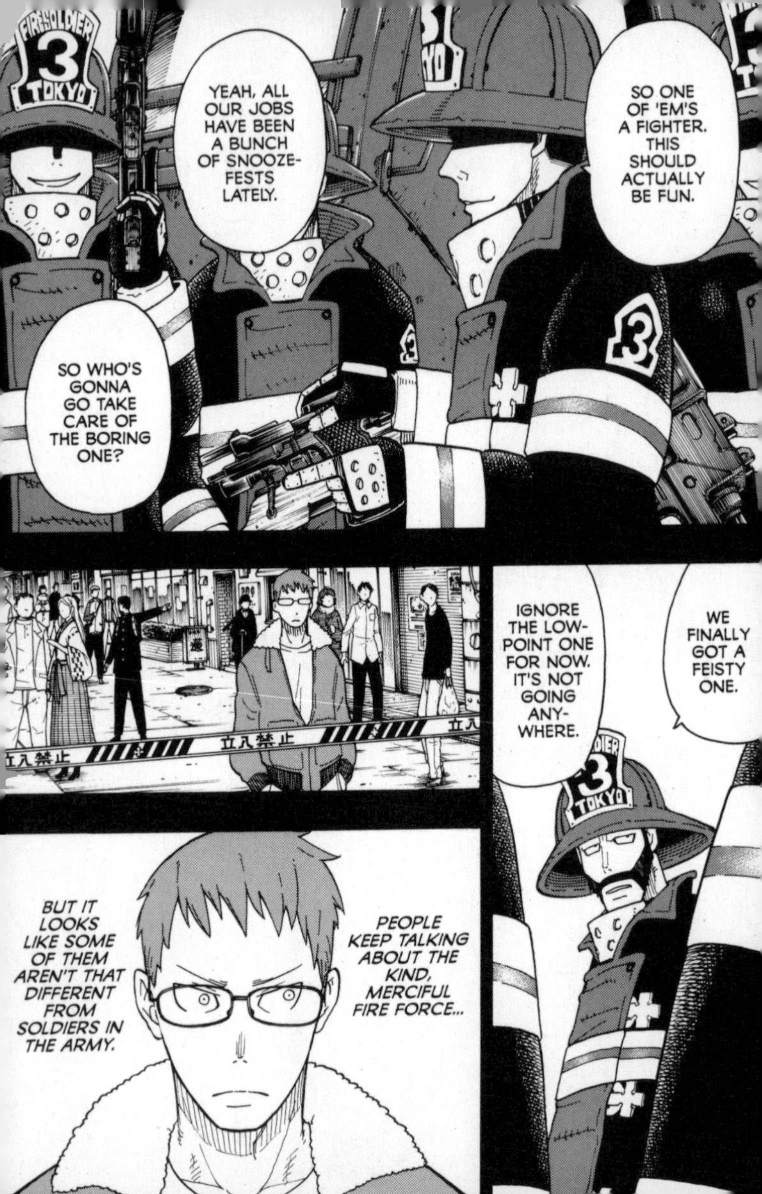
SO ONE OF 'EM'S A FIGHTER. THIS SHOULD ACTUALLY BE FUN.
YEAH, ALL OUR JOBS HAVE BEEN A BUNCH OF SNOOZE-FESTS LATELY.
SO WHO'S GONNA GO TAKE CARE OF THE BORING ONE?
WE FINALLY GOT A FEISTY ONE.
IGNORE THE LOW-POINT ONE FOR NOW. IT'S NOT GOING ANY-WHERE.
立入禁止
PEOPLE KEEP TALKING ABOUT THE KIND, MERCIFUL FIRE FORCE...
BUT IT LOOKS LIKE SOME OF THEM AREN'T THAT DIFFERENT FROM SOLDIERS IN THE ARMY.

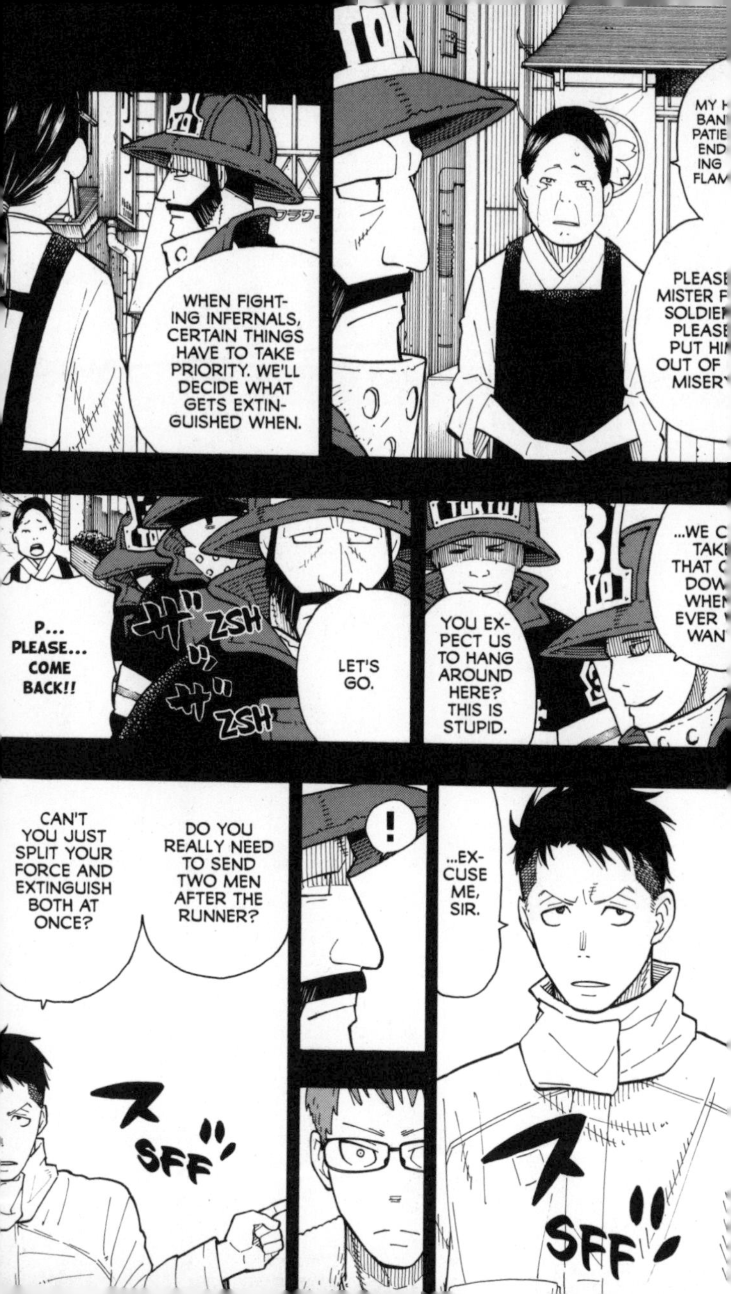
MY H BAN PATIE END ING FLAM
PLEASE MISTER F SOLDIER PLEASE PUT HIM OUT OF MISERY
WHEN FIGHTING INFERNALS, CERTAIN THINGS HAVE TO TAKE PRIORITY. WE'LL DECIDE WHAT GETS EXTINGUISHED WHEN.
...WE C TAKE THAT C DOW WHEN EVER WAN
YOU EXPECT US TO HANG AROUND HERE? THIS IS STUPID.
LET'S GO.
ZSH
ZSH
P... PLEASE... COME BACK!!
...EXCUSE ME, SIR.
SFF
!
DO YOU REALLY NEED TO SEND TWO MEN AFTER THE RUNNER?
CAN'T YOU JUST SPLIT YOUR FORCE AND EXTINGUISH BOTH AT ONCE?
SFF

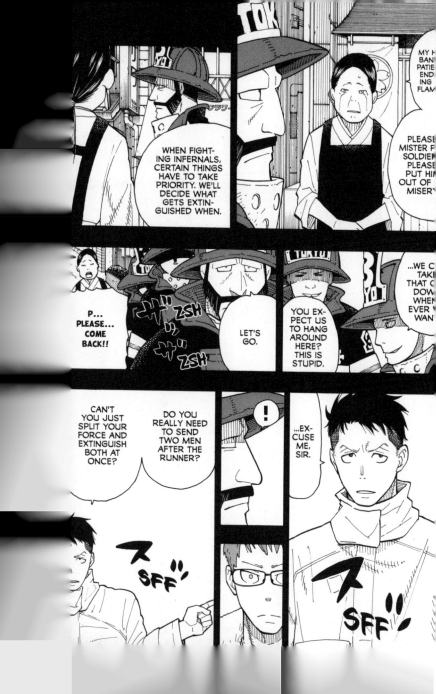

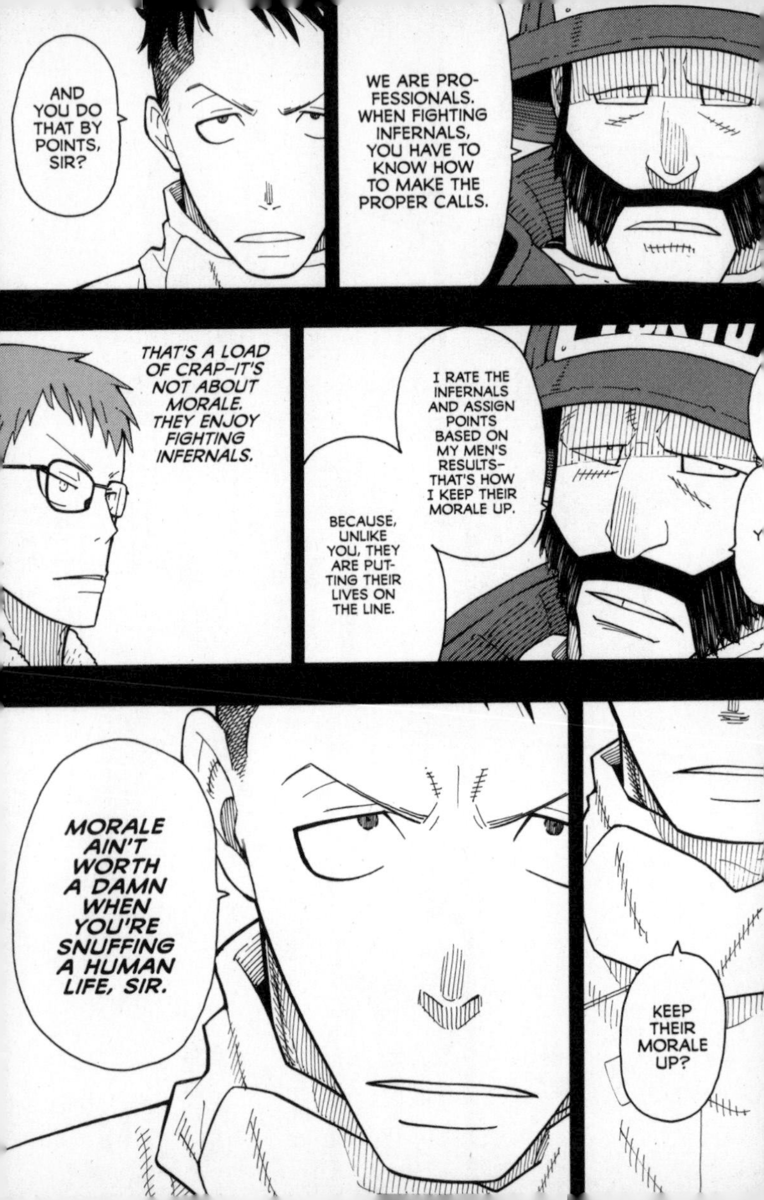
WE ARE PROFESSIONALS. WHEN FIGHTING INFERNALS, YOU HAVE TO KNOW HOW TO MAKE THE PROPER CALLS.
AND YOU DO THAT BY POINTS, SIR?
I RATE THE INFERNALS AND ASSIGN POINTS BASED ON MY MEN'S RESULTS–THAT'S HOW I KEEP THEIR MORALE UP.
BECAUSE, UNLIKE YOU, THEY ARE PUTTING THEIR LIVES ON THE LINE.
THAT'S A LOAD OF CRAP–IT'S NOT ABOUT MORALE. THEY ENJOY FIGHTING INFERNALS.
KEEP THEIR MORALE UP?
MORALE AIN'T WORTH A DAMN WHEN YOU'RE SNUFFING A HUMAN LIFE, SIR.

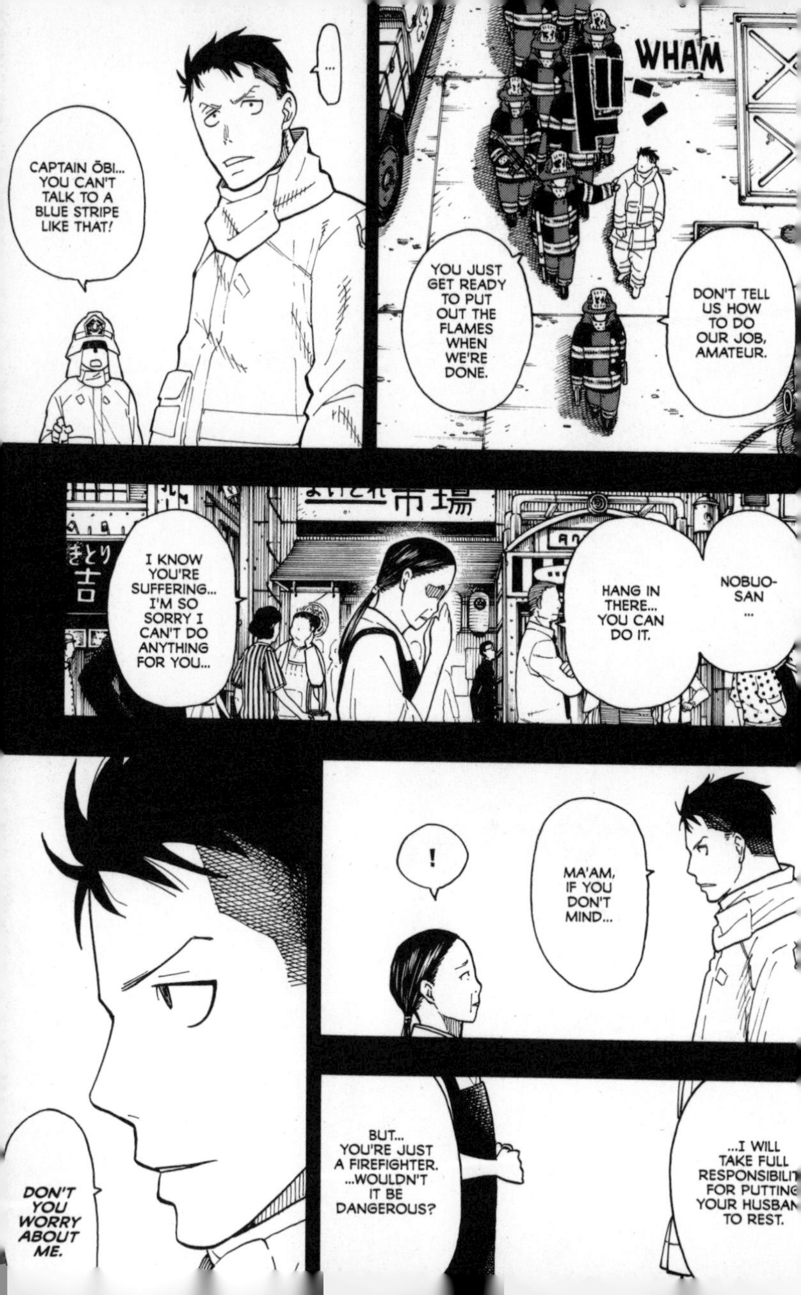
WHAM
DON'T TELL US HOW TO DO OUR JOB, AMATEUR.
YOU JUST GET READY TO PUT OUT THE FLAMES WHEN WE'RE DONE.
...
CAPTAIN ŌBI... YOU CAN'T TALK TO A BLUE STRIPE LIKE THAT!
NOBUO-SAN ...
HANG IN THERE... YOU CAN DO IT.
I KNOW YOU'RE SUFFERING... I'M SO SORRY I CAN'T DO ANYTHING FOR YOU...
MA'AM, IF YOU DON'T MIND...
!
...I WILL TAKE FULL RESPONSIBILIT FOR PUTTING YOUR HUSBAN TO REST.
BUT... YOU'RE JUST A FIREFIGHTER. ...WOULDN'T IT BE DANGEROUS?
DON'T YOU WORRY ABOUT ME.

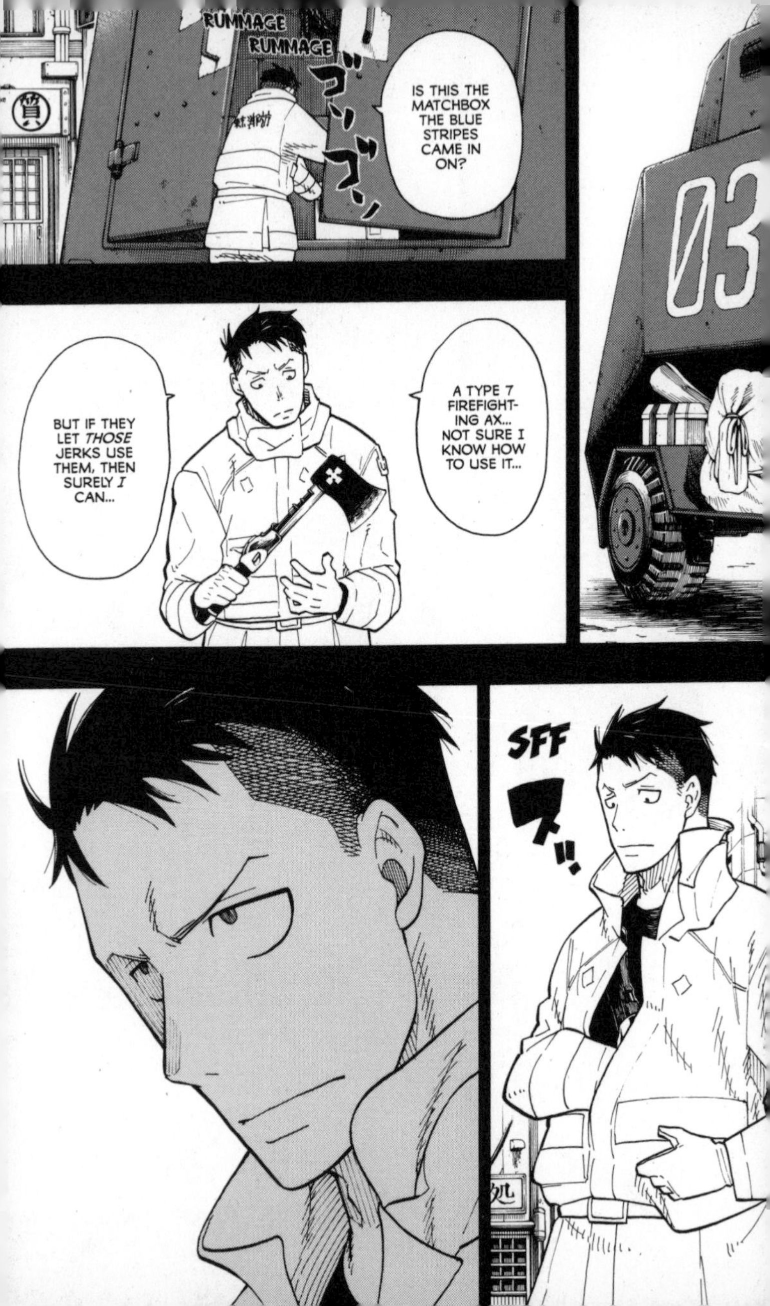

03
RUMMAGE
RUMMAGE
ゴソッ ゴソッ
IS THIS THE MATCHBOX THE BLUE STRIPES CAME IN ON?
A TYPE 7 FIREFIGHTING AX... NOT SURE I KNOW HOW TO USE IT...
BUT IF THEY LET *THOSE* JERKS USE THEM, THEN SURELY *I* CAN...
SFF
スッ!!

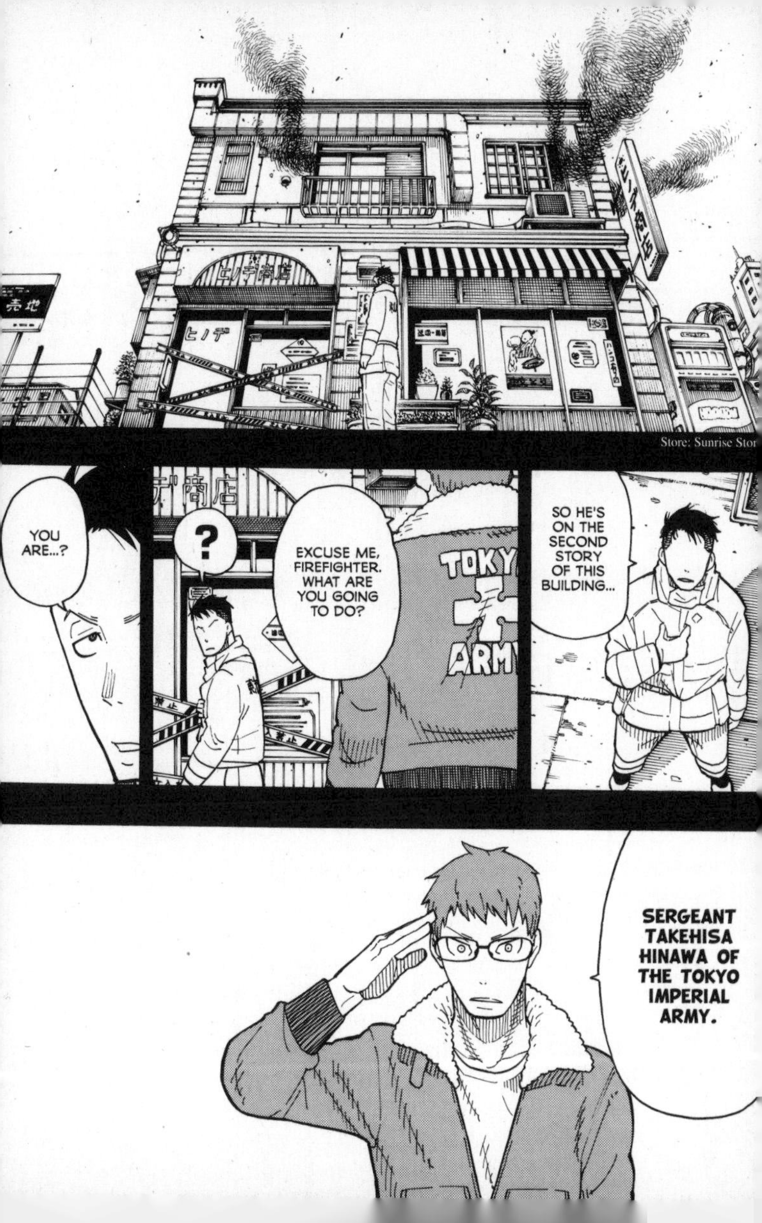
ヒノデ商店
ヒノデ
売地
Store: Sunrise Stor
SO HE'S ON THE SECOND STORY OF THIS BUILDING...
EXCUSE ME, FIREFIGHTER. WHAT ARE YOU GOING TO DO?
?
YOU ARE...?
SERGEANT TAKEHISA HINAWA OF THE TOKYO IMPERIAL ARMY.

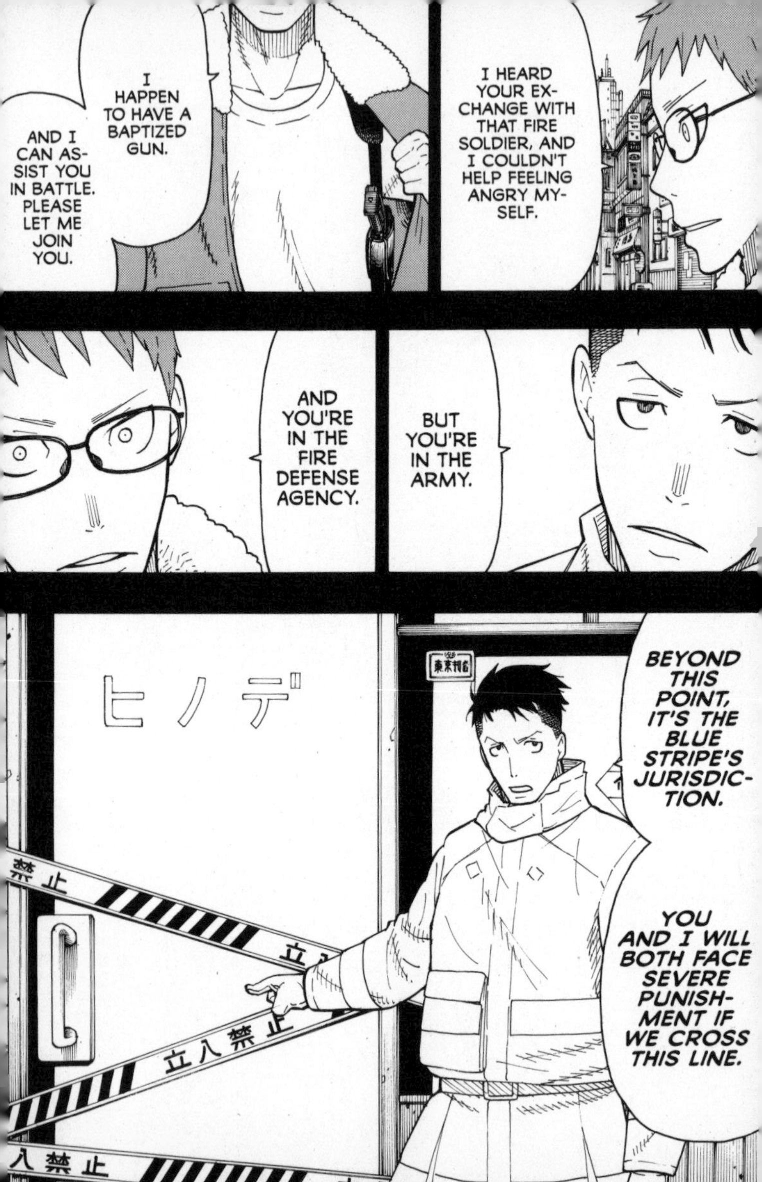
I HEARD YOUR EXCHANGE WITH THAT FIRE SOLDIER, AND I COULDN'T HELP FEELING ANGRY MYSELF.
I HAPPEN TO HAVE A BAPTIZED GUN.
AND I CAN ASSIST YOU IN BATTLE. PLEASE LET ME JOIN YOU.
BUT YOU'RE IN THE ARMY.
AND YOU'RE IN THE FIRE DEFENSE AGENCY.
BEYOND THIS POINT, IT'S THE BLUE STRIPE'S JURISDICTION.
YOU AND I WILL BOTH FACE SEVERE PUNISHMENT IF WE CROSS THIS LINE.
ヒノデ
立入禁止

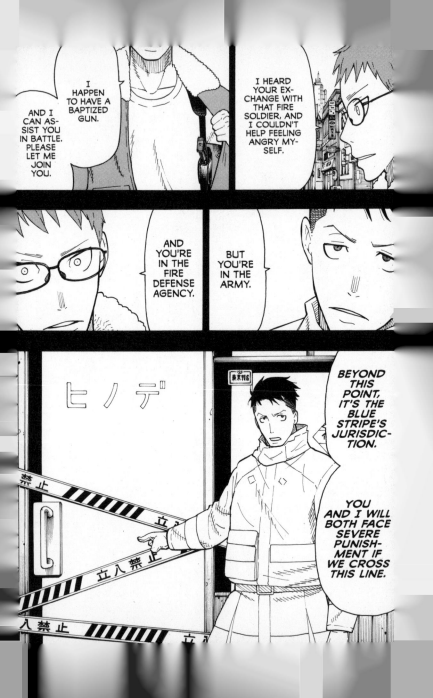

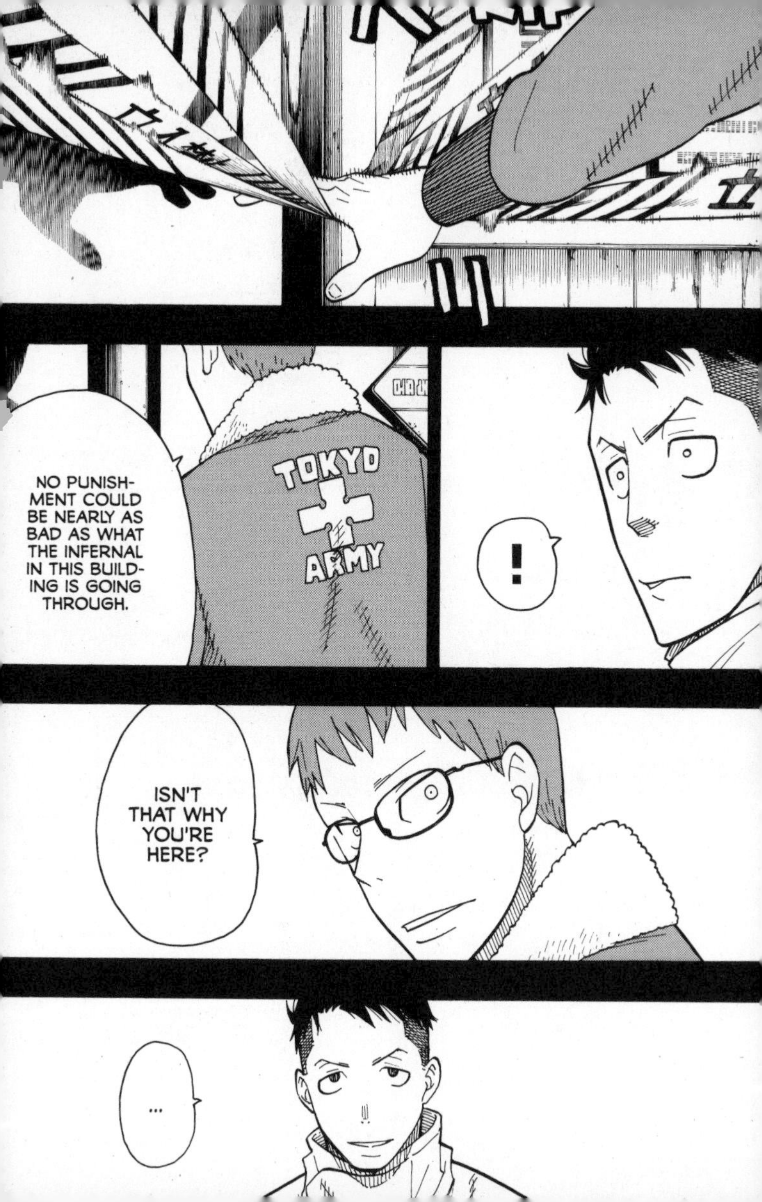

!
TOKYO
ARMY
NO PUNISHMENT COULD BE NEARLY AS BAD AS WHAT THE INFERNAL IN THIS BUILDING IS GOING THROUGH.
ISN'T THAT WHY YOU'RE HERE?
...

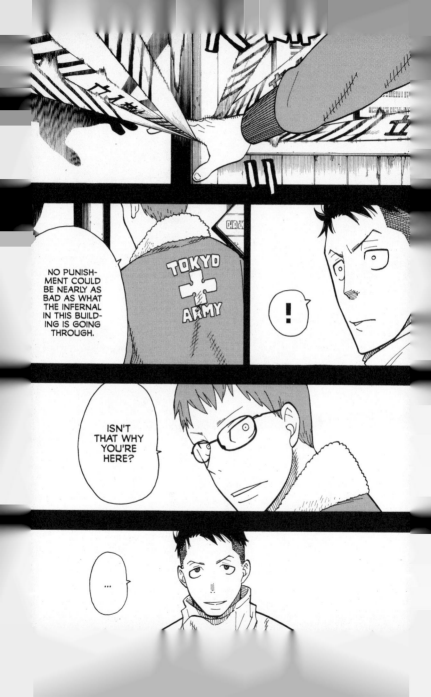

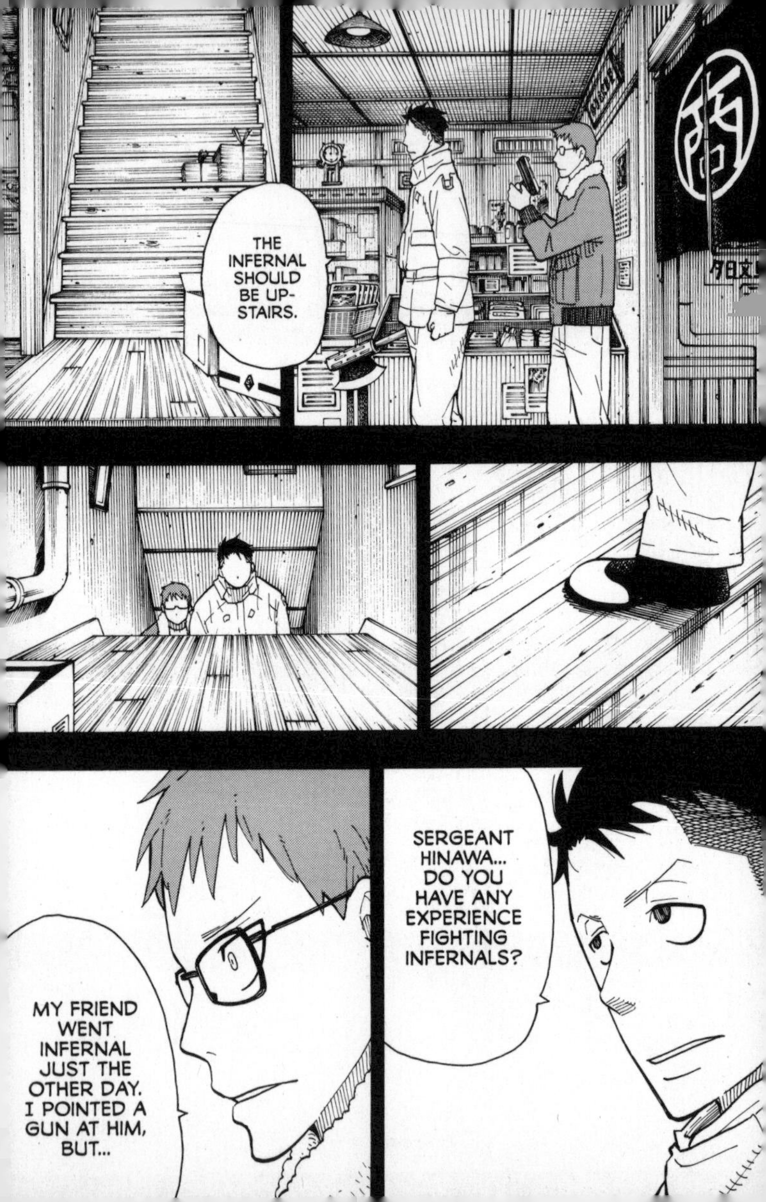
THE INFERNAL SHOULD BE UP-STAIRS.
SERGEANT HINAWA... DO YOU HAVE ANY EXPERIENCE FIGHTING INFERNALS?
MY FRIEND WENT INFERNAL JUST THE OTHER DAY. I POINTED A GUN AT HIM, BUT...

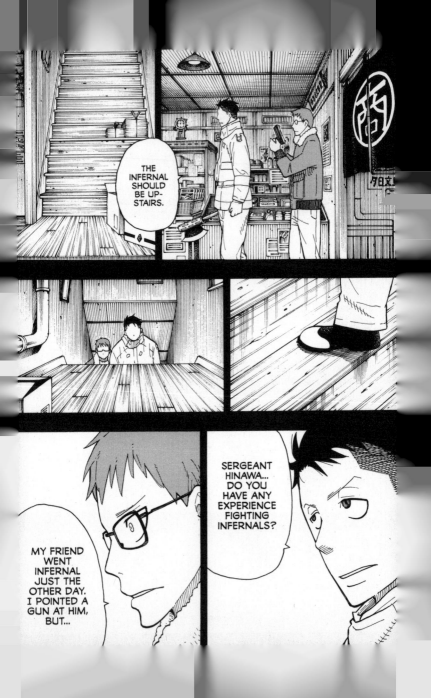

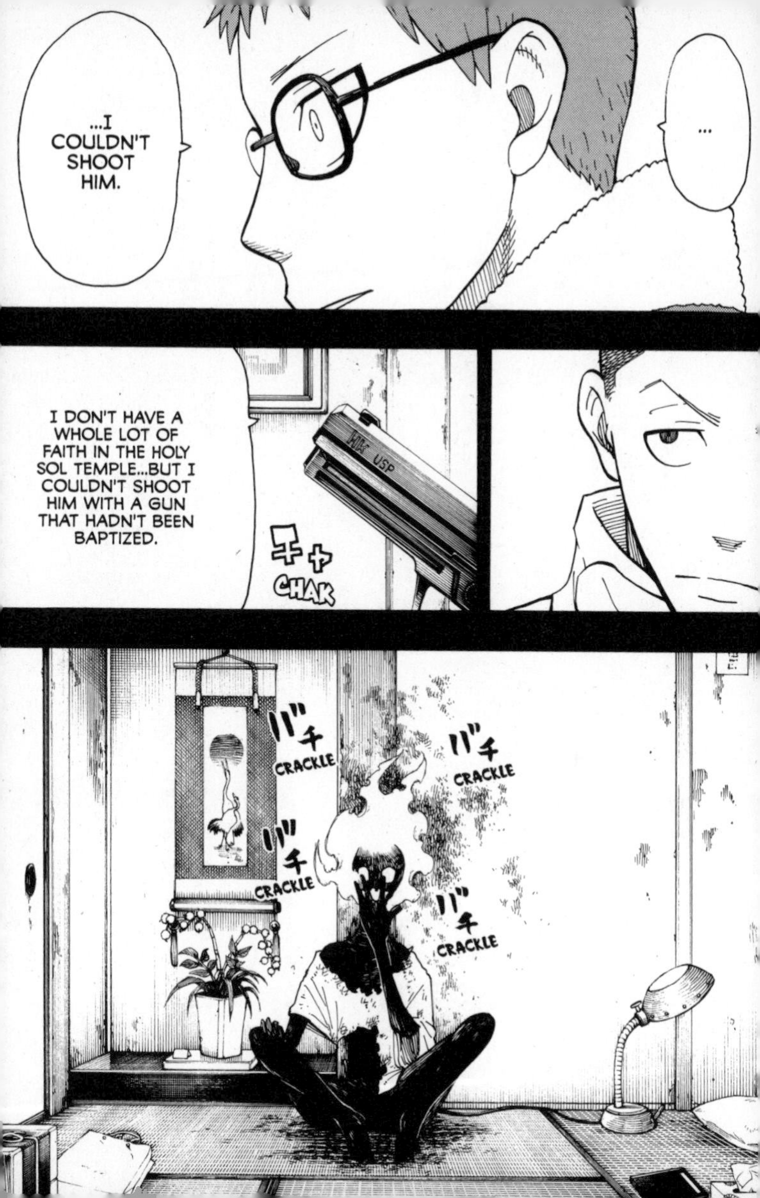
...
...I COULDN'T SHOOT HIM.
I DON'T HAVE A WHOLE LOT OF FAITH IN THE HOLY SOL TEMPLE...BUT I COULDN'T SHOOT HIM WITH A GUN THAT HADN'T BEEN BAPTIZED.
HK USP
チャ
CHAK
バチ
CRACKLE
バチ
CRACKLE
バチ
CRACKLE
バチ
CRACKLE

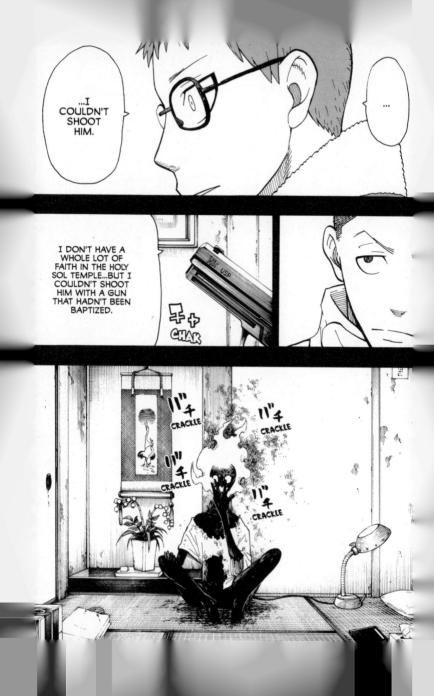

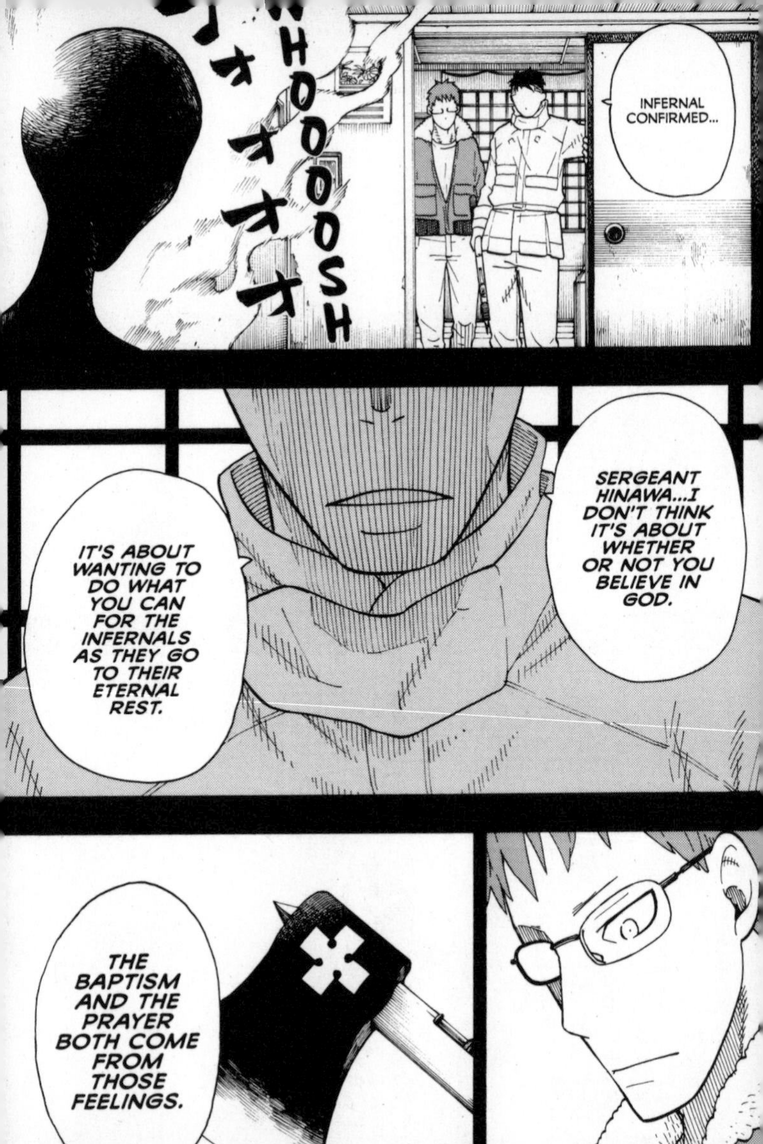
INFERNAL CONFIRMED...
WHOOOOSH
オオオオ
SERGEANT HINAWA...I DON'T THINK IT'S ABOUT WHETHER OR NOT YOU BELIEVE IN GOD.
IT'S ABOUT WANTING TO DO WHAT YOU CAN FOR THE INFERNALS AS THEY GO TO THEIR ETERNAL REST.
THE BAPTISM AND THE PRAYER BOTH COME FROM THOSE FEELINGS.

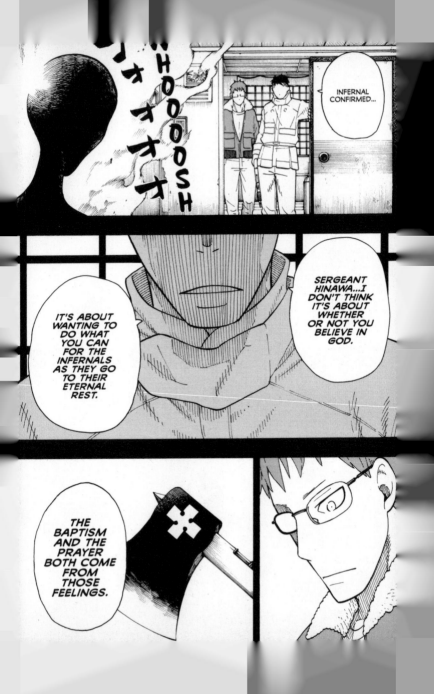

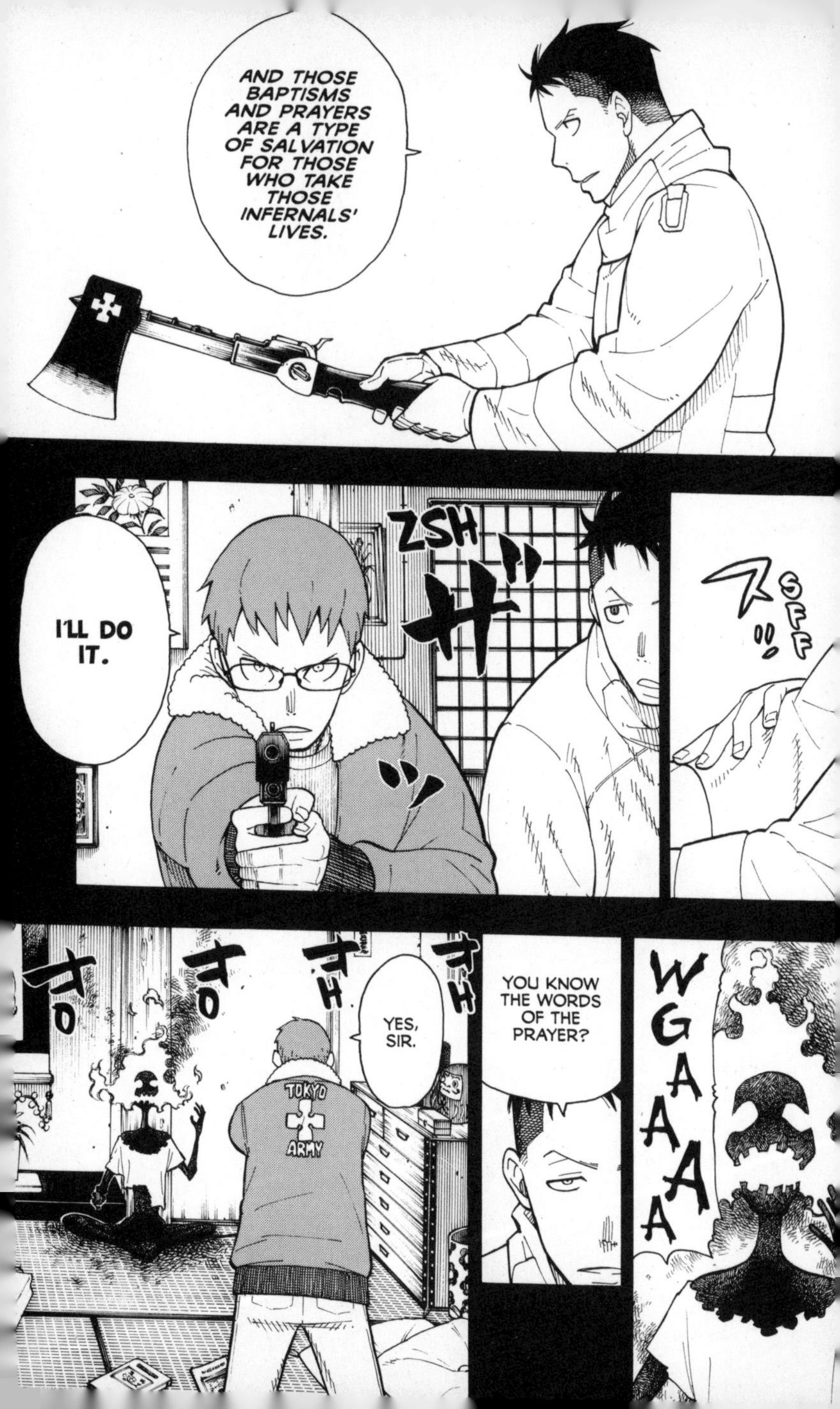
AND THOSE BAPTISMS AND PRAYERS ARE A TYPE OF SALVATION FOR THOSE WHO TAKE THOSE INFERNALS' LIVES.
SFF
ZSH
I'LL DO IT.
WGAAAAA
YOU KNOW THE WORDS OF THE PRAYER?
H
YES, SIR.
H
O
O
TOKYO ARMY

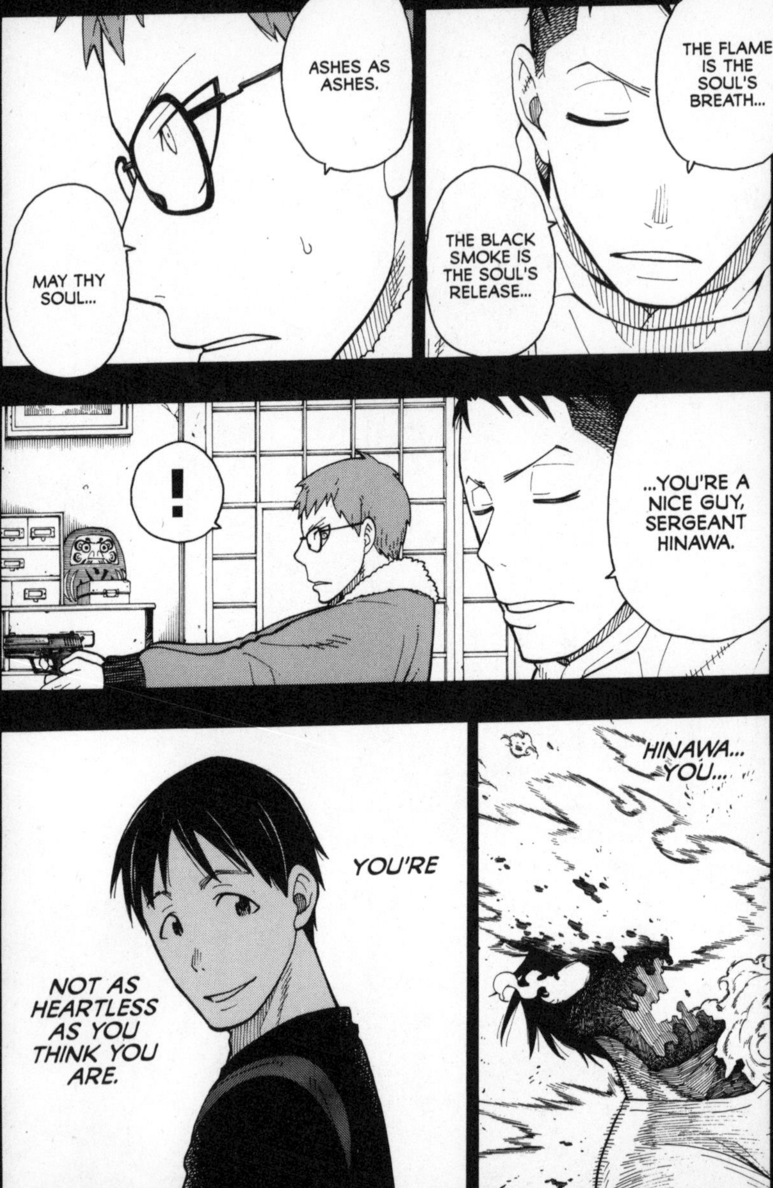
THE FLAME IS THE SOUL'S BREATH...
THE BLACK SMOKE IS THE SOUL'S RELEASE...
ASHES AS ASHES.
MAY THY SOUL...
...YOU'RE A NICE GUY, SERGEANT HINAWA.
!
HINAWA... YOU...
YOU'RE
NOT AS HEARTLESS AS YOU THINK YOU ARE.

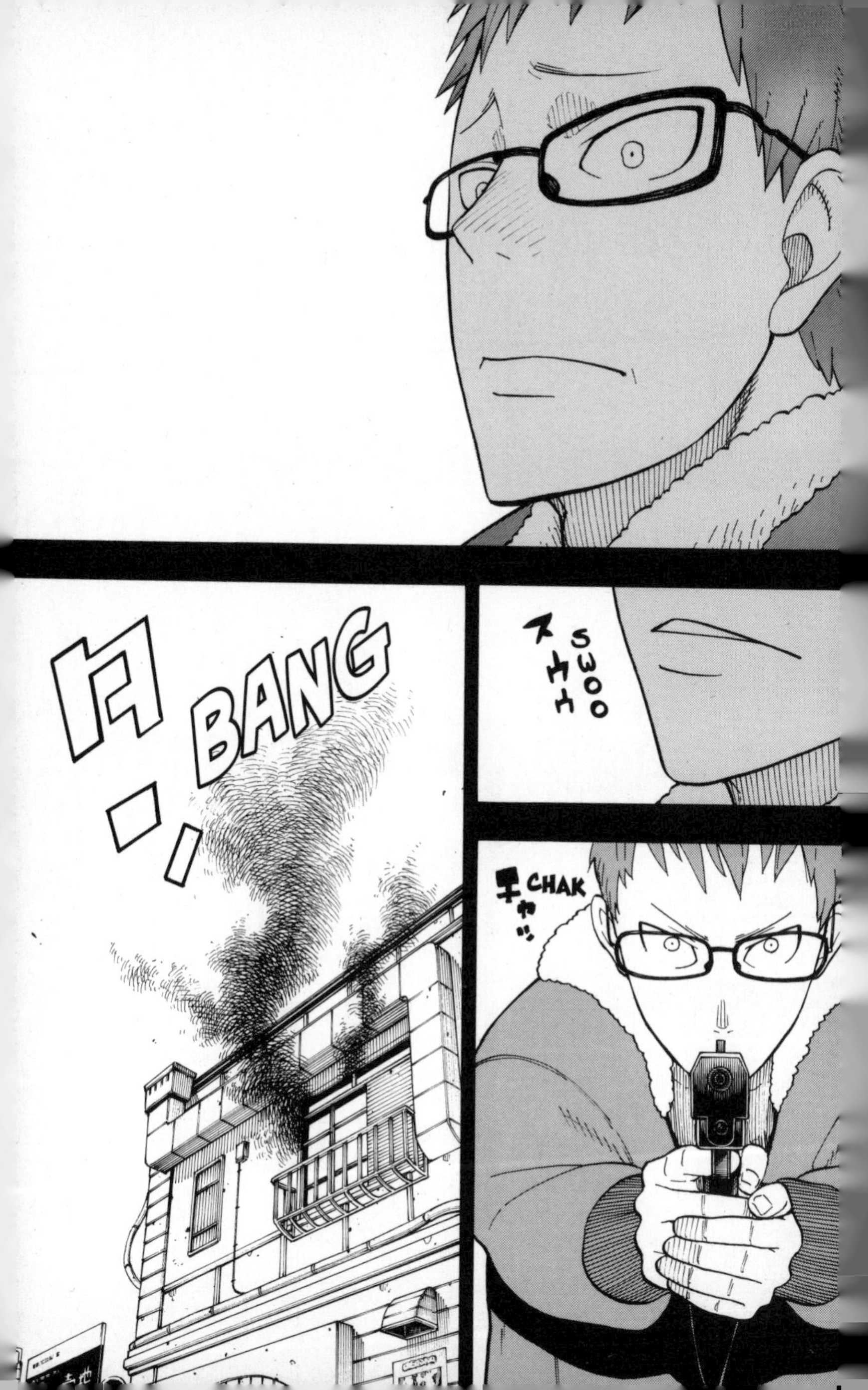

SWOO
CHAK
BANG

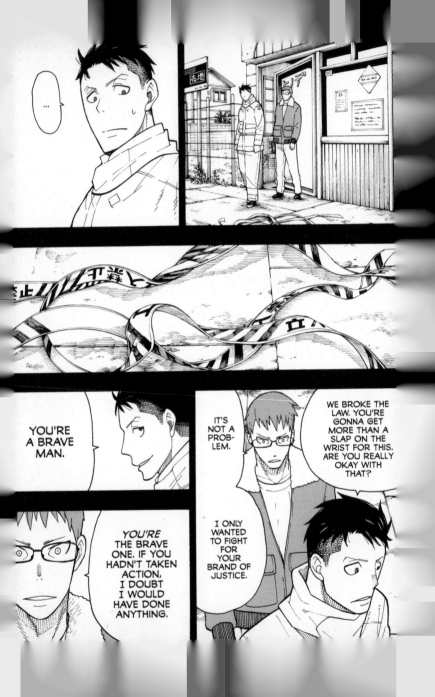

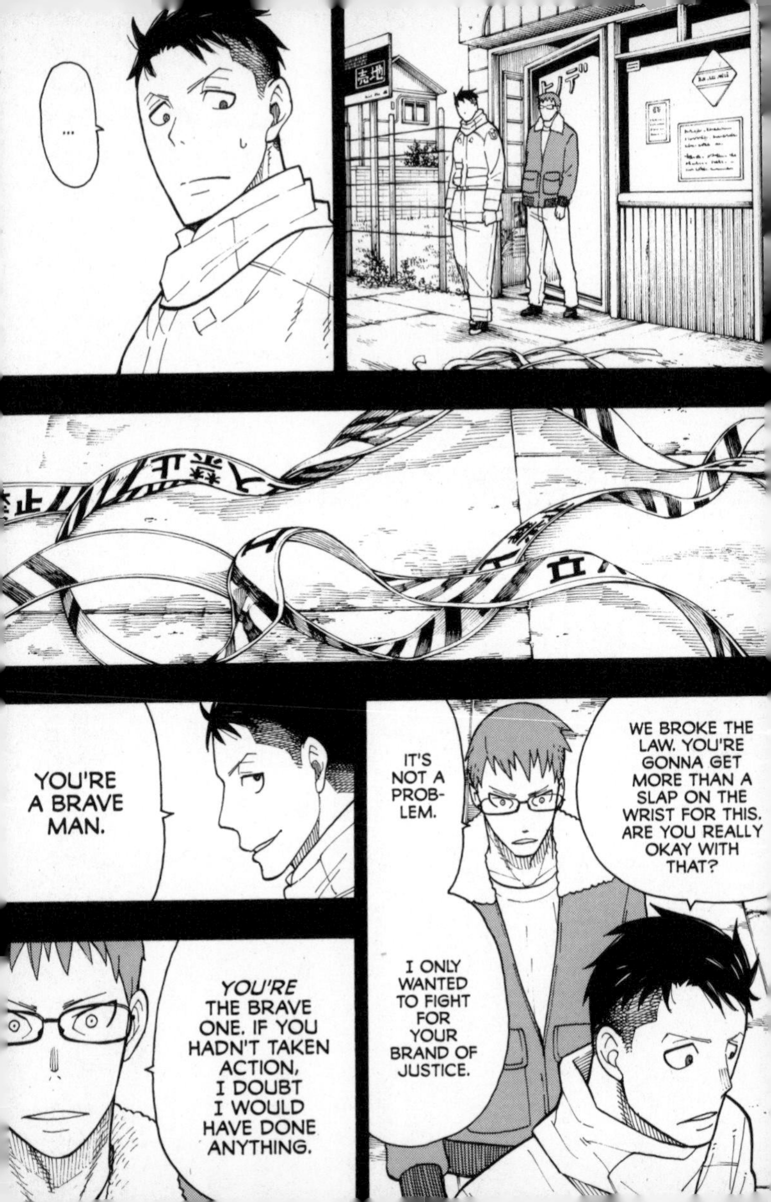
売地
...
WE BROKE THE LAW. YOU'RE GONNA GET MORE THAN A SLAP ON THE WRIST FOR THIS. ARE YOU REALLY OKAY WITH THAT?
IT'S NOT A PROB-LEM.
I ONLY WANTED TO FIGHT FOR YOUR BRAND OF JUSTICE.
YOU'RE A BRAVE MAN.
YOU'RE THE BRAVE ONE. IF YOU HADN'T TAKEN ACTION, I DOUBT I WOULD HAVE DONE ANYTHING.

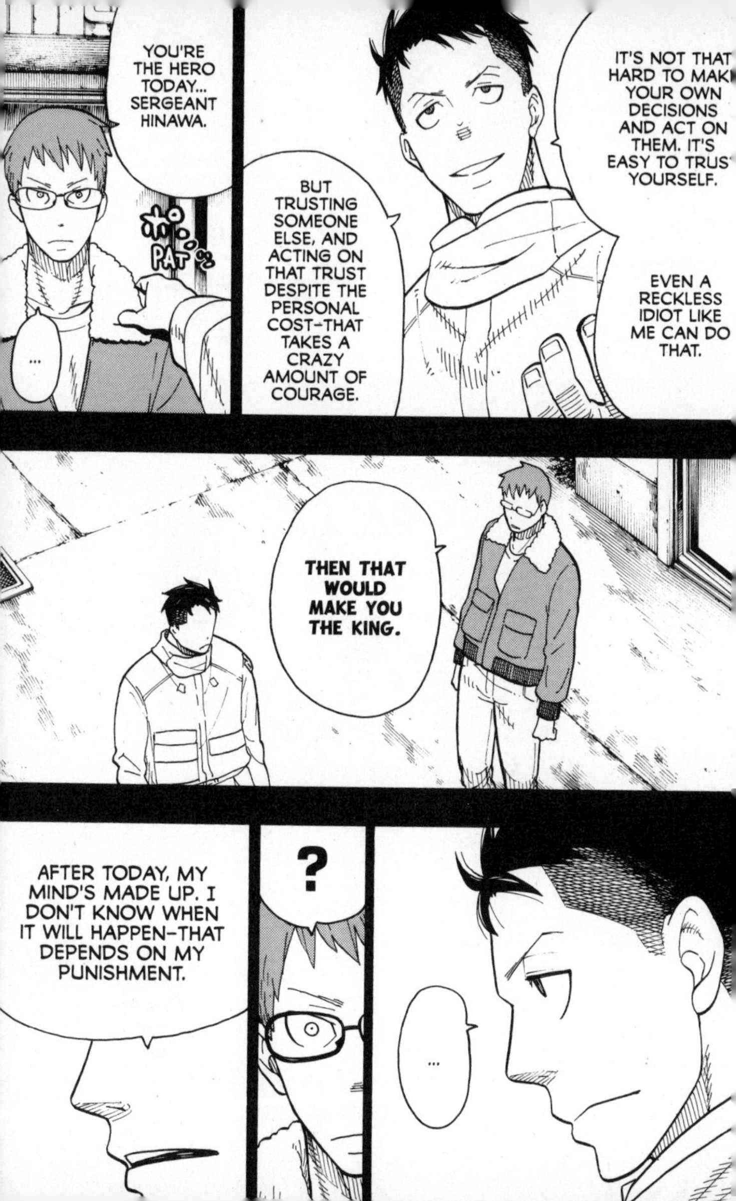
IT'S NOT THAT HARD TO MAK YOUR OWN DECISIONS AND ACT ON THEM. IT'S EASY TO TRUS YOURSELF.
EVEN A RECKLESS IDIOT LIKE ME CAN DO THAT.
BUT TRUSTING SOMEONE ELSE, AND ACTING ON THAT TRUST DESPITE THE PERSONAL COST–THAT TAKES A CRAZY AMOUNT OF COURAGE.
YOU'RE THE HERO TODAY... SERGEANT HINAWA.
PAT
...
THEN THAT WOULD MAKE YOU THE KING.
...
?
AFTER TODAY, MY MIND'S MADE UP. I DON'T KNOW WHEN IT WILL HAPPEN–THAT DEPENDS ON MY PUNISHMENT.

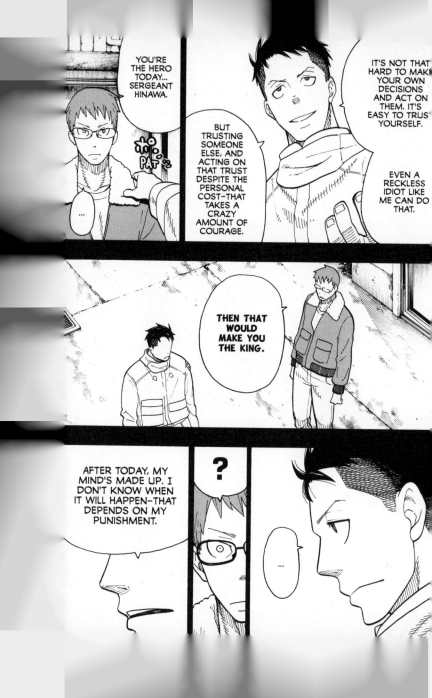

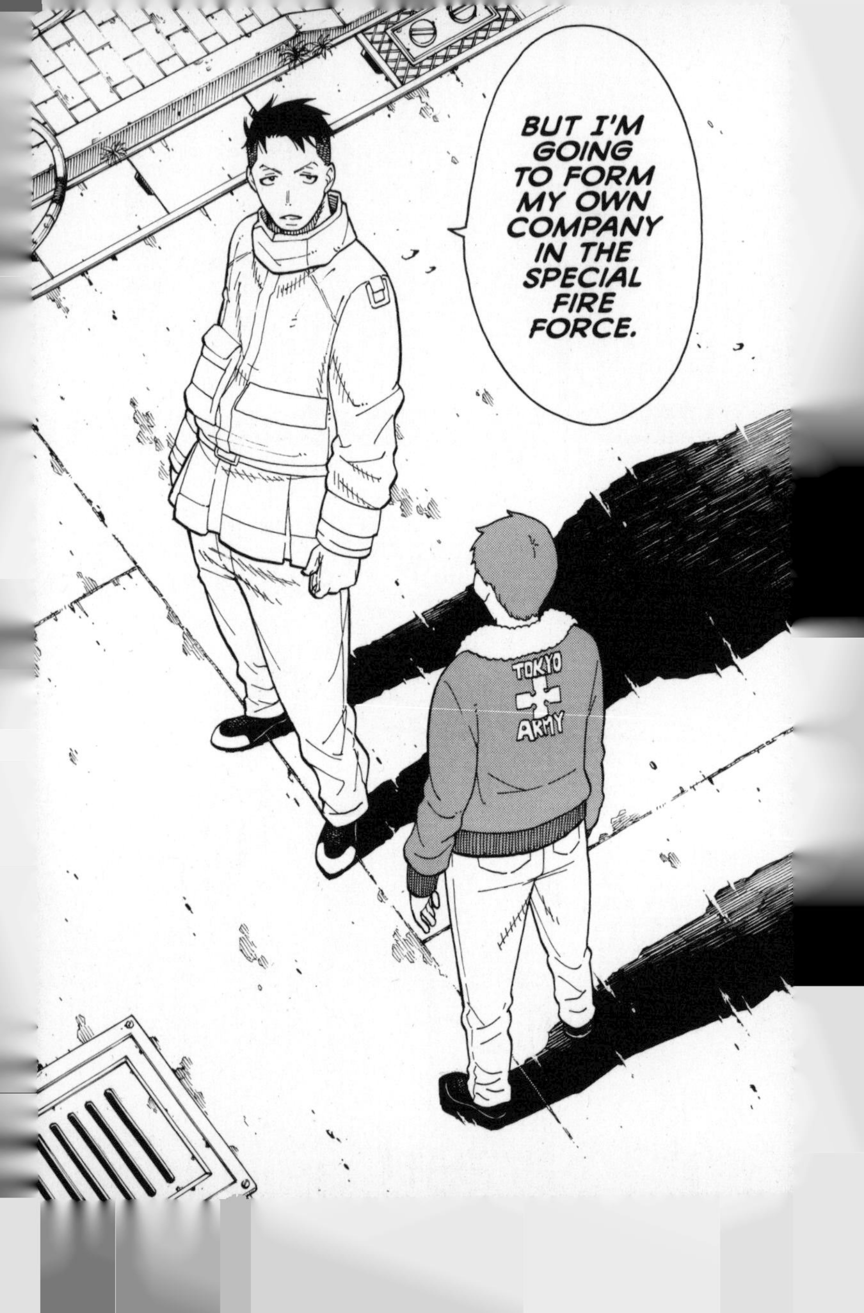
BUT I'M GOING TO FORM MY OWN COMPANY IN THE SPECIAL FIRE FORCE.
TOKYO
ARMY

FIRE FORCE

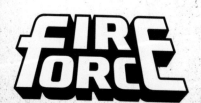

FIRE FORCE

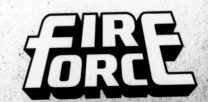

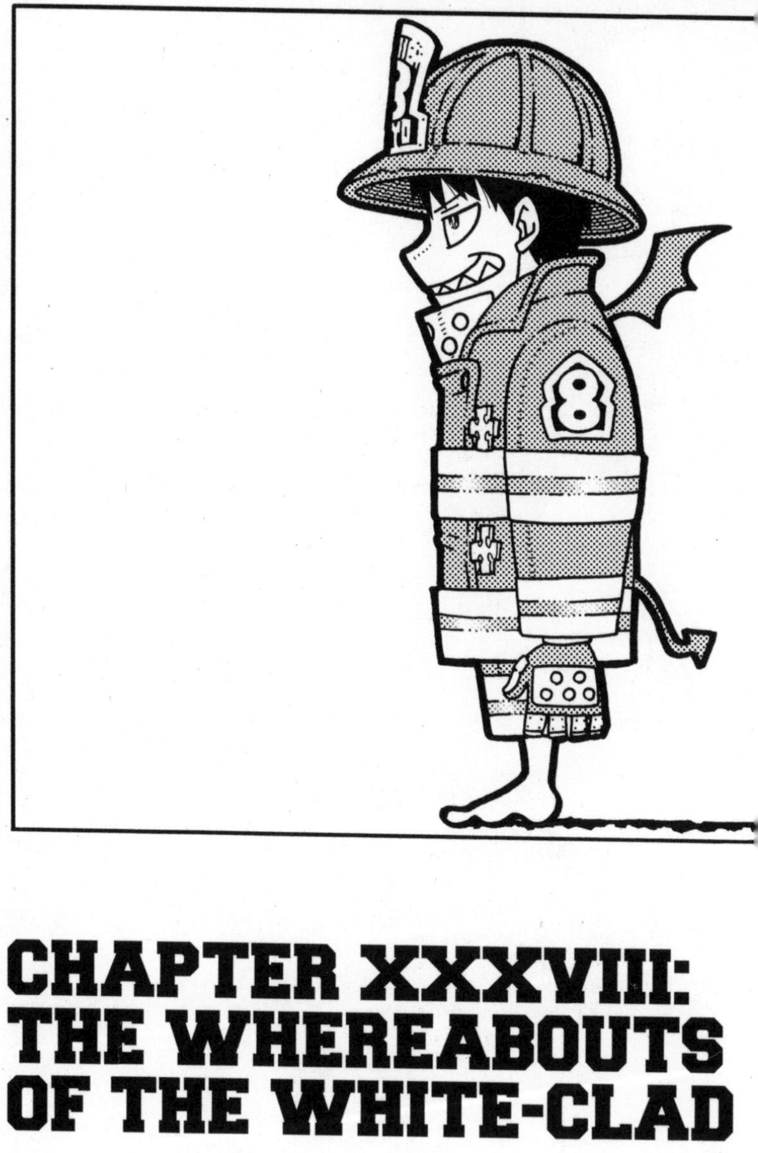

CHAPTER XXXVIII: THE WHEREABOUTS OF THE WHITE-CLAD

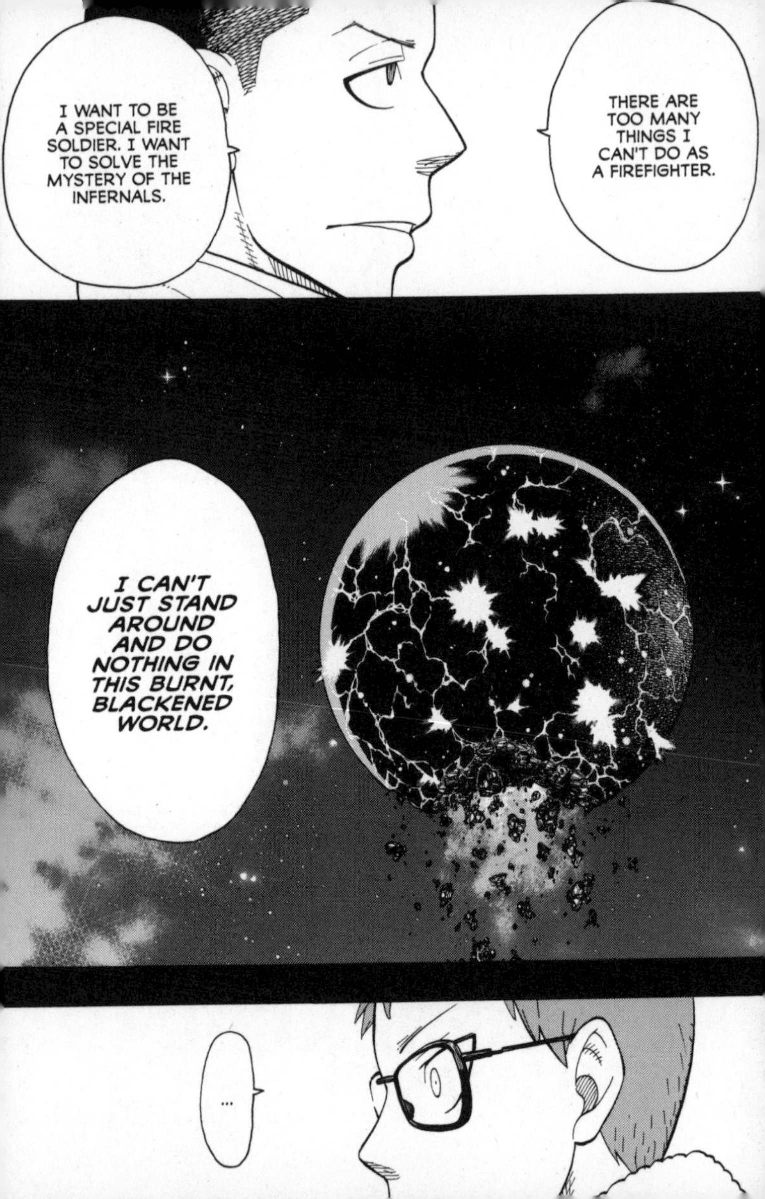
THERE ARE TOO MANY THINGS I CAN'T DO AS A FIREFIGHTER.
I WANT TO BE A SPECIAL FIRE SOLDIER. I WANT TO SOLVE THE MYSTERY OF THE INFERNALS.
I CAN'T JUST STAND AROUND AND DO NOTHING IN THIS BURNT, BLACKENED WORLD.
...

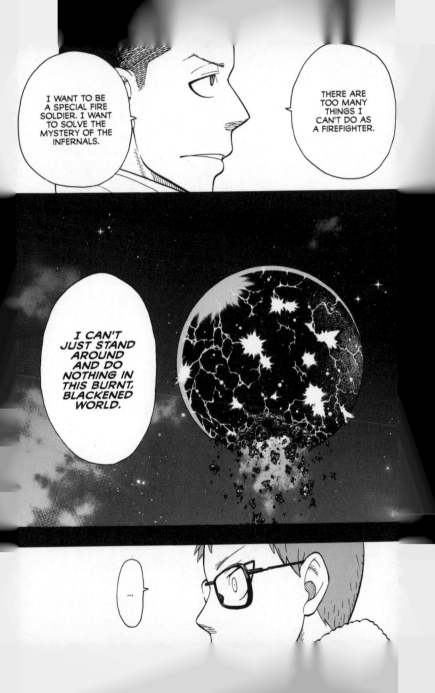

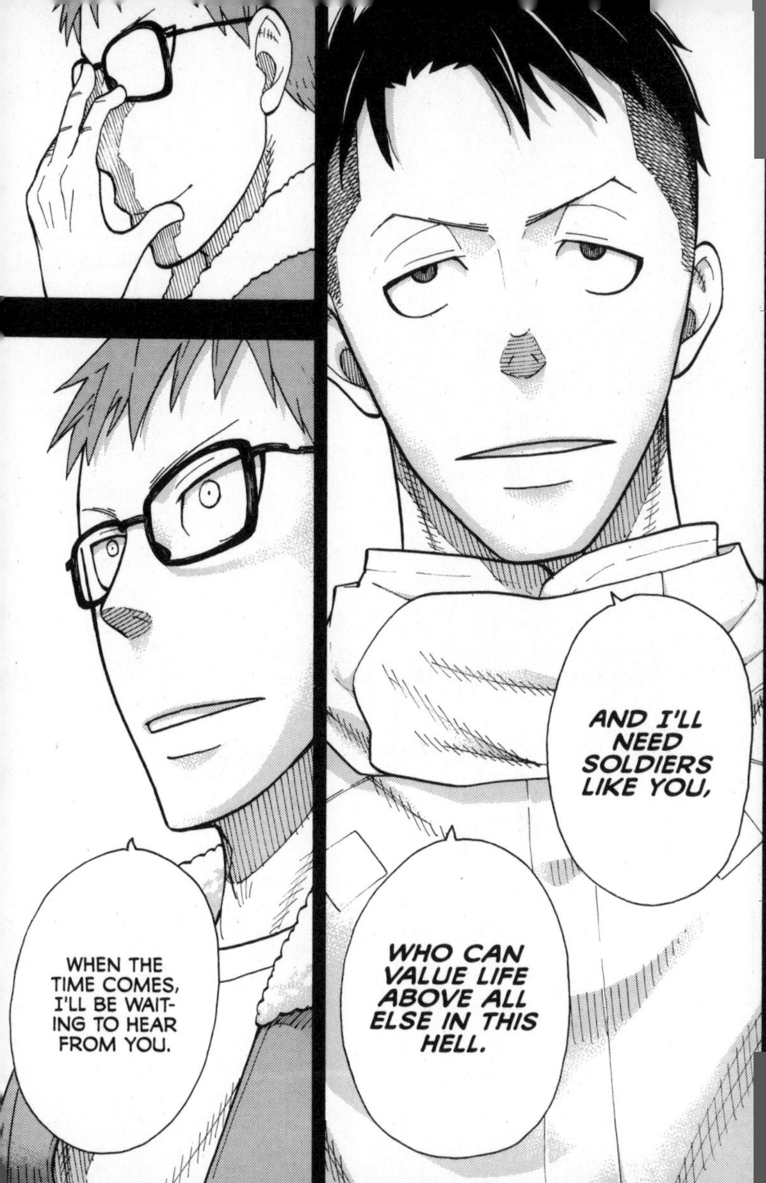
AND I'LL NEED SOLDIERS LIKE YOU,
WHO CAN VALUE LIFE ABOVE ALL ELSE IN THIS HELL.
WHEN THE TIME COMES, I'LL BE WAITING TO HEAR FROM YOU.

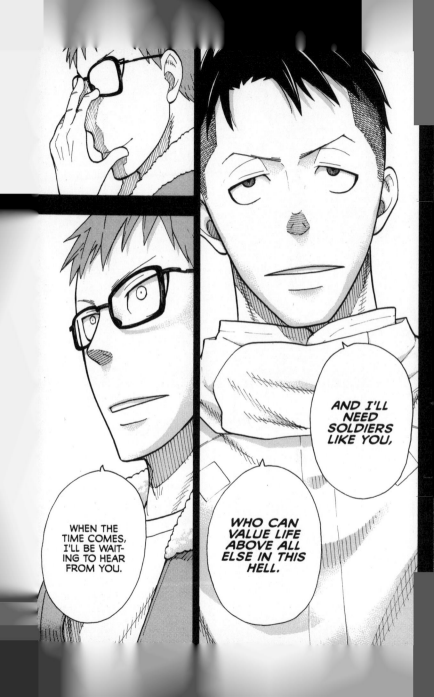

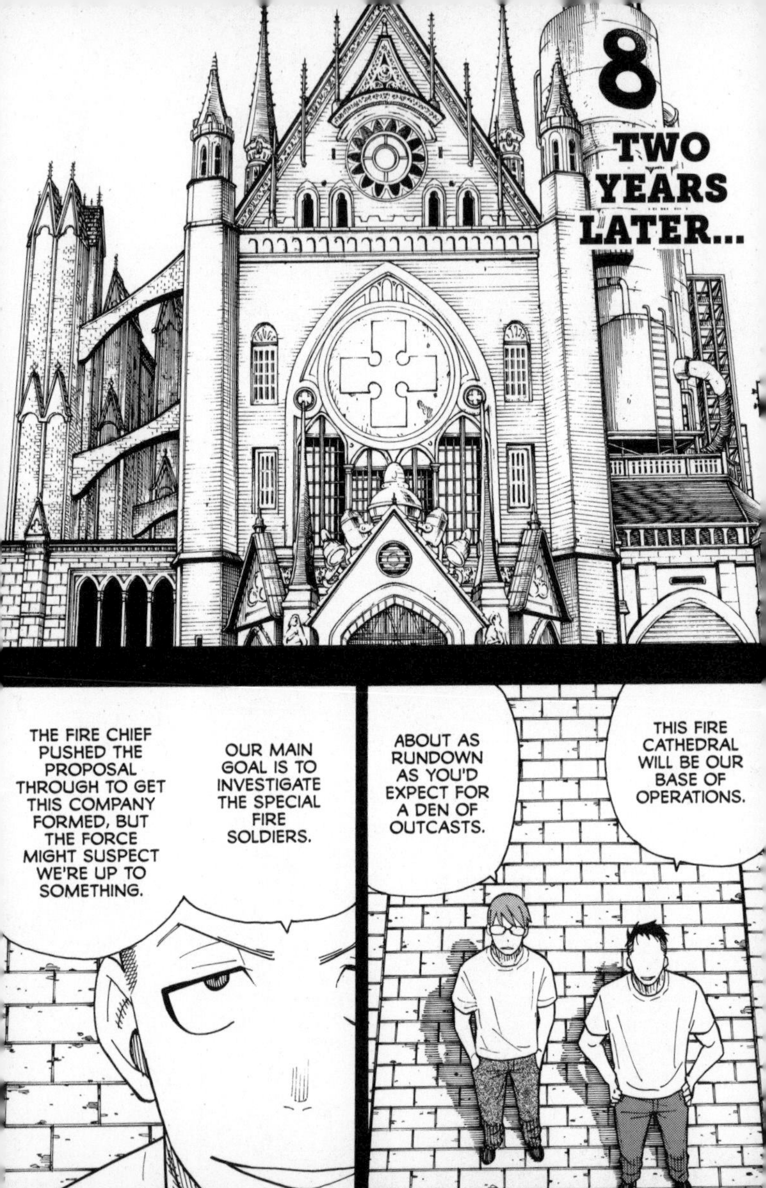
8
TWO YEARS LATER...
THIS FIRE CATHEDRAL WILL BE OUR BASE OF OPERATIONS.
ABOUT AS RUNDOWN AS YOU'D EXPECT FOR A DEN OF OUTCASTS.
OUR MAIN GOAL IS TO INVESTIGATE THE SPECIAL FIRE SOLDIERS.
THE FIRE CHIEF PUSHED THE PROPOSAL THROUGH TO GET THIS COMPANY FORMED, BUT THE FORCE MIGHT SUSPECT WE'RE UP TO SOMETHING.

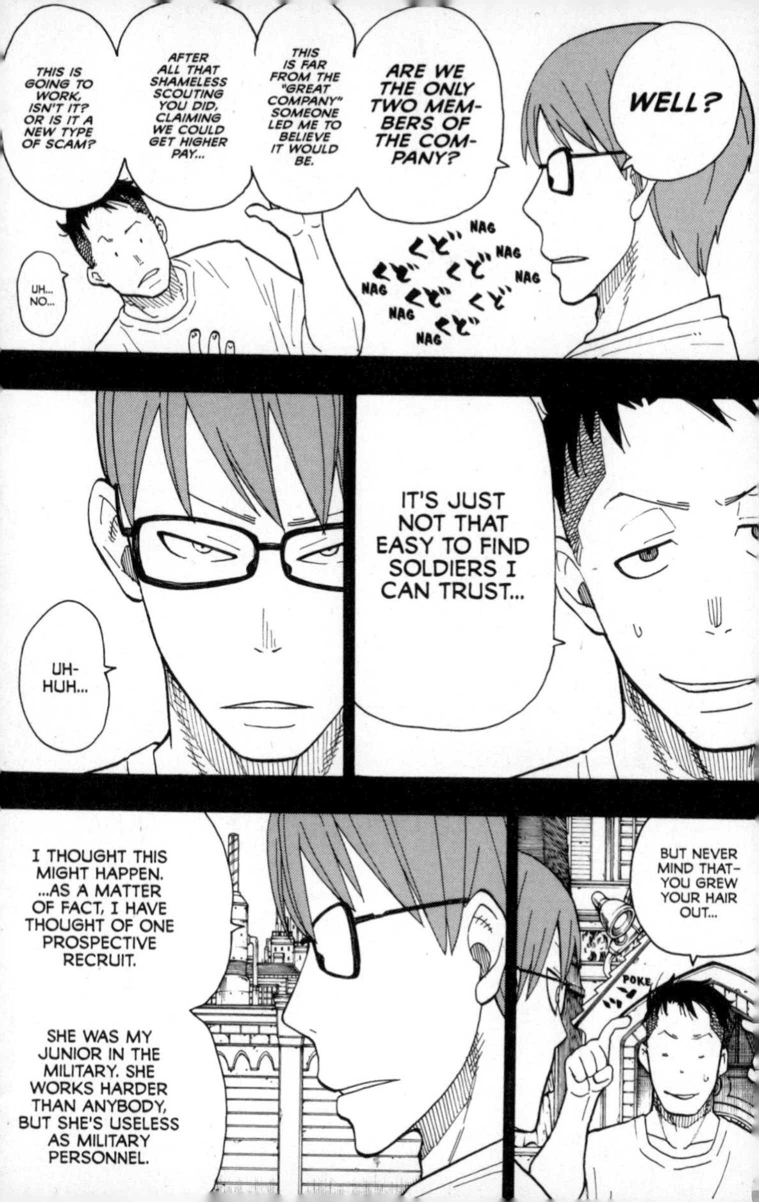
WELL?
ARE WE THE ONLY TWO MEMBERS OF THE COMPANY?
THIS IS FAR FROM THE "GREAT COMPANY" SOMEONE LED ME TO BELIEVE IT WOULD BE.
AFTER ALL THAT SHAMELESS SCOUTING YOU DID, CLAIMING WE COULD GET HIGHER PAY...
THIS IS GOING TO WORK, ISN'T IT? OR IS IT A NEW TYPE OF SCAM?
NAG NAG NAG NAG NAG NAG
UH... NO...
IT'S JUST NOT THAT EASY TO FIND SOLDIERS I CAN TRUST...
UH-HUH...
BUT NEVER MIND THAT- YOU GREW YOUR HAIR OUT...
POKE
I THOUGHT THIS MIGHT HAPPEN. ...AS A MATTER OF FACT, I HAVE THOUGHT OF ONE PROSPECTIVE RECRUIT.
SHE WAS MY JUNIOR IN THE MILITARY. SHE WORKS HARDER THAN ANYBODY, BUT SHE'S USELESS AS MILITARY PERSONNEL.

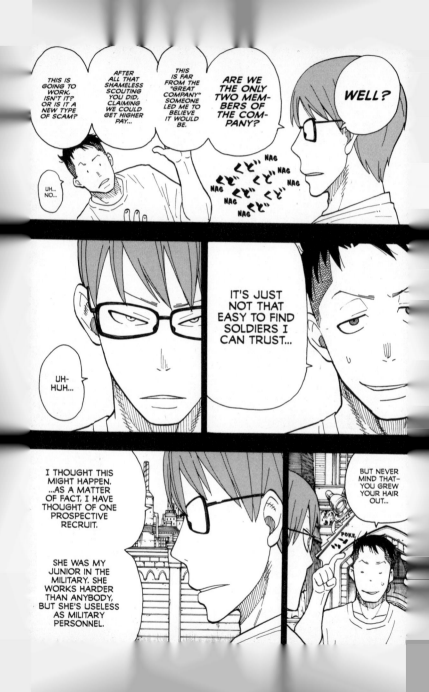

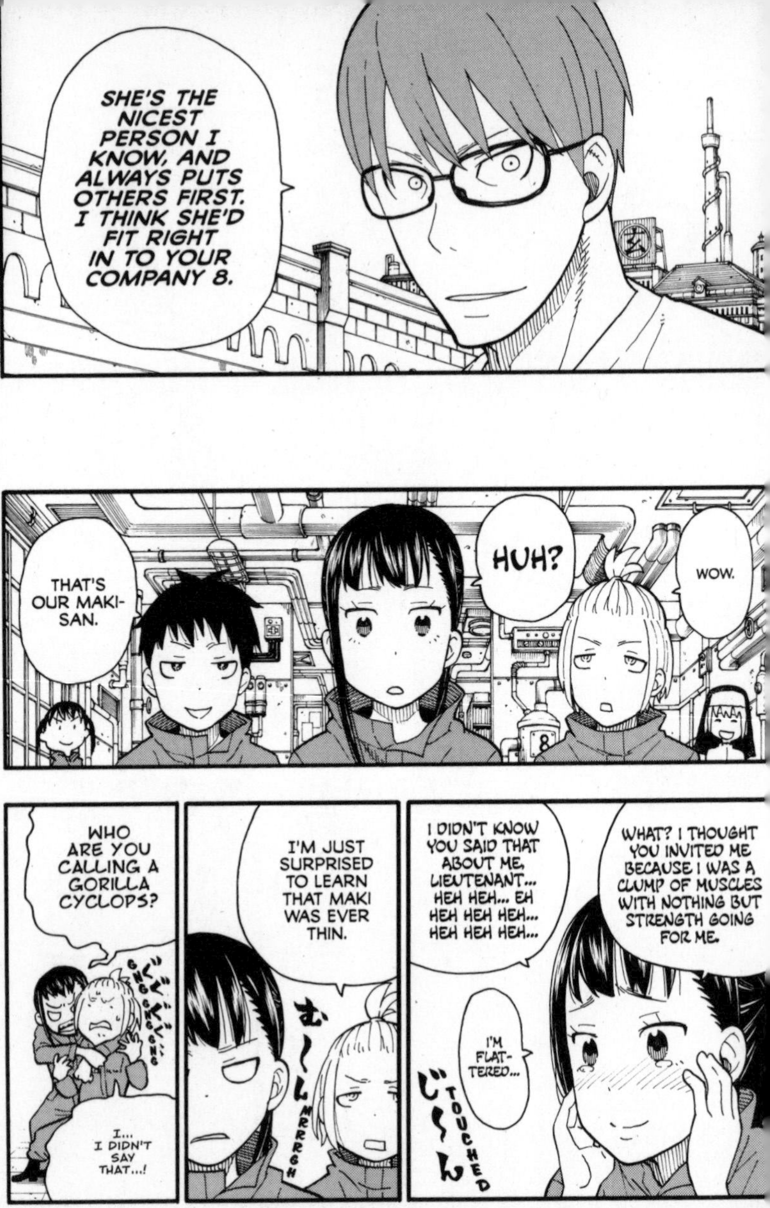
SHE'S THE NICEST PERSON I KNOW, AND ALWAYS PUTS OTHERS FIRST. I THINK SHE'D FIT RIGHT IN TO YOUR COMPANY 8.
WOW.
HUH?
THAT'S OUR MAKI-SAN.
WHAT? I THOUGHT YOU INVITED ME BECAUSE I WAS A CLUMP OF MUSCLES WITH NOTHING BUT STRENGTH GOING FOR ME.
I DIDN'T KNOW YOU SAID THAT ABOUT ME, LIEUTENANT... HEH HEH... EH HEH HEH HEH... HEH HEH HEH...
I'M FLAT-TERED...
TOUCHED
I'M JUST SURPRISED TO LEARN THAT MAKI WAS EVER THIN.
MRRRGH
WHO ARE YOU CALLING A GORILLA CYCLOPS?
GNG GNG GNG
I... I DIDN'T SAY THAT...!

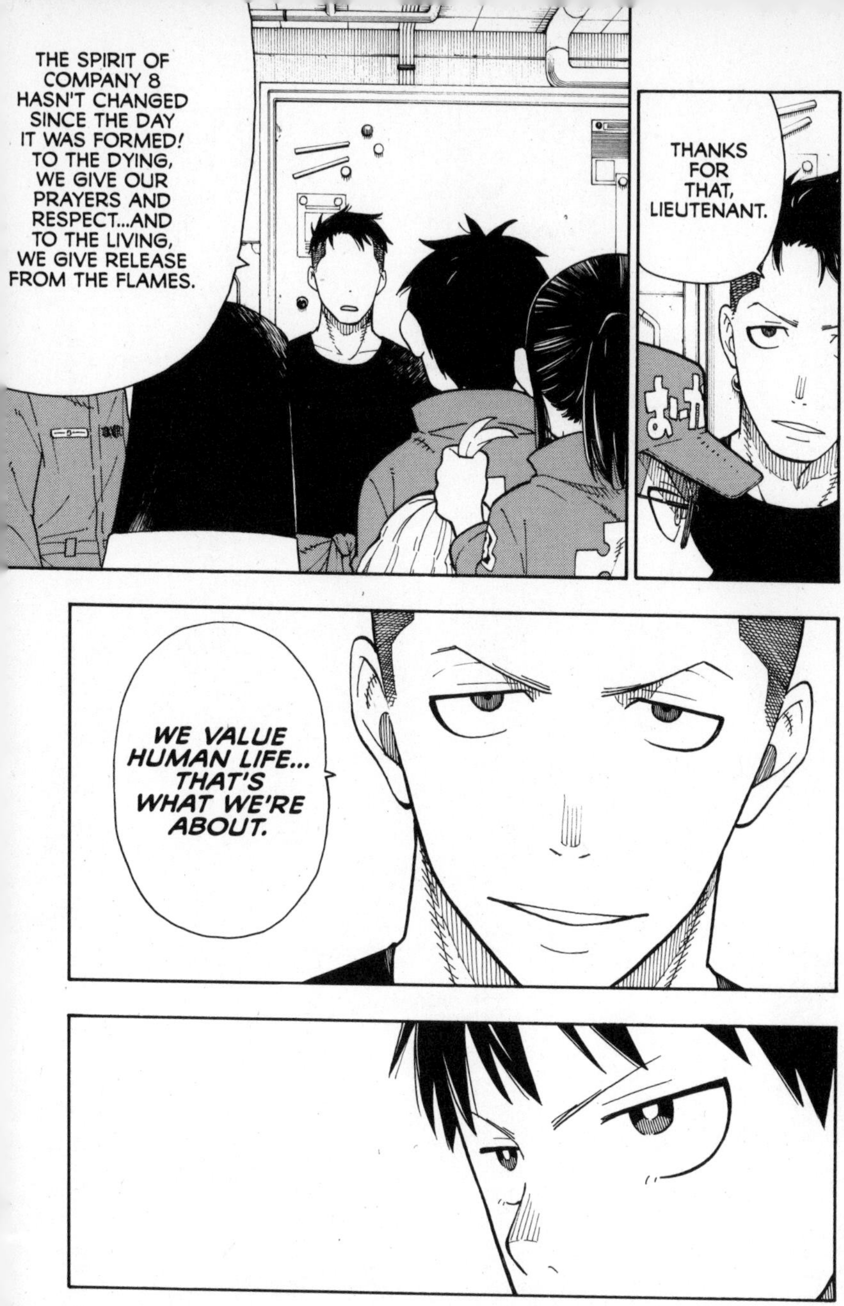
THANKS FOR THAT, LIEUTENANT.
THE SPIRIT OF COMPANY 8 HASN'T CHANGED SINCE THE DAY IT WAS FORMED! TO THE DYING, WE GIVE OUR PRAYERS AND RESPECT...AND TO THE LIVING, WE GIVE RELEASE FROM THE FLAMES.
WE VALUE HUMAN LIFE... THAT'S WHAT WE'RE ABOUT.

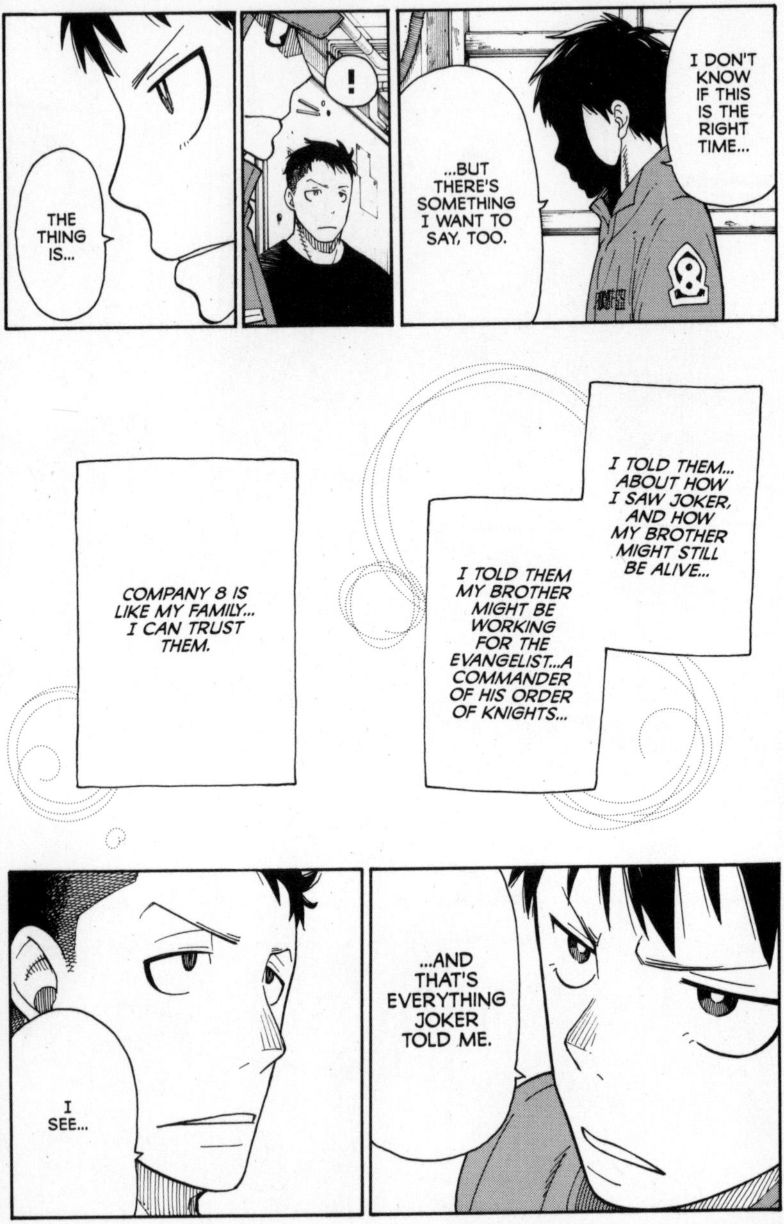
I DON'T KNOW IF THIS IS THE RIGHT TIME...
...BUT THERE'S SOMETHING I WANT TO SAY, TOO.
!
THE THING IS...
I TOLD THEM... ABOUT HOW I SAW JOKER, AND HOW MY BROTHER MIGHT STILL BE ALIVE...
I TOLD THEM MY BROTHER MIGHT BE WORKING FOR THE EVANGELIST...A COMMANDER OF HIS ORDER OF KNIGHTS...
COMPANY 8 IS LIKE MY FAMILY... I CAN TRUST THEM.
...AND THAT'S EVERYTHING JOKER TOLD ME.
I SEE...

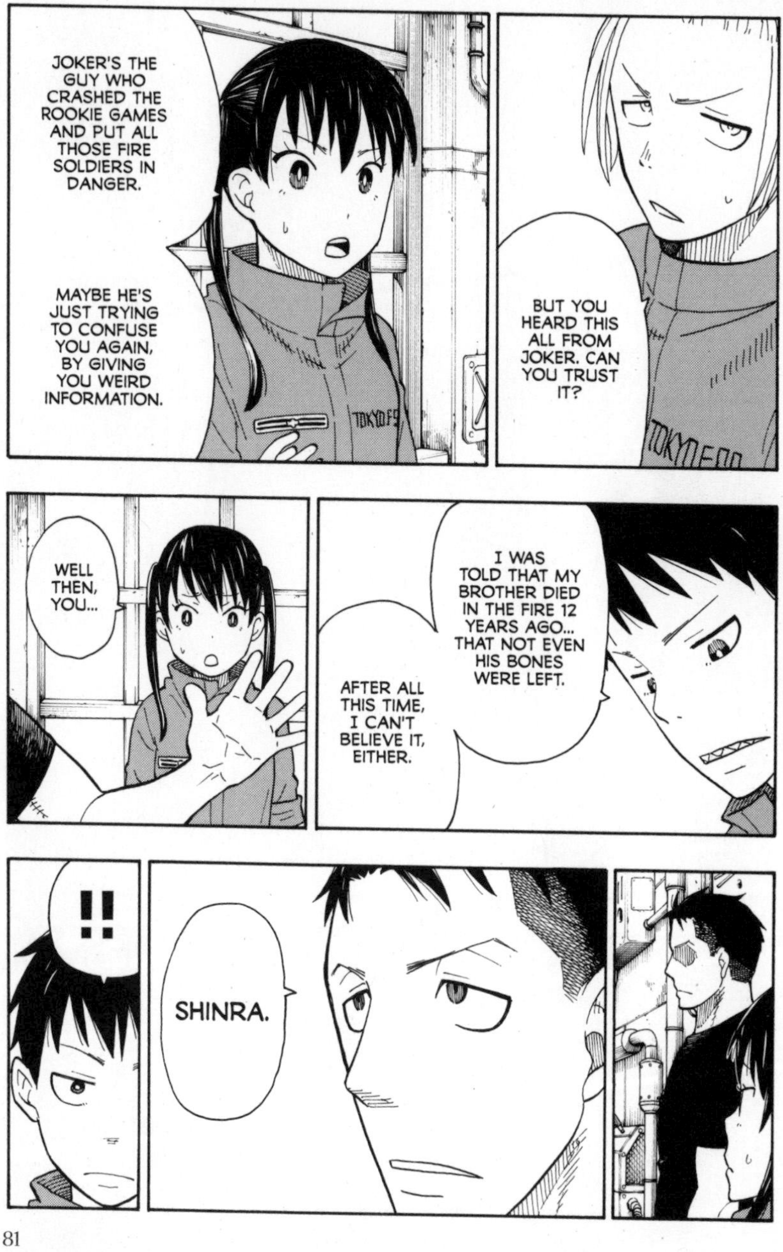
BUT YOU HEARD THIS ALL FROM JOKER. CAN YOU TRUST IT?
JOKER'S THE GUY WHO CRASHED THE ROOKIE GAMES AND PUT ALL THOSE FIRE SOLDIERS IN DANGER.
MAYBE HE'S JUST TRYING TO CONFUSE YOU AGAIN, BY GIVING YOU WEIRD INFORMATION.
I WAS TOLD THAT MY BROTHER DIED IN THE FIRE 12 YEARS AGO... THAT NOT EVEN HIS BONES WERE LEFT.
AFTER ALL THIS TIME, I CAN'T BELIEVE IT, EITHER.
WELL THEN, YOU...
SHINRA.
!!

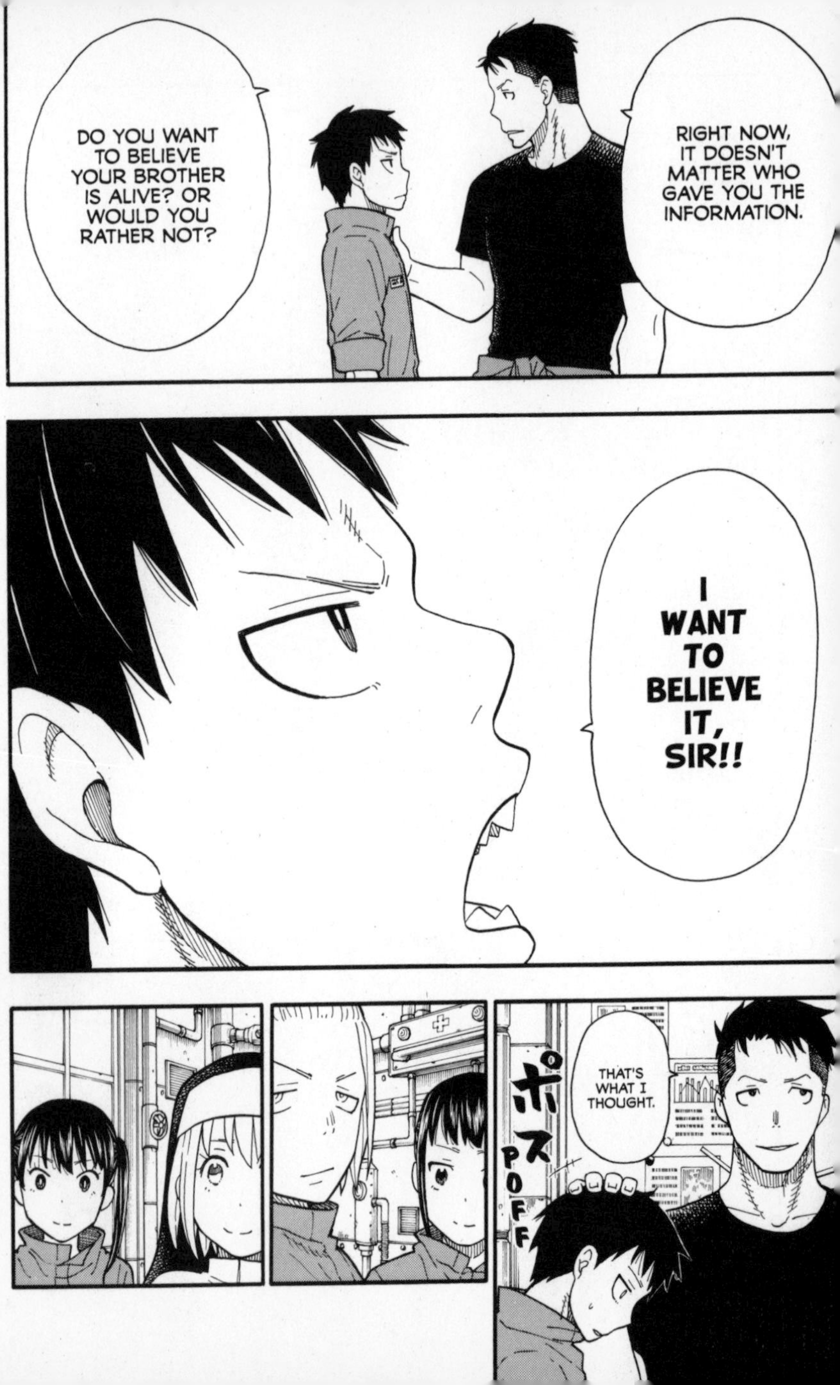
RIGHT NOW, IT DOESN'T MATTER WHO GAVE YOU THE INFORMATION.
DO YOU WANT TO BELIEVE YOUR BROTHER IS ALIVE? OR WOULD YOU RATHER NOT?
I WANT TO BELIEVE IT, SIR!!
THAT'S WHAT I THOUGHT.
ポス
POFF

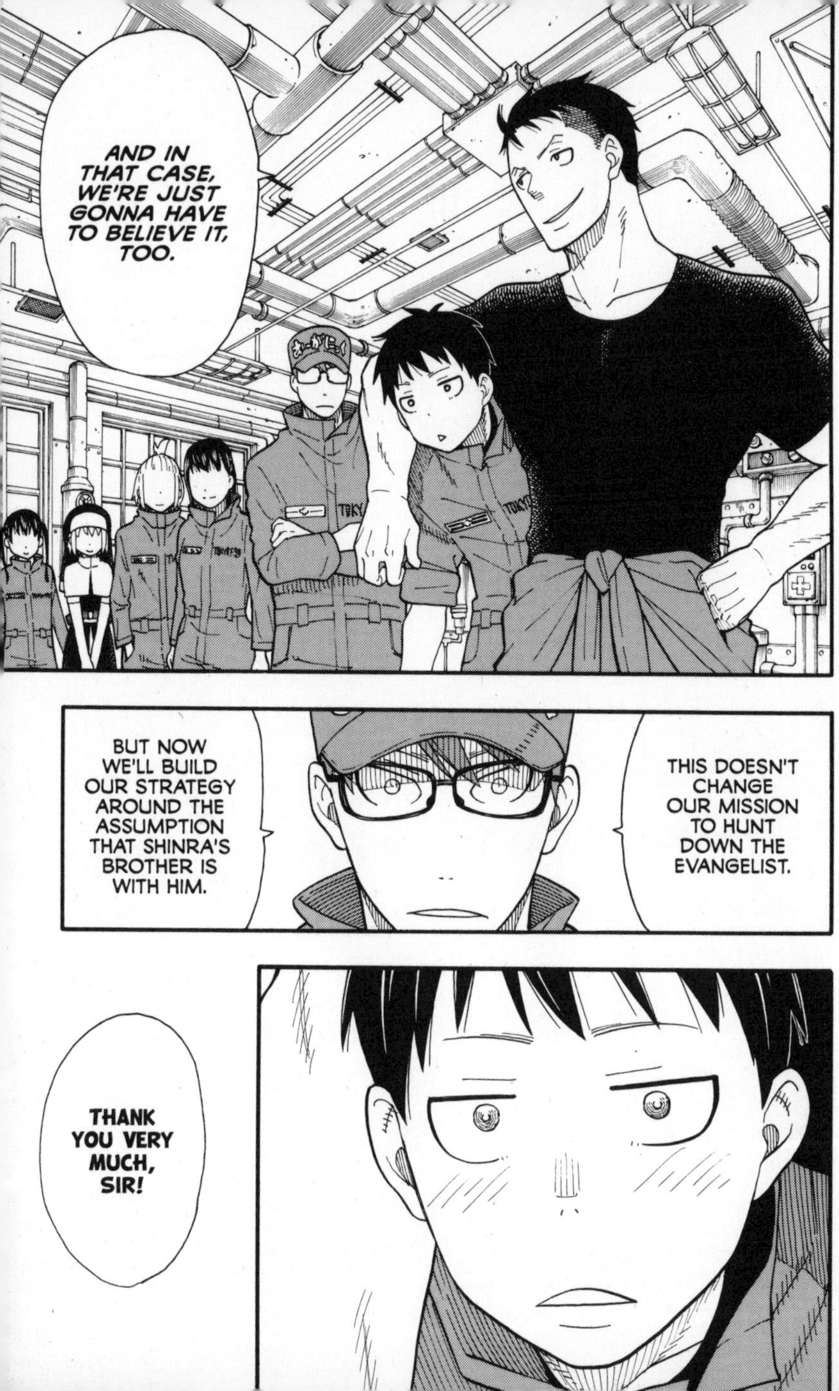
AND IN THAT CASE, WE'RE JUST GONNA HAVE TO BELIEVE IT, TOO.
THIS DOESN'T CHANGE OUR MISSION TO HUNT DOWN THE EVANGELIST.
BUT NOW WE'LL BUILD OUR STRATEGY AROUND THE ASSUMPTION THAT SHINRA'S BROTHER IS WITH HIM.
THANK YOU VERY MUCH, SIR!

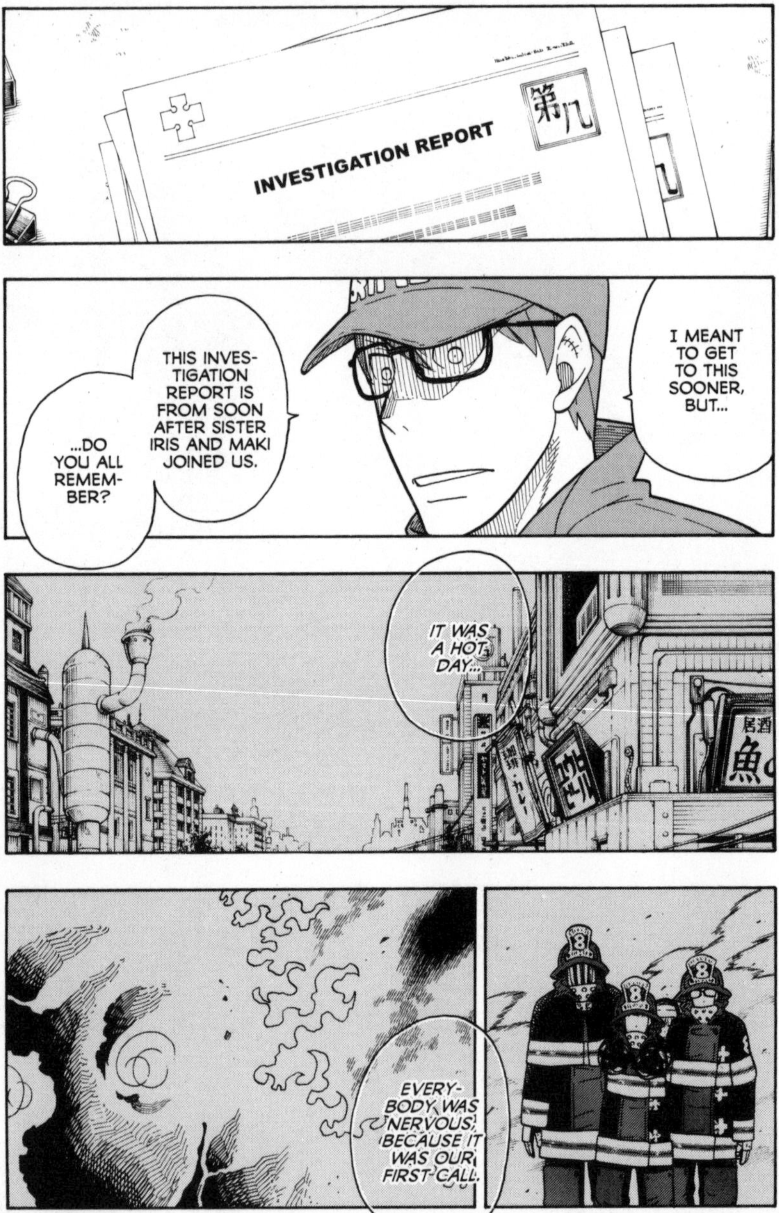
第八
INVESTIGATION REPORT
I MEANT TO GET TO THIS SOONER, BUT...
THIS INVES-TIGATION REPORT IS FROM SOON AFTER SISTER IRIS AND MAKI JOINED US.
...DO YOU ALL REMEM-BER?
IT WAS A HOT DAY...
EVERY-BODY WAS NERVOUS, BECAUSE IT WAS OUR FIRST CALL.

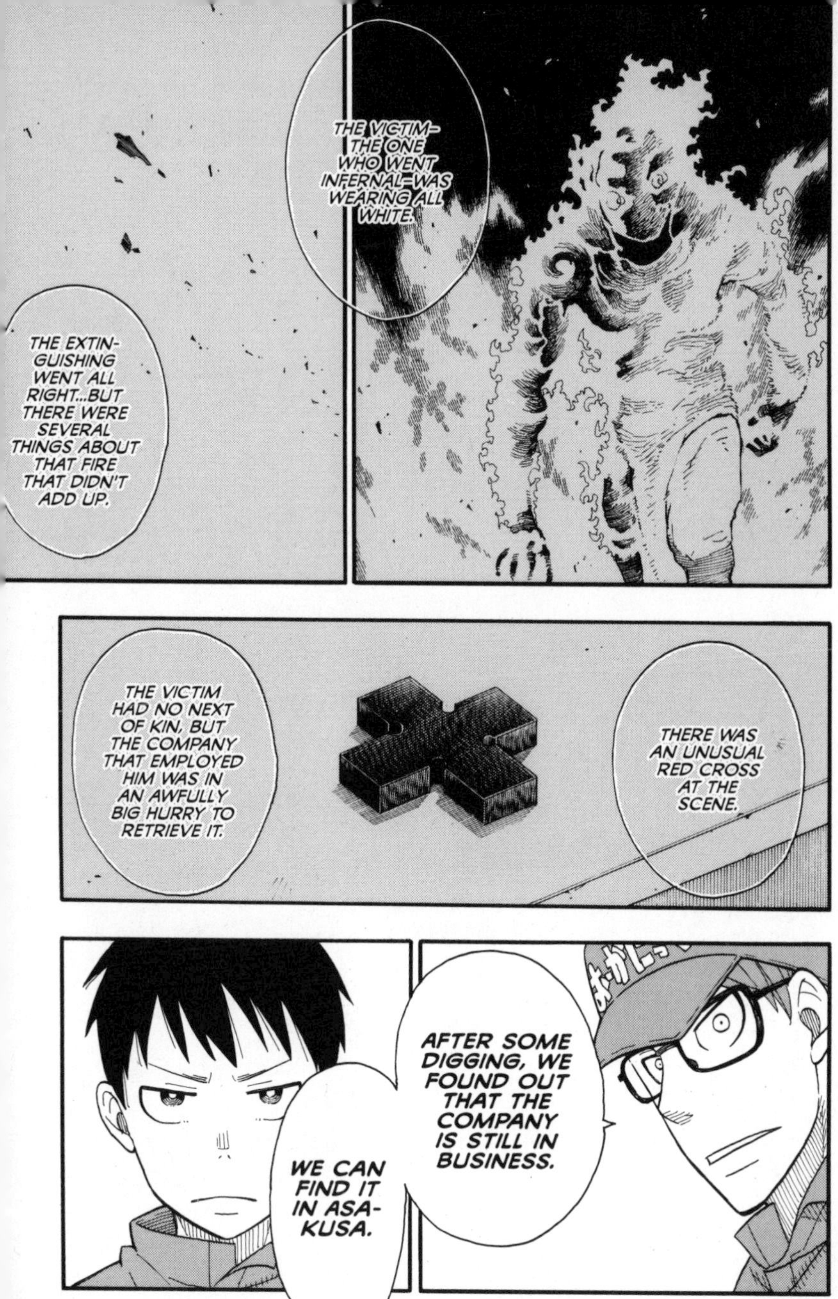
THE VICTIM—THE ONE WHO WENT INFERNAL—WAS WEARING ALL WHITE.
THE EXTIN-GUISHING WENT ALL RIGHT...BUT THERE WERE SEVERAL THINGS ABOUT THAT FIRE THAT DIDN'T ADD UP.
THERE WAS AN UNUSUAL RED CROSS AT THE SCENE.
THE VICTIM HAD NO NEXT OF KIN, BUT THE COMPANY THAT EMPLOYED HIM WAS IN AN AWFULLY BIG HURRY TO RETRIEVE IT.
AFTER SOME DIGGING, WE FOUND OUT THAT THE COMPANY IS STILL IN BUSINESS.
WE CAN FIND IT IN ASA-KUSA.

ASAKUSA

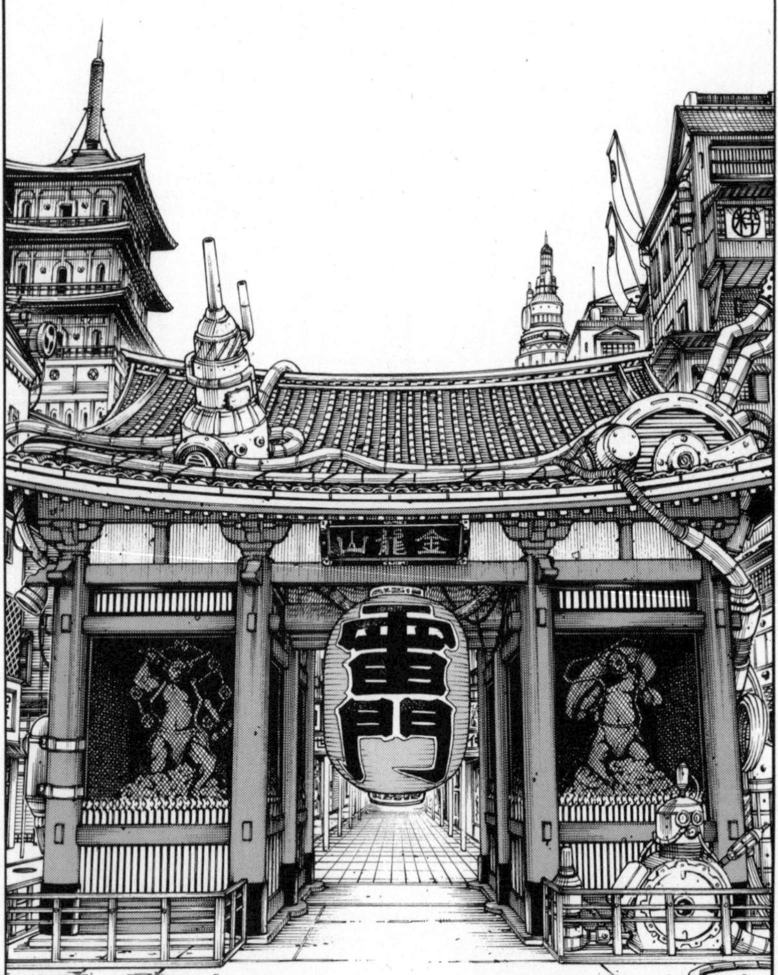
金龍山
雷門

Sign: Kinryūzan

Lamp: Kaminarimon

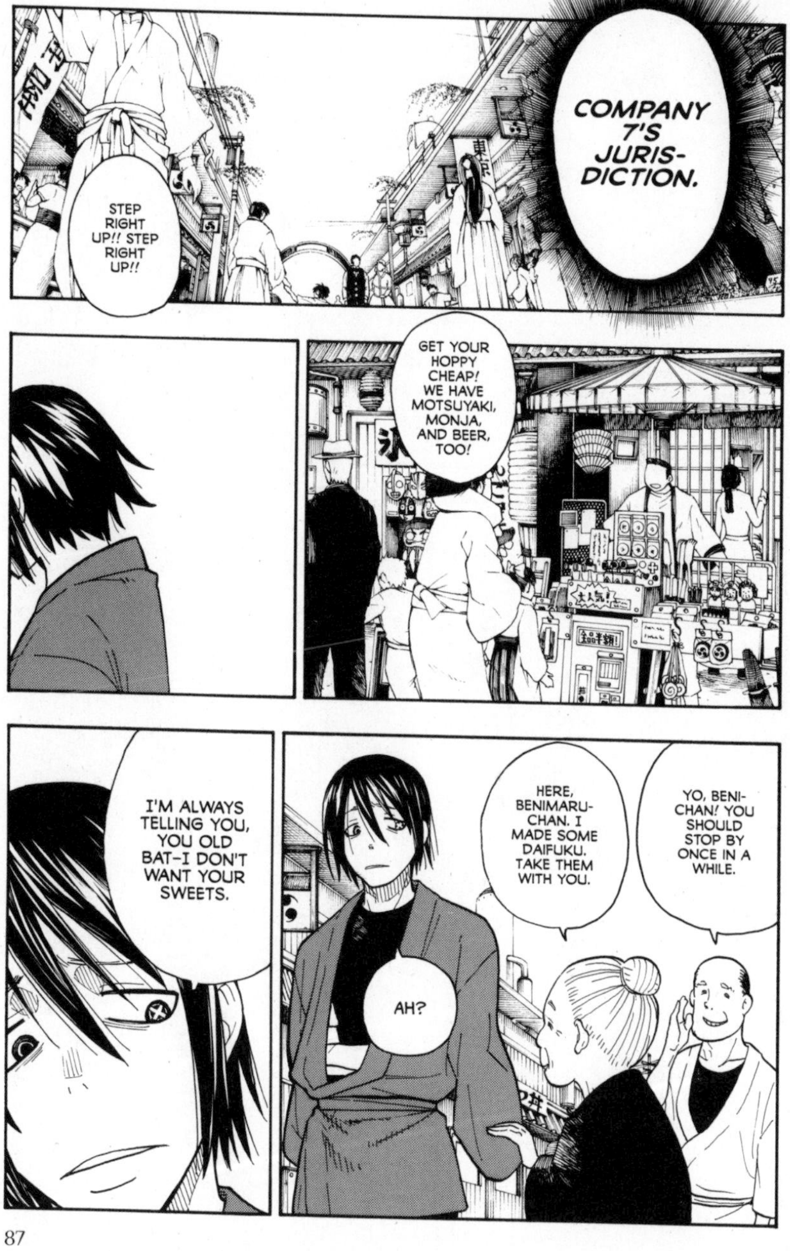

COMPANY 7'S JURIS-DICTION.
STEP RIGHT UP!! STEP RIGHT UP!!
GET YOUR HOPPY CHEAP! WE HAVE MOTSUYAKI, MONJA, AND BEER, TOO!
YO, BENI-CHAN! YOU SHOULD STOP BY ONCE IN A WHILE.
HERE, BENIMARU-CHAN. I MADE SOME DAIFUKU. TAKE THEM WITH YOU.
AH?
I'M ALWAYS TELLING YOU, YOU OLD BAT–I DON'T WANT YOUR SWEETS.

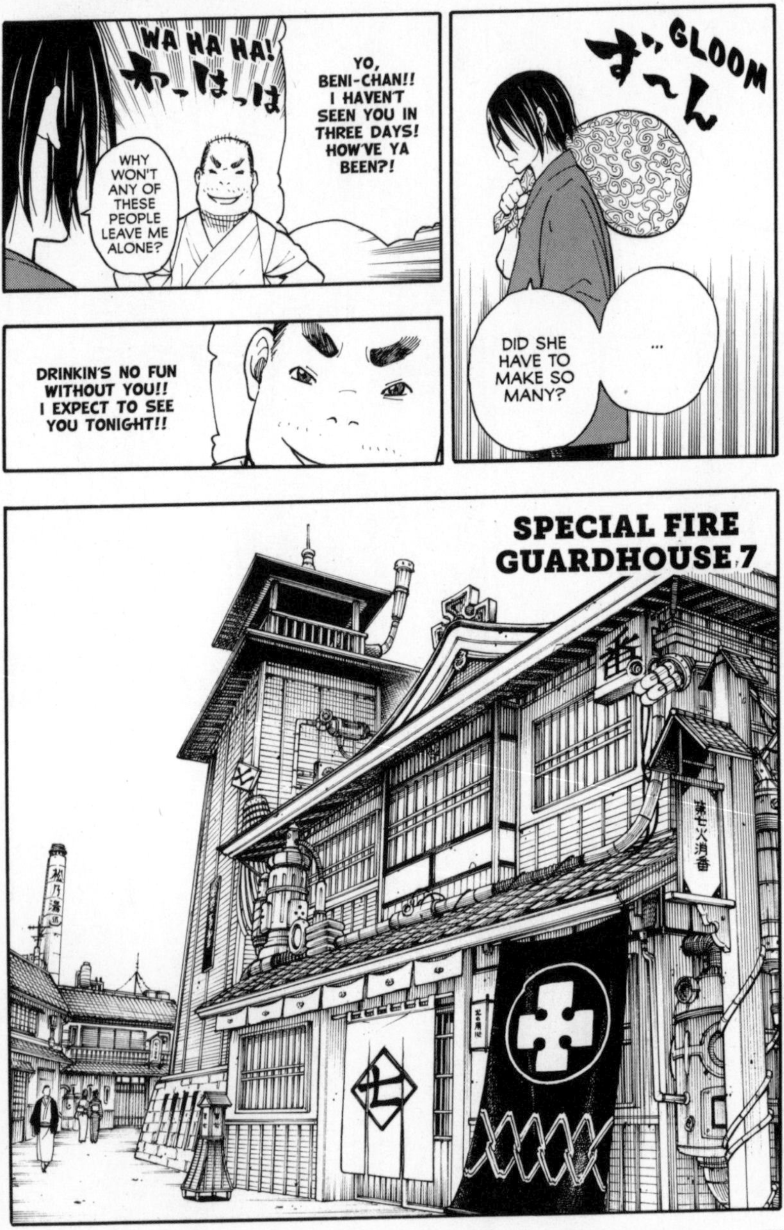
GLOOM
ず〜ん
DID SHE HAVE TO MAKE SO MANY?
...
WA HA HA!
わっはっは
YO, BENI-CHAN!! I HAVEN'T SEEN YOU IN THREE DAYS! HOW'VE YA BEEN?!
WHY WON'T ANY OF THESE PEOPLE LEAVE ME ALONE?
DRINKIN'S NO FUN WITHOUT YOU!! I EXPECT TO SEE YOU TONIGHT!!
SPECIAL FIRE GUARDHOUSE 7

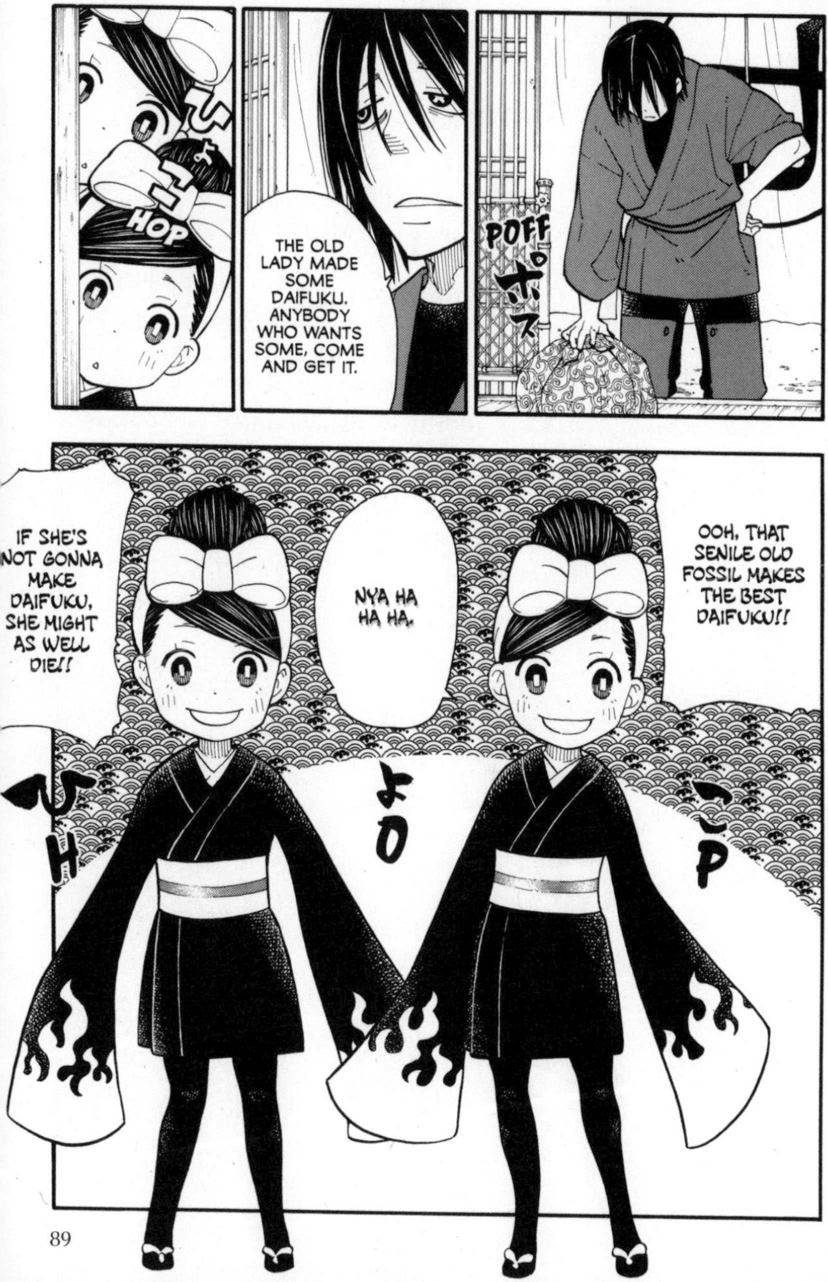
POFF
ポス
THE OLD LADY MADE SOME DAIFUKU. ANYBODY WHO WANTS SOME, COME AND GET IT.
HOP
OOH, THAT SENILE OLD FOSSIL MAKES THE BEST DAIFUKU!!
P
NYA HA HA HA.
O
IF SHE'S NOT GONNA MAKE DAIFUKU, SHE MIGHT AS WELL DIE!!
H

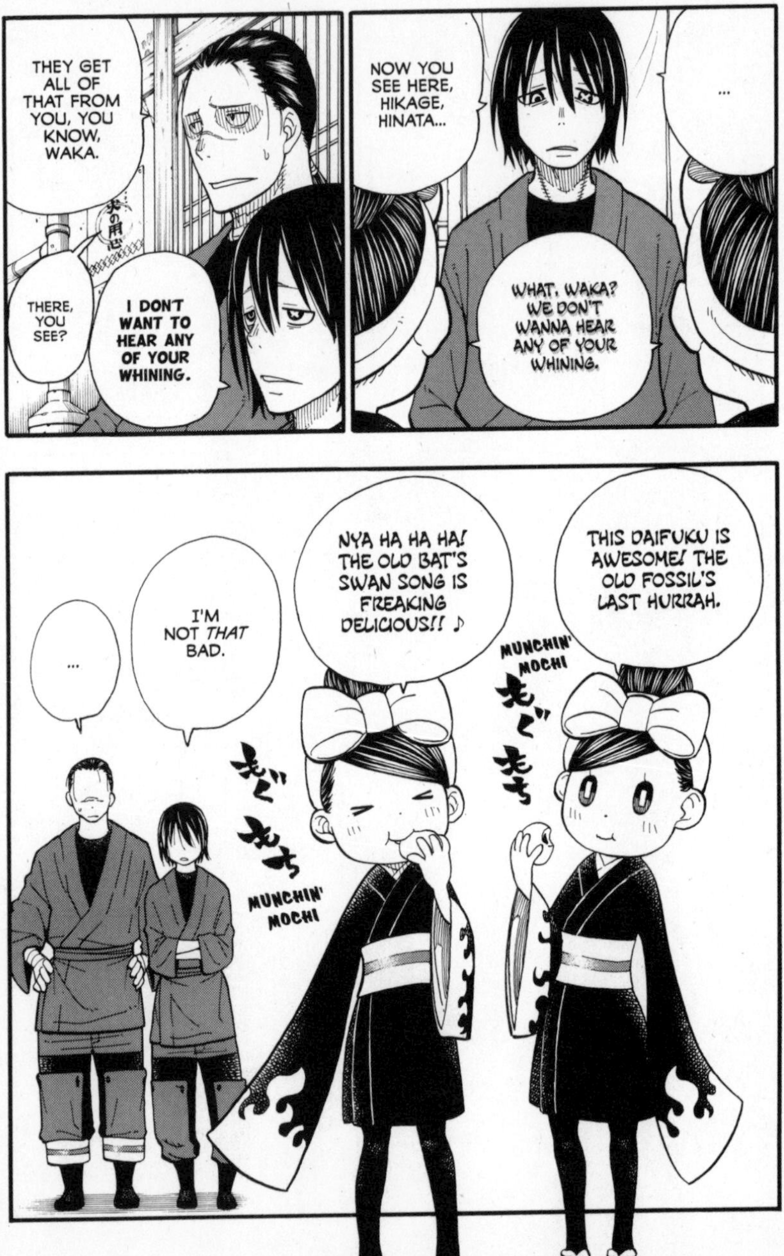
...
NOW YOU SEE HERE, HIKAGE, HINATA...
WHAT, WAKA? WE DON'T WANNA HEAR ANY OF YOUR WHINING.
THEY GET ALL OF THAT FROM YOU, YOU KNOW, WAKA.
I DON'T WANT TO HEAR ANY OF YOUR WHINING.
THERE, YOU SEE?
THIS DAIFUKU IS AWESOME! THE OLD FOSSIL'S LAST HURRAH.
MUNCHIN' MOCHI
NYA HA HA HA! THE OLD BAT'S SWAN SONG IS FREAKING DELICIOUS!! ♪
MUNCHIN' MOCHI
I'M NOT *THAT* BAD.
...

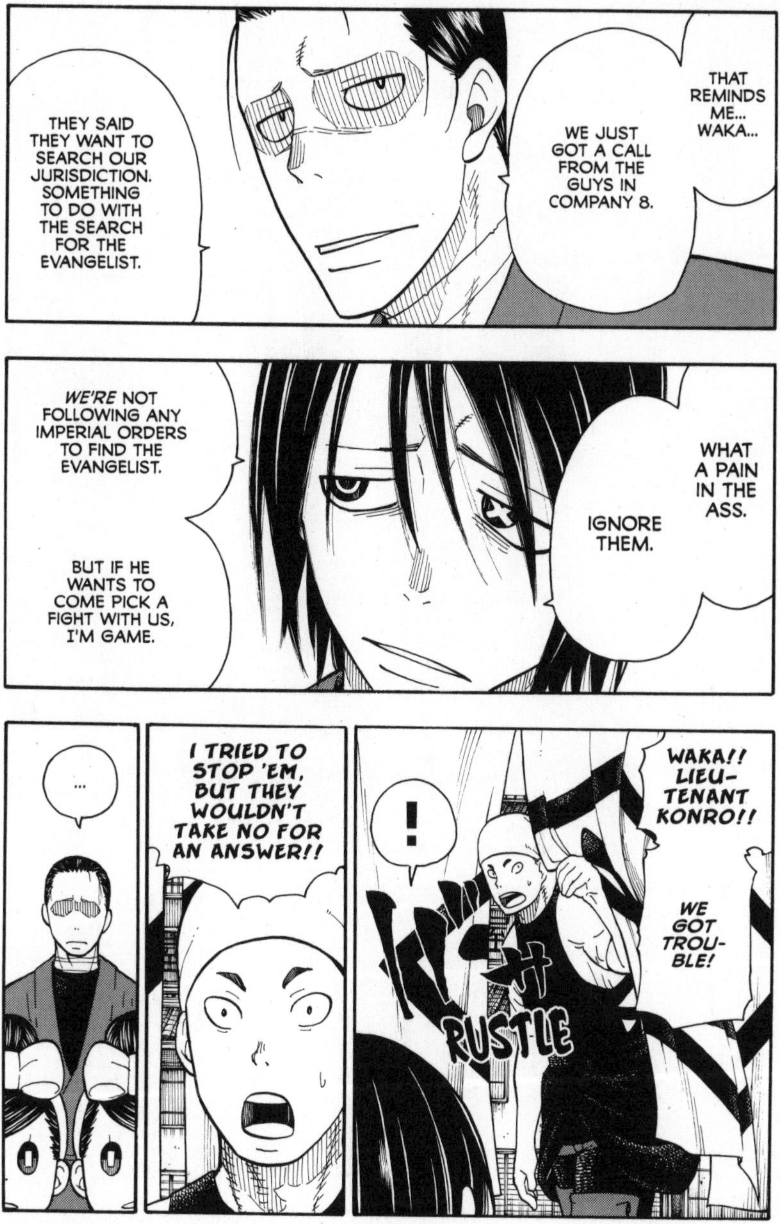
THAT REMINDS ME... WAKA...
WE JUST GOT A CALL FROM THE GUYS IN COMPANY 8.
THEY SAID THEY WANT TO SEARCH OUR JURISDICTION. SOMETHING TO DO WITH THE SEARCH FOR THE EVANGELIST.
WHAT A PAIN IN THE ASS.
IGNORE THEM.
WE'RE NOT FOLLOWING ANY IMPERIAL ORDERS TO FIND THE EVANGELIST.
BUT IF HE WANTS TO COME PICK A FIGHT WITH US, I'M GAME.
WAKA!! LIEU-TENANT KONRO!!
WE GOT TROU-BLE!
!
RUSTLE
I TRIED TO STOP 'EM, BUT THEY WOULDN'T TAKE NO FOR AN ANSWER!!
...

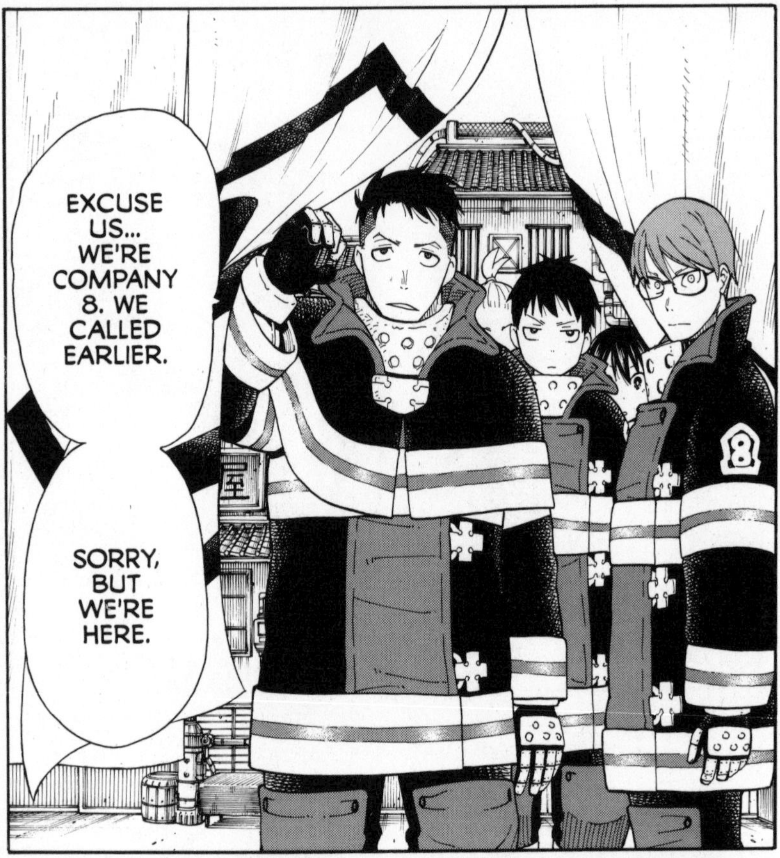
EXCUSE US... WE'RE COMPANY 8. WE CALLED EARLIER.
SORRY, BUT WE'RE HERE.
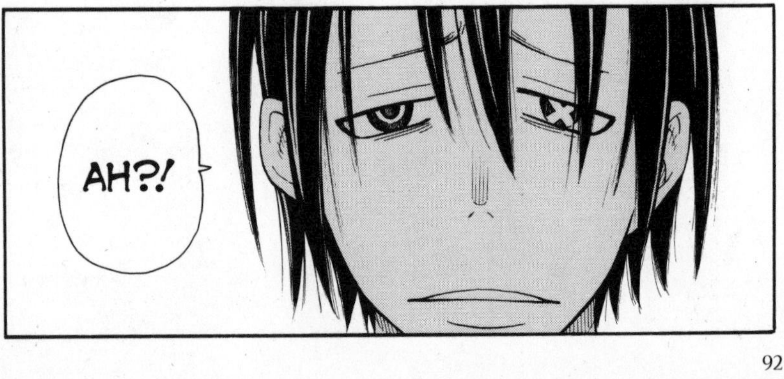
AH?!

FIRE FORCE

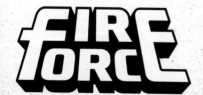

FIRE FORCE

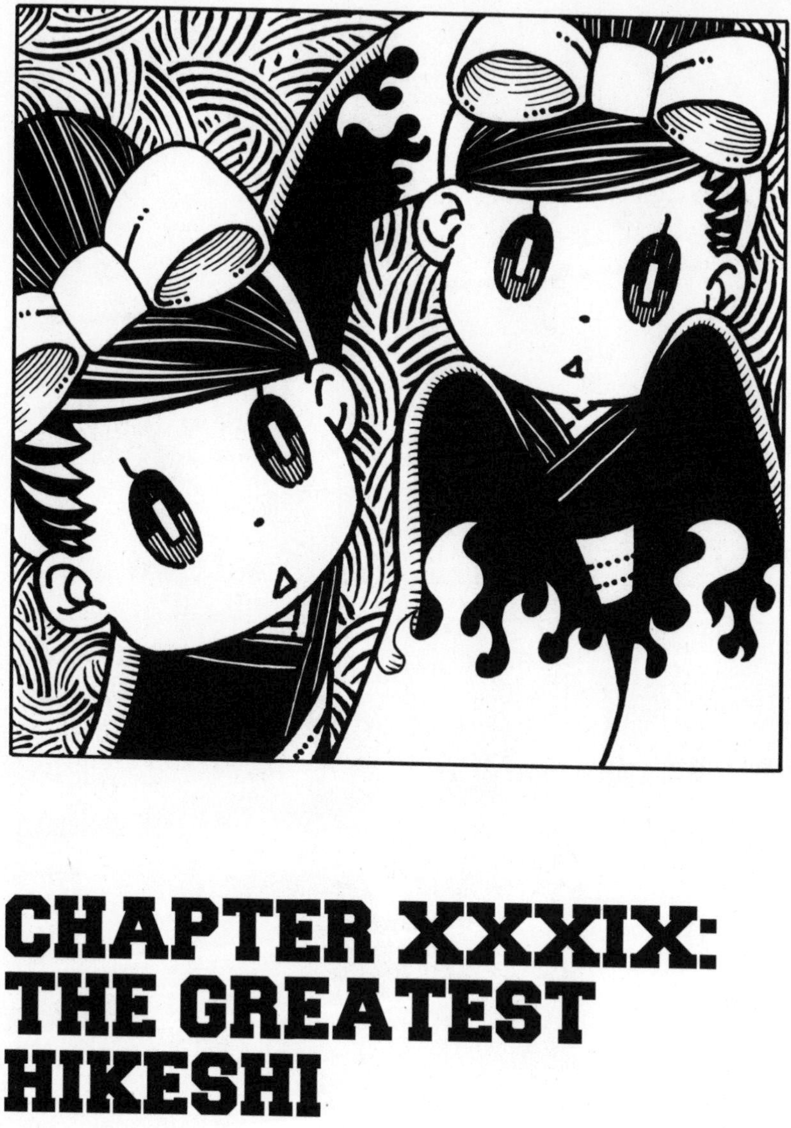

CHAPTER XXXIX: THE GREATEST HIKESHI

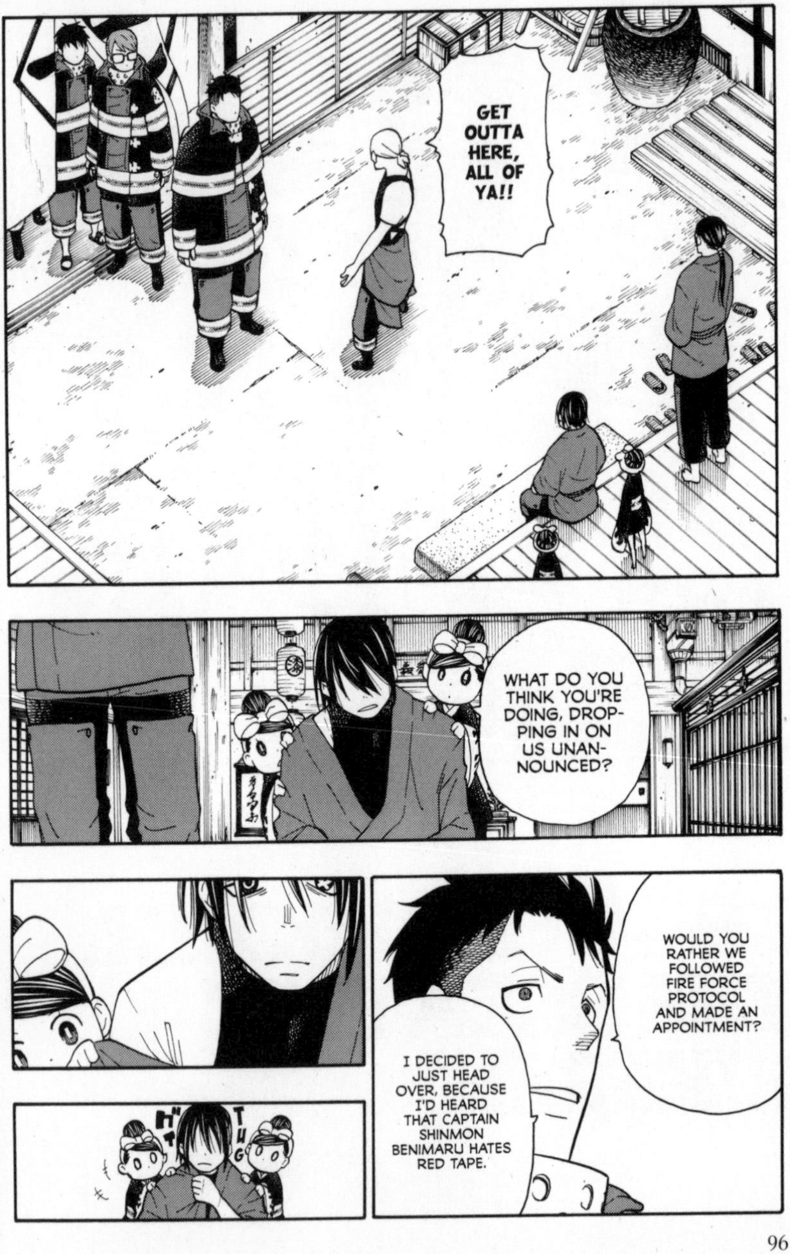
GET OUTTA HERE, ALL OF YA!!
WHAT DO YOU THINK YOU'RE DOING, DROP-PING IN ON US UNAN-NOUNCED?
WOULD YOU RATHER WE FOLLOWED FIRE FORCE PROTOCOL AND MADE AN APPOINTMENT?
I DECIDED TO JUST HEAD OVER, BECAUSE I'D HEARD THAT CAPTAIN SHINMON BENIMARU HATES RED TAPE.
TUG

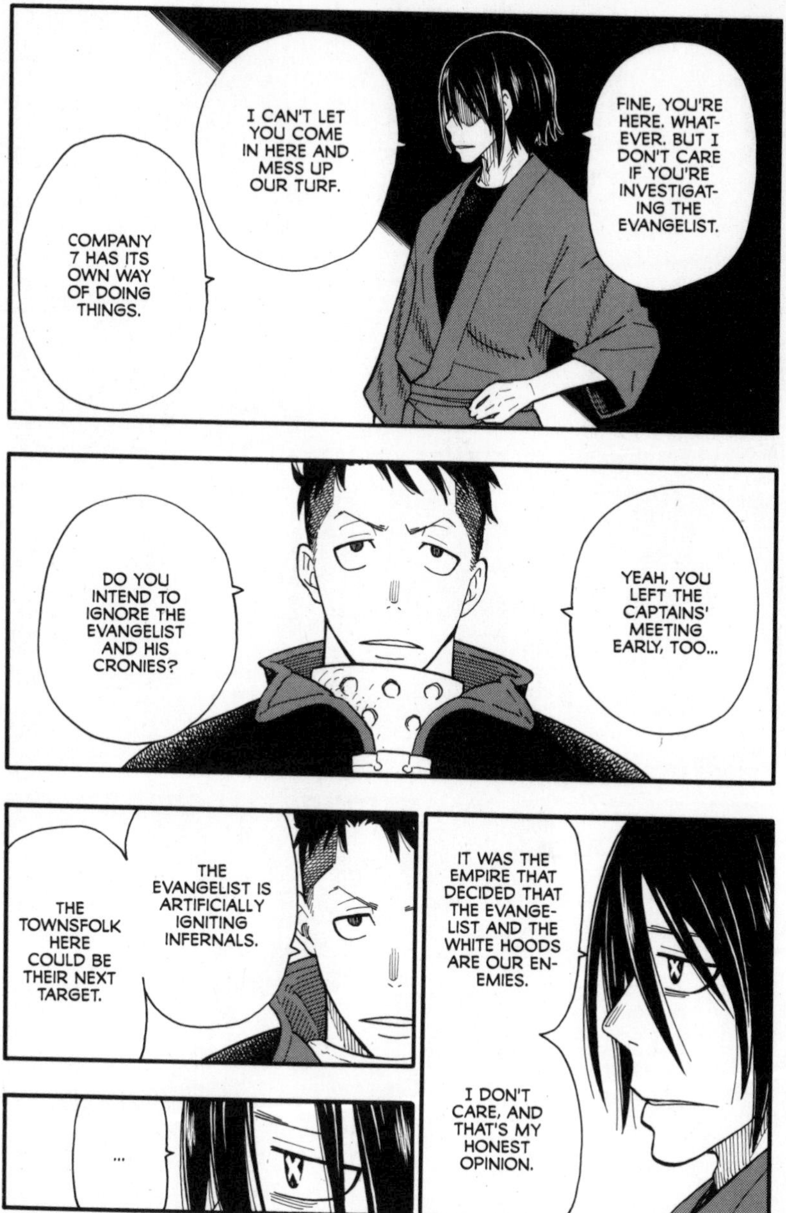
FINE, YOU'RE HERE. WHATEVER. BUT I DON'T CARE IF YOU'RE INVESTIGATING THE EVANGELIST.
I CAN'T LET YOU COME IN HERE AND MESS UP OUR TURF.
COMPANY 7 HAS ITS OWN WAY OF DOING THINGS.
YEAH, YOU LEFT THE CAPTAINS' MEETING EARLY, TOO...
DO YOU INTEND TO IGNORE THE EVANGELIST AND HIS CRONIES?
IT WAS THE EMPIRE THAT DECIDED THAT THE EVANGELIST AND THE WHITE HOODS ARE OUR ENEMIES.
I DON'T CARE, AND THAT'S MY HONEST OPINION.
THE EVANGELIST IS ARTIFICIALLY IGNITING INFERNALS.
THE TOWNSFOLK HERE COULD BE THEIR NEXT TARGET.
...

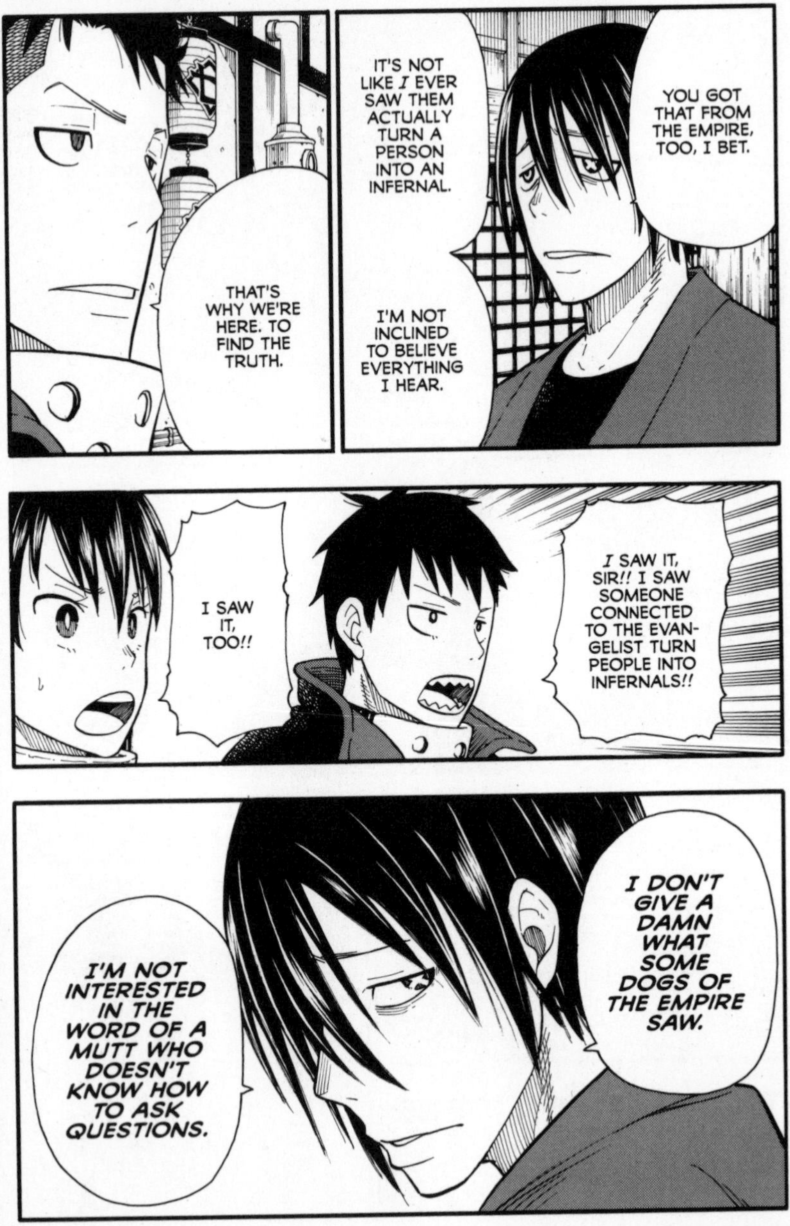
YOU GOT THAT FROM THE EMPIRE, TOO, I BET.
IT'S NOT LIKE *I* EVER SAW THEM ACTUALLY TURN A PERSON INTO AN INFERNAL.
I'M NOT INCLINED TO BELIEVE EVERYTHING I HEAR.
THAT'S WHY WE'RE HERE. TO FIND THE TRUTH.
I SAW IT, SIR!! I SAW SOMEONE CONNECTED TO THE EVAN-GELIST TURN PEOPLE INTO INFERNALS!!
I SAW IT, TOO!!
I DON'T GIVE A DAMN WHAT SOME DOGS OF THE EMPIRE SAW.
I'M NOT INTERESTED IN THE WORD OF A MUTT WHO DOESN'T KNOW HOW TO ASK QUESTIONS.

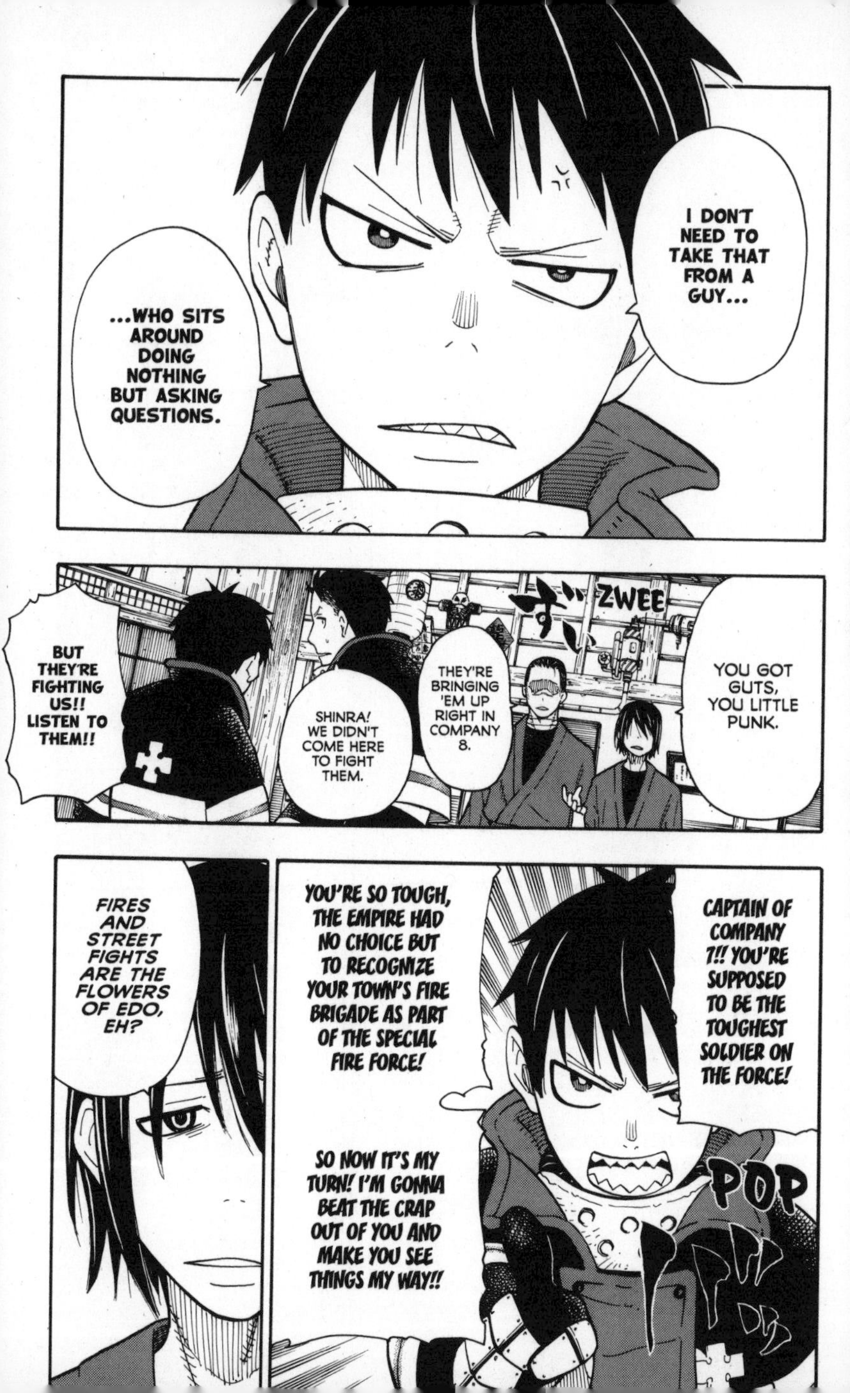
I DON'T NEED TO TAKE THAT FROM A GUY...
...WHO SITS AROUND DOING NOTHING BUT ASKING QUESTIONS.
YOU GOT GUTS, YOU LITTLE PUNK.
ZWEE
THEY'RE BRINGING 'EM UP RIGHT IN COMPANY 8.
SHINRA! WE DIDN'T COME HERE TO FIGHT THEM.
BUT THEY'RE FIGHTING US!! LISTEN TO THEM!!
CAPTAIN OF COMPANY 7!! YOU'RE SUPPOSED TO BE THE TOUGHEST SOLDIER ON THE FORCE!
YOU'RE SO TOUGH, THE EMPIRE HAD NO CHOICE BUT TO RECOGNIZE YOUR TOWN'S FIRE BRIGADE AS PART OF THE SPECIAL FIRE FORCE!
SO NOW IT'S MY TURN! I'M GONNA BEAT THE CRAP OUT OF YOU AND MAKE YOU SEE THINGS MY WAY!!
POP
FIRES AND STREET FIGHTS ARE THE FLOWERS OF EDO, EH?

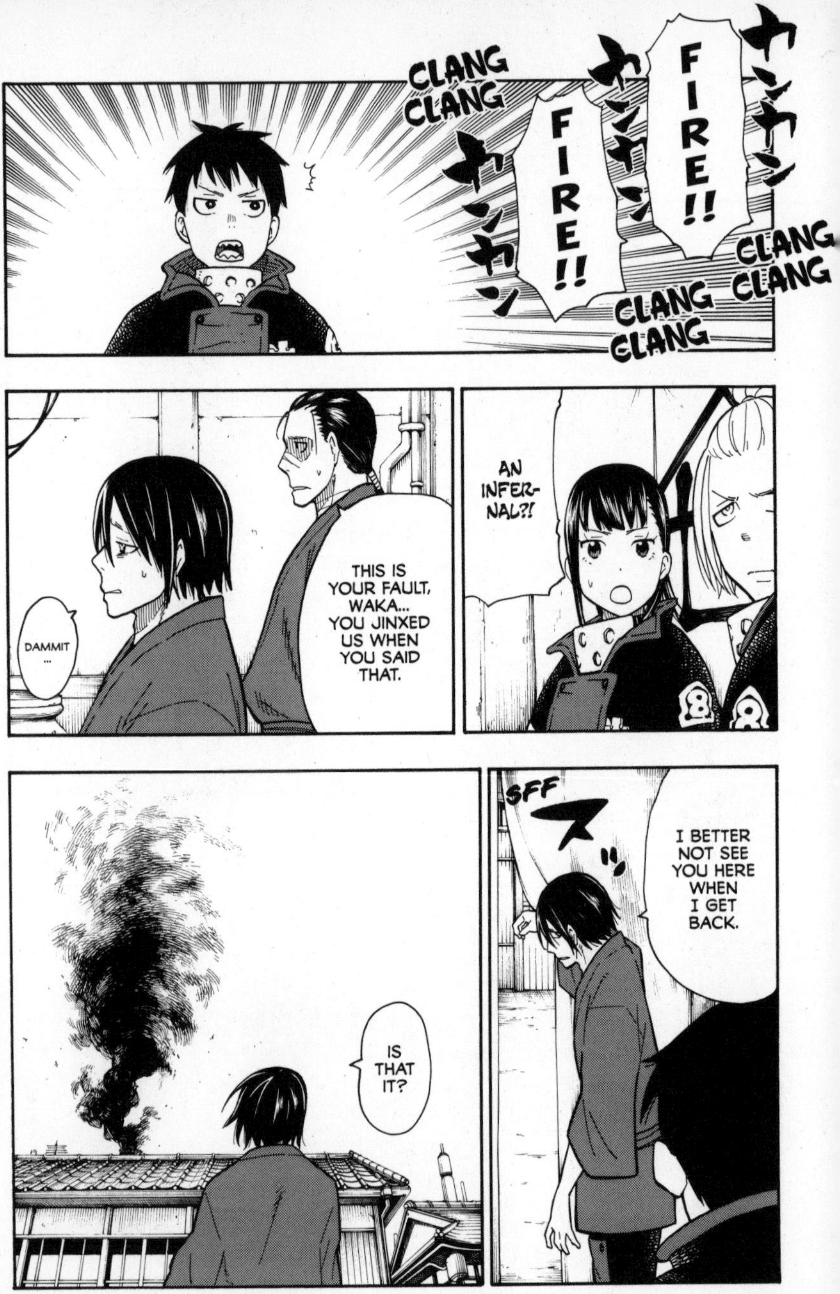
カンカン
FIRE!!
カンカン
FIRE!!
カンカン
CLANG CLANG
CLANG CLANG
CLANG CLANG
CLANG CLANG
AN INFER-NAL?!
THIS IS YOUR FAULT, WAKA... YOU JINXED US WHEN YOU SAID THAT.
DAMMIT ...
SFF
ス
I BETTER NOT SEE YOU HERE WHEN I GET BACK.
IS THAT IT?

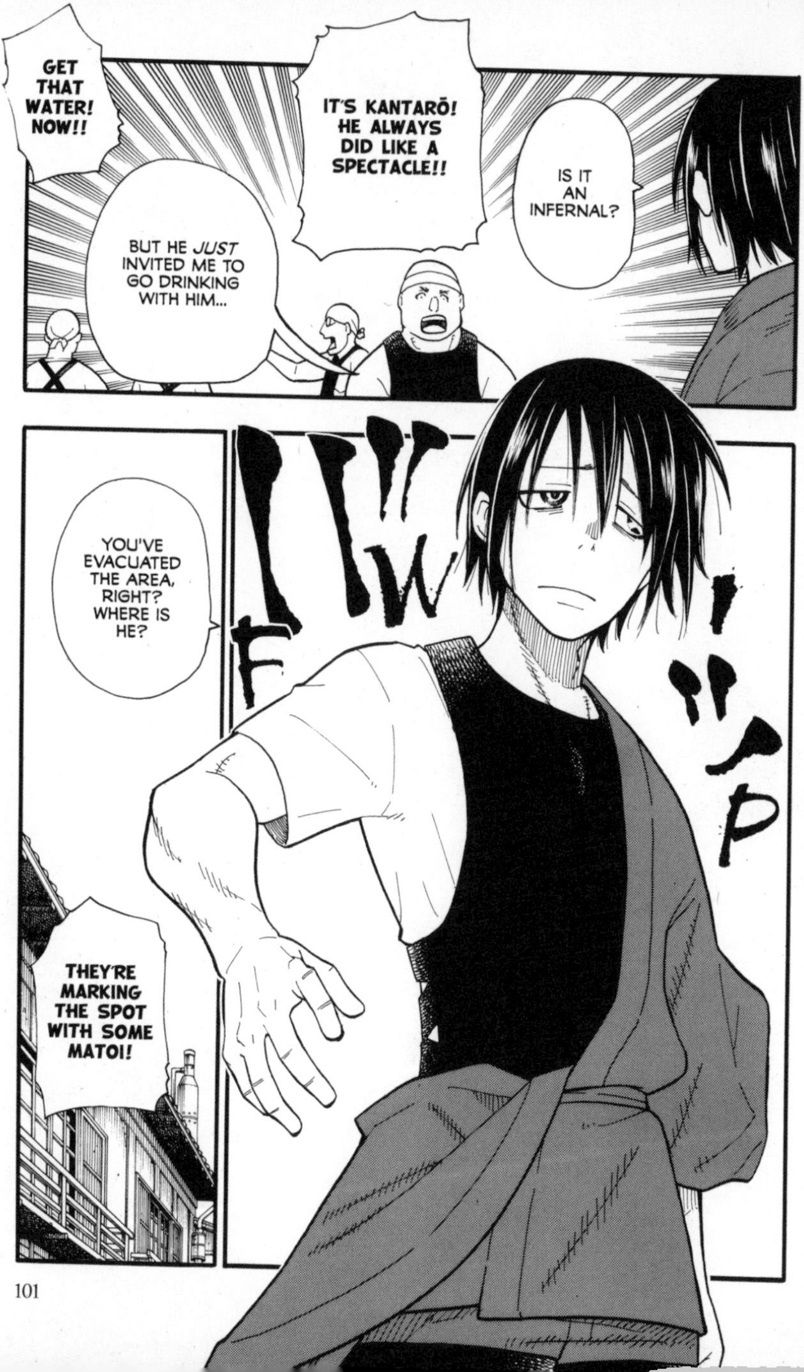
IS IT AN INFERNAL?
IT'S KANTARŌ! HE ALWAYS DID LIKE A SPECTACLE!!
BUT HE *JUST* INVITED ME TO GO DRINKING WITH HIM...
GET THAT WATER! NOW!!
YOU'VE EVACUATED THE AREA, RIGHT? WHERE IS HE?
THEY'RE MARKING THE SPOT WITH SOME MATOI!

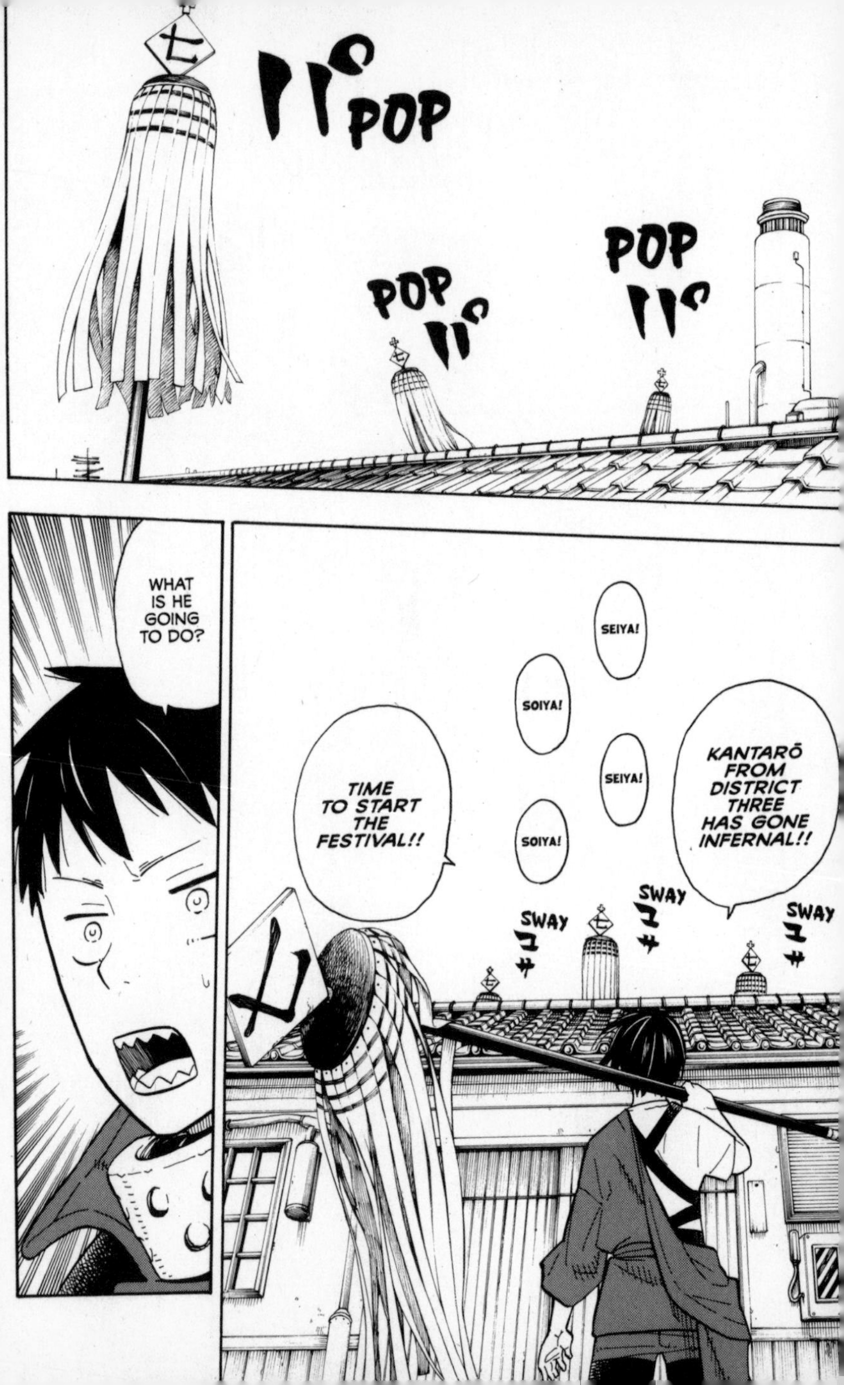
POP
POP
POP
KANTARŌ FROM DISTRICT THREE HAS GONE INFERNAL!!
SEIYA!
SOIYA!
SEIYA!
SOIYA!
TIME TO START THE FESTIVAL!!
SWAY
SWAY
SWAY
WHAT IS HE GOING TO DO?

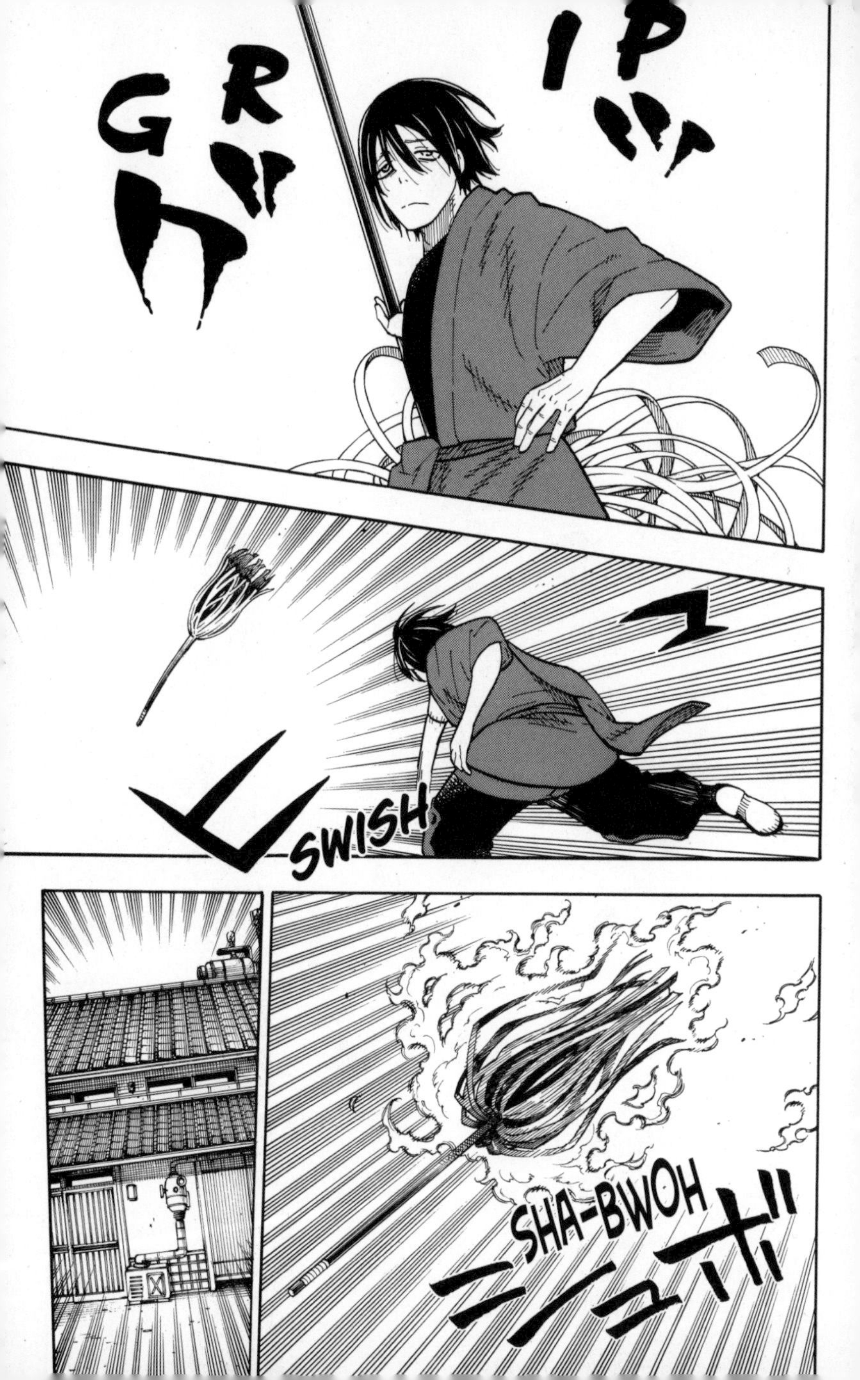
IP
GR
SWISH
SHA-BWOH

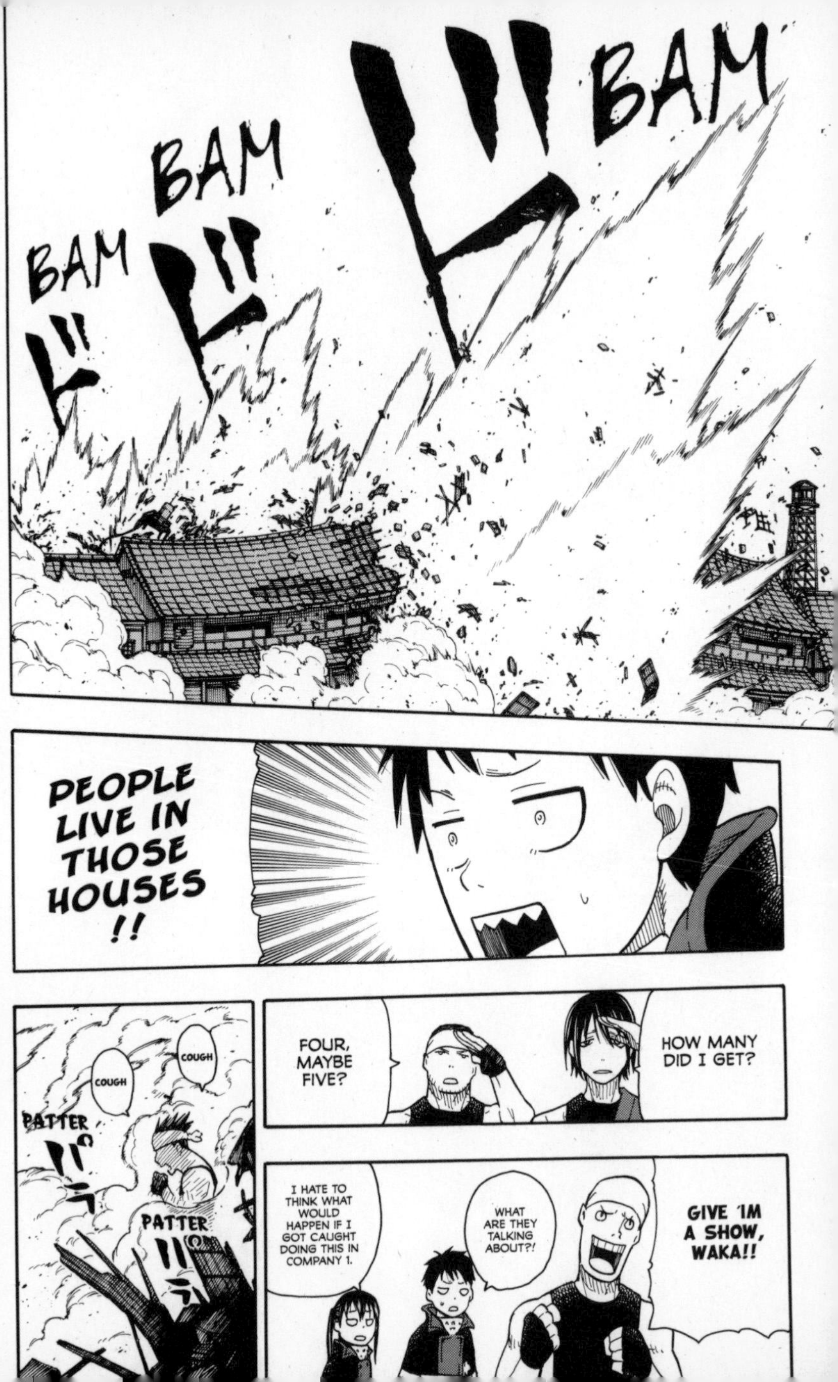
BAM
BAM
BAM
PEOPLE LIVE IN THOSE HOUSES!!
HOW MANY DID I GET?
FOUR, MAYBE FIVE?
GIVE 'IM A SHOW, WAKA!!
WHAT ARE THEY TALKING ABOUT?!
I HATE TO THINK WHAT WOULD HAPPEN IF I GOT CAUGHT DOING THIS IN COMPANY 1.
COUGH
COUGH
PATTER
PATTER

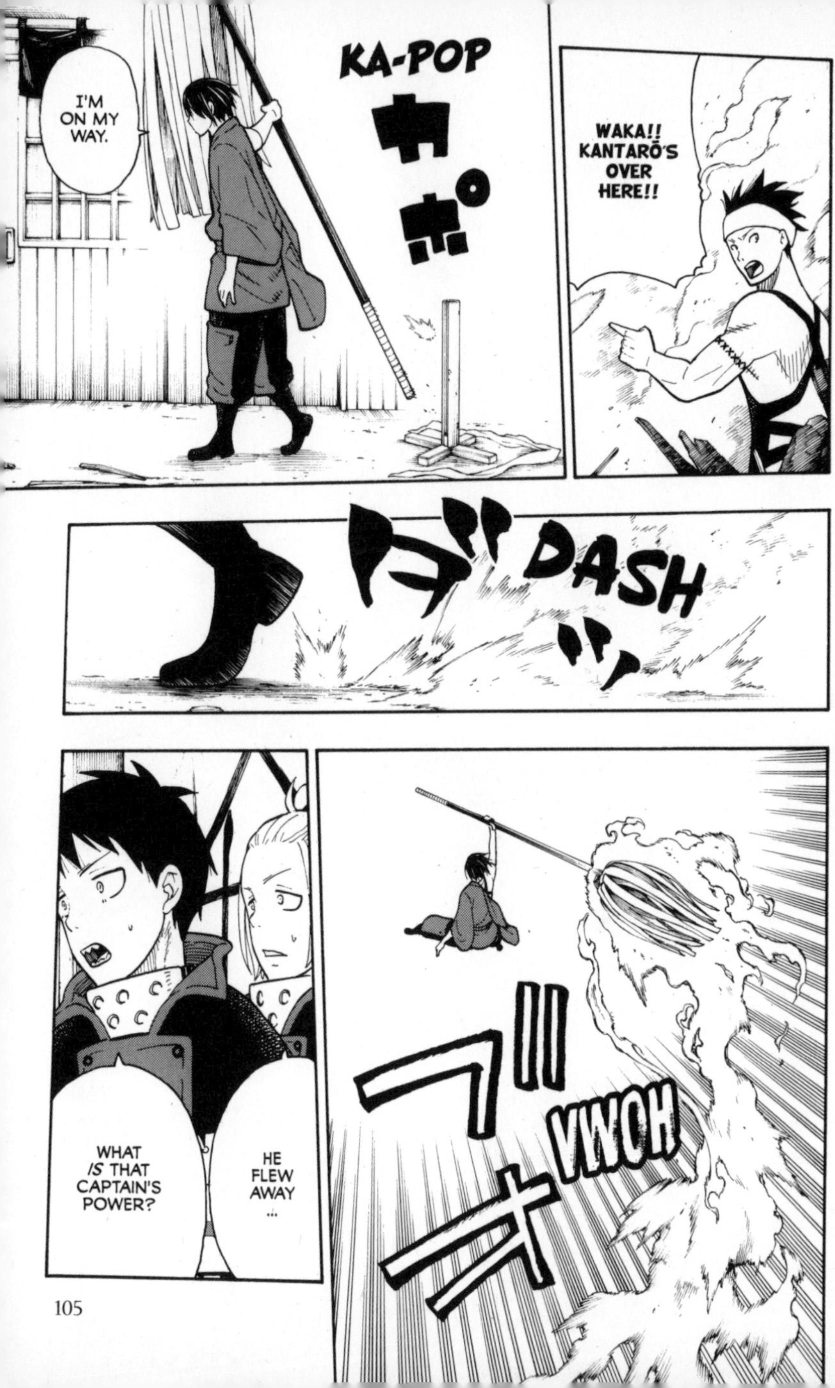
WAKA!! KANTARŌ'S OVER HERE!!
KA-POP
I'M ON MY WAY.
DASH
VWOH
HE FLEW AWAY ...
WHAT *IS* THAT CAPTAIN'S POWER?

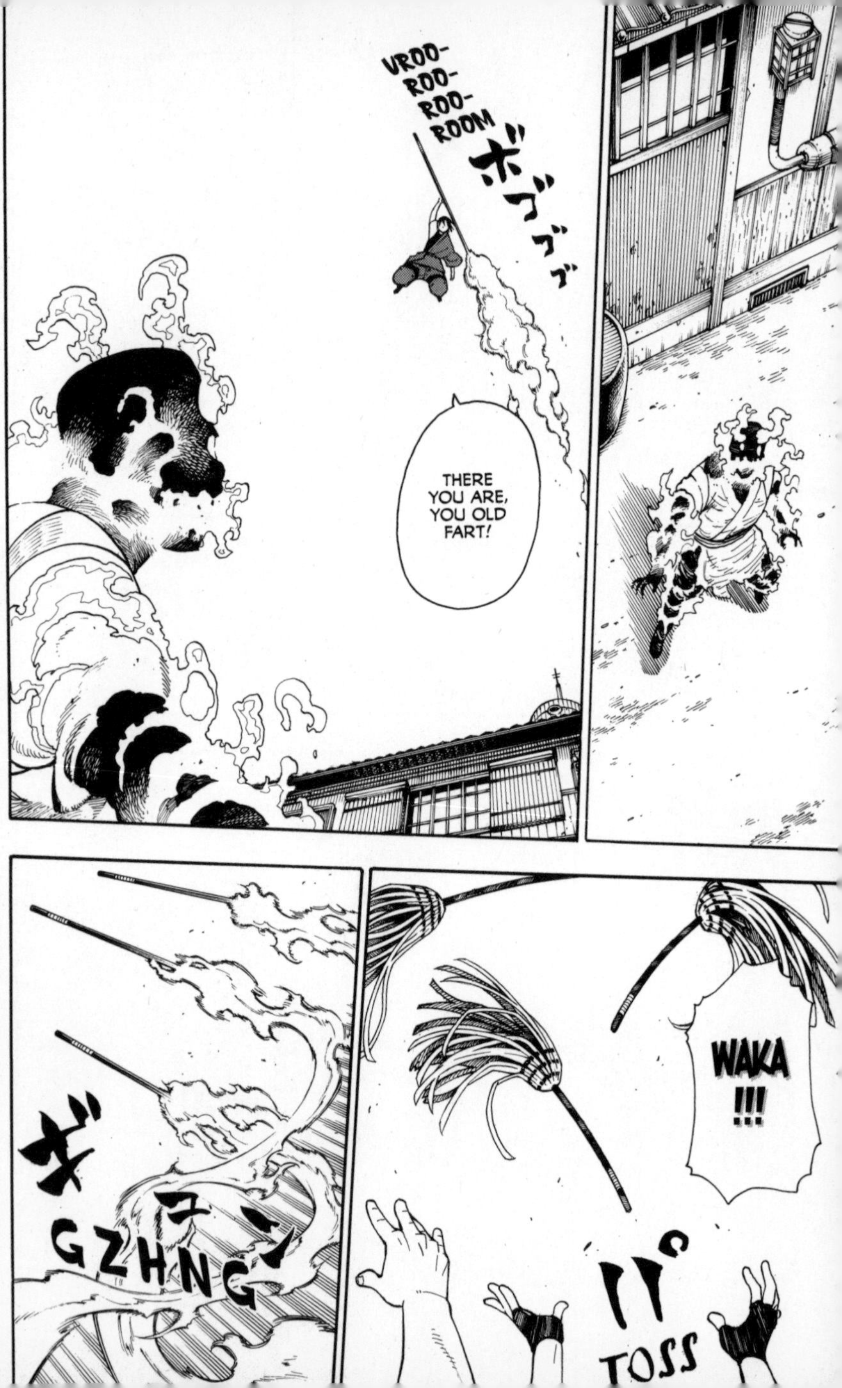
VROO-
ROO-
ROO-
ROOM
ボゴゴゴ
THERE YOU ARE, YOU OLD FART!
WAKA !!!
TOSS
GZHNG

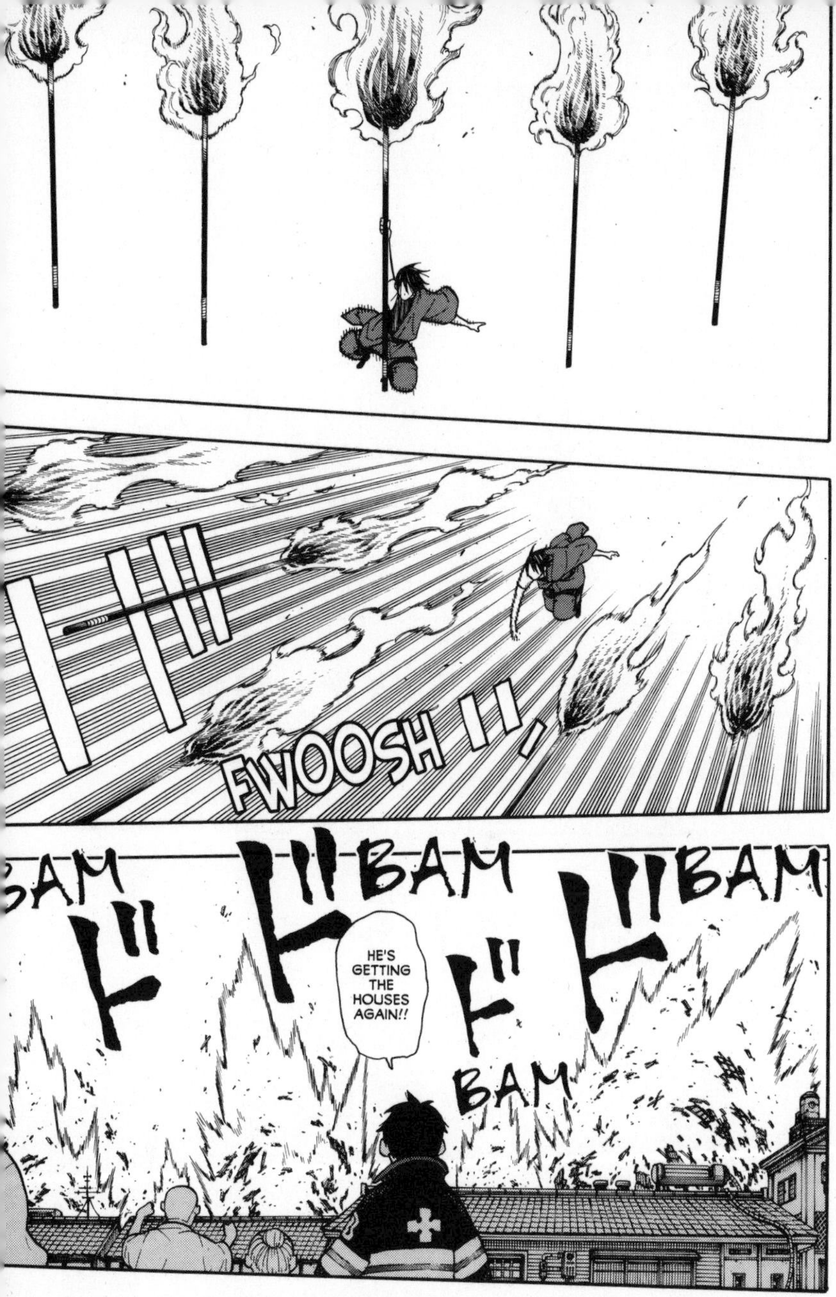
FWOOSH
ド
BAM
ド
BAM
HE'S GETTING THE HOUSES AGAIN!!
ド
BAM
ド
BAM

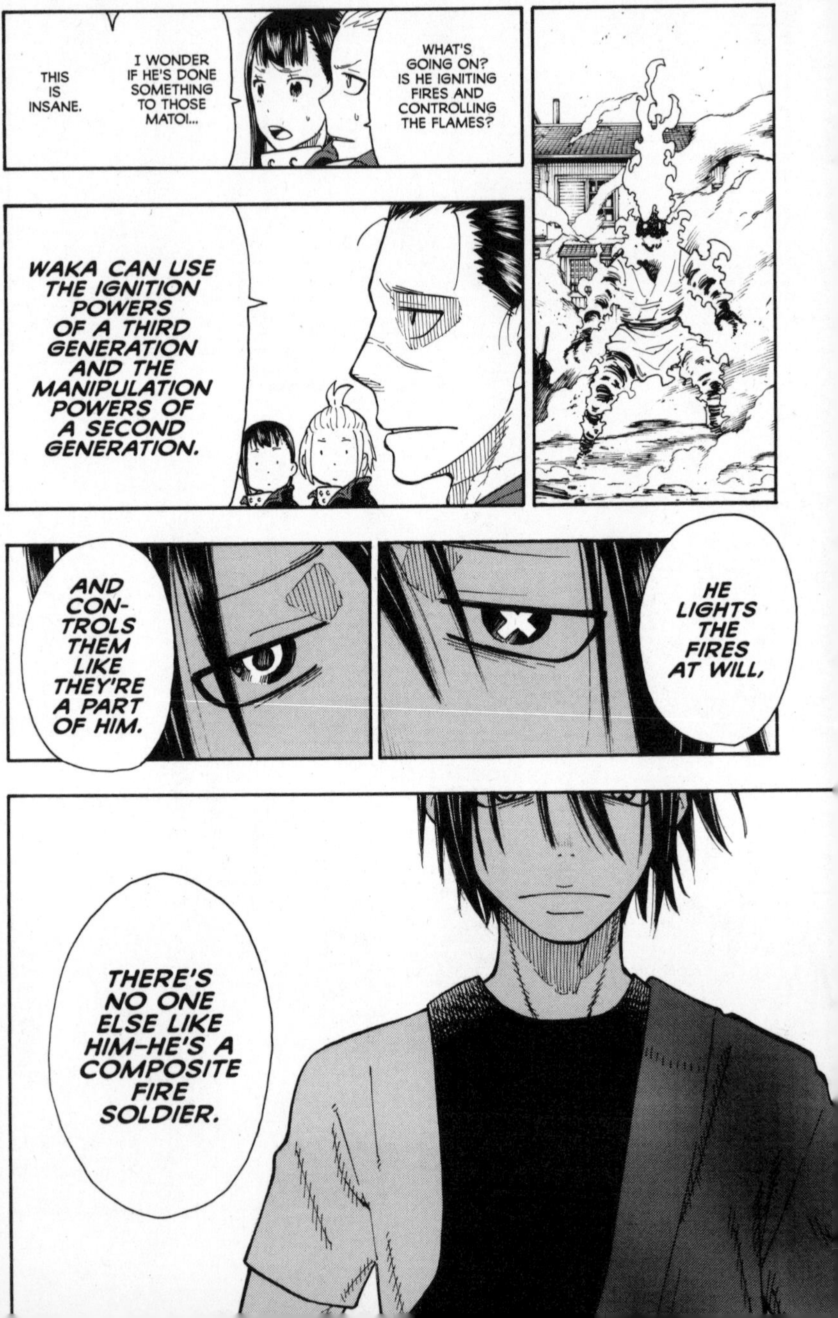
WHAT'S GOING ON? IS HE IGNITING FIRES AND CONTROLLING THE FLAMES?
I WONDER IF HE'S DONE SOMETHING TO THOSE MATOI...
THIS IS INSANE.
WAKA CAN USE THE IGNITION POWERS OF A THIRD GENERATION AND THE MANIPULATION POWERS OF A SECOND GENERATION.
HE LIGHTS THE FIRES AT WILL,
AND CONTROLS THEM LIKE THEY'RE A PART OF HIM.
THERE'S NO ONE ELSE LIKE HIM—HE'S A COMPOSITE FIRE SOLDIER.

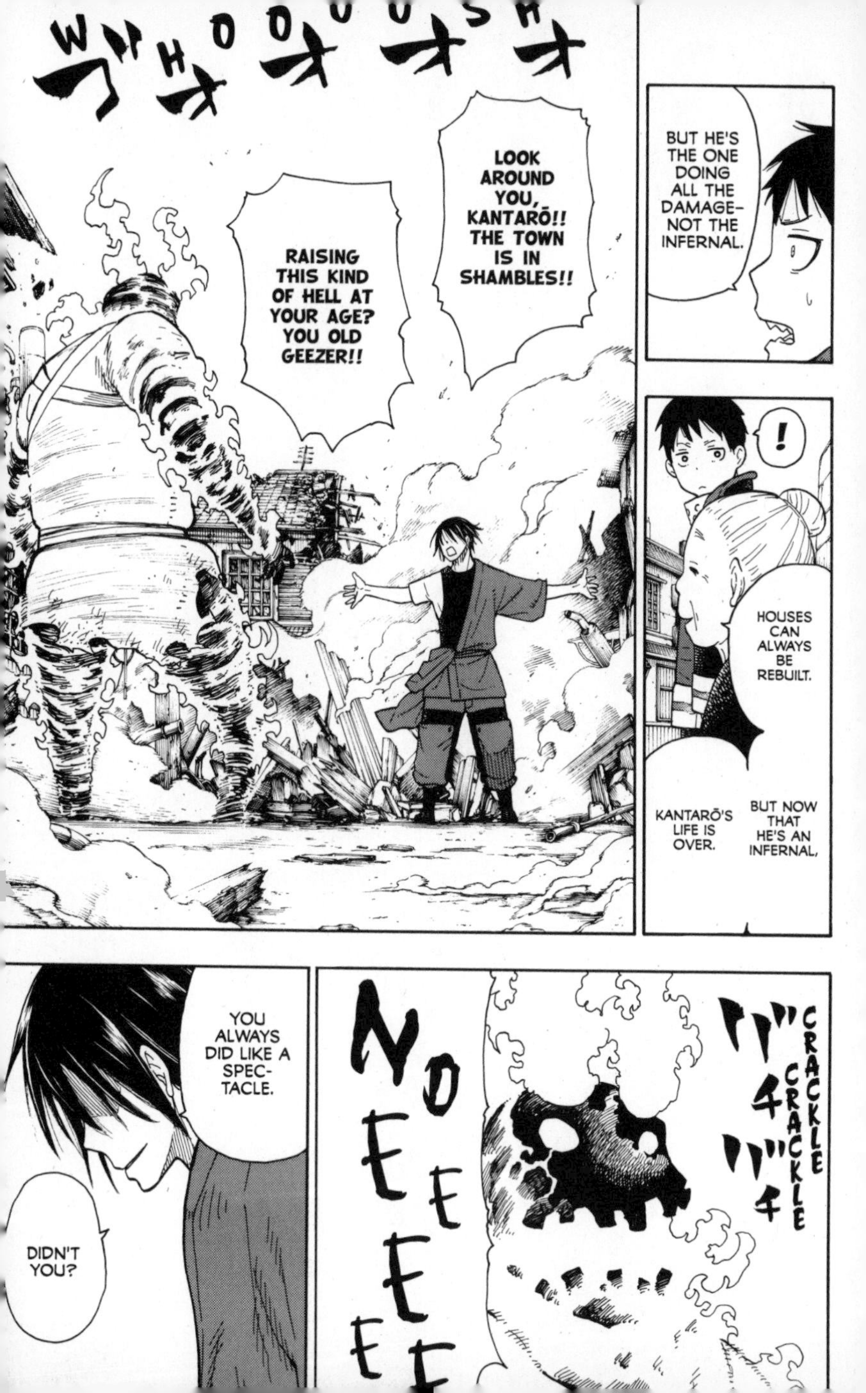
BUT HE'S THE ONE DOING ALL THE DAMAGE—NOT THE INFERNAL.
!
HOUSES CAN ALWAYS BE REBUILT.
BUT NOW THAT HE'S AN INFERNAL,
KANTARŌ'S LIFE IS OVER.
WHOOUUSH
LOOK AROUND YOU, KANTARŌ!! THE TOWN IS IN SHAMBLES!!
RAISING THIS KIND OF HELL AT YOUR AGE? YOU OLD GEEZER!!
CRACKLE CRACKLE
NOEEEEE
YOU ALWAYS DID LIKE A SPECTACLE.
DIDN'T YOU?

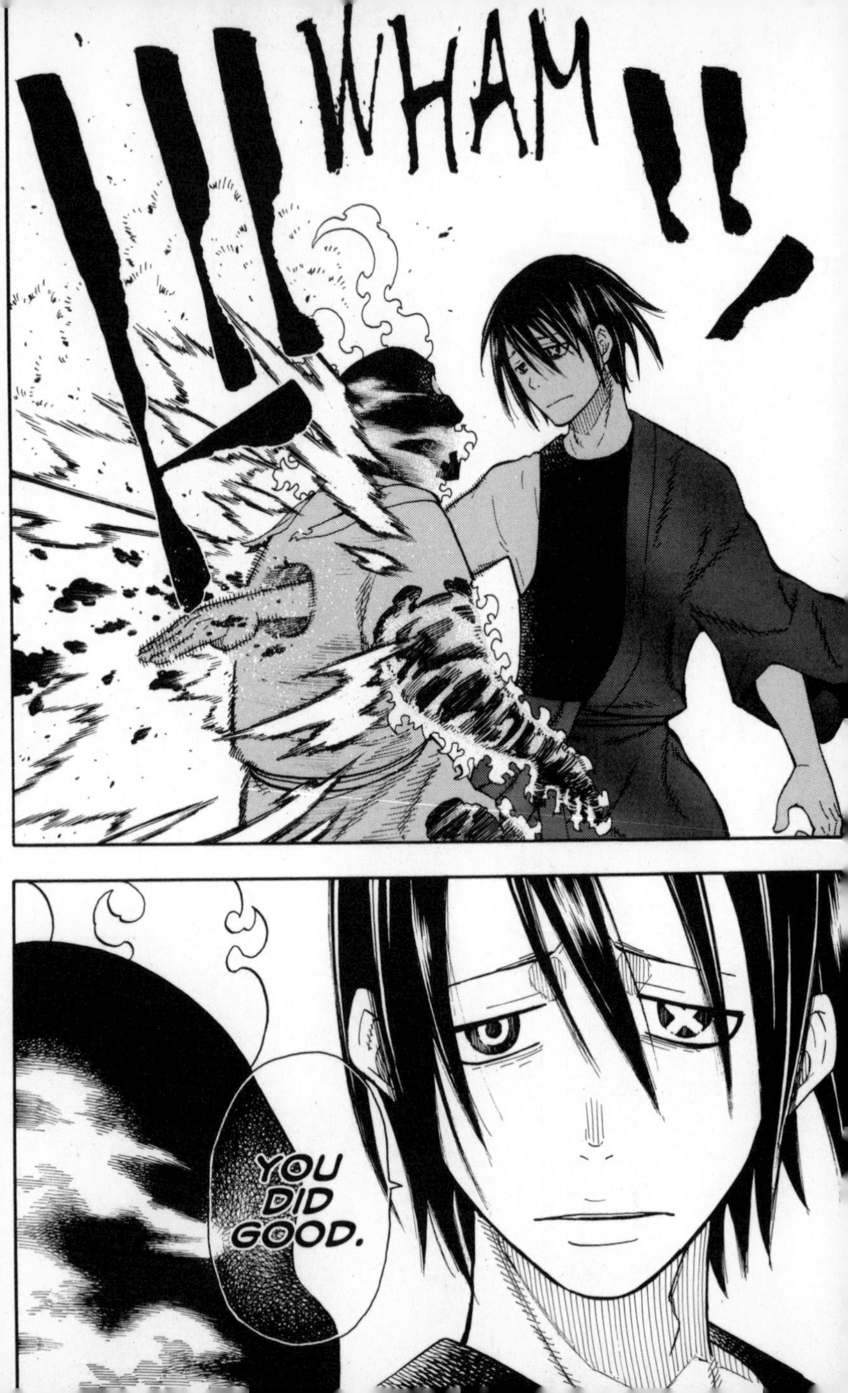
WHAM!!
YOU DID GOOD.

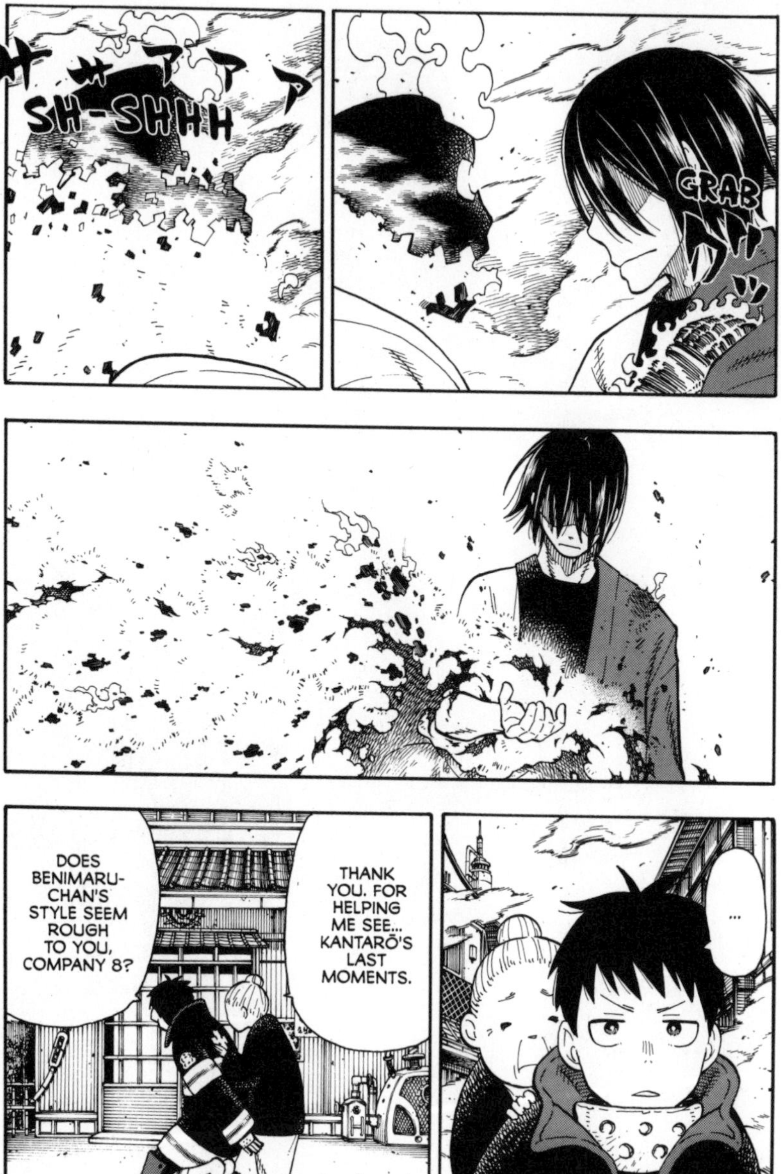
GRAB
SH-SHHH
...
THANK YOU. FOR HELPING ME SEE... KANTARŌ'S LAST MOMENTS.
DOES BENIMARU-CHAN'S STYLE SEEM ROUGH TO YOU, COMPANY 8?

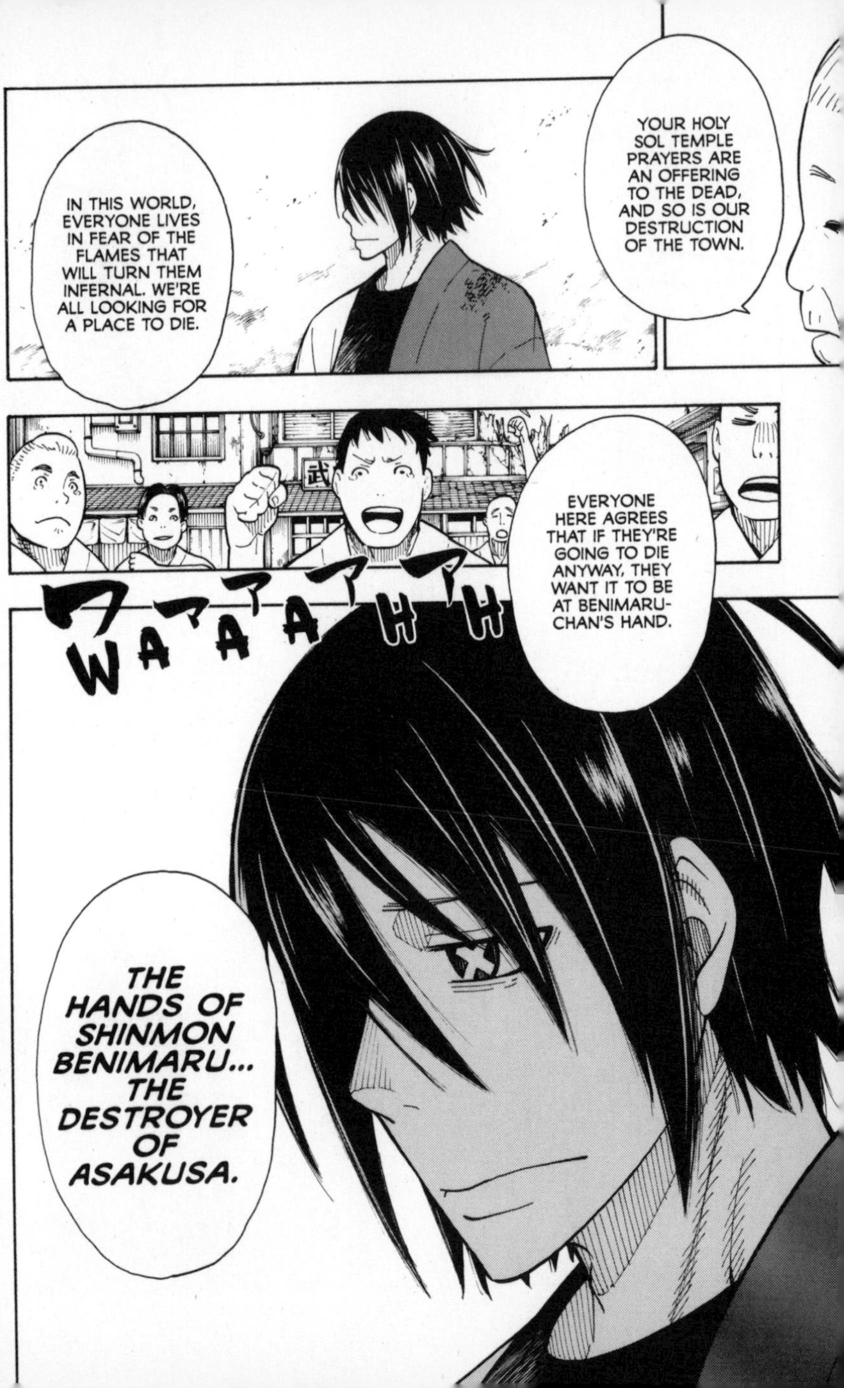
YOUR HOLY SOL TEMPLE PRAYERS ARE AN OFFERING TO THE DEAD, AND SO IS OUR DESTRUCTION OF THE TOWN.
IN THIS WORLD, EVERYONE LIVES IN FEAR OF THE FLAMES THAT WILL TURN THEM INFERNAL. WE'RE ALL LOOKING FOR A PLACE TO DIE.
EVERYONE HERE AGREES THAT IF THEY'RE GOING TO DIE ANYWAY, THEY WANT IT TO BE AT BENIMARU-CHAN'S HAND.
ワアアア
WAAAHH
THE HANDS OF SHINMON BENIMARU... THE DESTROYER OF ASAKUSA.

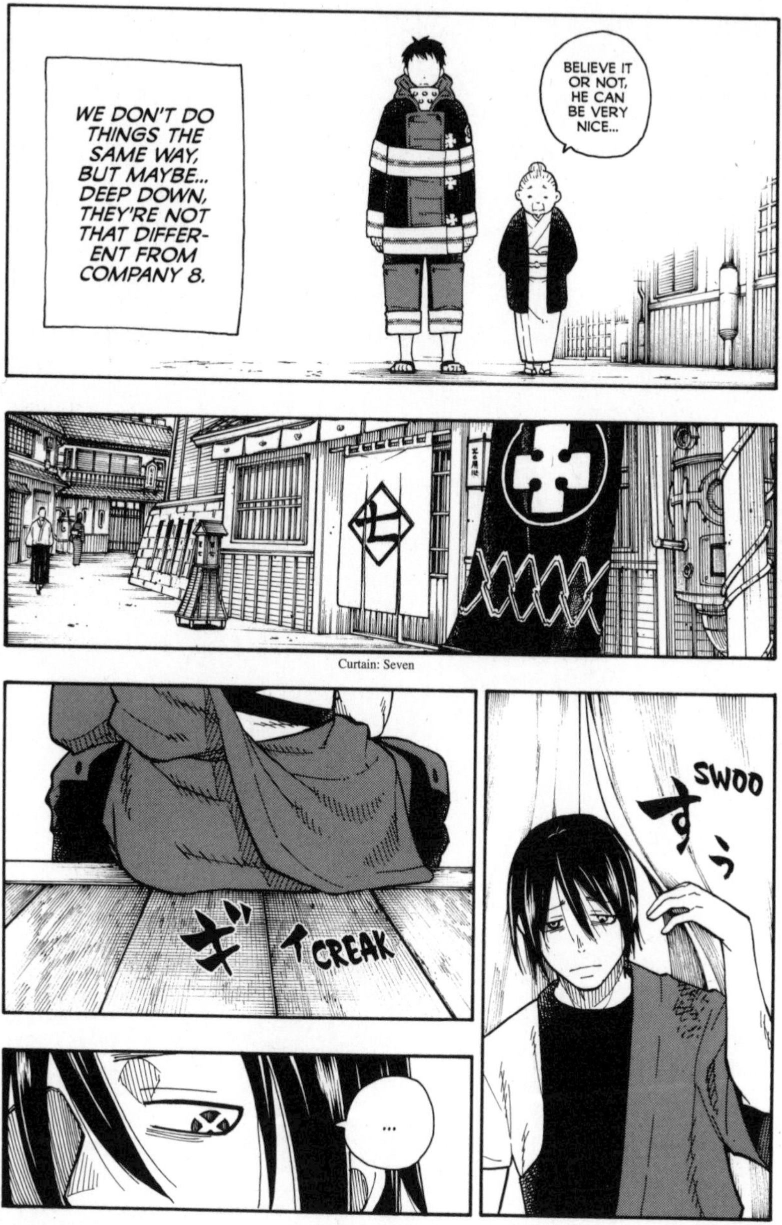
BELIEVE IT OR NOT, HE CAN BE VERY NICE...
WE DON'T DO THINGS THE SAME WAY, BUT MAYBE... DEEP DOWN, THEY'RE NOT THAT DIFFER-ENT FROM COMPANY 8.
SWOO
すう
ギイ
CREAK
...

Curtain: Seven

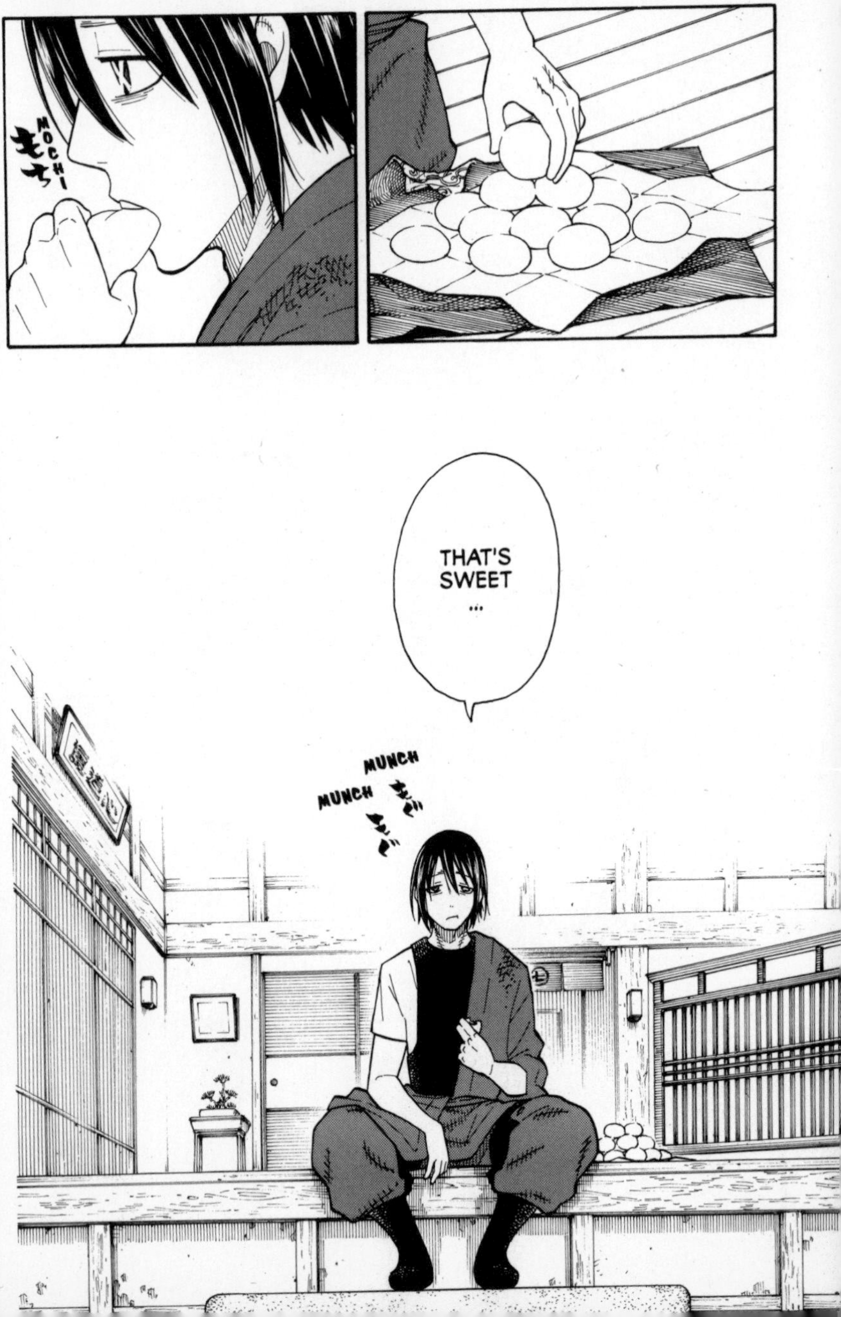
もち
MOCHI
THAT'S SWEET ...
MUNCH
もぐ
MUNCH
もぐ

FIRE FORCE

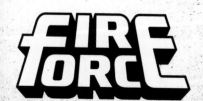

FIRE FORCE

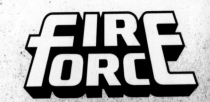

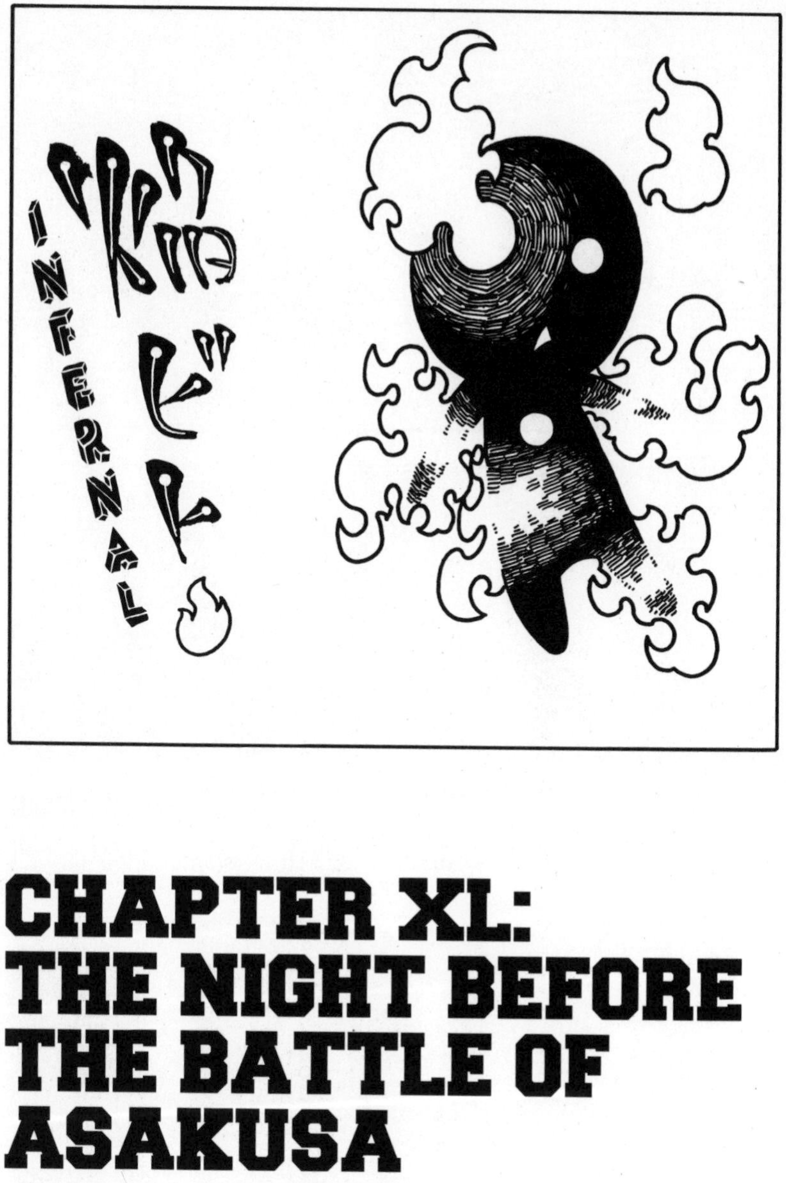
INFERNAL

CHAPTER XL: THE NIGHT BEFORE THE BATTLE OF ASAKUSA

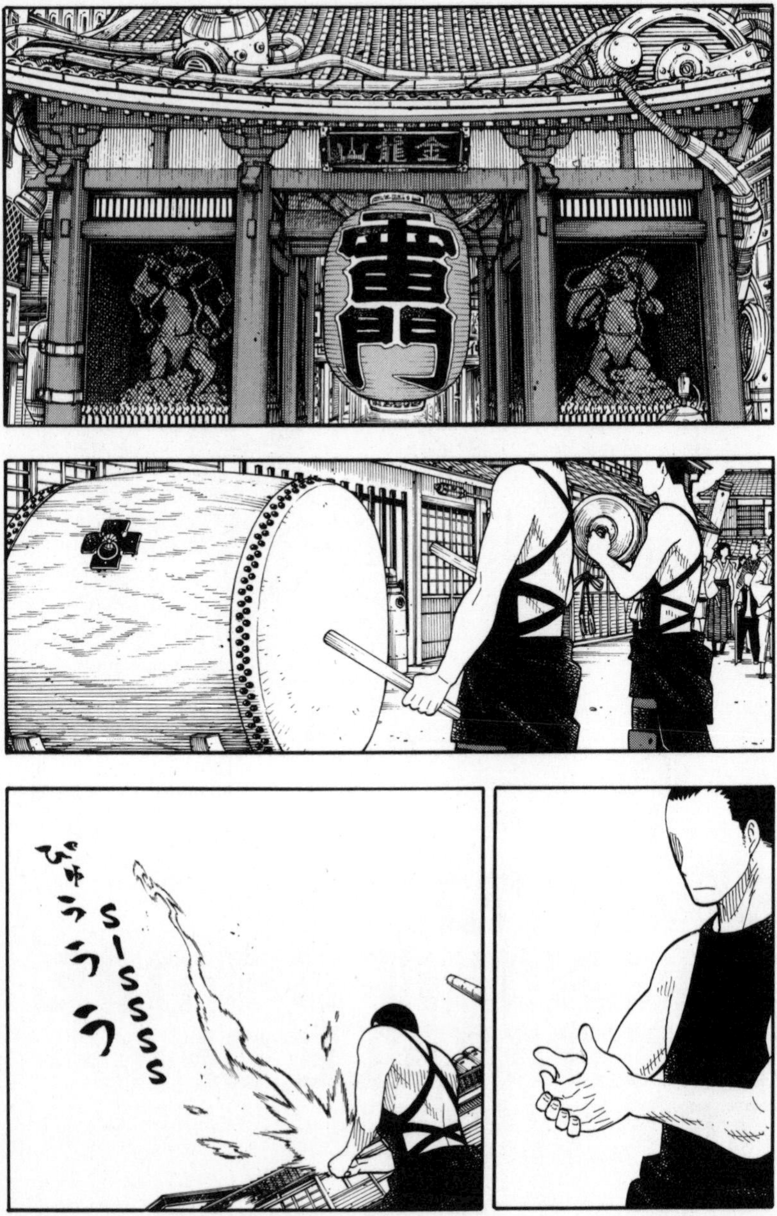
金龍山
雷門
S-SSSS
ぴゅううう

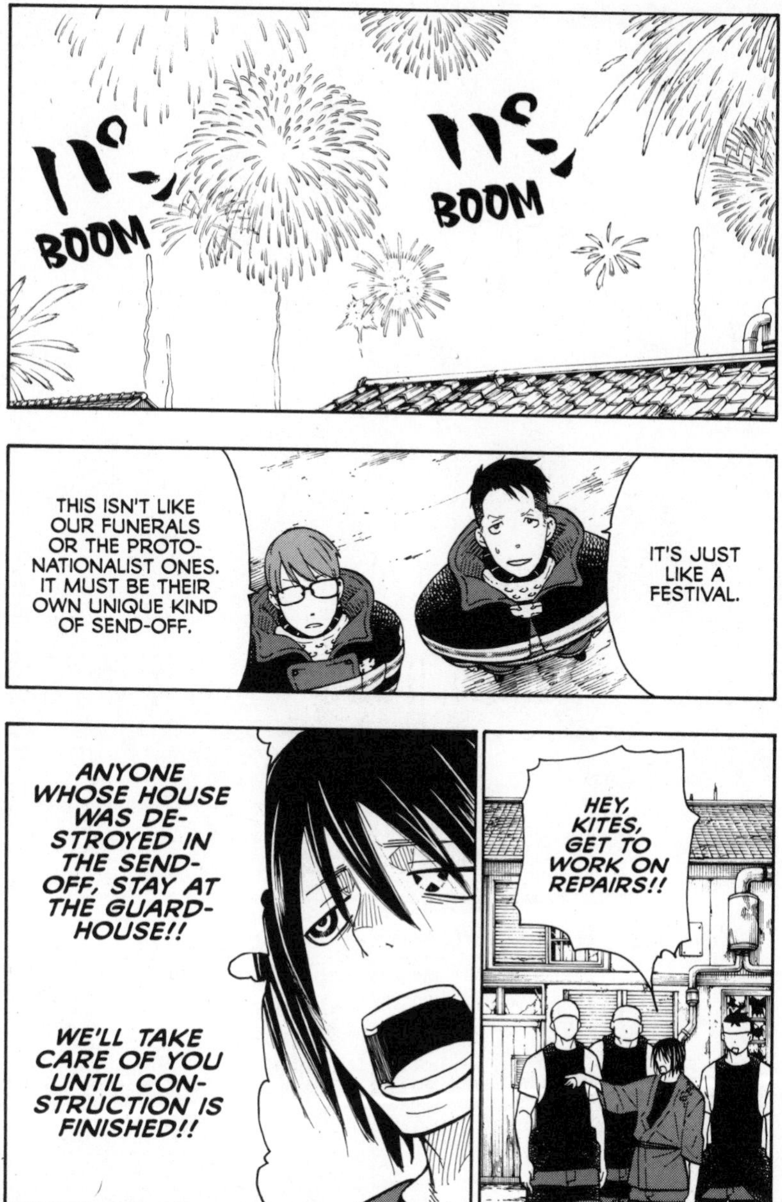
BOOM
BOOM
IT'S JUST LIKE A FESTIVAL.
THIS ISN'T LIKE OUR FUNERALS OR THE PROTO-NATIONALIST ONES. IT MUST BE THEIR OWN UNIQUE KIND OF SEND-OFF.
HEY, KITES, GET TO WORK ON REPAIRS!!
ANYONE WHOSE HOUSE WAS DE-STROYED IN THE SEND-OFF, STAY AT THE GUARD-HOUSE!!
WE'LL TAKE CARE OF YOU UNTIL CON-STRUCTION IS FINISHED!!

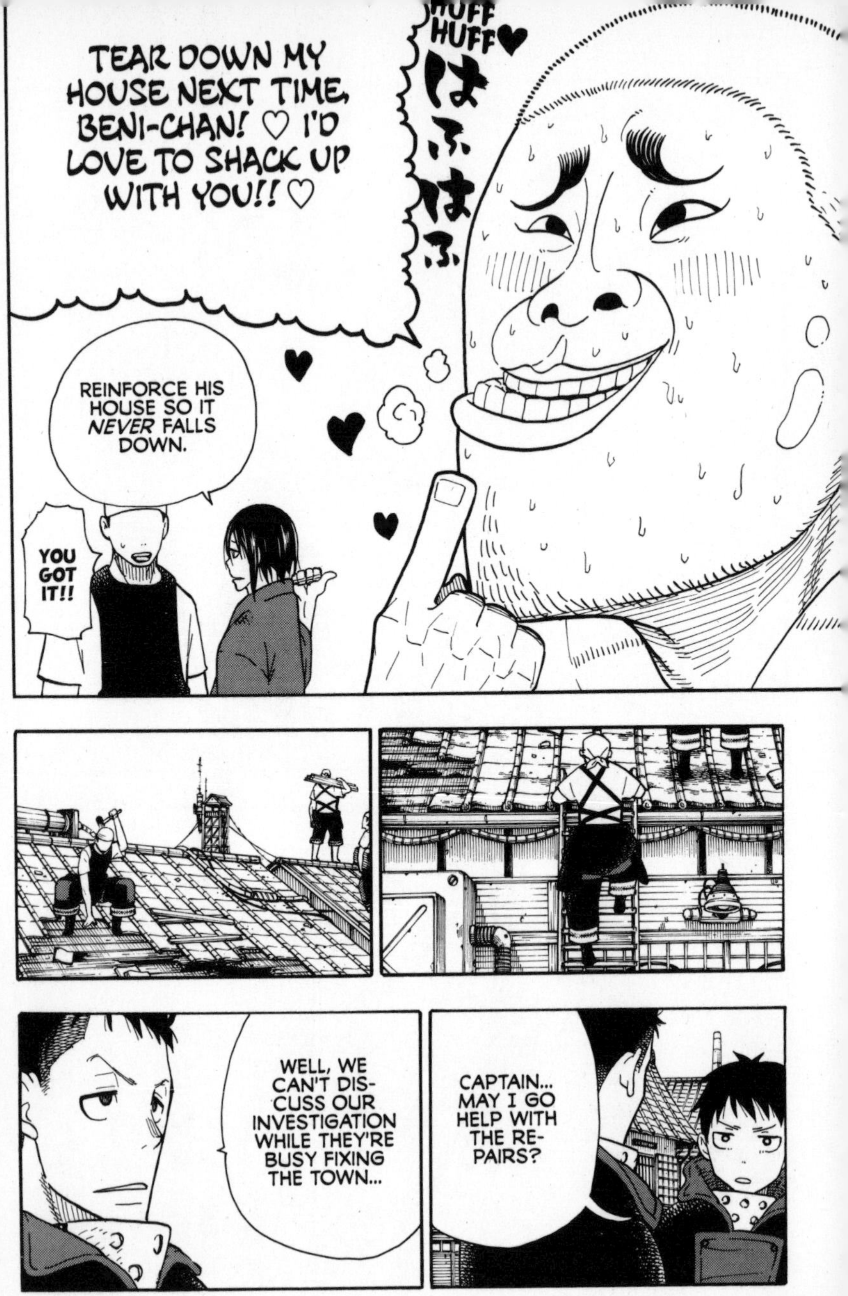
HUFF HUFF
はふはふ
TEAR DOWN MY HOUSE NEXT TIME, BENI-CHAN! ♡ I'D LOVE TO SHACK UP WITH YOU!! ♡
REINFORCE HIS HOUSE SO IT *NEVER* FALLS DOWN.
YOU GOT IT!!
CAPTAIN... MAY I GO HELP WITH THE RE-PAIRS?
WELL, WE CAN'T DIS-CUSS OUR INVESTIGATION WHILE THEY'RE BUSY FIXING THE TOWN...

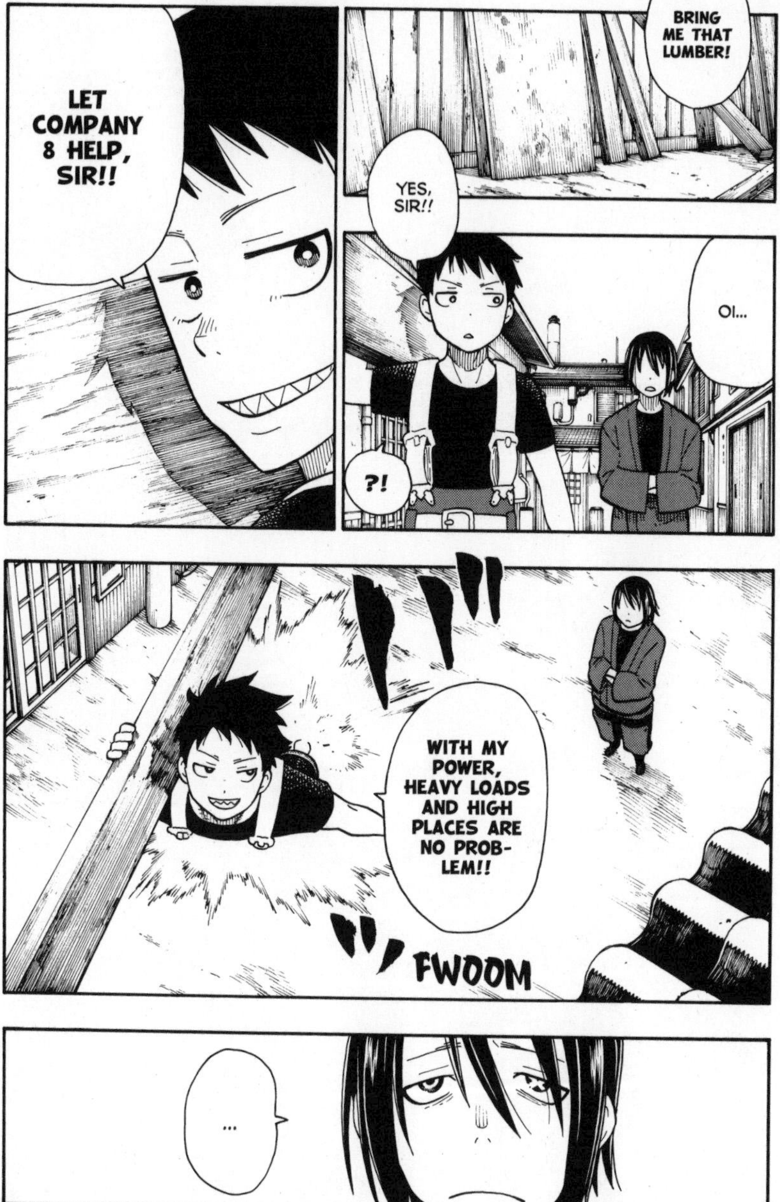
BRING ME THAT LUMBER!
YES, SIR!!
OI...
?!
LET COMPANY 8 HELP, SIR!!
WITH MY POWER, HEAVY LOADS AND HIGH PLACES ARE NO PROB-LEM!!
FWOOM
...

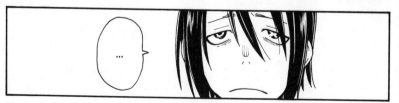

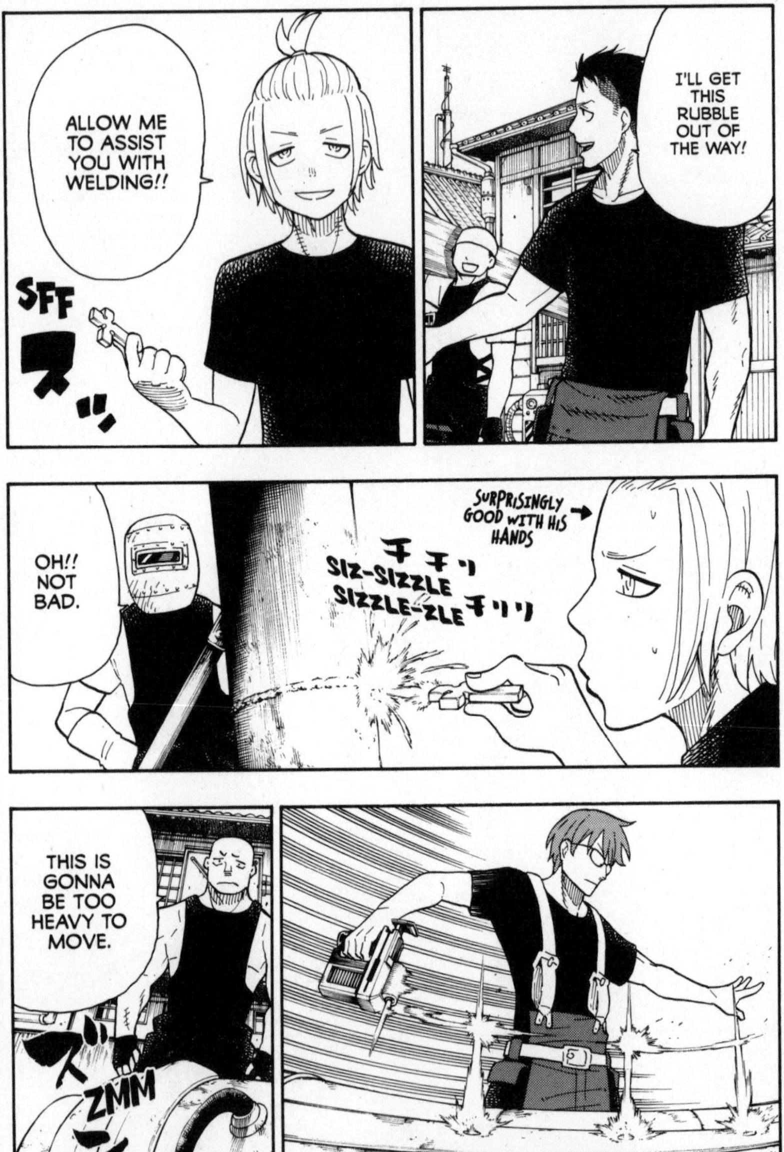
I'LL GET THIS RUBBLE OUT OF THE WAY!
ALLOW ME TO ASSIST YOU WITH WELDING!!
SFF
スッ
SURPRISINGLY GOOD WITH HIS HANDS
チチリ
SIZ-SIZZLE
SIZZLE-ZLE
チリリ
OH!! NOT BAD.
TAK タ TAK タ TAK タン
THIS IS GONNA BE TOO HEAVY TO MOVE.
ズン
ZMM

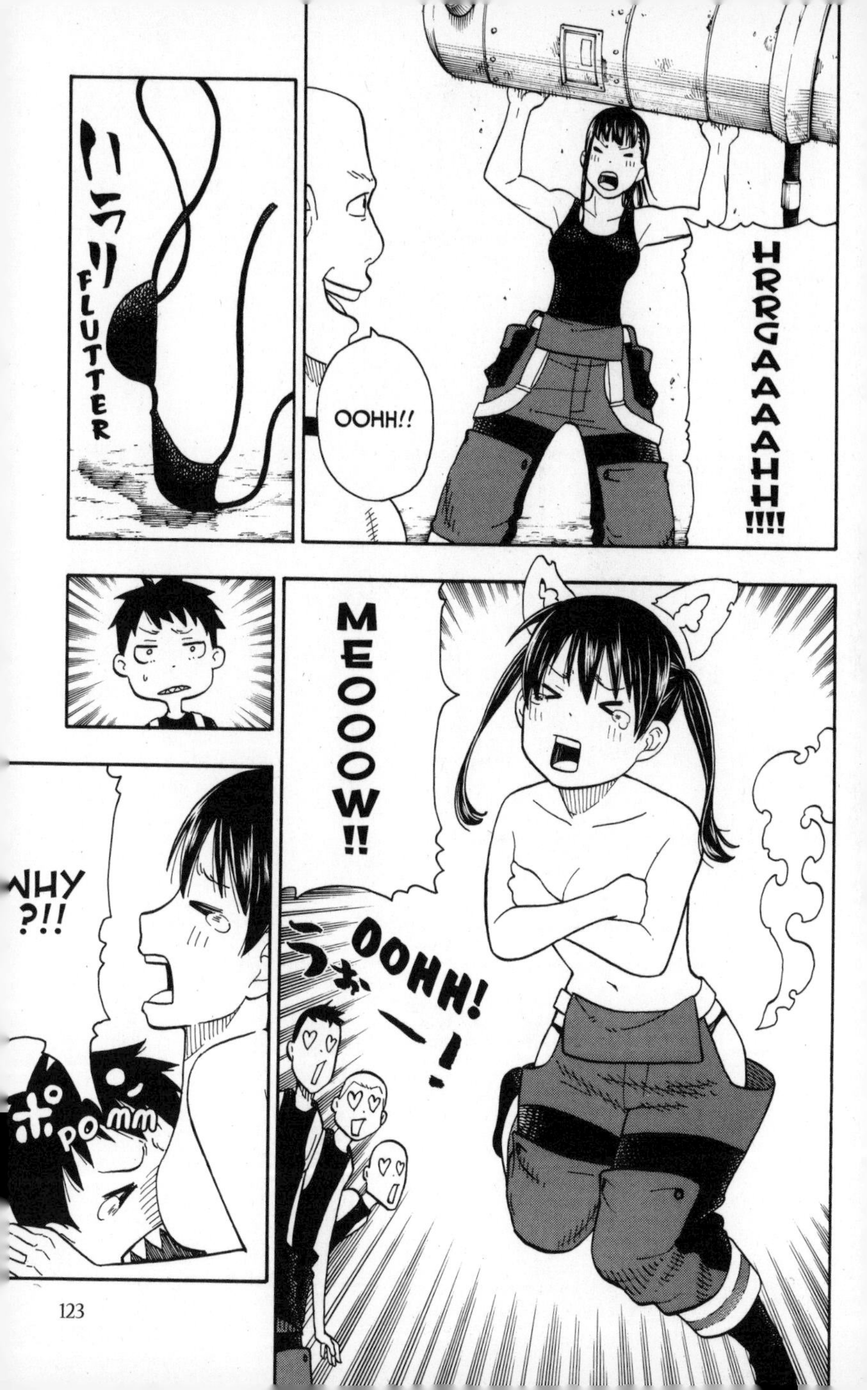
HRRGAAAAHH!!!!
OOHH!!
ハラリ
FLUTTER
MEOOOOW!!
うぉー!
OOHH!
WHY?!!
ポ
POMM

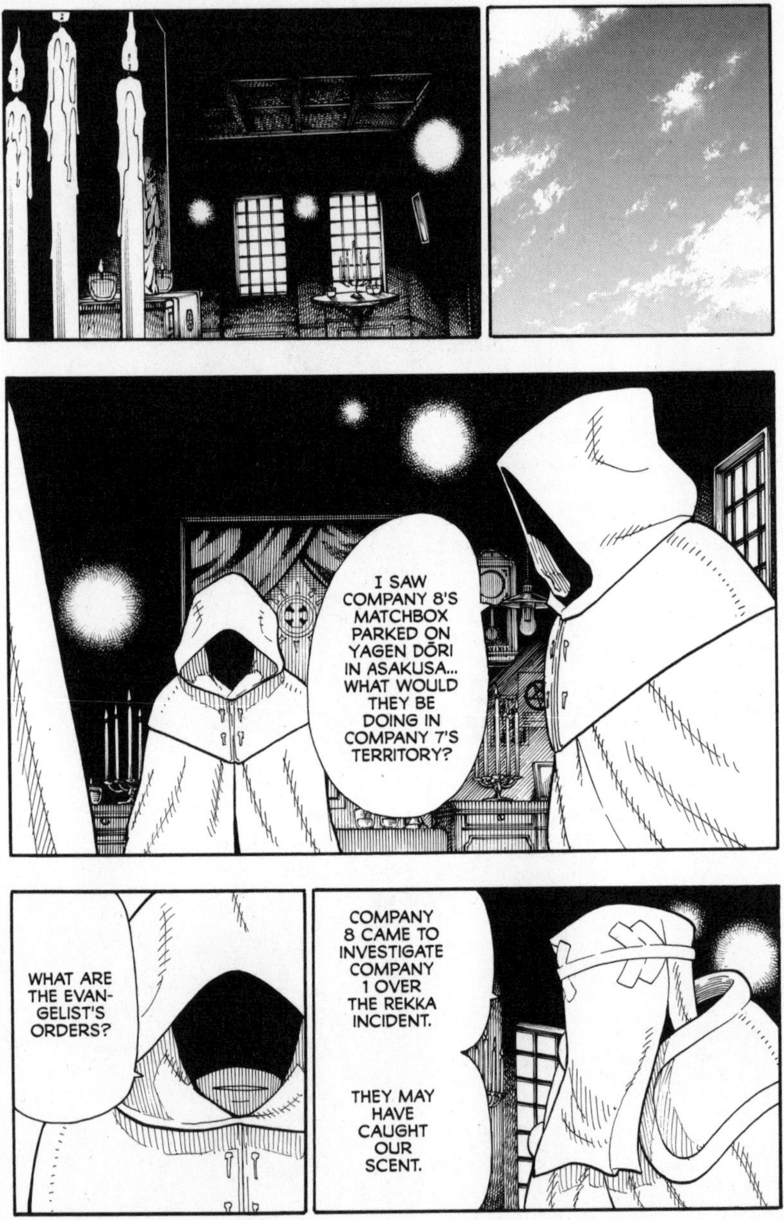
I SAW COMPANY 8'S MATCHBOX PARKED ON YAGEN DŌRI IN ASAKUSA... WHAT WOULD THEY BE DOING IN COMPANY 7'S TERRITORY?
COMPANY 8 CAME TO INVESTIGATE COMPANY 1 OVER THE REKKA INCIDENT.
THEY MAY HAVE CAUGHT OUR SCENT.
WHAT ARE THE EVAN-GELIST'S ORDERS?

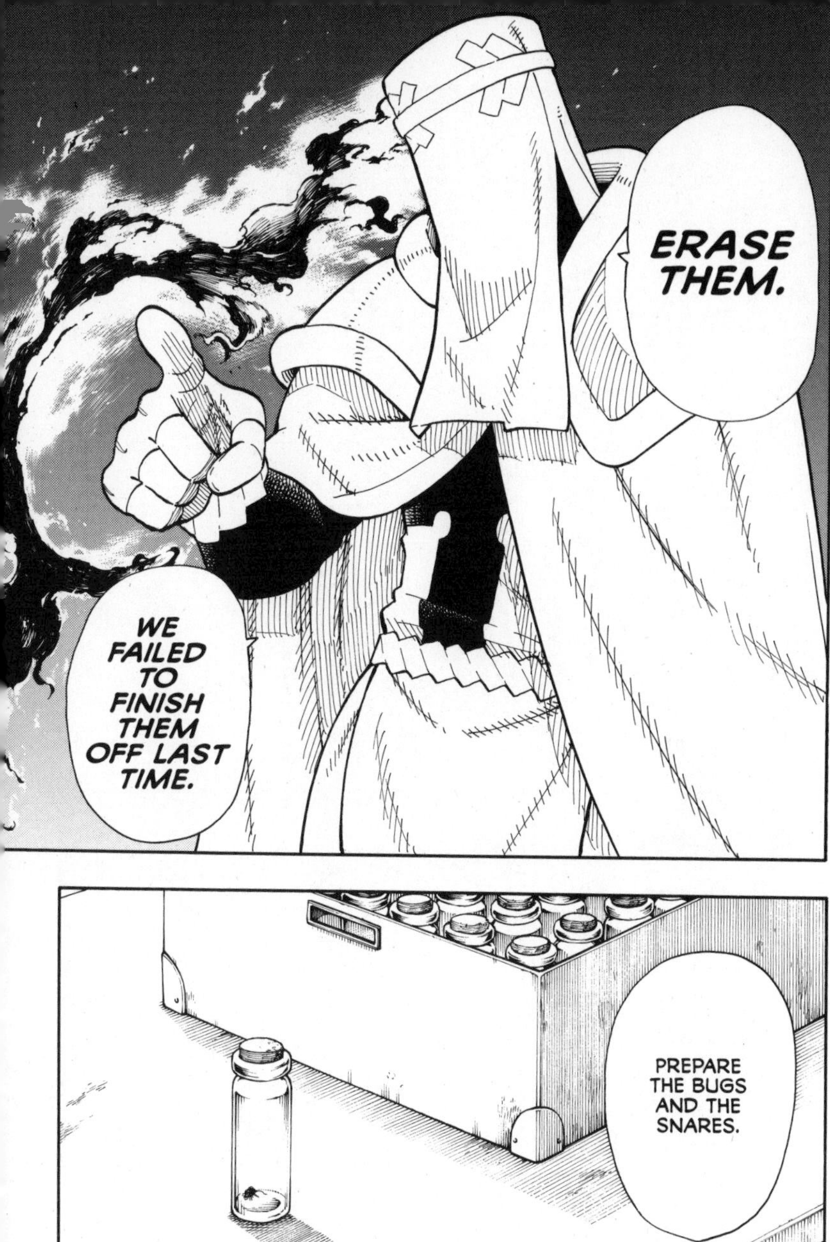
ERASE THEM.
WE FAILED TO FINISH THEM OFF LAST TIME.
PREPARE THE BUGS AND THE SNARES.

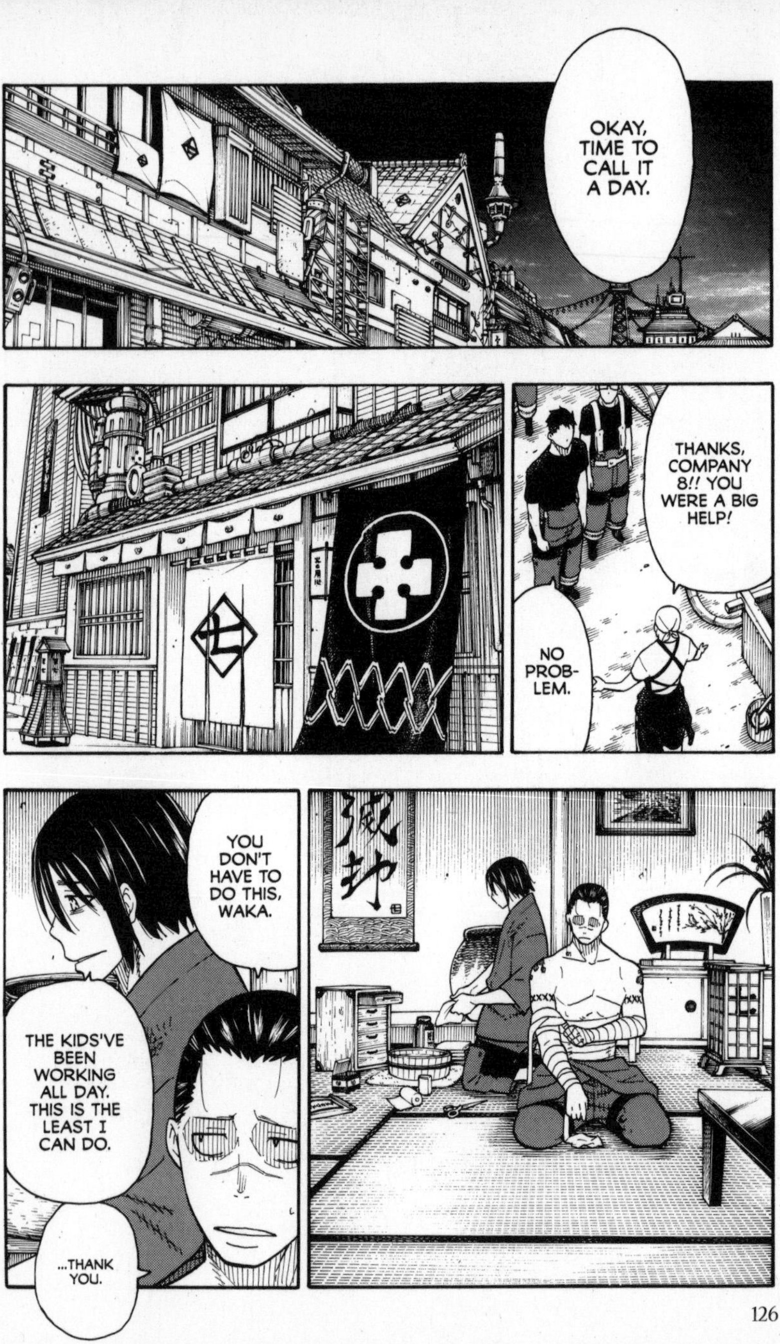
OKAY, TIME TO CALL IT A DAY.
THANKS, COMPANY 8!! YOU WERE A BIG HELP!
NO PROBLEM.
YOU DON'T HAVE TO DO THIS, WAKA.
THE KIDS'VE BEEN WORKING ALL DAY. THIS IS THE LEAST I CAN DO.
...THANK YOU.

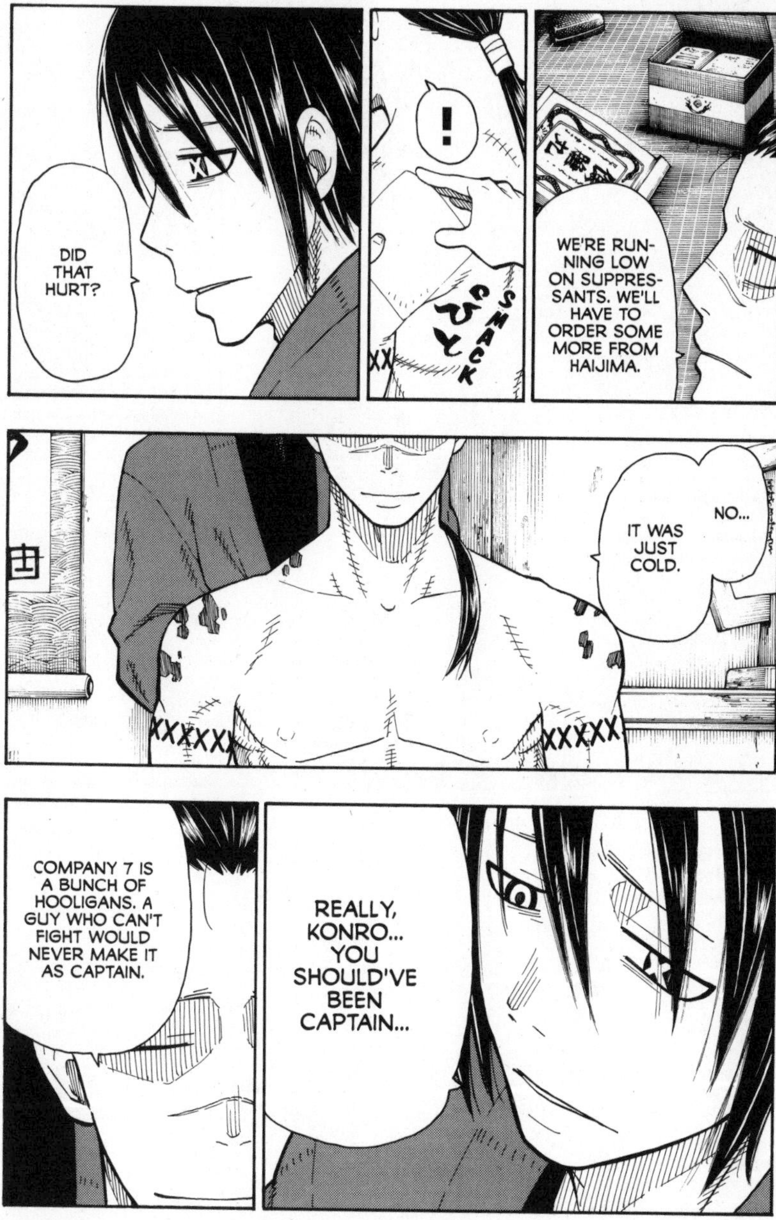
WE'RE RUN-NING LOW ON SUPPRES-SANTS. WE'LL HAVE TO ORDER SOME MORE FROM HAIJIMA.
!
SMACK
DID THAT HURT?
NO...
IT WAS JUST COLD.
REALLY, KONRO... YOU SHOULD'VE BEEN CAPTAIN...
COMPANY 7 IS A BUNCH OF HOOLIGANS. A GUY WHO CAN'T FIGHT WOULD NEVER MAKE IT AS CAPTAIN.

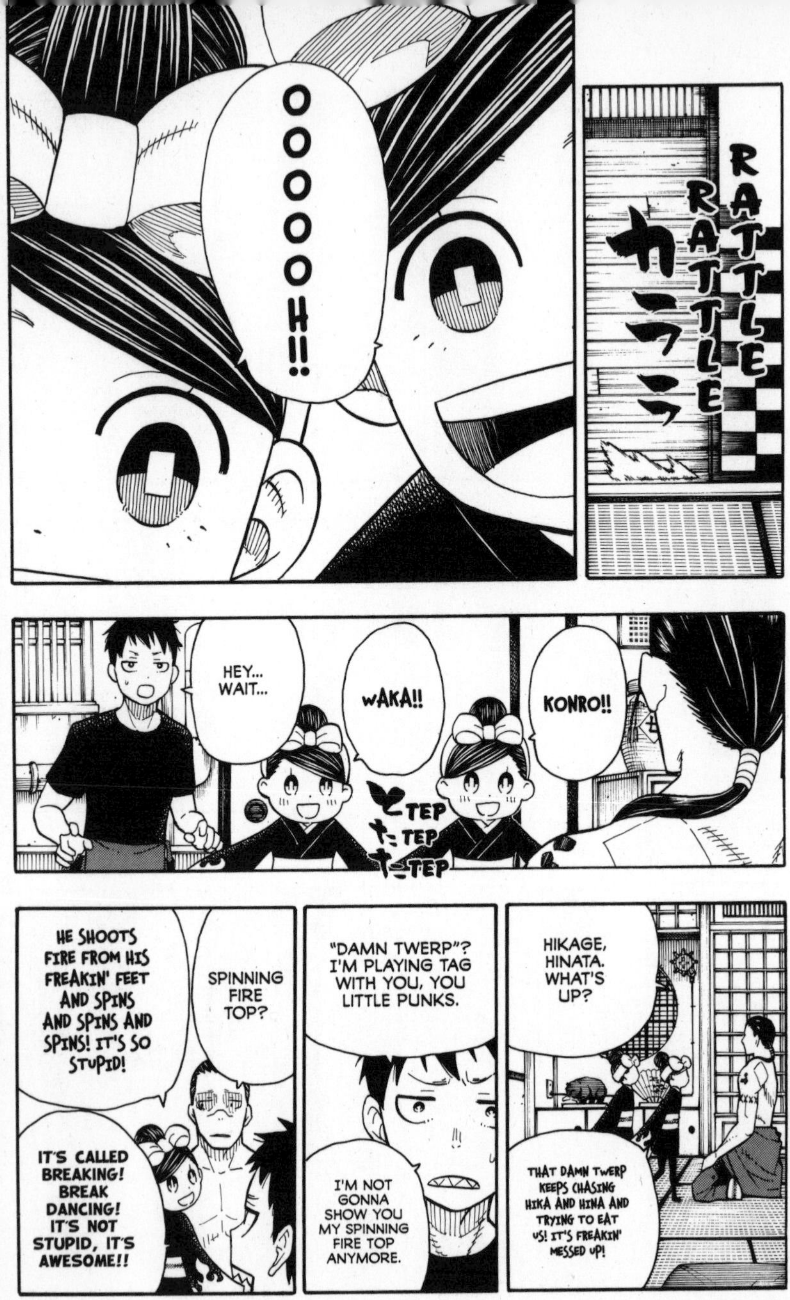
RATTLE RATTLE
カラララ
OOOOOH!!
KONRO!!
WAKA!!
HEY... WAIT...
TEP TEP TEP
HIKAGE, HINATA. WHAT'S UP?
THAT DAMN TWERP KEEPS CHASING HIKA AND HINA AND TRYING TO EAT US! IT'S FREAKIN' MESSED UP!
"DAMN TWERP"? I'M PLAYING TAG WITH YOU, YOU LITTLE PUNKS.
I'M NOT GONNA SHOW YOU MY SPINNING FIRE TOP ANYMORE.
SPINNING FIRE TOP?
HE SHOOTS FIRE FROM HIS FREAKIN' FEET AND SPINS AND SPINS AND SPINS! IT'S SO STUPID!
IT'S CALLED BREAKING! BREAK DANCING! IT'S NOT STUPID, IT'S AWESOME!!

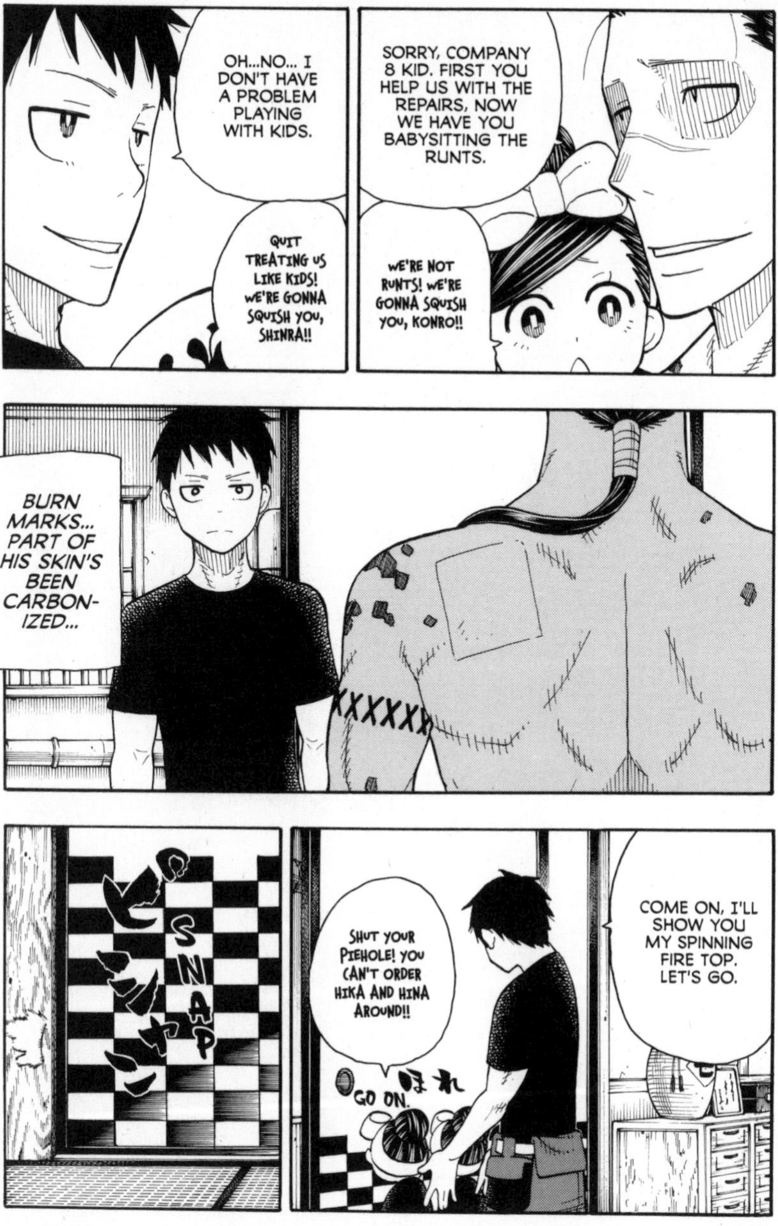
SORRY, COMPANY 8 KID. FIRST YOU HELP US WITH THE REPAIRS, NOW WE HAVE YOU BABYSITTING THE RUNTS.
WE'RE NOT RUNTS! WE'RE GONNA SQUISH YOU, KONRO!!
OH...NO... I DON'T HAVE A PROBLEM PLAYING WITH KIDS.
QUIT TREATING US LIKE KIDS! WE'RE GONNA SQUISH YOU, SHINRA!!
BURN MARKS... PART OF HIS SKIN'S BEEN CARBON-IZED...
COME ON, I'LL SHOW YOU MY SPINNING FIRE TOP. LET'S GO.
SHUT YOUR PIEHOLE! YOU CAN'T ORDER HIKA AND HINA AROUND!!
ほれ
GO ON.
SNAP

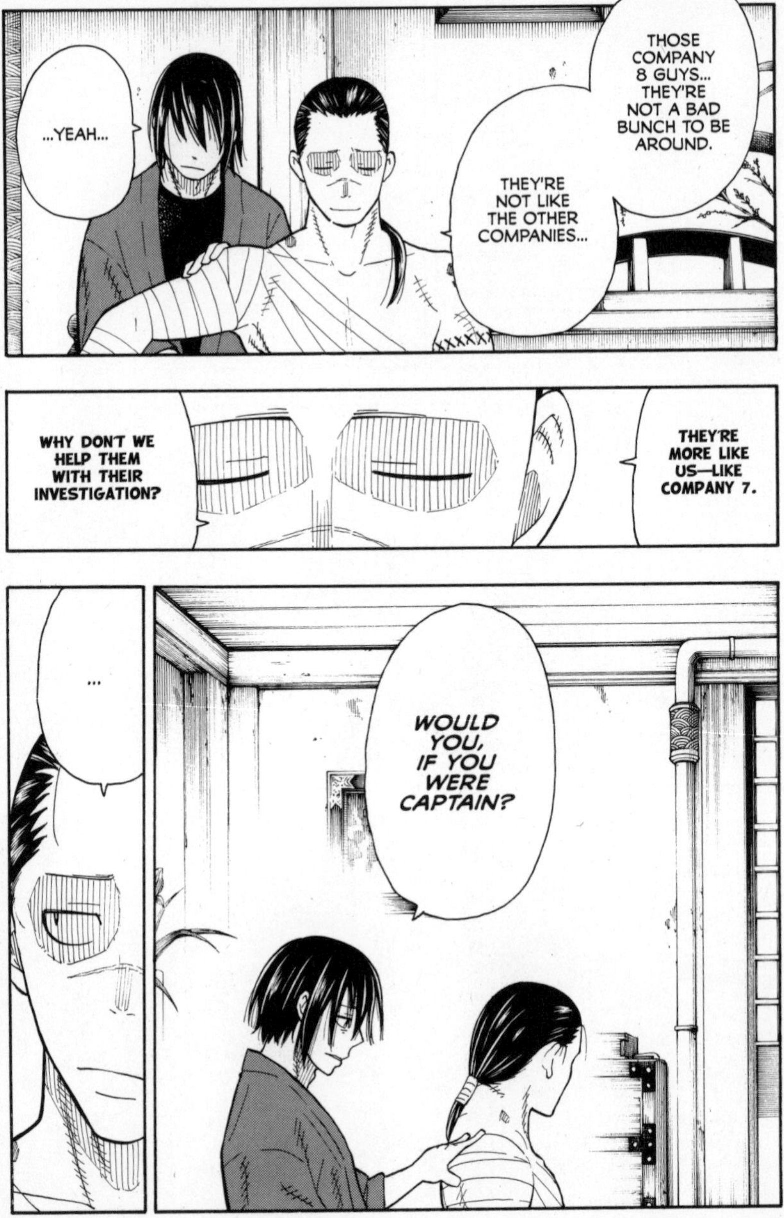
THOSE COMPANY 8 GUYS... THEY'RE NOT A BAD BUNCH TO BE AROUND.
THEY'RE NOT LIKE THE OTHER COMPANIES...
...YEAH...
THEY'RE MORE LIKE US—LIKE COMPANY 7.
WHY DON'T WE HELP THEM WITH THEIR INVESTIGATION?
WOULD YOU, IF YOU WERE CAPTAIN?
...

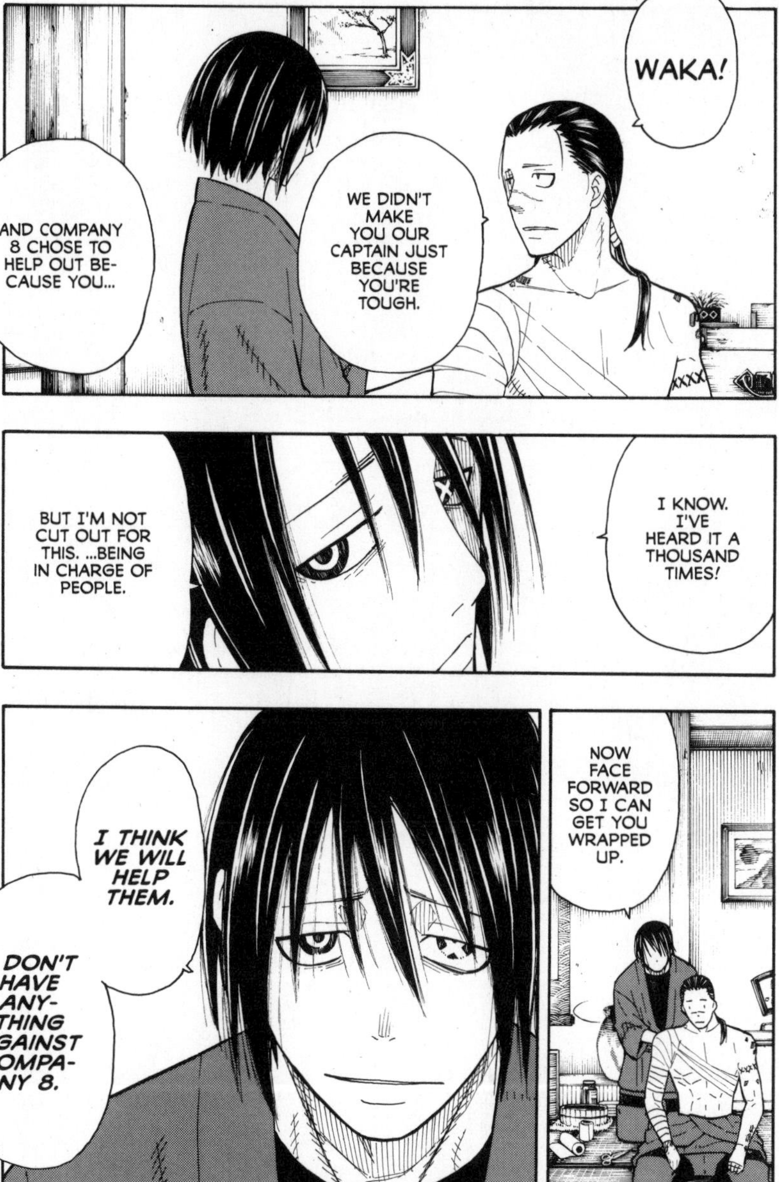
WAKA!
WE DIDN'T MAKE YOU OUR CAPTAIN JUST BECAUSE YOU'RE TOUGH.
AND COMPANY 8 CHOSE TO HELP OUT BE-CAUSE YOU...
I KNOW. I'VE HEARD IT A THOUSAND TIMES!
BUT I'M NOT CUT OUT FOR THIS. ...BEING IN CHARGE OF PEOPLE.
NOW FACE FORWARD SO I CAN GET YOU WRAPPED UP.
I THINK WE WILL HELP THEM.
I DON'T HAVE ANY-THING AGAINST COMPA-NY 8.

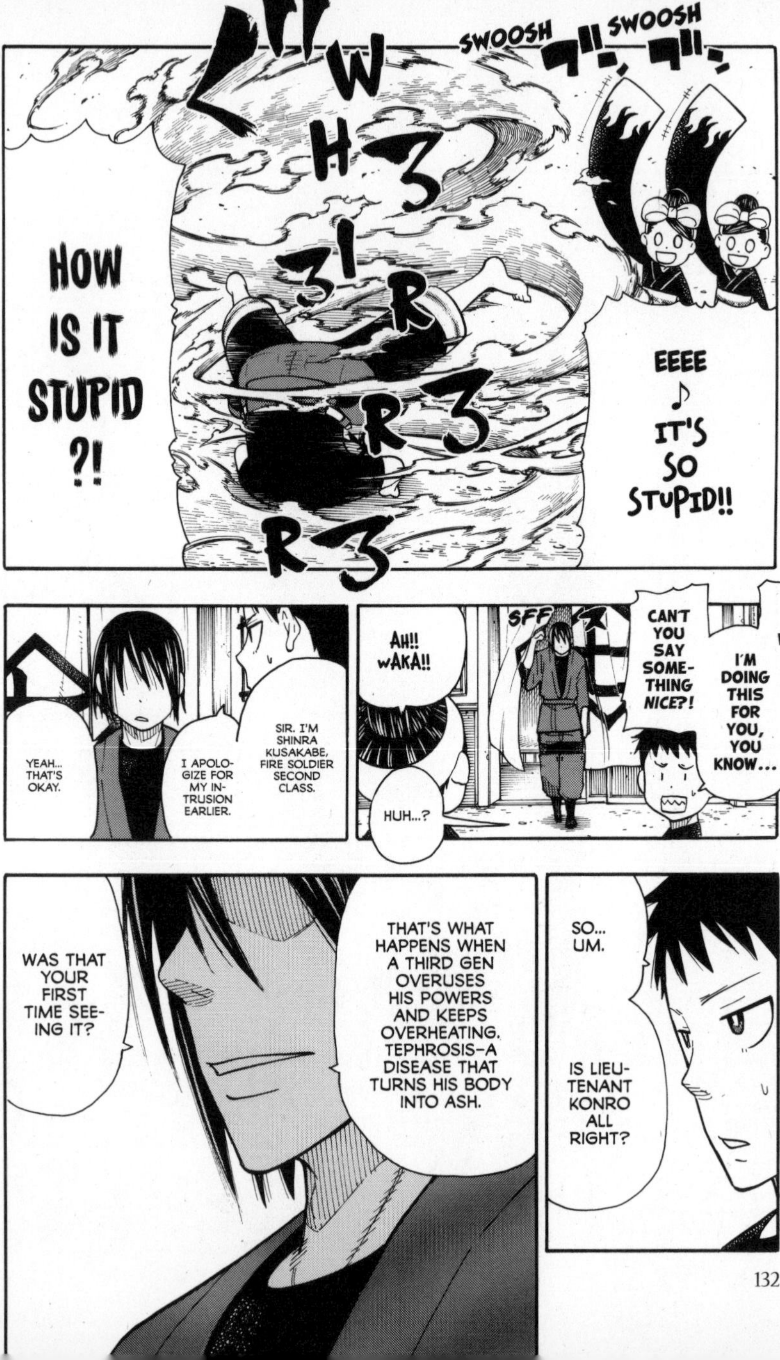
SWOOSH
SWOOSH
EEEE ♪ IT'S SO STUPID!!
HOW IS IT STUPID?!
WHIRRR
WHY?!
I'M DOING THIS FOR YOU, YOU KNOW...
CAN'T YOU SAY SOMETHING NICE?!
SFF
AH!! WAKA!!
HUH...?
SIR. I'M SHINRA KUSAKABE, FIRE SOLDIER SECOND CLASS.
I APOLOGIZE FOR MY INTRUSION EARLIER.
YEAH... THAT'S OKAY.
SO... UM.
IS LIEUTENANT KONRO ALL RIGHT?
THAT'S WHAT HAPPENS WHEN A THIRD GEN OVERUSES HIS POWERS AND KEEPS OVERHEATING. TEPHROSIS–A DISEASE THAT TURNS HIS BODY INTO ASH.
WAS THAT YOUR FIRST TIME SEEING IT?

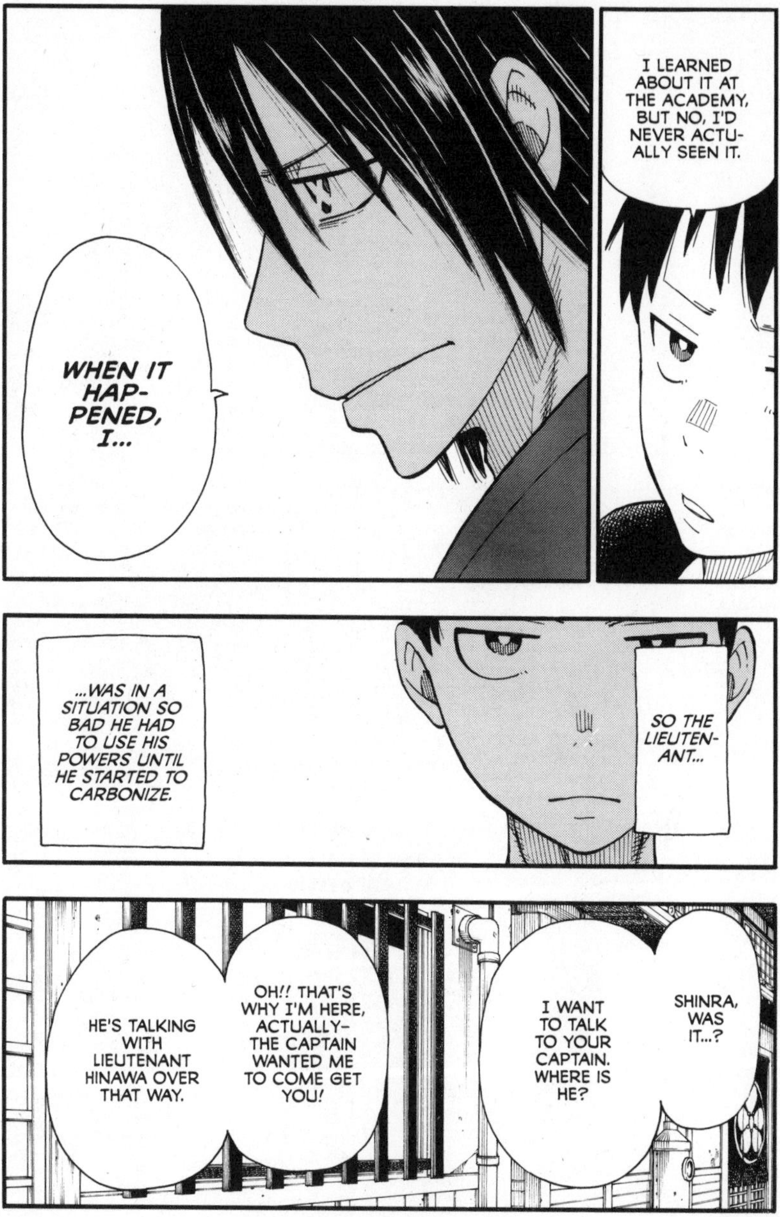
I LEARNED ABOUT IT AT THE ACADEMY, BUT NO, I'D NEVER ACTUALLY SEEN IT.
WHEN IT HAPPENED, I...
SO THE LIEUTENANT...
...WAS IN A SITUATION SO BAD HE HAD TO USE HIS POWERS UNTIL HE STARTED TO CARBONIZE.
SHINRA, WAS IT...?
I WANT TO TALK TO YOUR CAPTAIN. WHERE IS HE?
OH!! THAT'S WHY I'M HERE, ACTUALLY– THE CAPTAIN WANTED ME TO COME GET YOU!
HE'S TALKING WITH LIEUTENANT HINAWA OVER THAT WAY.

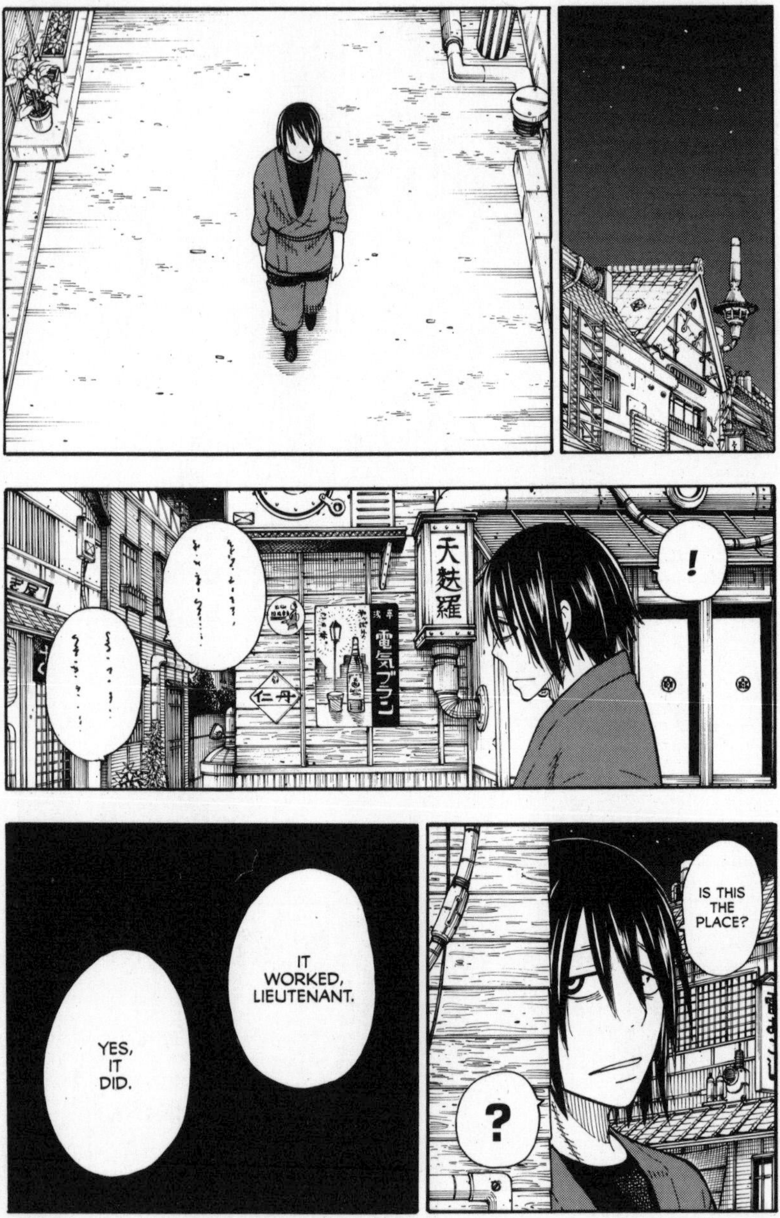
!
天麩羅
電気ブラン
仁丹
IS THIS THE PLACE?
?
IT WORKED, LIEUTENANT.
YES, IT DID.

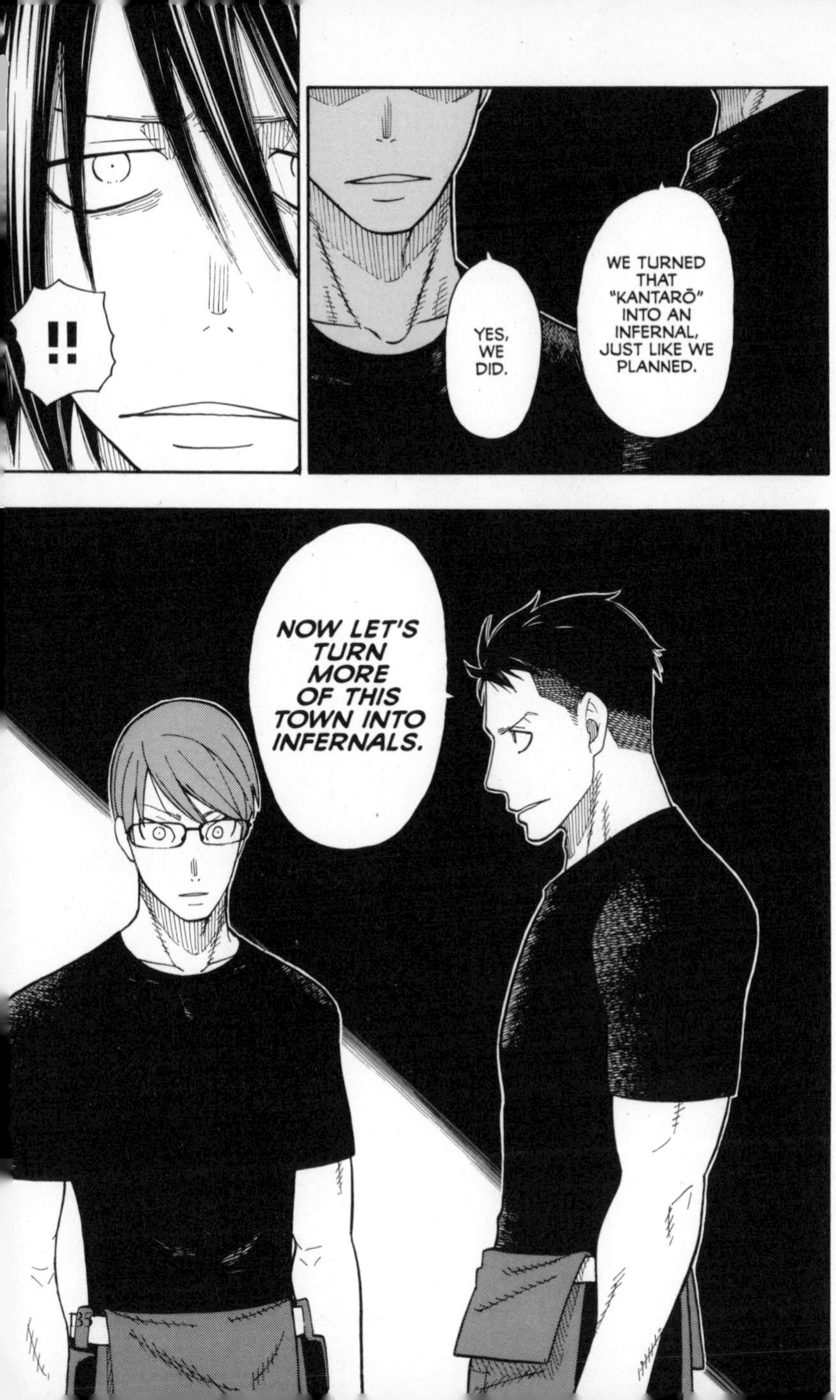
WE TURNED THAT "KANTARŌ" INTO AN INFERNAL, JUST LIKE WE PLANNED.
YES, WE DID.
!!
NOW LET'S TURN MORE OF THIS TOWN INTO INFERNALS.

FIRE FORCE

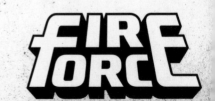

CHAPTER XLI:
A COMPOSITE FIRE
SOLDIER ENRAGED

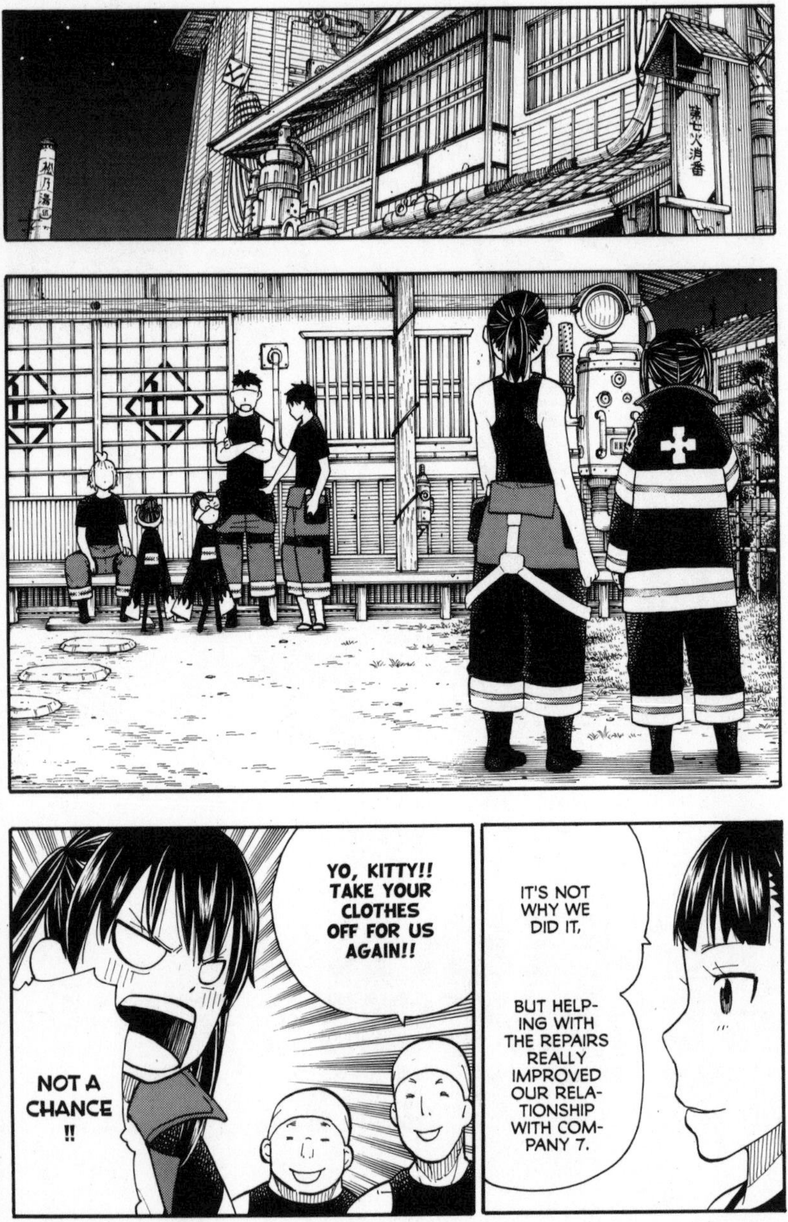
IT'S NOT WHY WE DID IT,
BUT HELPING WITH THE REPAIRS REALLY IMPROVED OUR RELATIONSHIP WITH COMPANY 7.
YO, KITTY!! TAKE YOUR CLOTHES OFF FOR US AGAIN!!
NOT A CHANCE!!

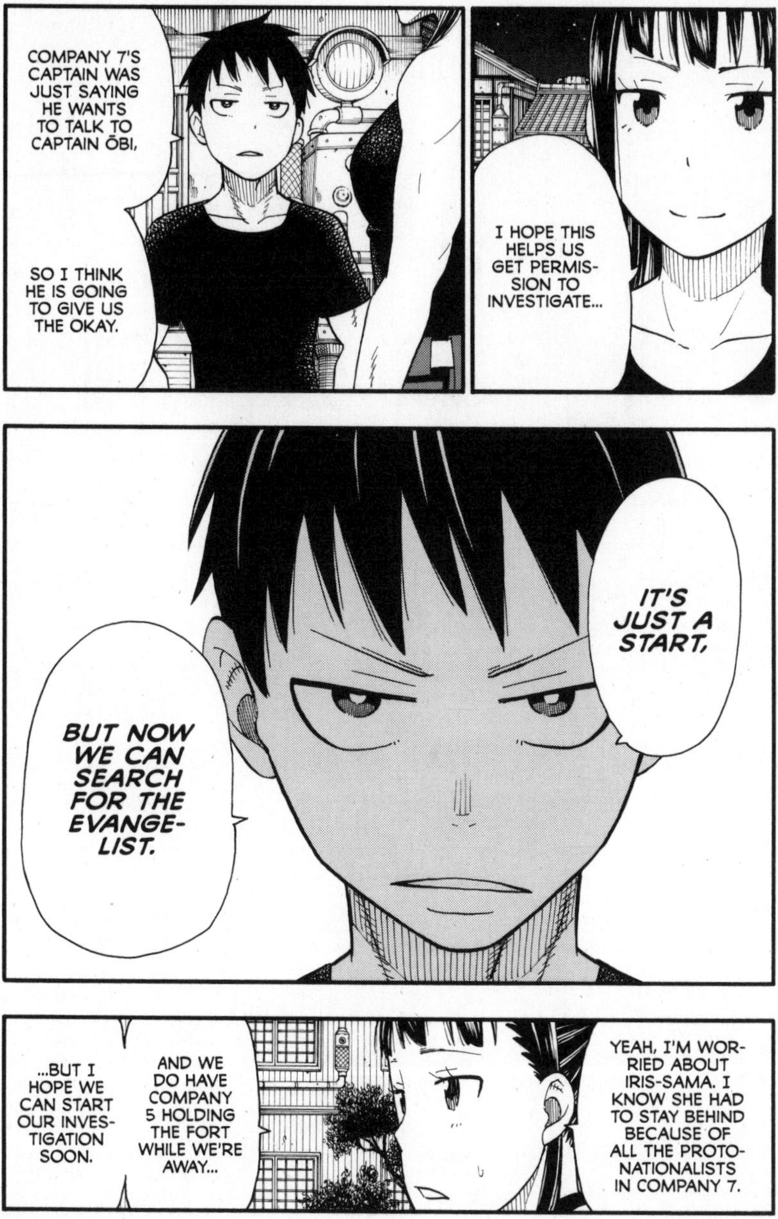
I HOPE THIS HELPS US GET PERMISSION TO INVESTIGATE...
COMPANY 7'S CAPTAIN WAS JUST SAYING HE WANTS TO TALK TO CAPTAIN ŌBI,
SO I THINK HE IS GOING TO GIVE US THE OKAY.
IT'S JUST A START,
BUT NOW WE CAN SEARCH FOR THE EVANGELIST.
YEAH, I'M WORRIED ABOUT IRIS-SAMA. I KNOW SHE HAD TO STAY BEHIND BECAUSE OF ALL THE PROTO-NATIONALISTS IN COMPANY 7.
AND WE DO HAVE COMPANY 5 HOLDING THE FORT WHILE WE'RE AWAY...
...BUT I HOPE WE CAN START OUR INVESTIGATION SOON.

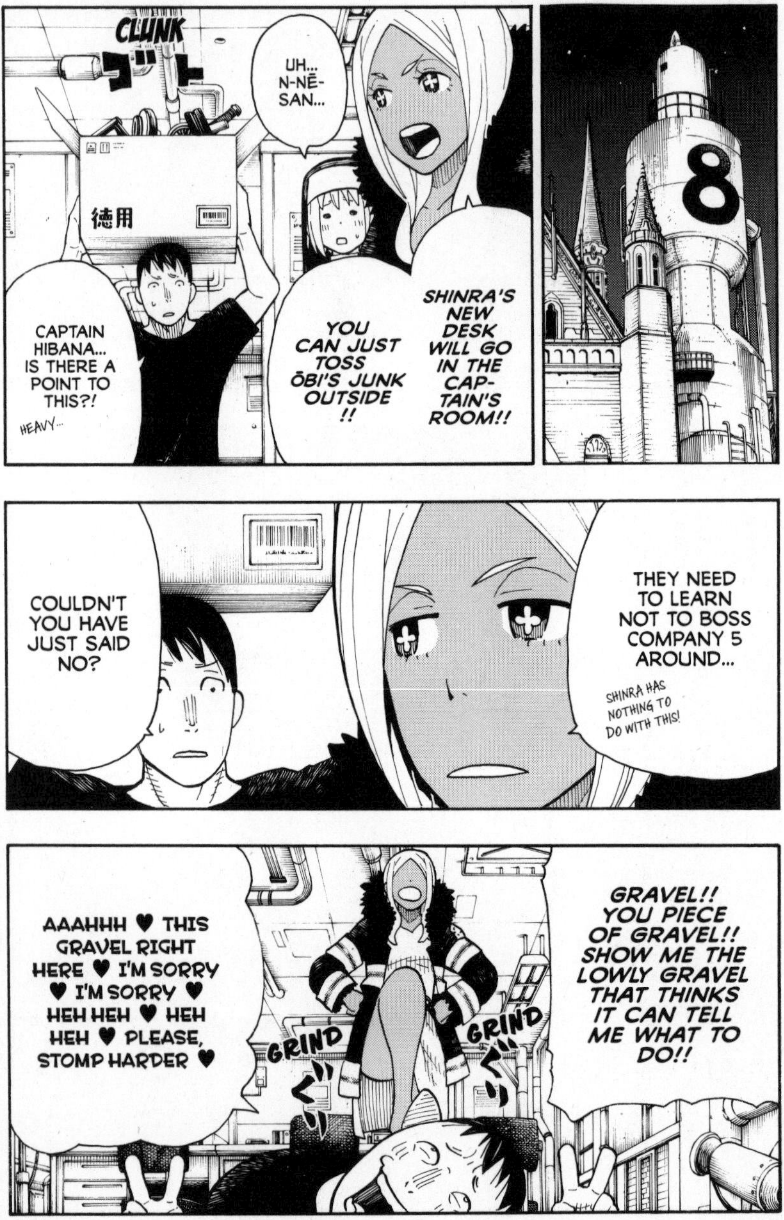
UH... N-NĒ-SAN...
SHINRA'S NEW DESK WILL GO IN THE CAP-TAIN'S ROOM!!
YOU CAN JUST TOSS ŌBI'S JUNK OUTSIDE !!
CLUNK
徳用
CAPTAIN HIBANA... IS THERE A POINT TO THIS?!
HEAVY...
THEY NEED TO LEARN NOT TO BOSS COMPANY 5 AROUND...
SHINRA HAS NOTHING TO DO WITH THIS!
COULDN'T YOU HAVE JUST SAID NO?
GRAVEL!! YOU PIECE OF GRAVEL!! SHOW ME THE LOWLY GRAVEL THAT THINKS IT CAN TELL ME WHAT TO DO!!
GRIND
GRIND
AAAHHH ♥ THIS GRAVEL RIGHT HERE ♥ I'M SORRY ♥ I'M SORRY ♥ HEH HEH ♥ HEH HEH ♥ PLEASE, STOMP HARDER ♥

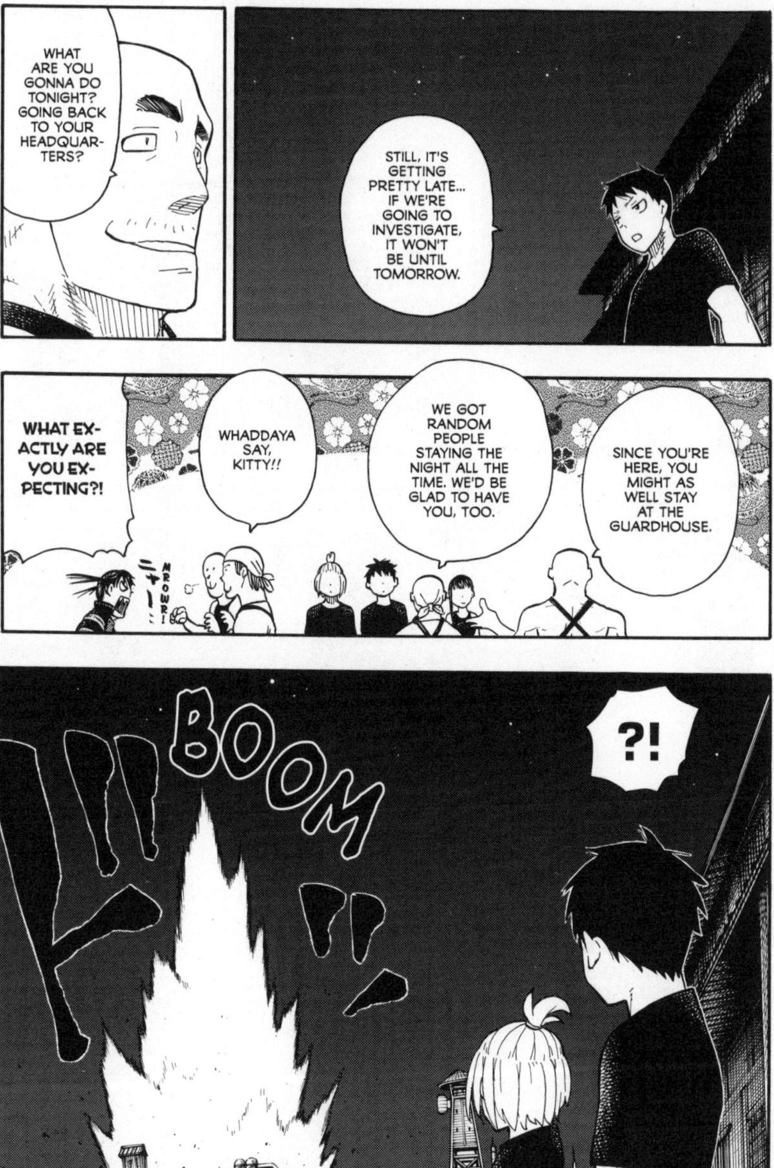
STILL, IT'S GETTING PRETTY LATE... IF WE'RE GOING TO INVESTIGATE, IT WON'T BE UNTIL TOMORROW.
WHAT ARE YOU GONNA DO TONIGHT? GOING BACK TO YOUR HEADQUARTERS?
SINCE YOU'RE HERE, YOU MIGHT AS WELL STAY AT THE GUARDHOUSE.
WE GOT RANDOM PEOPLE STAYING THE NIGHT ALL THE TIME. WE'D BE GLAD TO HAVE YOU, TOO.
WHADDAYA SAY, KITTY!!
WHAT EXACTLY ARE YOU EXPECTING?!
MROWR!
?!
BOOM

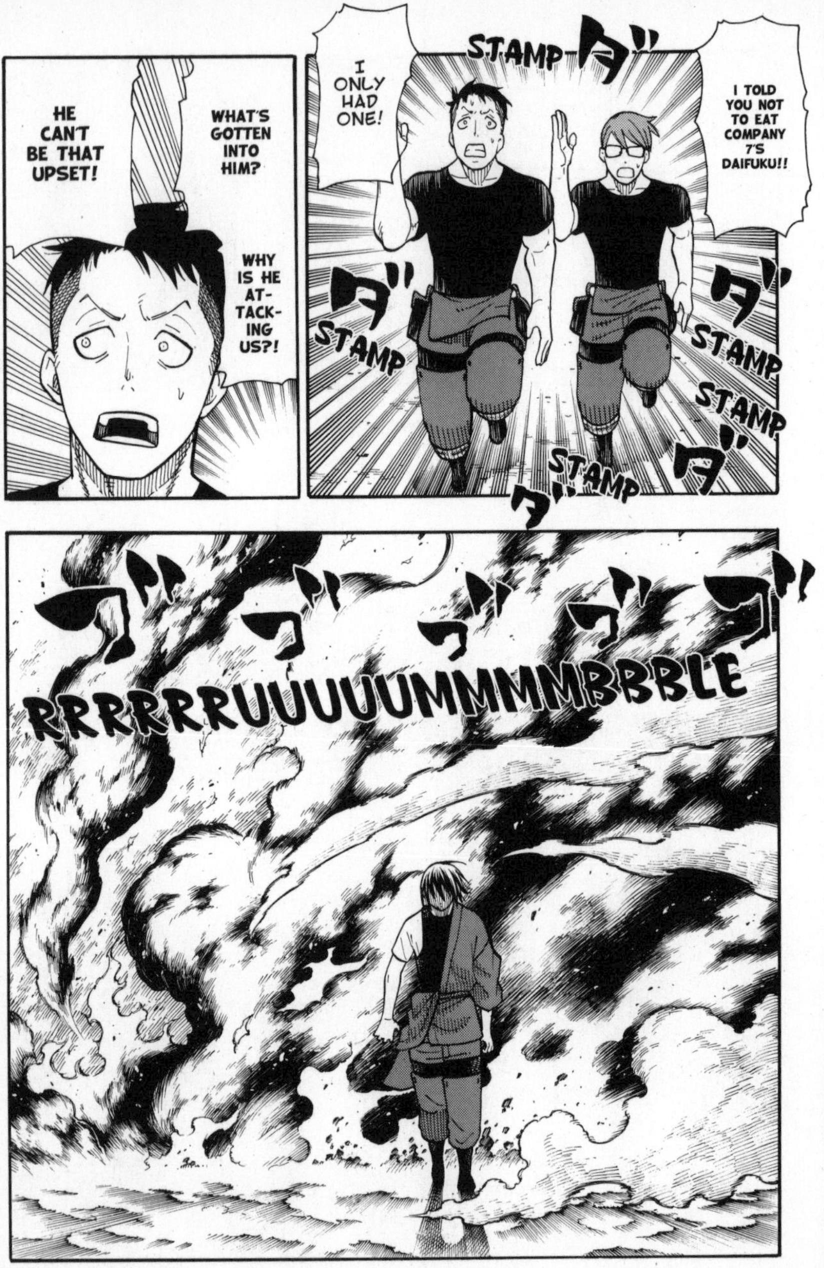
I TOLD YOU NOT TO EAT COMPANY 7'S DAIFUKU!!
STAMP
I ONLY HAD ONE!
STAMP
STAMP
STAMP
STAMP
STAMP
WHAT'S GOTTEN INTO HIM?
HE CAN'T BE THAT UPSET!
WHY IS HE AT-TACK-ING US?!
RRRRRRUUUUUMMMMBBBLE

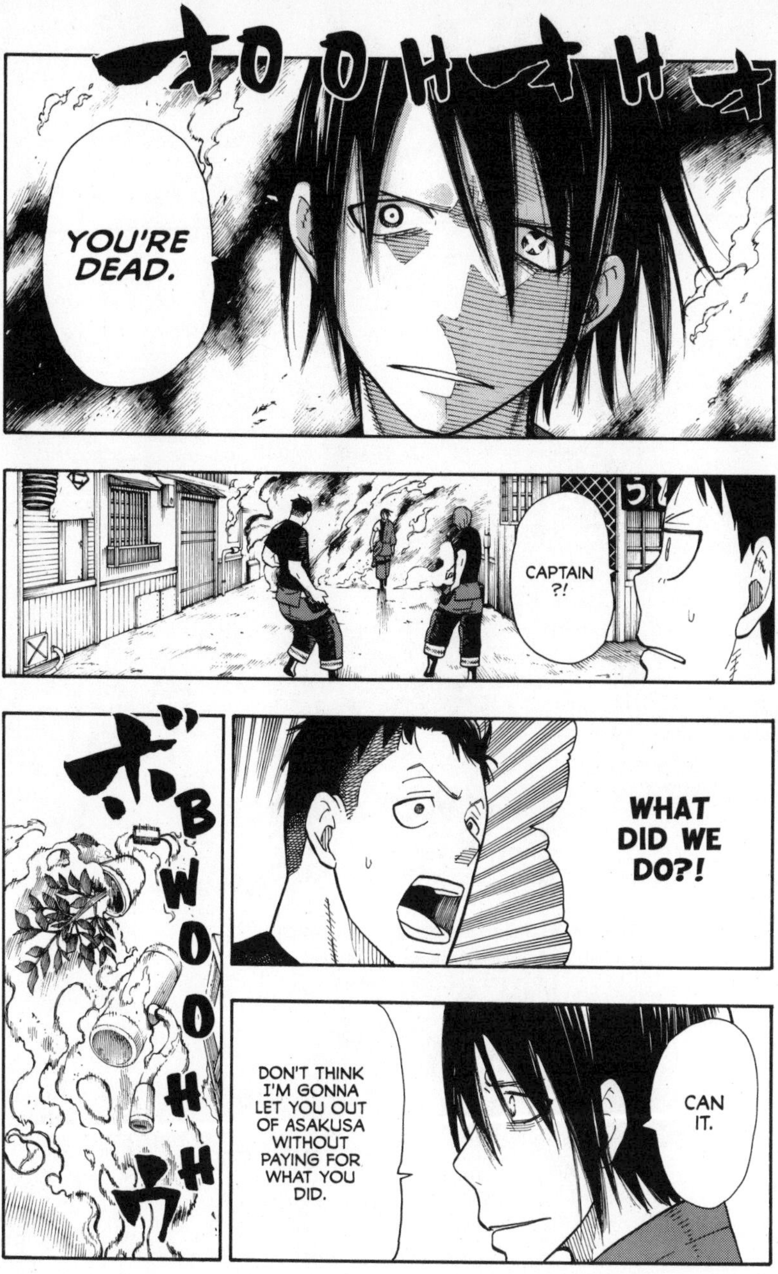
YOU'RE DEAD.
CAPTAIN ?!
WHAT DID WE DO?!
CAN IT.
DON'T THINK I'M GONNA LET YOU OUT OF ASAKUSA WITHOUT PAYING FOR WHAT YOU DID.
BWOOHH

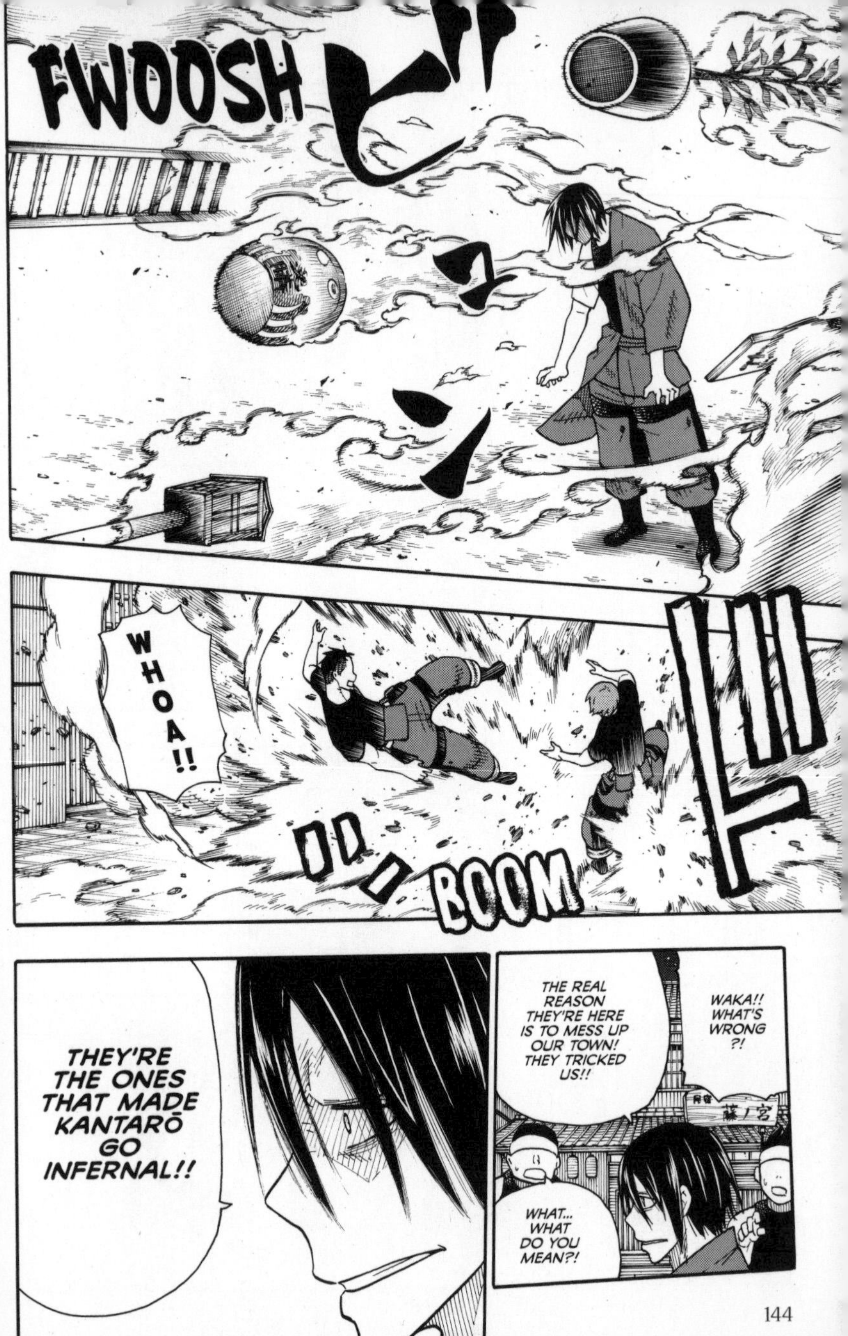
FWOOSH
BOOM
WHOA!!
WAKA!! WHAT'S WRONG?!
THE REAL REASON THEY'RE HERE IS TO MESS UP OUR TOWN! THEY TRICKED US!!
WHAT... WHAT DO YOU MEAN?!
THEY'RE THE ONES THAT MADE KANTARŌ GO INFERNAL!!

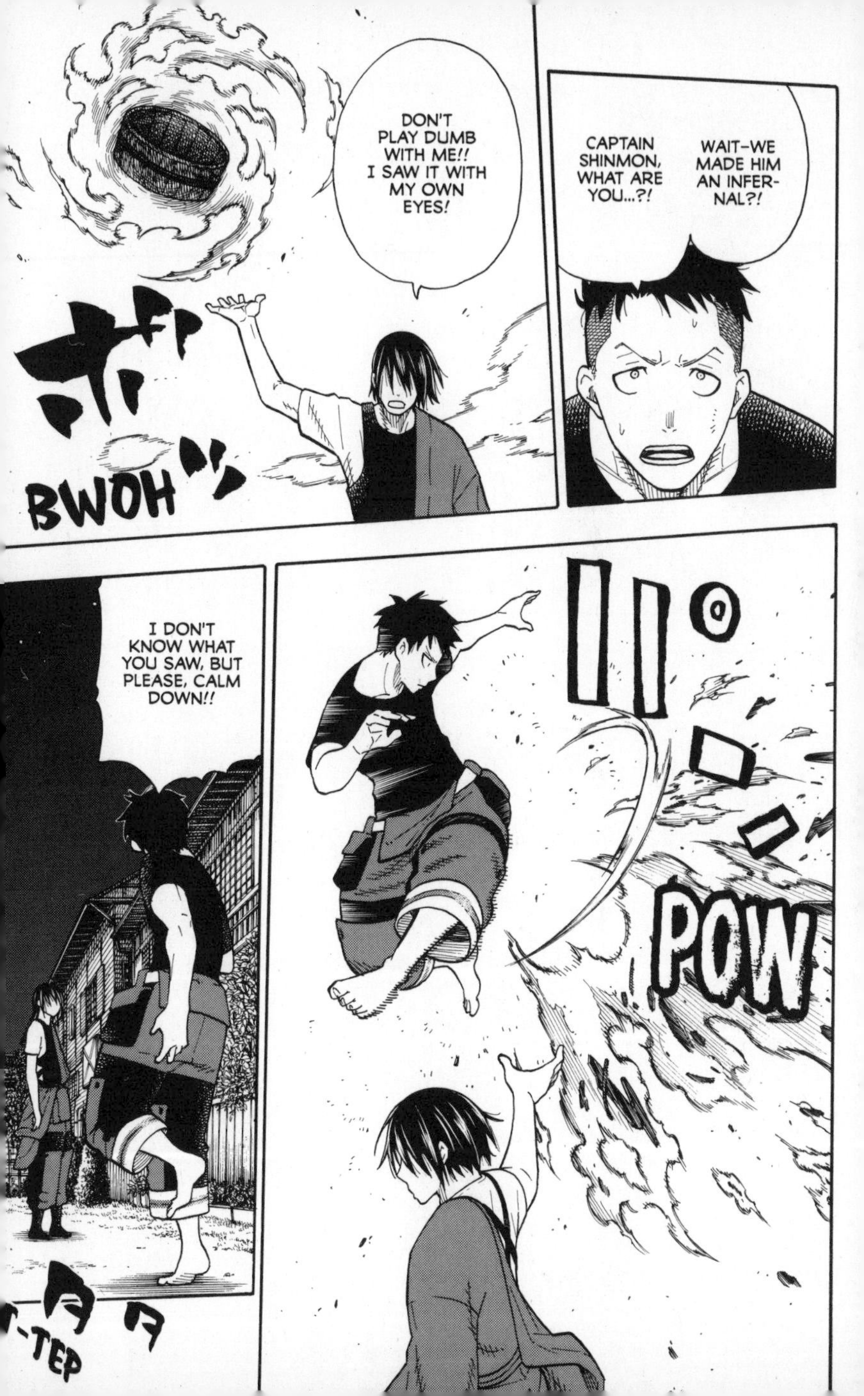
WAIT—WE MADE HIM AN INFERNAL?!
CAPTAIN SHINMON, WHAT ARE YOU...?!
DON'T PLAY DUMB WITH ME!! I SAW IT WITH MY OWN EYES!
BWOH
POW
I DON'T KNOW WHAT YOU SAW, BUT PLEASE, CALM DOWN!!
T-TEP

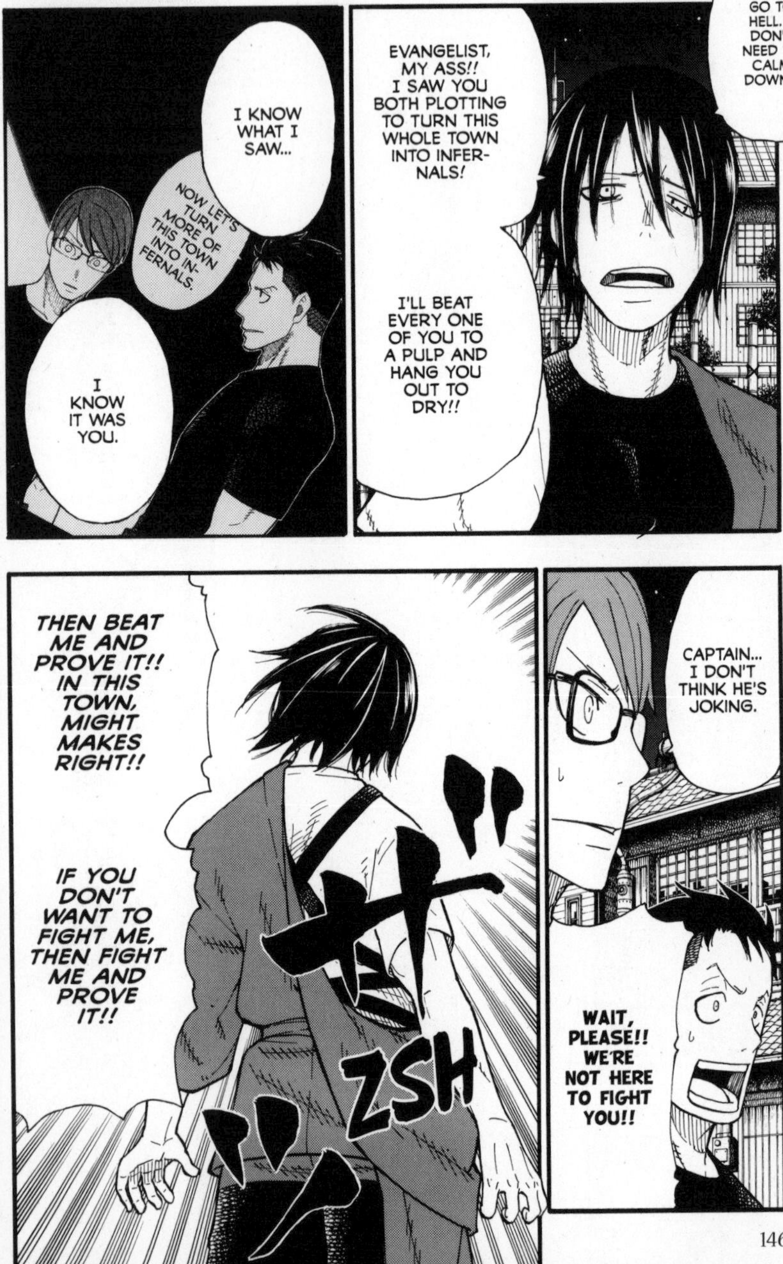
GO TO HELL. I DON'T NEED TO CALM DOWN!!
EVANGELIST, MY ASS!! I SAW YOU BOTH PLOTTING TO TURN THIS WHOLE TOWN INTO INFER-NALS!
I'LL BEAT EVERY ONE OF YOU TO A PULP AND HANG YOU OUT TO DRY!!
I KNOW WHAT I SAW...
NOW LET'S TURN MORE OF THIS TOWN INTO IN-FERNALS.
I KNOW IT WAS YOU.
CAPTAIN... I DON'T THINK HE'S JOKING.
WAIT, PLEASE!! WE'RE NOT HERE TO FIGHT YOU!!
THEN BEAT ME AND PROVE IT!! IN THIS TOWN, MIGHT MAKES RIGHT!!
IF YOU DON'T WANT TO FIGHT ME, THEN FIGHT ME AND PROVE IT!!
ZSH

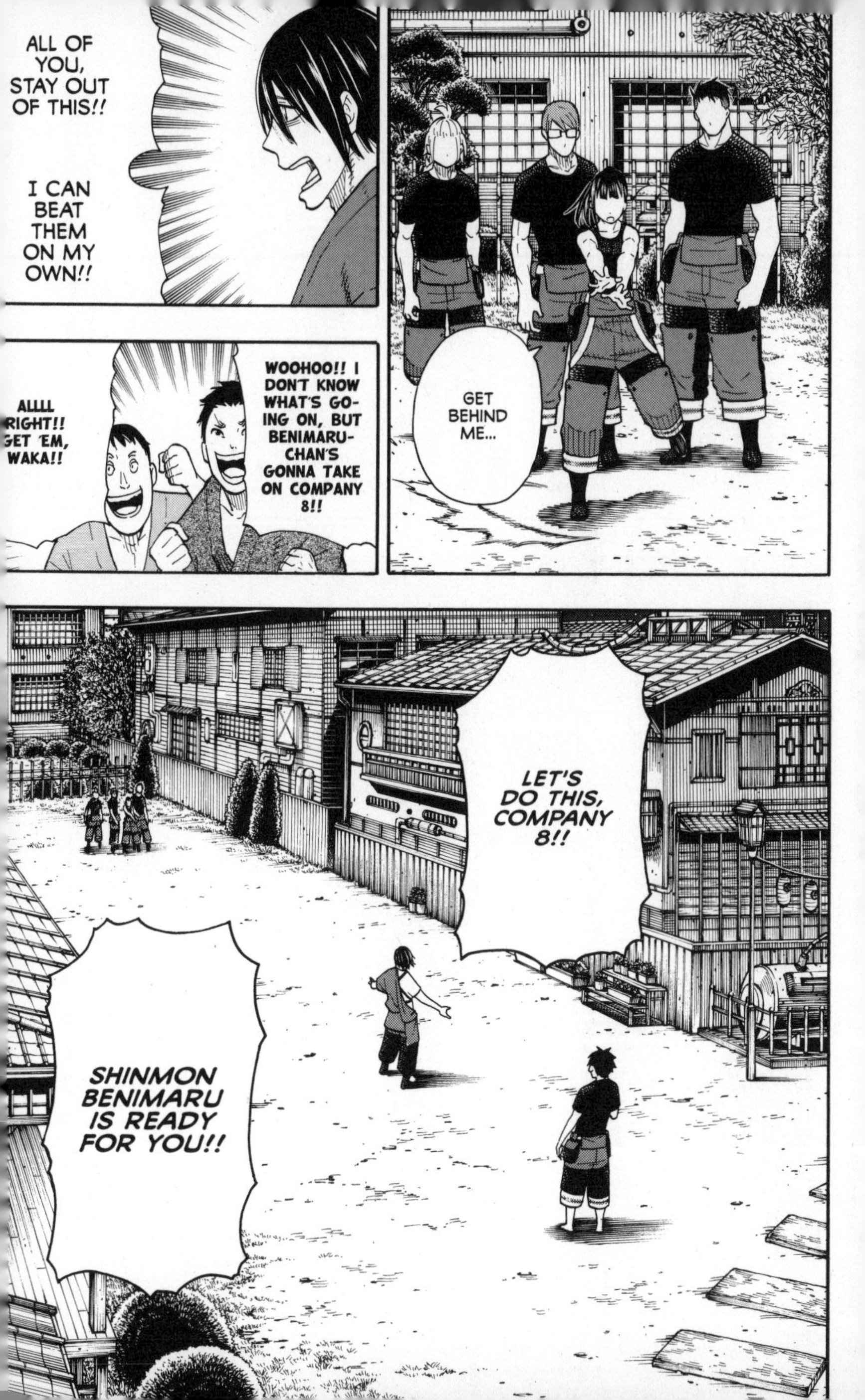
GET BEHIND ME...
ALL OF YOU, STAY OUT OF THIS!!
I CAN BEAT THEM ON MY OWN!!
WOOHOO!! I DON'T KNOW WHAT'S GO-ING ON, BUT BENIMARU-CHAN'S GONNA TAKE ON COMPANY 8!!
ALLLL RIGHT!! GET 'EM, WAKA!!
LET'S DO THIS, COMPANY 8!!
SHINMON BENIMARU IS READY FOR YOU!!

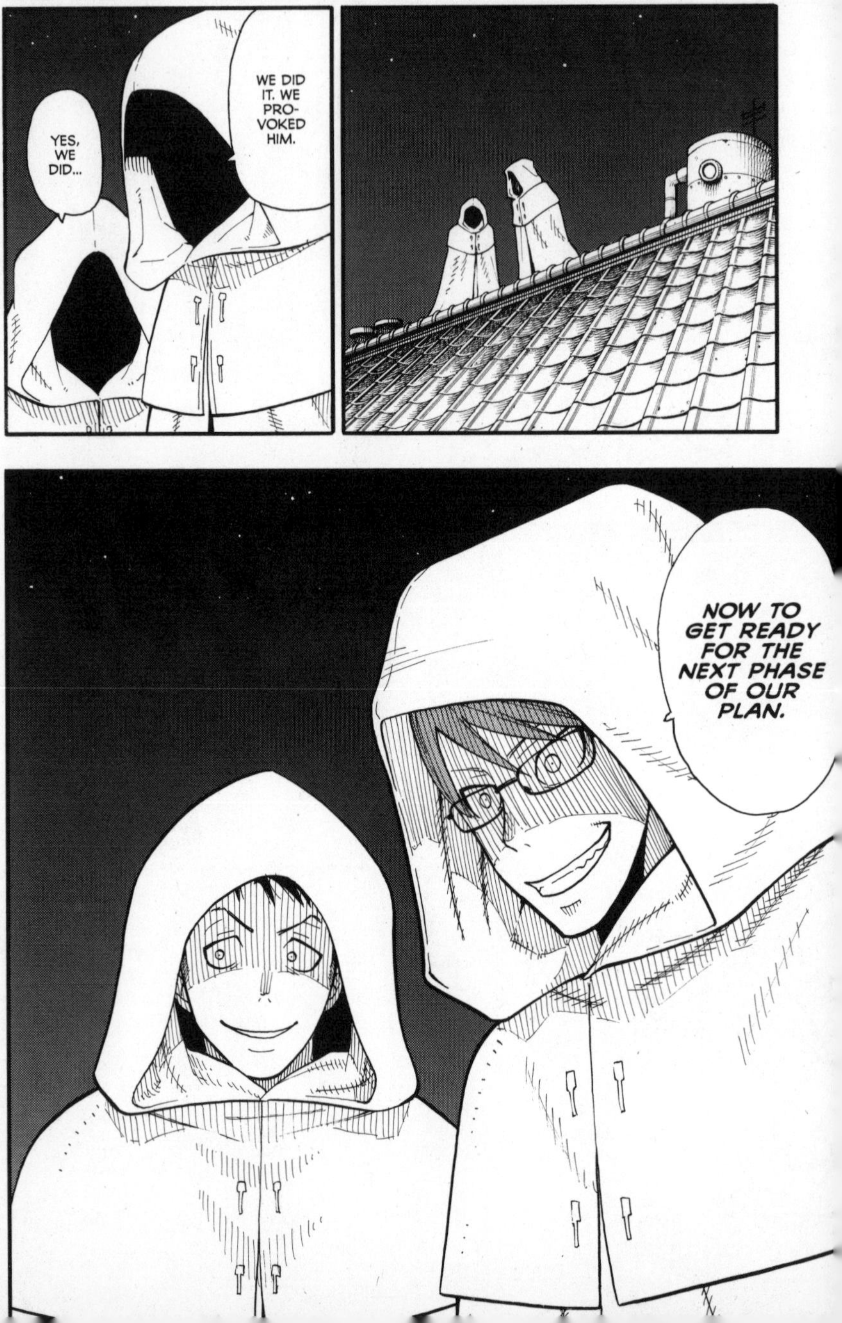
WE DID IT. WE PROVOKED HIM.
YES, WE DID...
NOW TO GET READY FOR THE NEXT PHASE OF OUR PLAN.

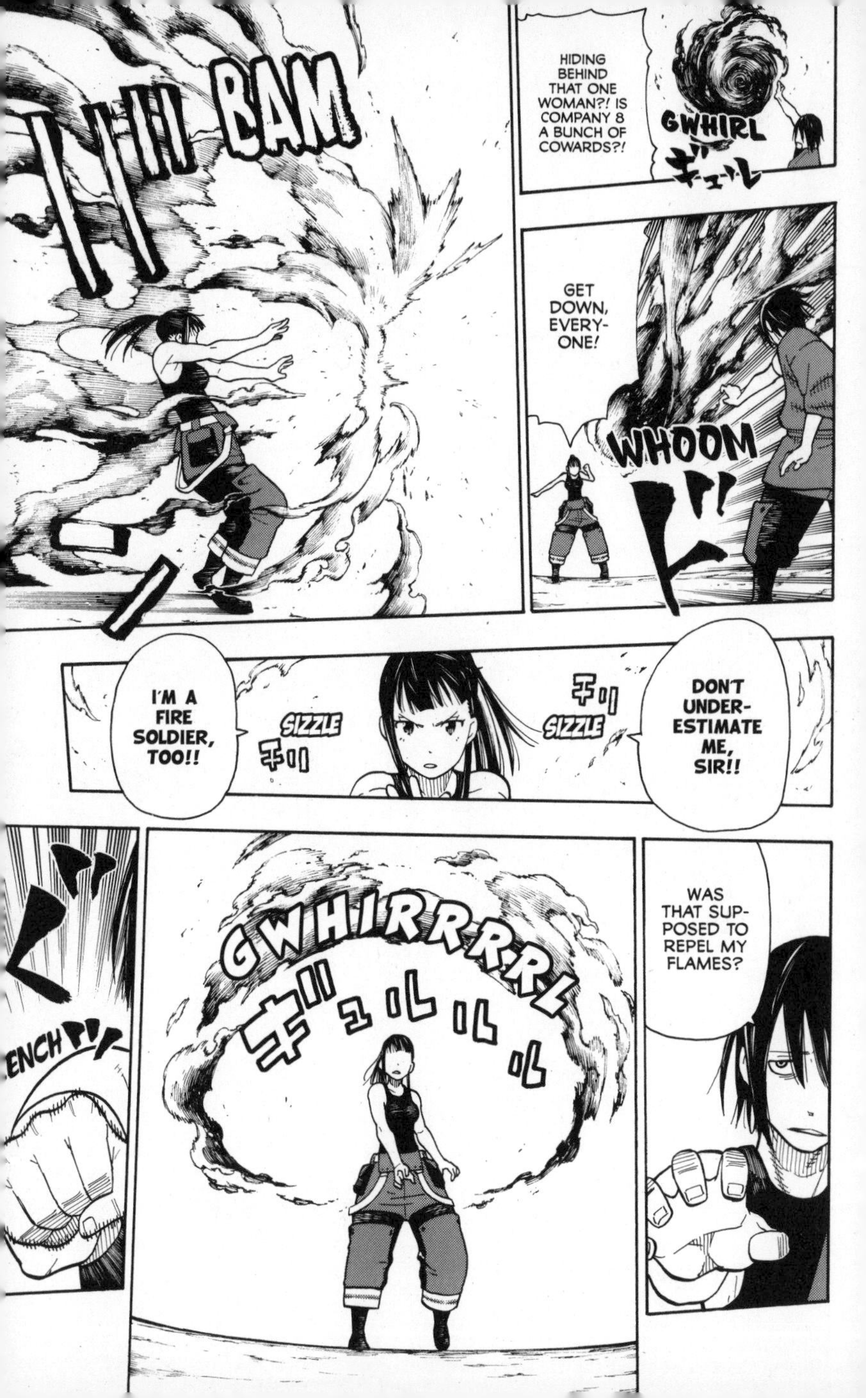
HIDING BEHIND THAT ONE WOMAN?! IS COMPANY 8 A BUNCH OF COWARDS?!
GWHIRL
ギュル
GET DOWN, EVERY-ONE!
WHOOM
BAM
DON'T UNDER-ESTIMATE ME, SIR!!
チリ
SIZZLE
I'M A FIRE SOLDIER, TOO!!
SIZZLE
チリ
WAS THAT SUP-POSED TO REPEL MY FLAMES?
GWHIRRRRRL
ギュルルル
ENCH

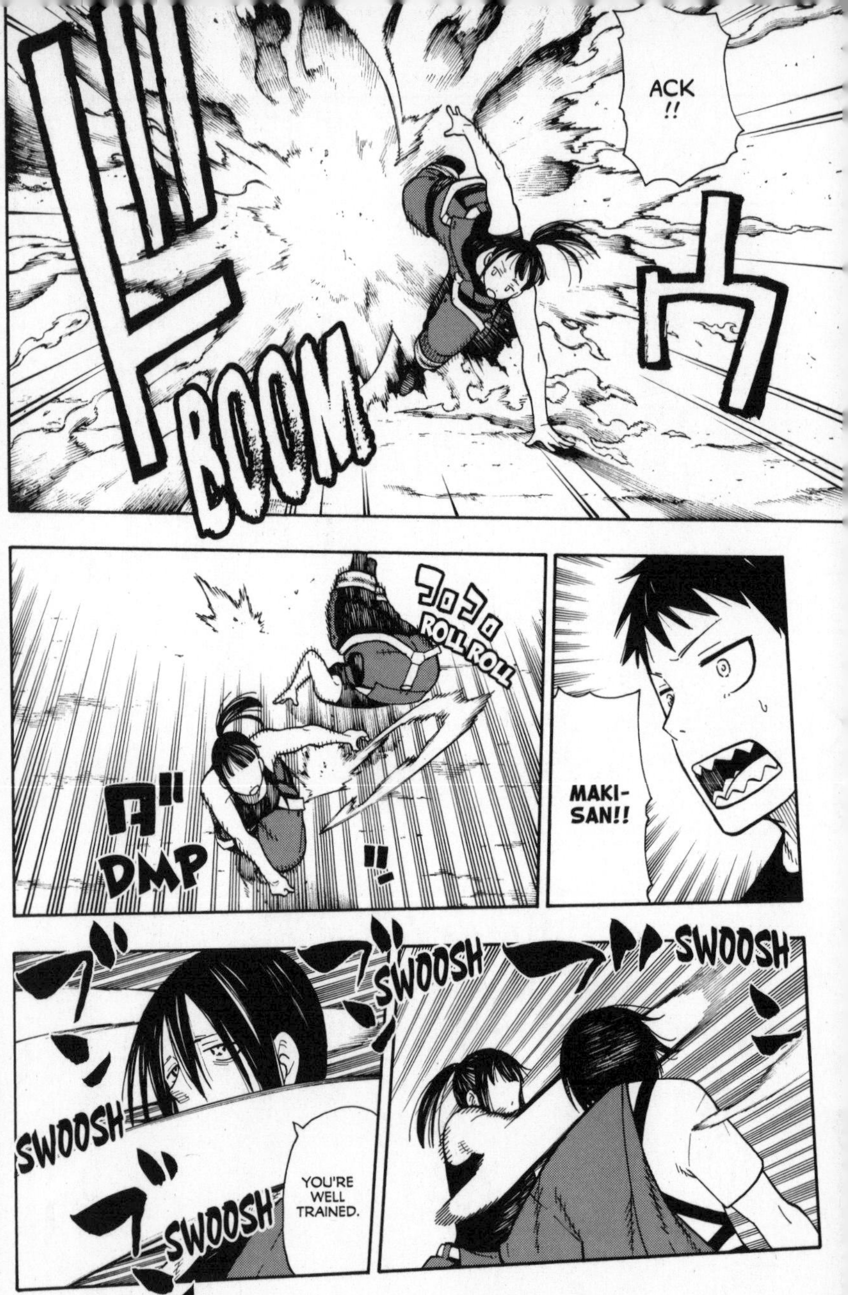
ACK!!
BOOM
MAKI-SAN!!
ROLL ROLL
DMP
SWOOSH
SWOOSH
SWOOSH
YOU'RE WELL TRAINED.
SWOOSH

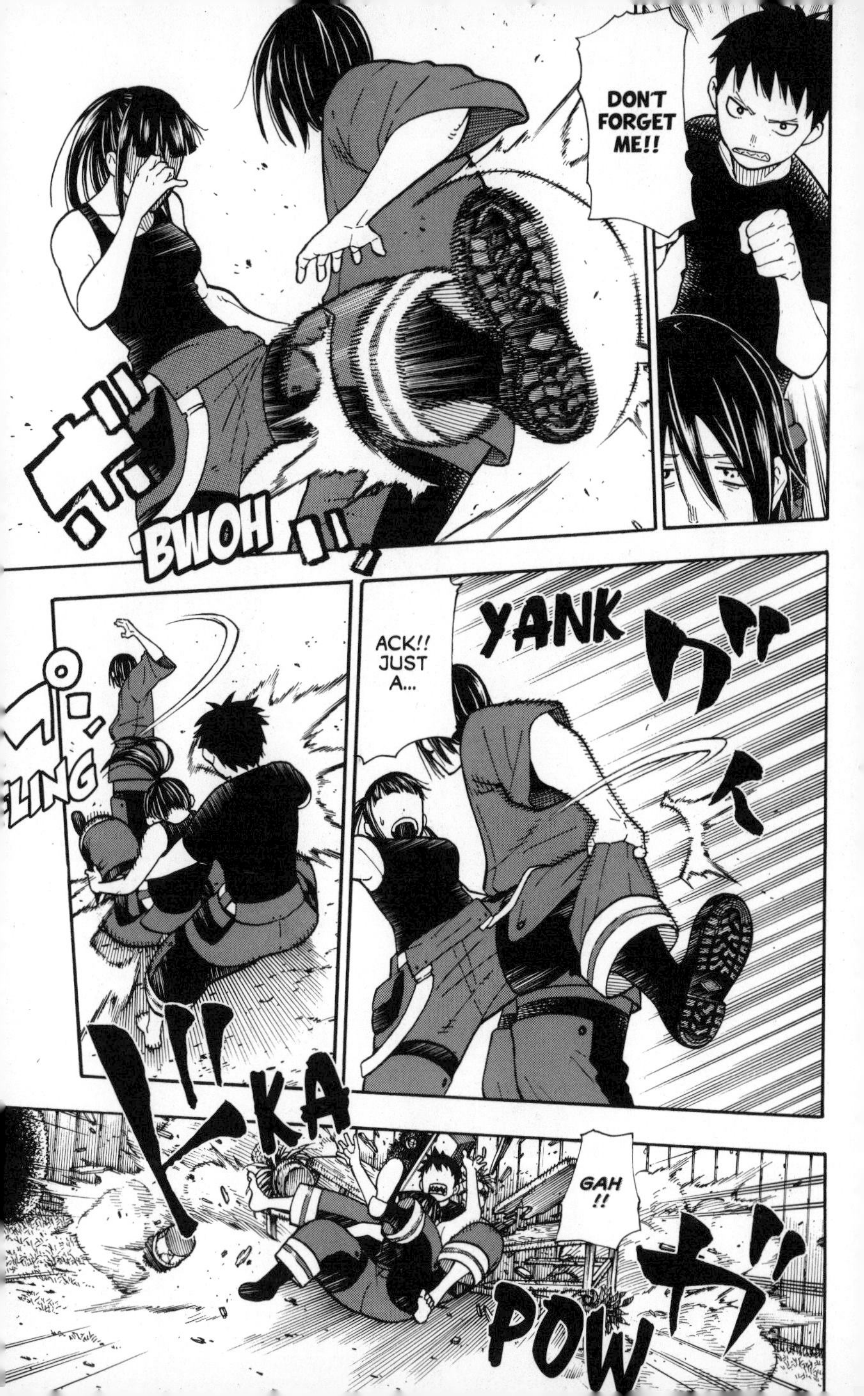
DON'T FORGET ME!!
BWOH
YANK
ACK!! JUST A...
LING
KA
GAH !!
POW

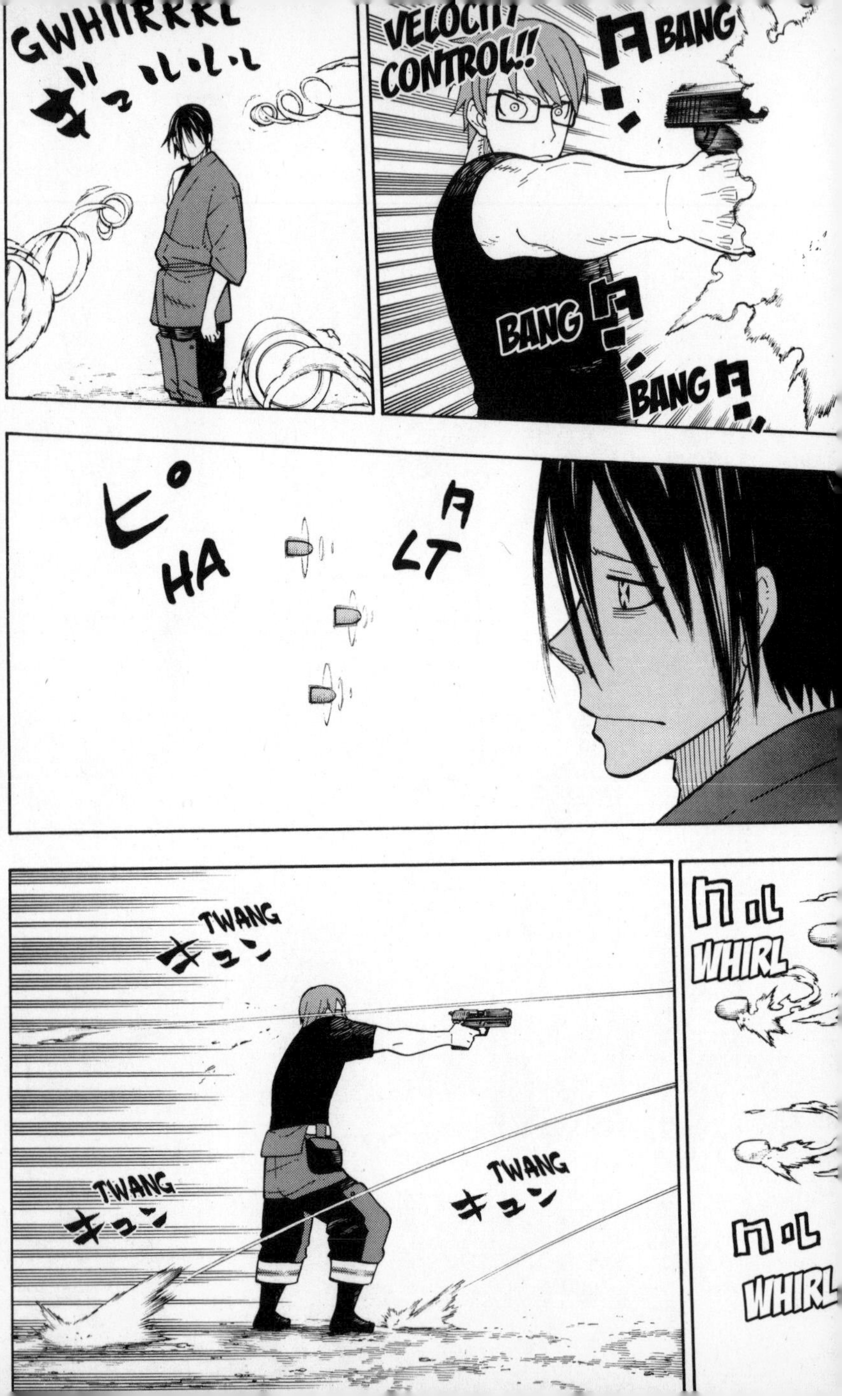
VELOCITY CONTROL!!
ダ BANG
BANG ダ
BANG ダ
GWHIIRRRL
ぎゅいいい
ピタ
HALT
クル
WHIRL
クル
WHIRL
TWANG
キュン
TWANG
キュン
TWANG
キュン

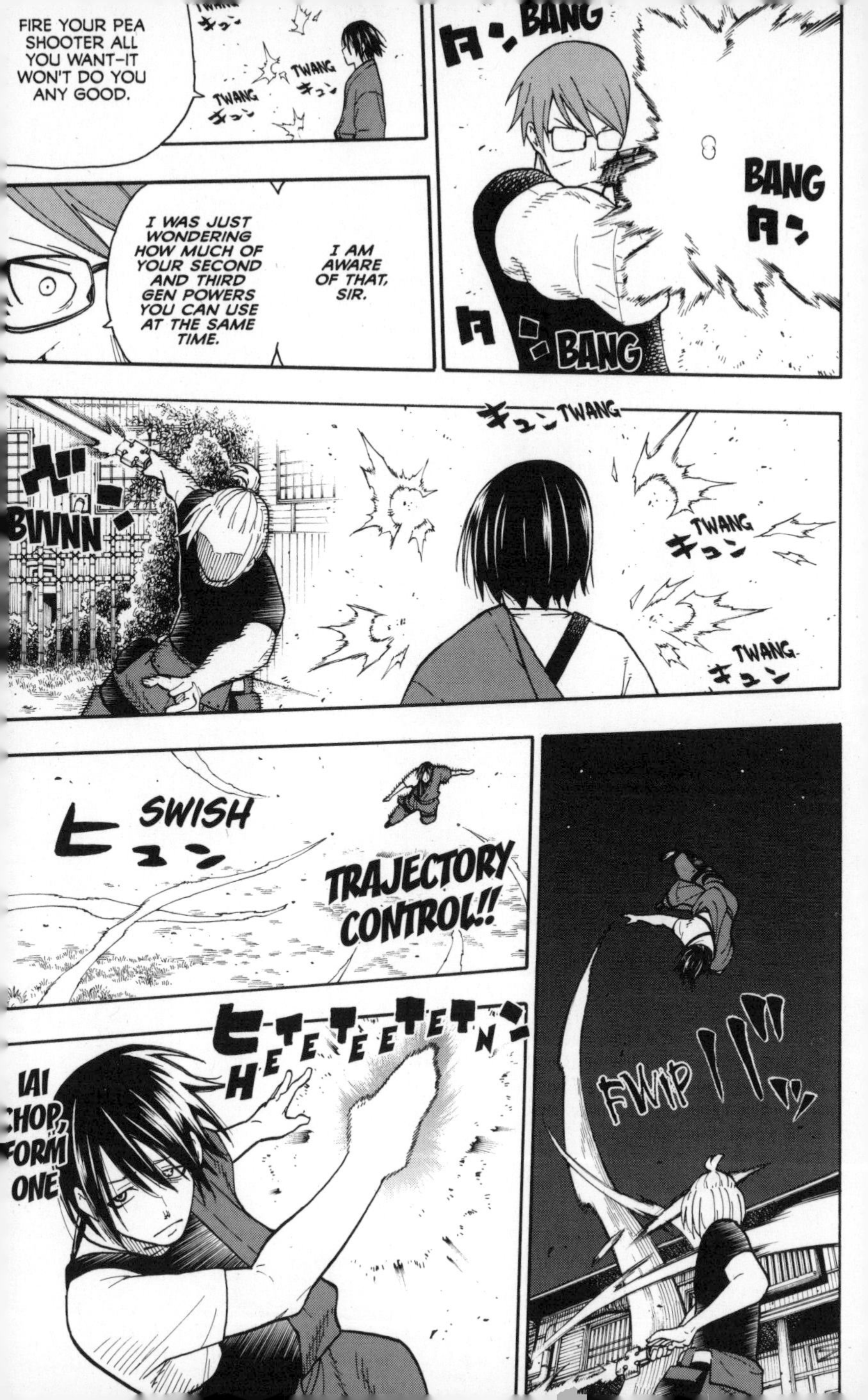
タン BANG
BANG タン
タン BANG
キュン
TWANG キュン
TWANG キュン
FIRE YOUR PEA SHOOTER ALL YOU WANT–IT WON'T DO YOU ANY GOOD.
I AM AWARE OF THAT, SIR.
I WAS JUST WONDERING HOW MUCH OF YOUR SECOND AND THIRD GEN POWERS YOU CAN USE AT THE SAME TIME.
キュン TWANG
TWANG キュン
TWANG キュン
BWNN
FWIP
SWISH ヒュン
TRAJECTORY CONTROL!!
HEEEEEEN
IAI CHOP, FORM ONE

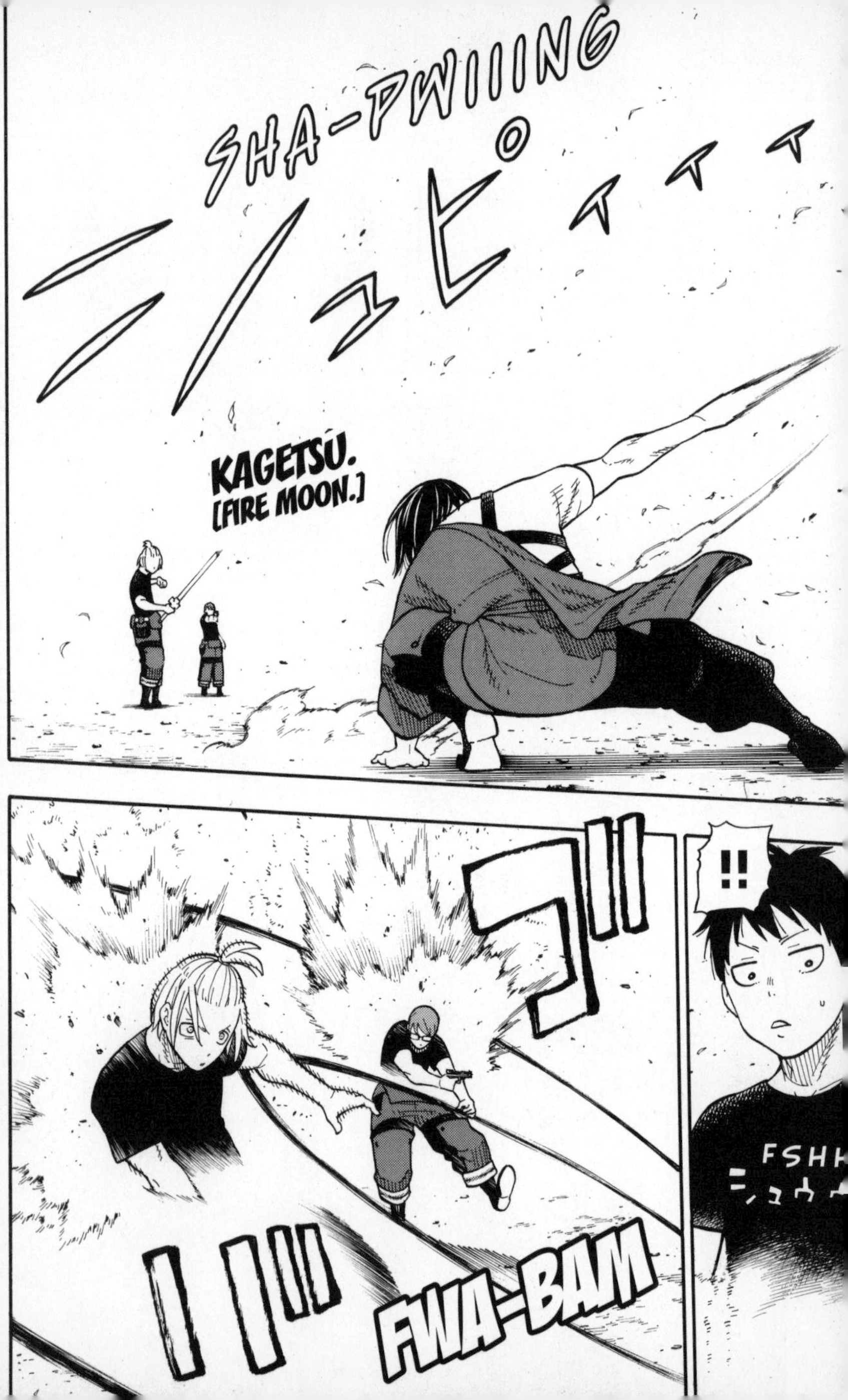
SHA-PWIIING
シュピイイイ
KAGETSU.
[FIRE MOON.]
!!
ゴ
FWA-BAM

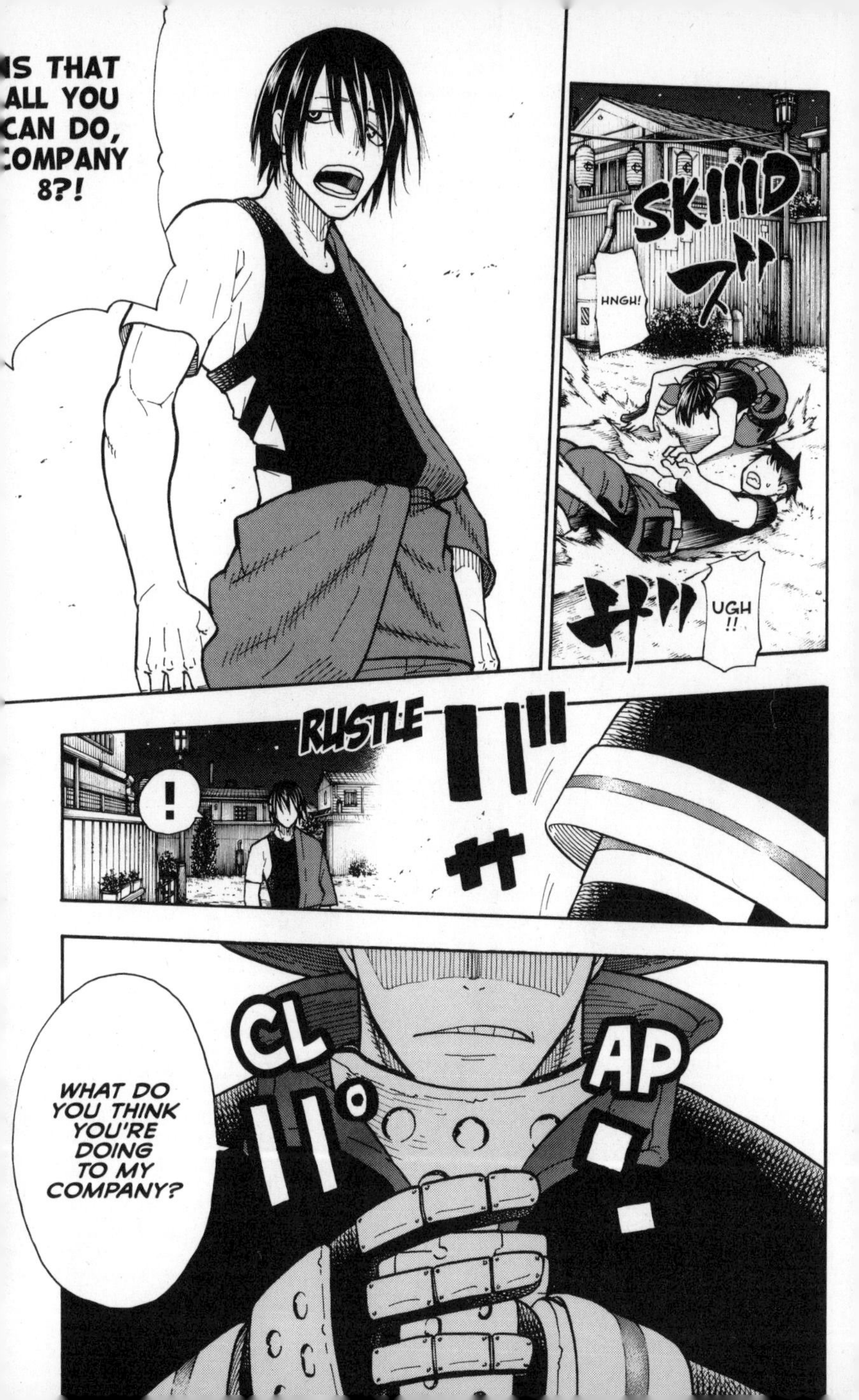
SKIIID
HNGH!
UGH!!
IS THAT ALL YOU CAN DO, COMPANY 8?!
RUSTLE
!
CLAP
WHAT DO YOU THINK YOU'RE DOING TO MY COMPANY?

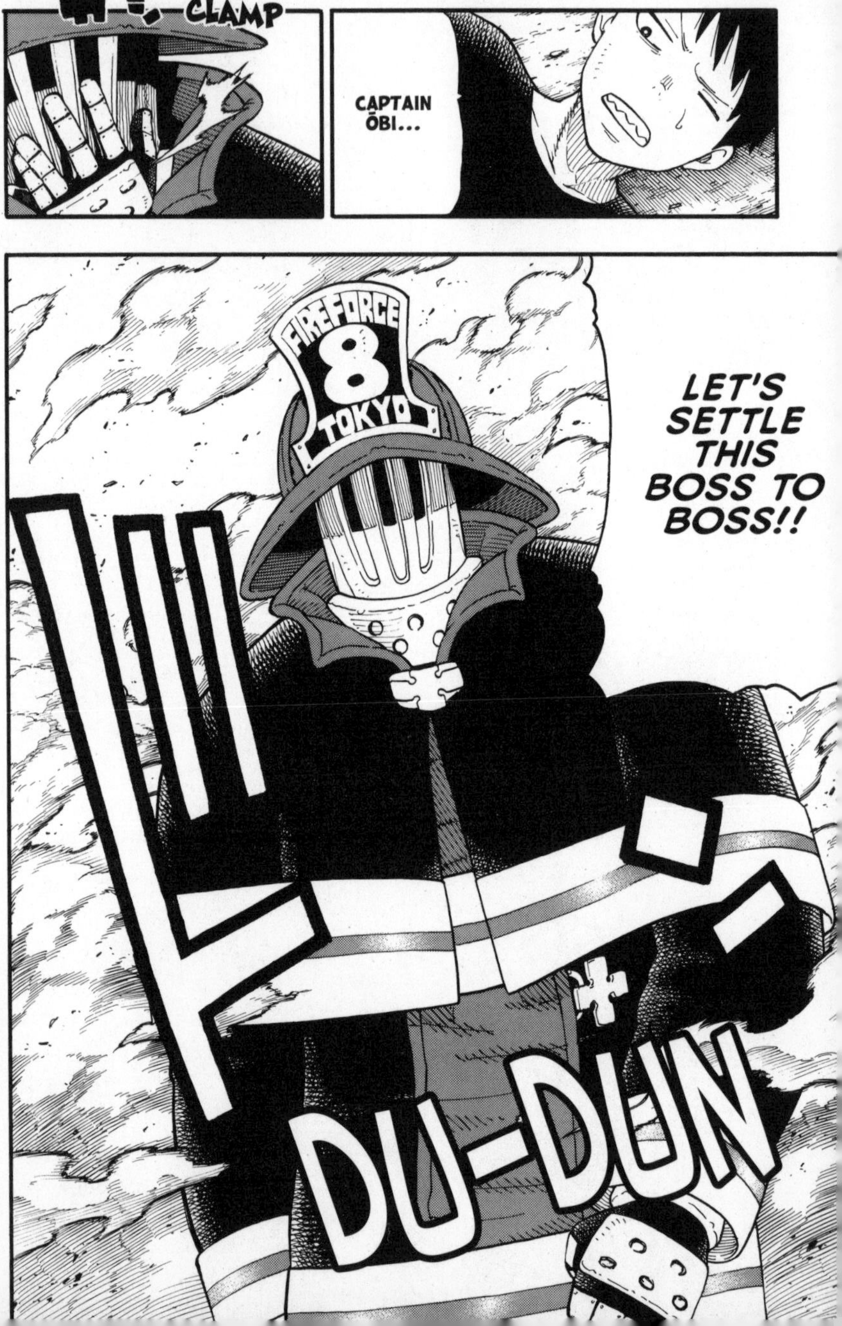
CAPTAIN ŌBI...
CLAMP
LET'S SETTLE THIS BOSS TO BOSS!!
DU-DUN

FIRE FORCE

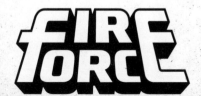

FIRE FORCE

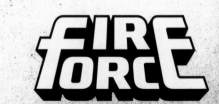

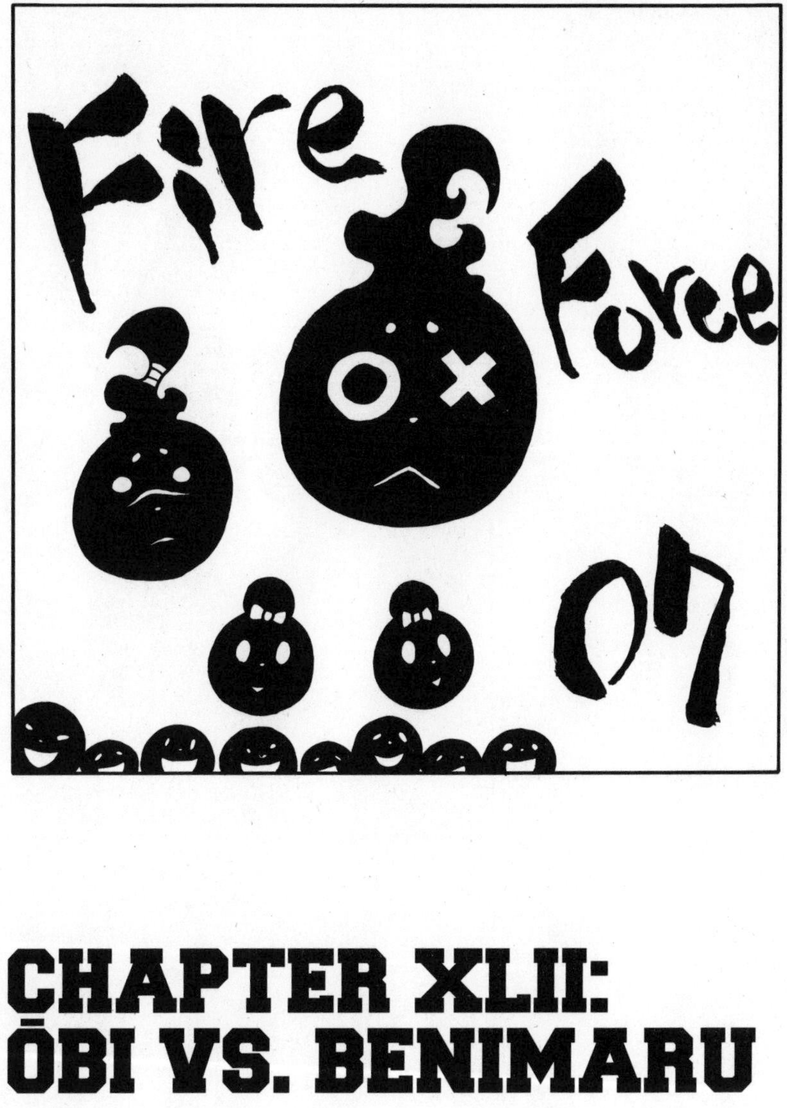
Fire Force
07

CHAPTER XLII:
ŌBI VS. BENIMARU

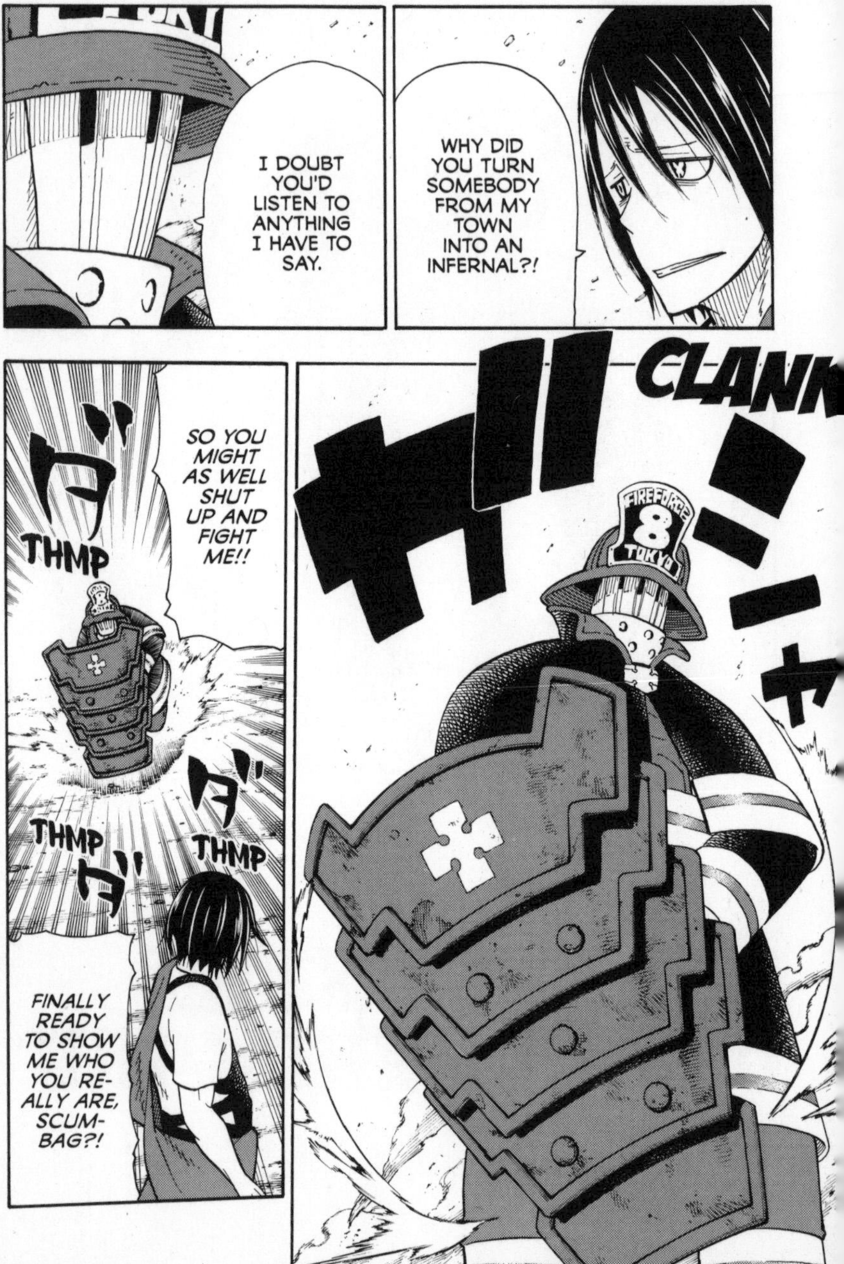
WHY DID YOU TURN SOMEBODY FROM MY TOWN INTO AN INFERNAL?!
I DOUBT YOU'D LISTEN TO ANYTHING I HAVE TO SAY.
CLANK
FIRE FORCE 8 TOKYO
SO YOU MIGHT AS WELL SHUT UP AND FIGHT ME!!
THMP
THMP
THMP
FINALLY READY TO SHOW ME WHO YOU RE-ALLY ARE, SCUM-BAG?!

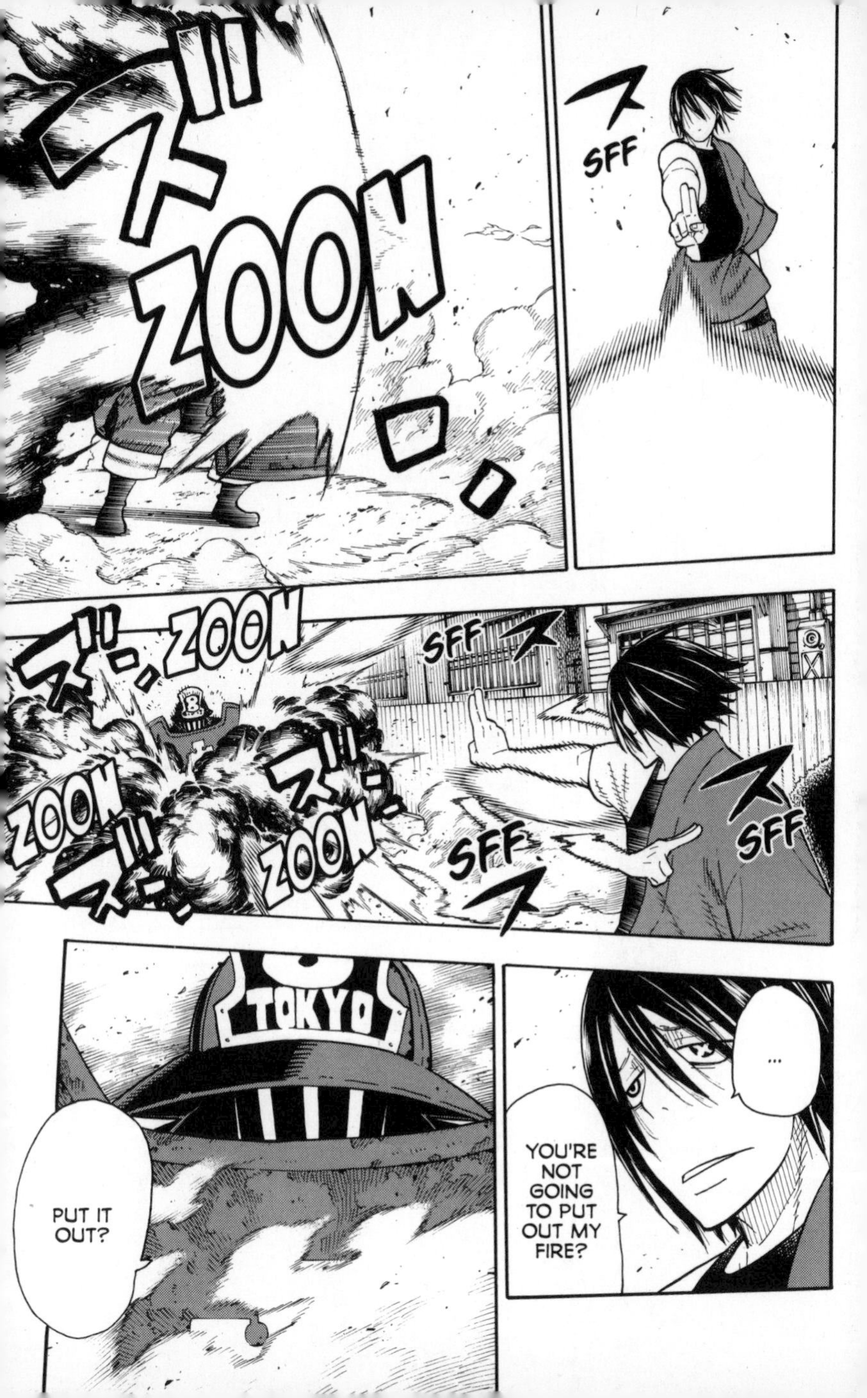

ス
SFF
ズ
ZOON
ス
SFF
ス
SFF
ス
SFF
ズ
ZOON
ズ
ZOON
ズ
ZOON
...
YOU'RE NOT GOING TO PUT OUT MY FIRE?
TOKYO
PUT IT OUT?

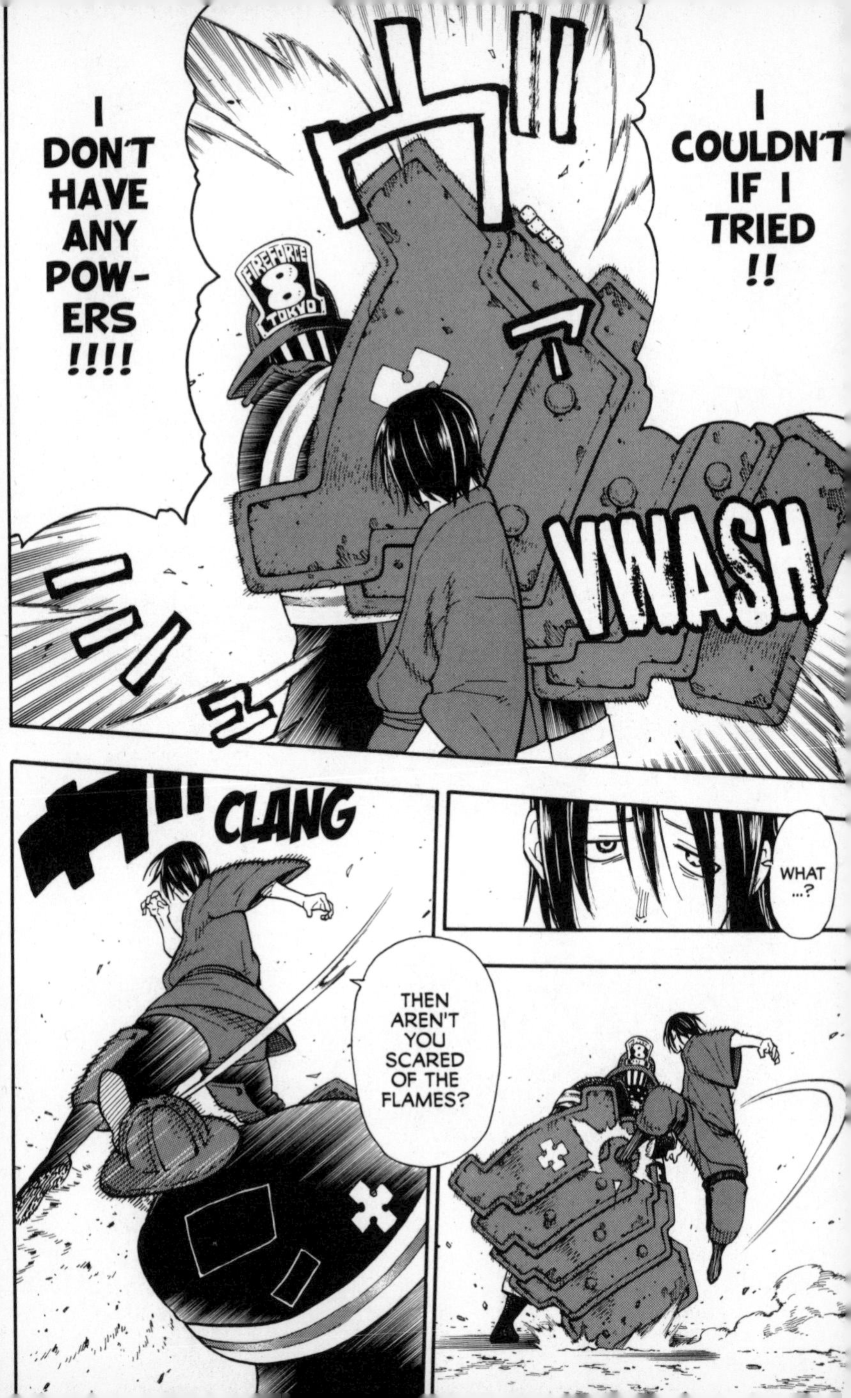
I COULDN'T IF I TRIED!!
I DON'T HAVE ANY POW-ERS!!!!
VWASH
WHAT ...?
THEN AREN'T YOU SCARED OF THE FLAMES?
CLANG

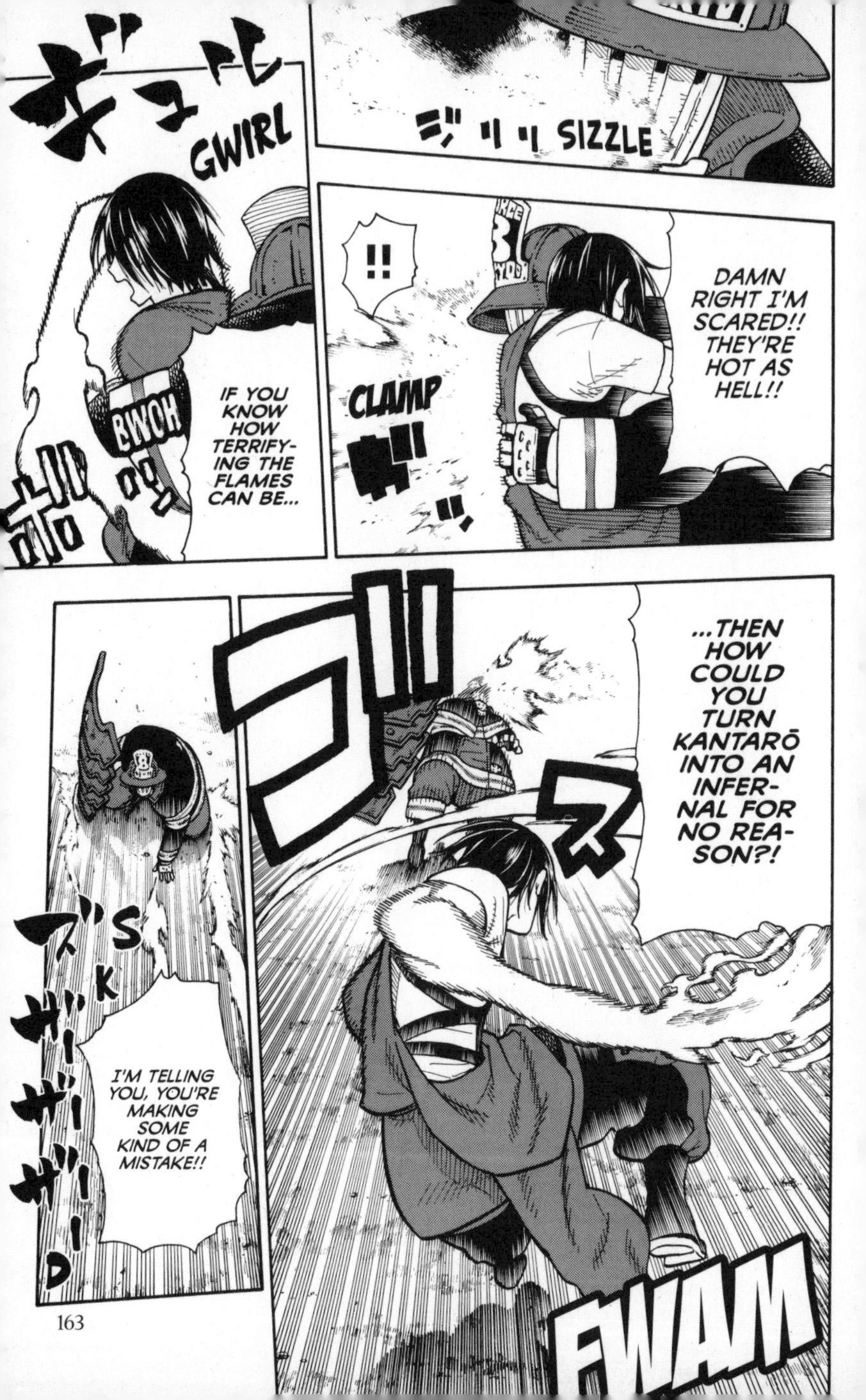
SIZZLE
!!
DAMN RIGHT I'M SCARED!! THEY'RE HOT AS HELL!!
CLAMP
GWIRL
IF YOU KNOW HOW TERRIFYING THE FLAMES CAN BE...
BWOH
...THEN HOW COULD YOU TURN KANTARŌ INTO AN INFERNAL FOR NO REASON?!
FWAM
SK
D
I'M TELLING YOU, YOU'RE MAKING SOME KIND OF A MISTAKE!!

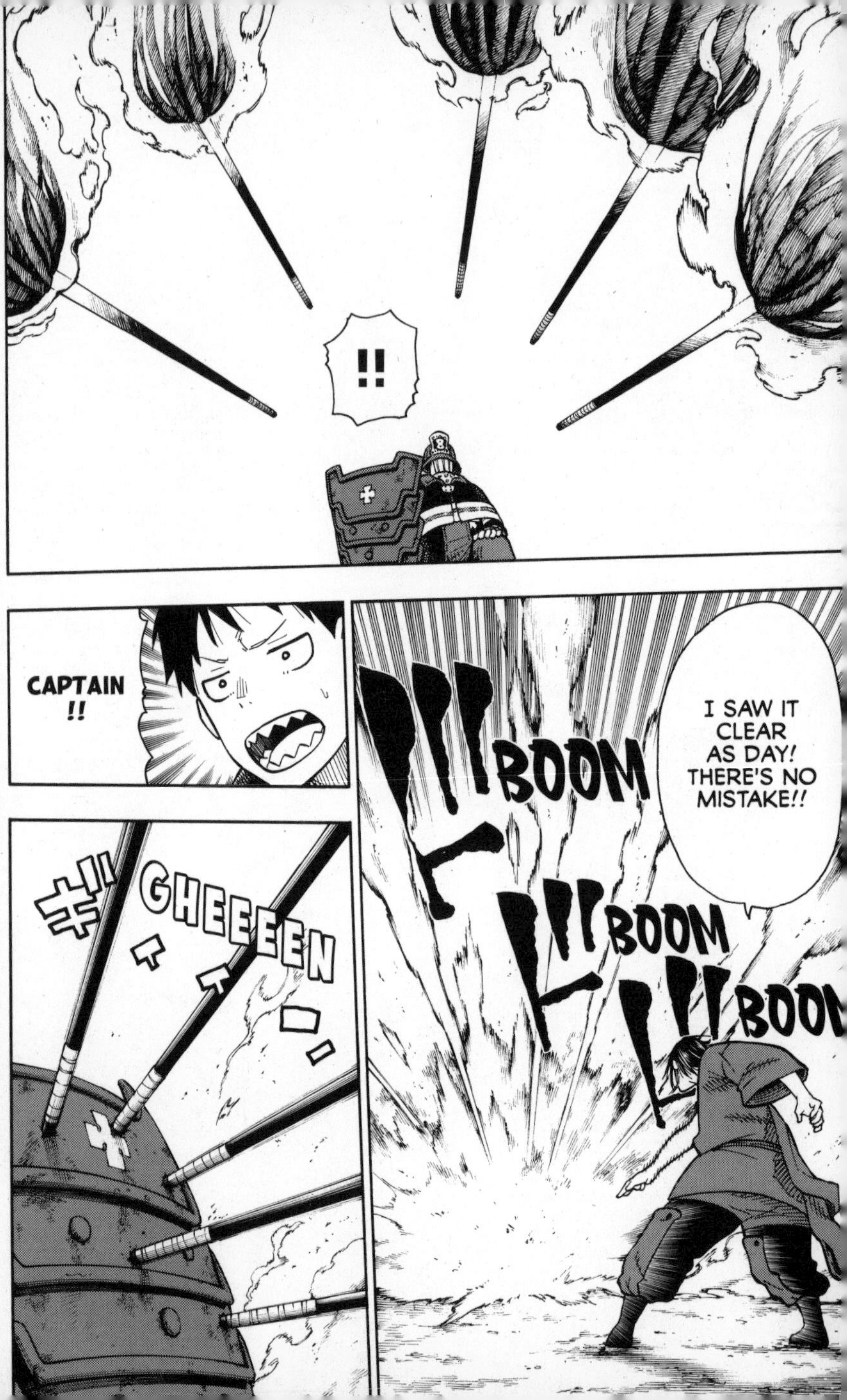
!!
I SAW IT CLEAR AS DAY! THERE'S NO MISTAKE!!
BOOM
BOOM
BOO
CAPTAIN !!
GHEEEEN

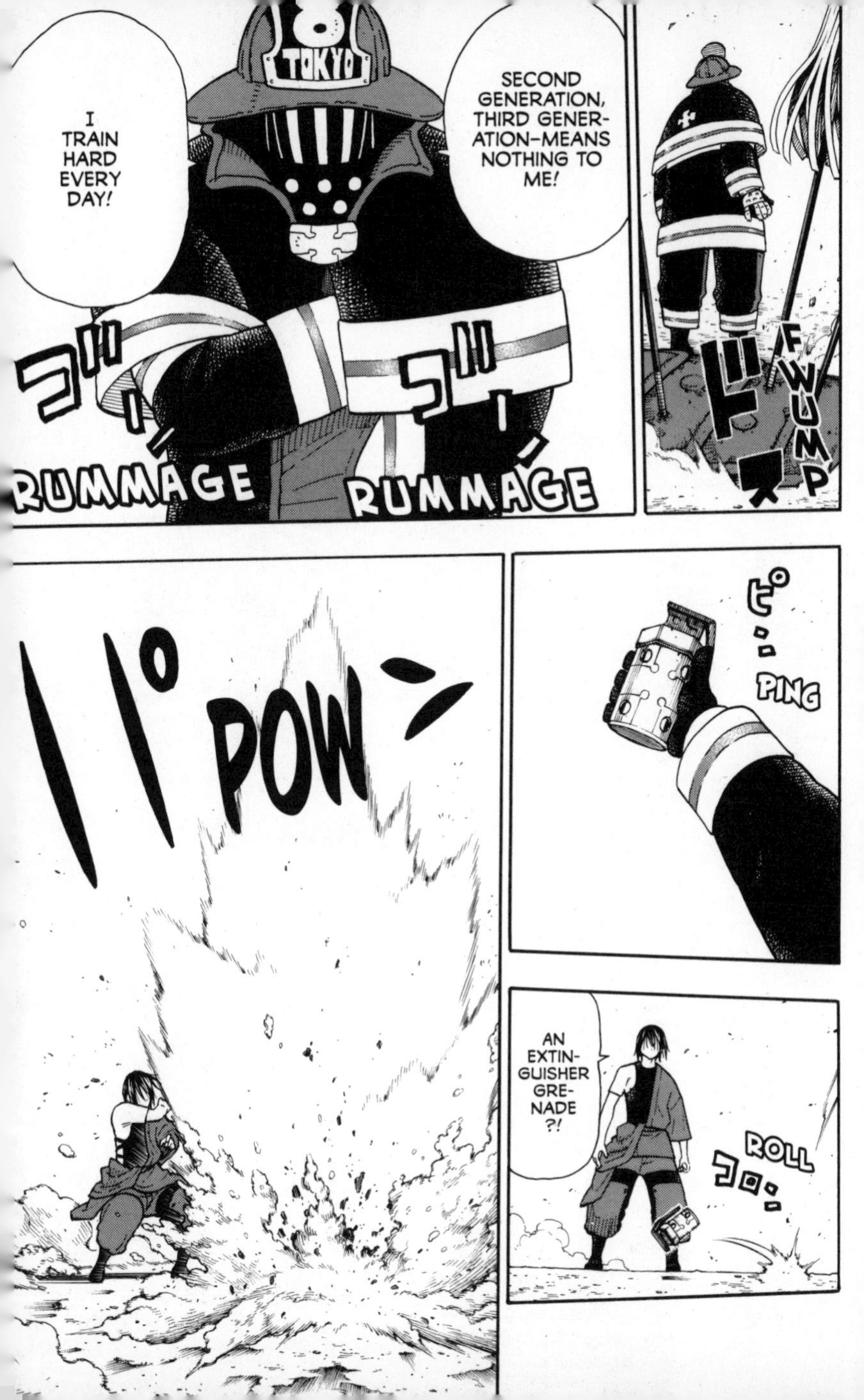
FWUMP
SECOND GENERATION, THIRD GENERATION–MEANS NOTHING TO ME!
I TRAIN HARD EVERY DAY!
RUMMAGE
RUMMAGE
PING
AN EXTINGUISHER GRENADE?!
ROLL
POW

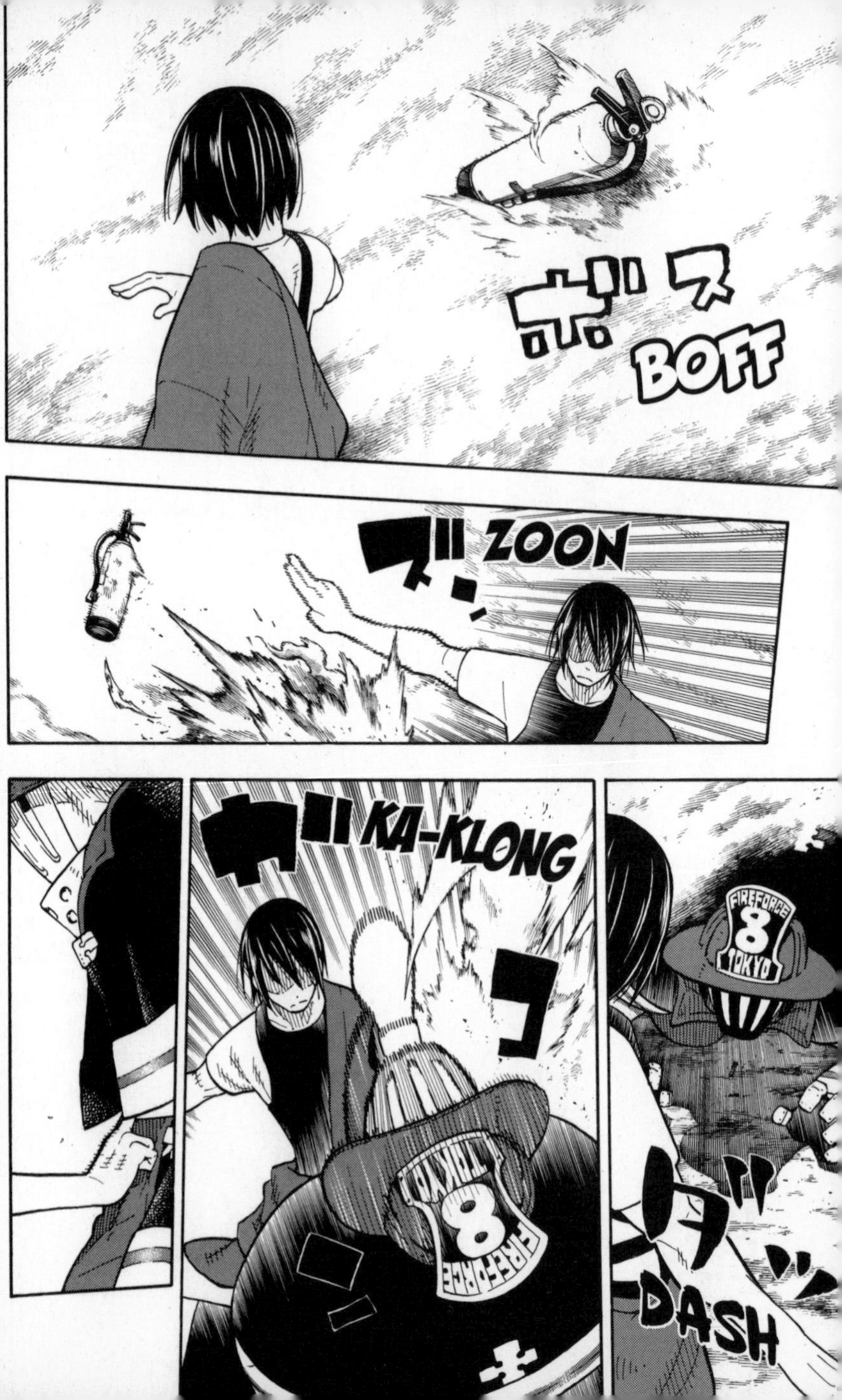
BOFF
ZOON
DASH
KA-KLONG

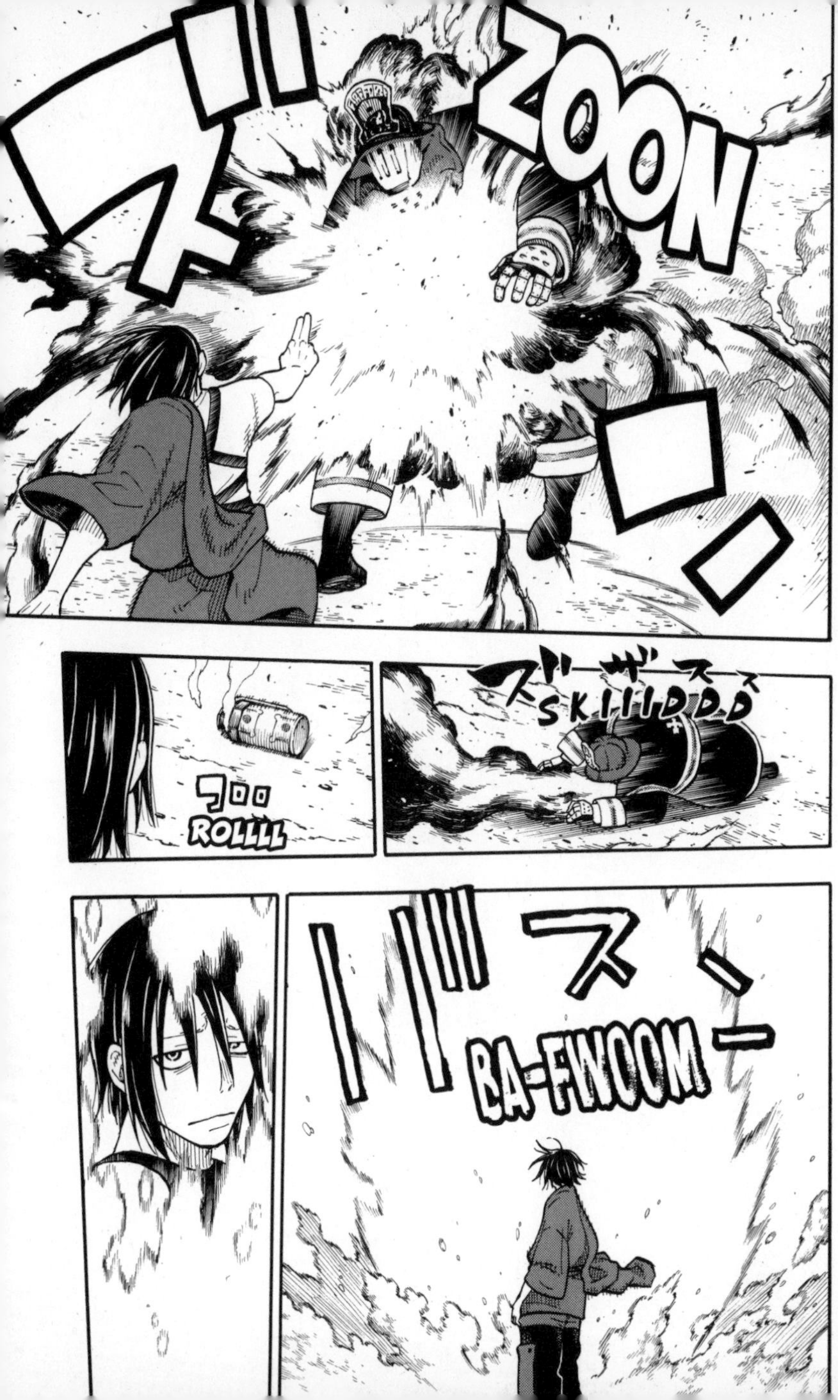
ZOOON
SKIIIDDD
ROLLLL
BA-FWOOM

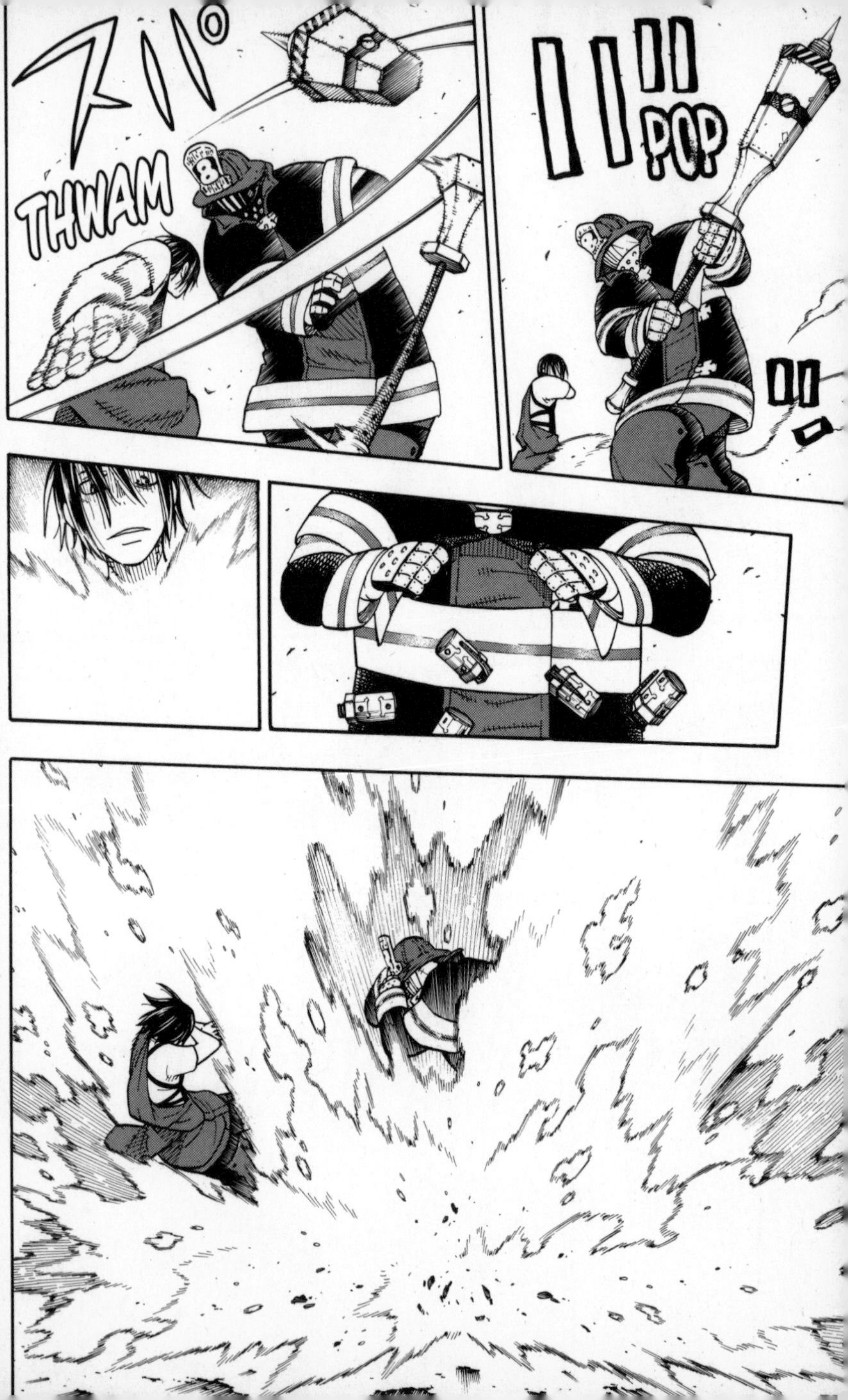
POP
スパ
THWAM

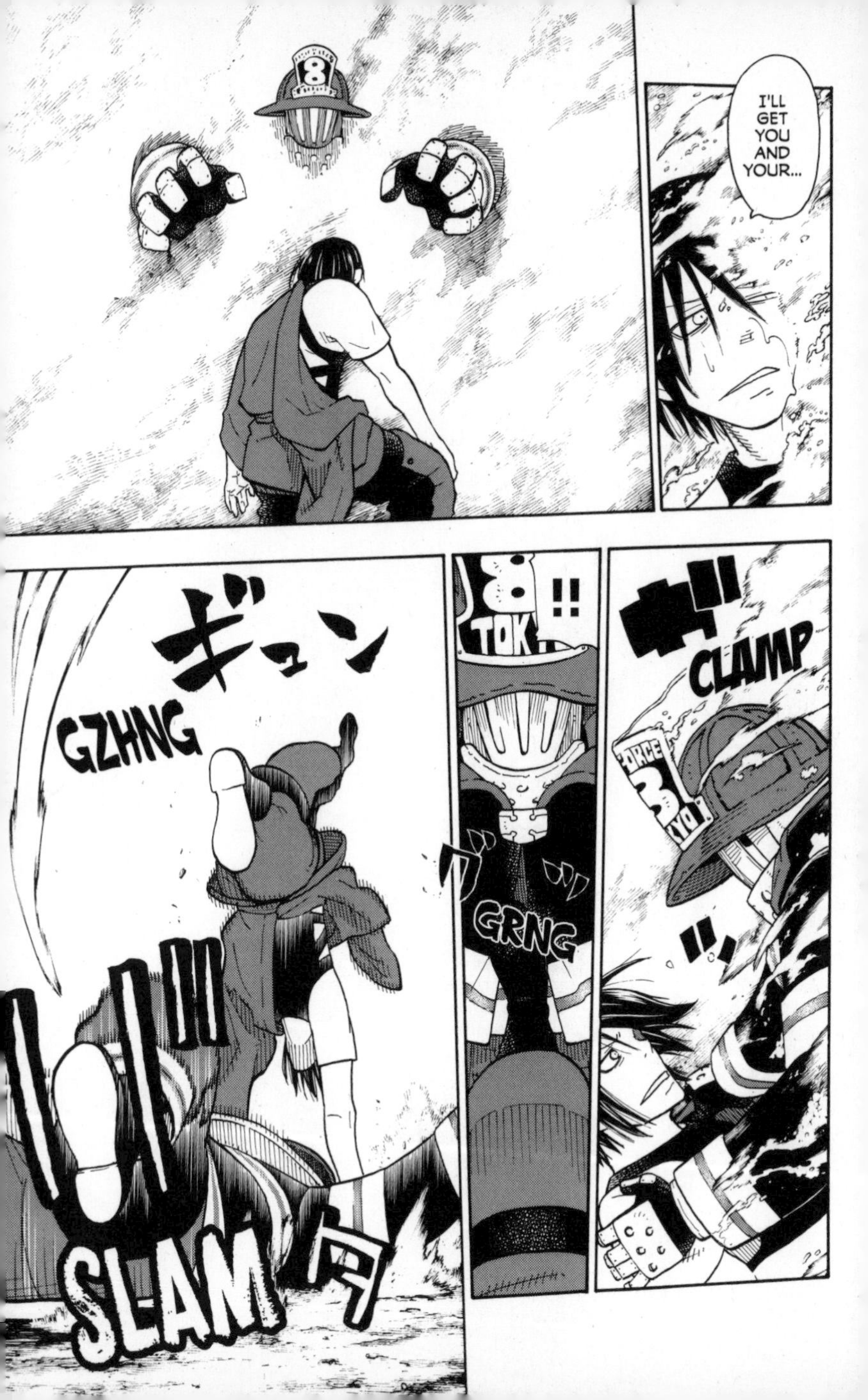
I'LL GET YOU AND YOUR...
キッ
CLAMP
TOK
GRNG
ギュン
GZHNG
SLAM

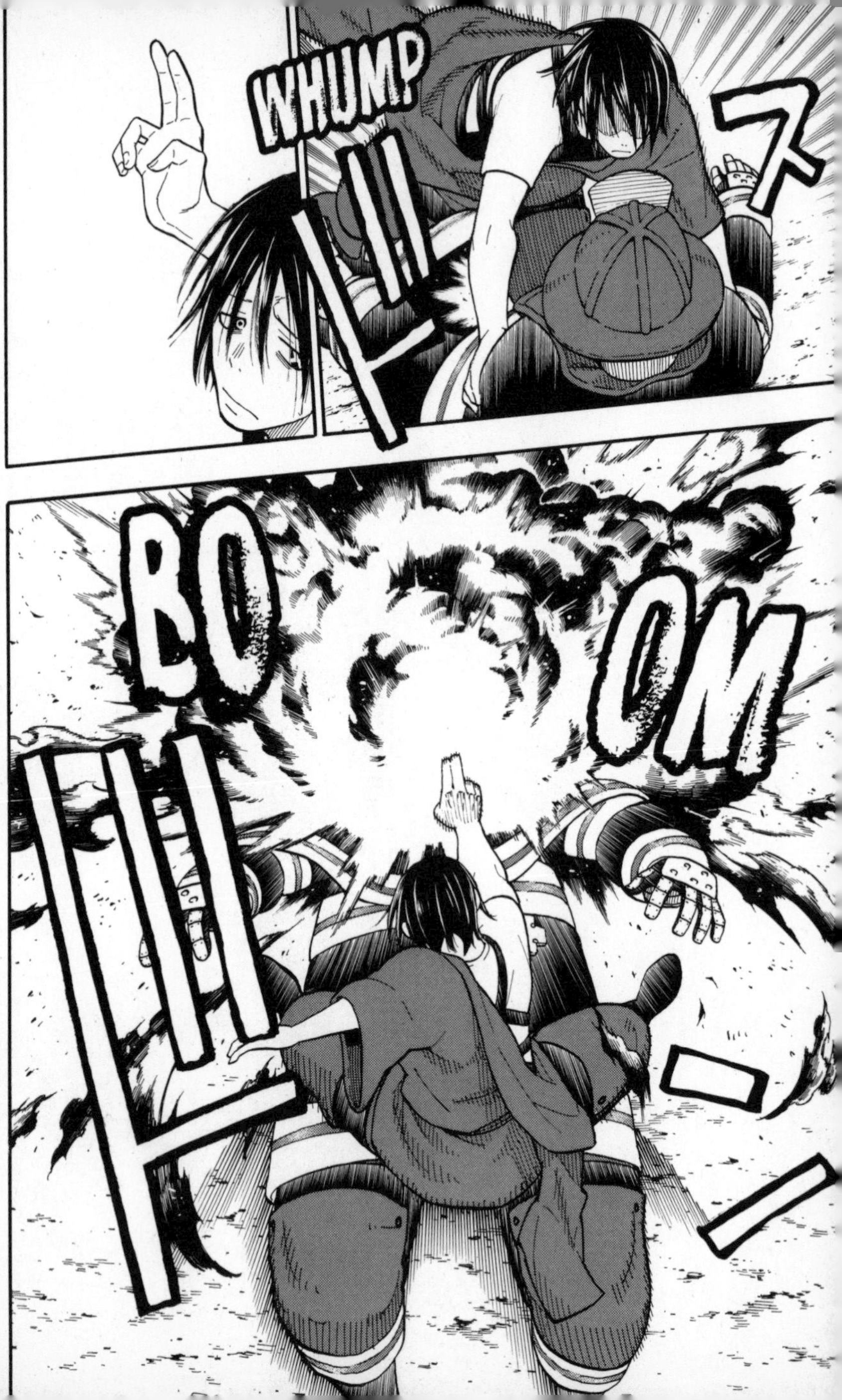
WHUMP
ス
BOOM

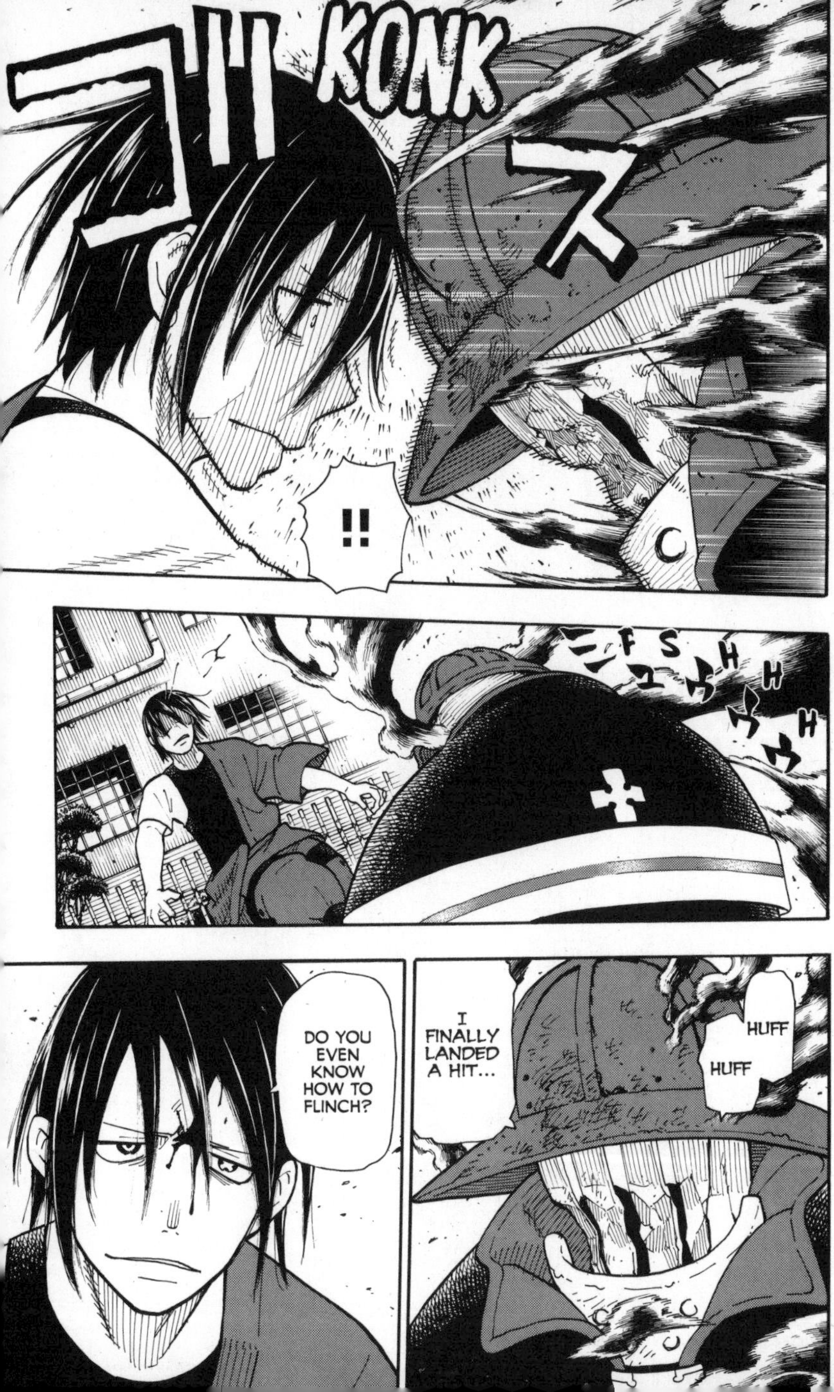
KONK
!!
FSHHHH
HUFF
HUFF
I FINALLY LANDED A HIT...
DO YOU EVEN KNOW HOW TO FLINCH?

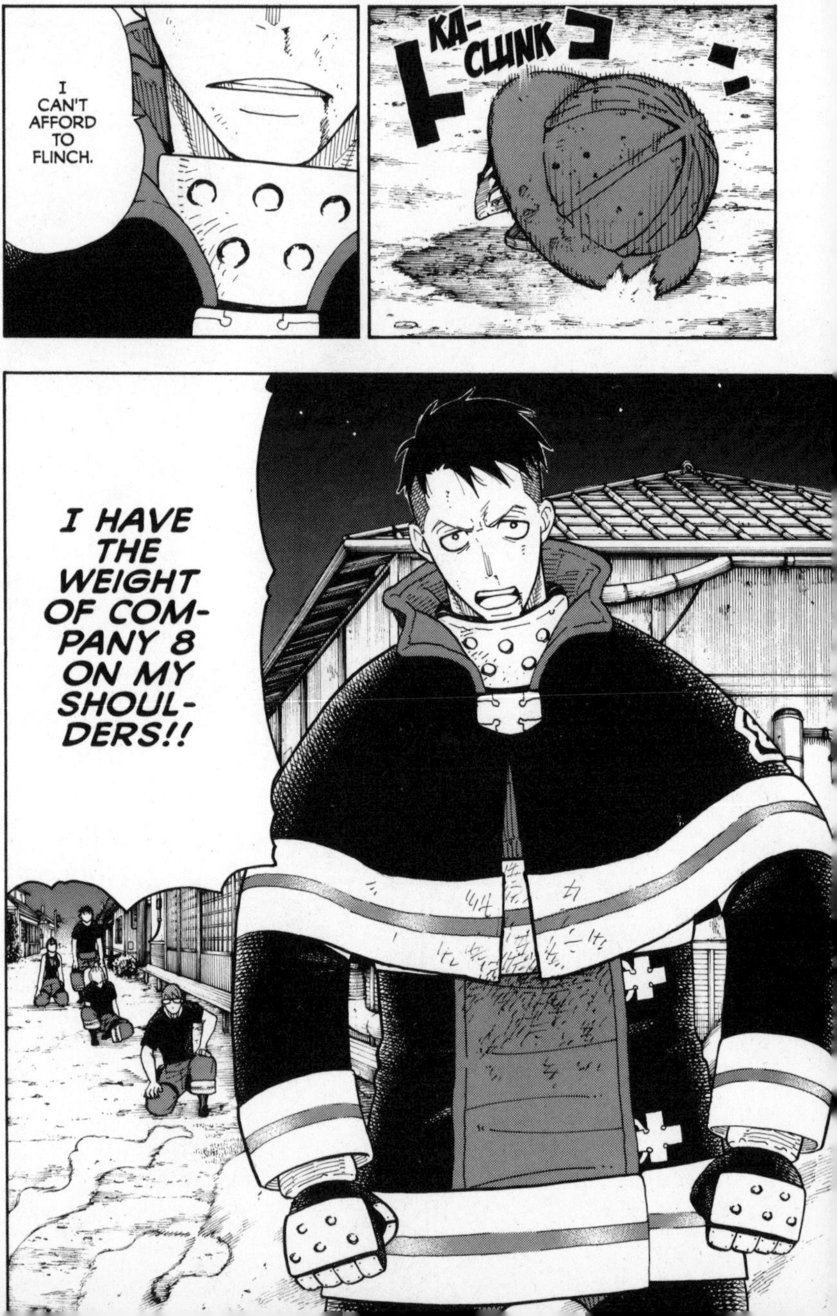
KA-CLUNK
I CAN'T AFFORD TO FLINCH.
I HAVE THE WEIGHT OF COMPANY 8 ON MY SHOULDERS!!

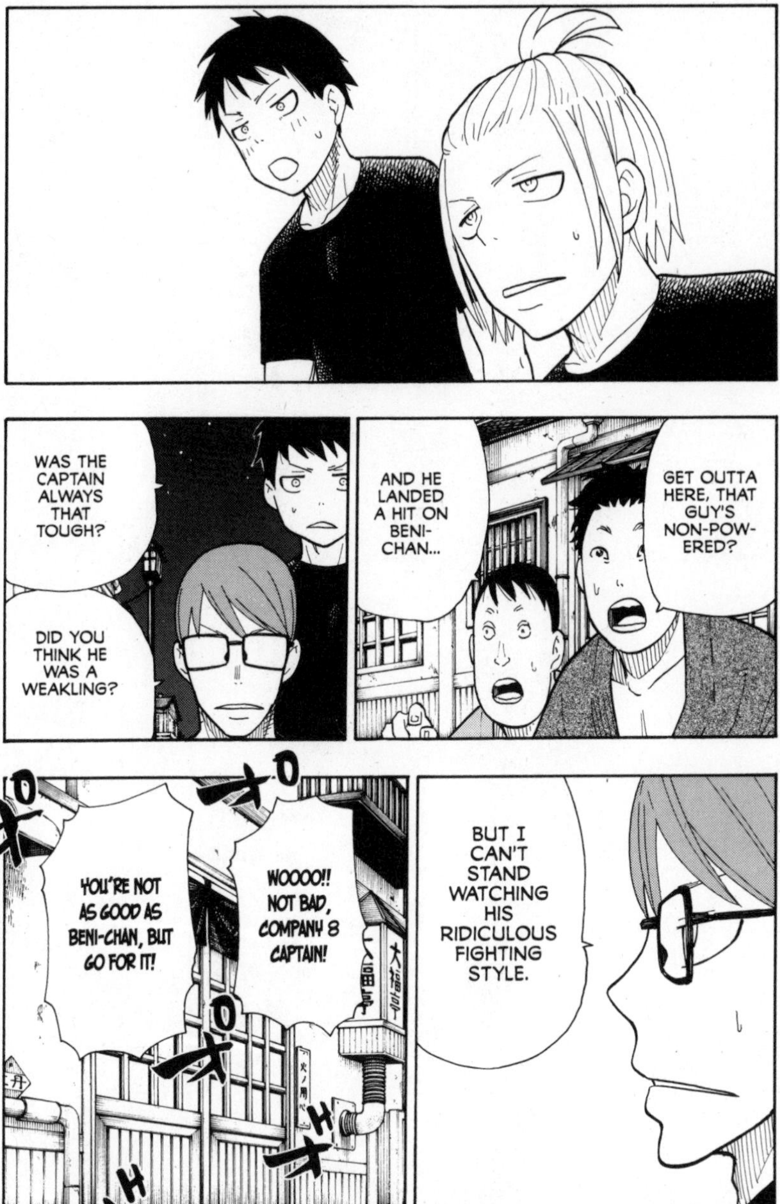
GET OUTTA HERE, THAT GUY'S NON-POWERED?
AND HE LANDED A HIT ON BENI-CHAN...
WAS THE CAPTAIN ALWAYS THAT TOUGH?
DID YOU THINK HE WAS A WEAKLING?
BUT I CAN'T STAND WATCHING HIS RIDICULOUS FIGHTING STYLE.
WOOOO!! NOT BAD, COMPANY 8 CAPTAIN!
YOU'RE NOT AS GOOD AS BENI-CHAN, BUT GO FOR IT!

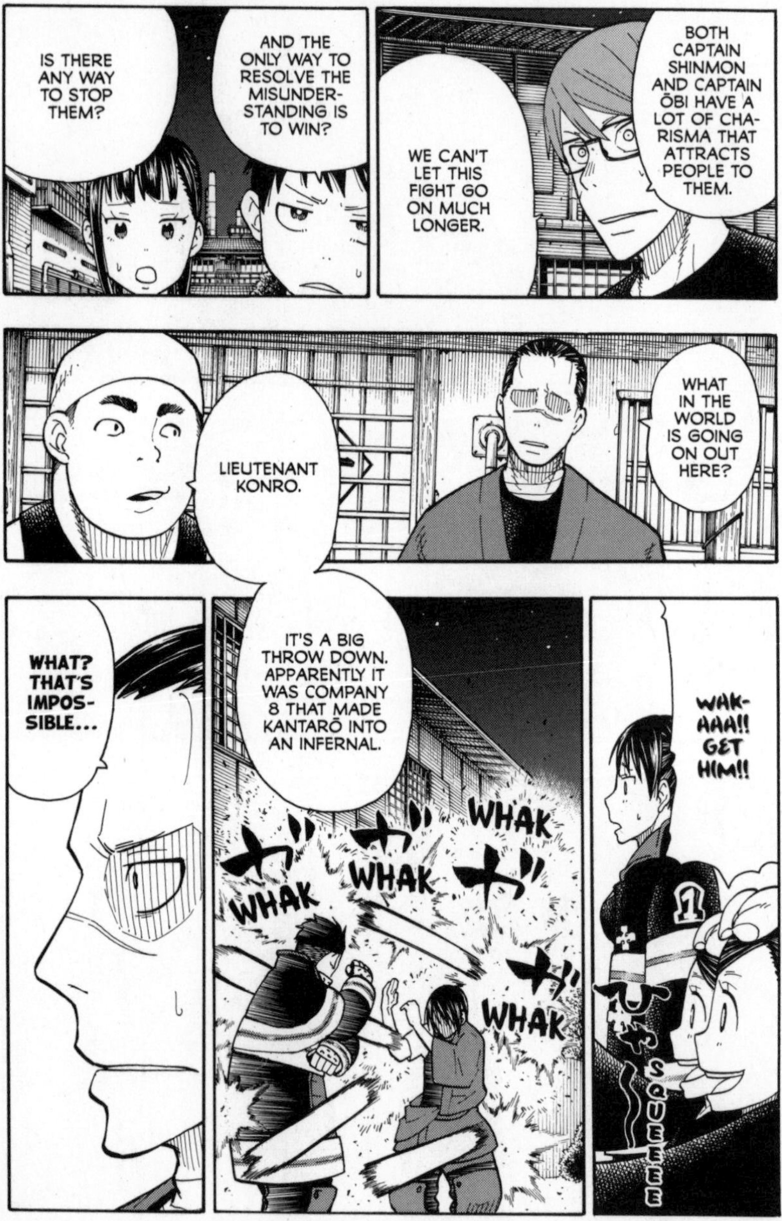
BOTH CAPTAIN SHINMON AND CAPTAIN ŌBI HAVE A LOT OF CHARISMA THAT ATTRACTS PEOPLE TO THEM.
WE CAN'T LET THIS FIGHT GO ON MUCH LONGER.
AND THE ONLY WAY TO RESOLVE THE MISUNDERSTANDING IS TO WIN?
IS THERE ANY WAY TO STOP THEM?
WHAT IN THE WORLD IS GOING ON OUT HERE?
LIEUTENANT KONRO.
WAK-AAA!! GET HIM!!
SQUEEEE
IT'S A BIG THROW DOWN. APPARENTLY IT WAS COMPANY 8 THAT MADE KANTARŌ INTO AN INFERNAL.
WHAK
WHAK
WHAK
WHAK
WHAT? THAT'S IMPOSSIBLE...

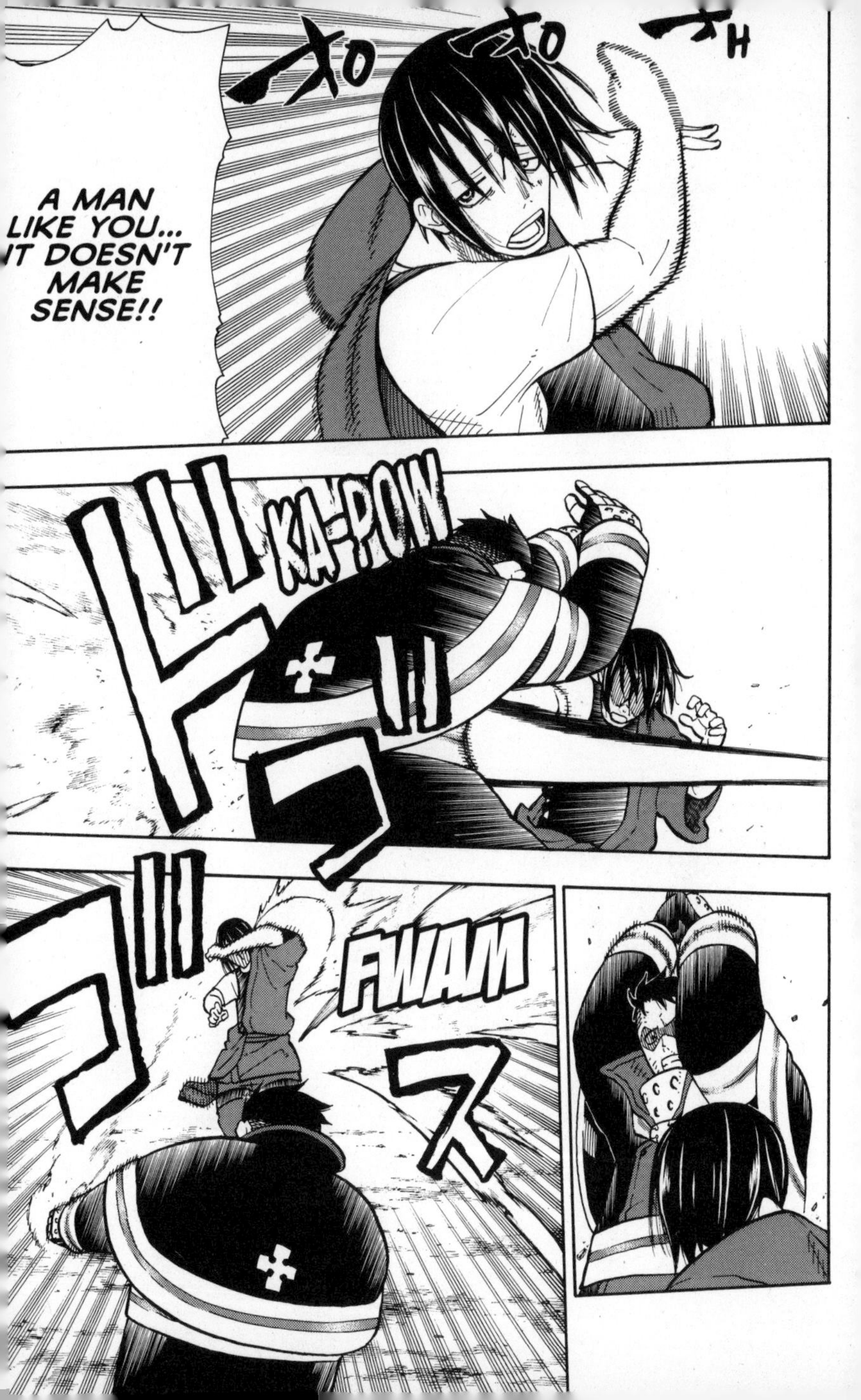
A MAN LIKE YOU... IT DOESN'T MAKE SENSE!!
KA-POW
FWAM

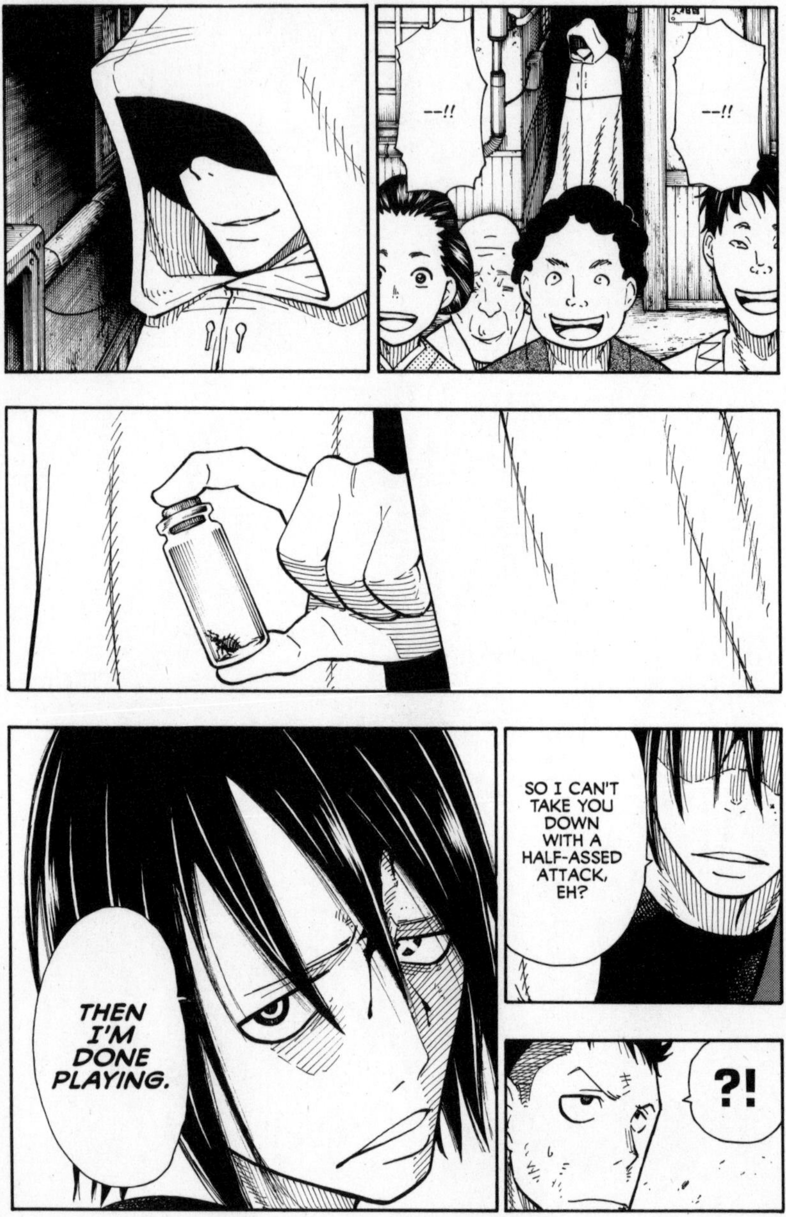
--!!
--!!
SO I CAN'T TAKE YOU DOWN WITH A HALF-ASSED ATTACK, EH?
?!
THEN I'M DONE PLAYING.

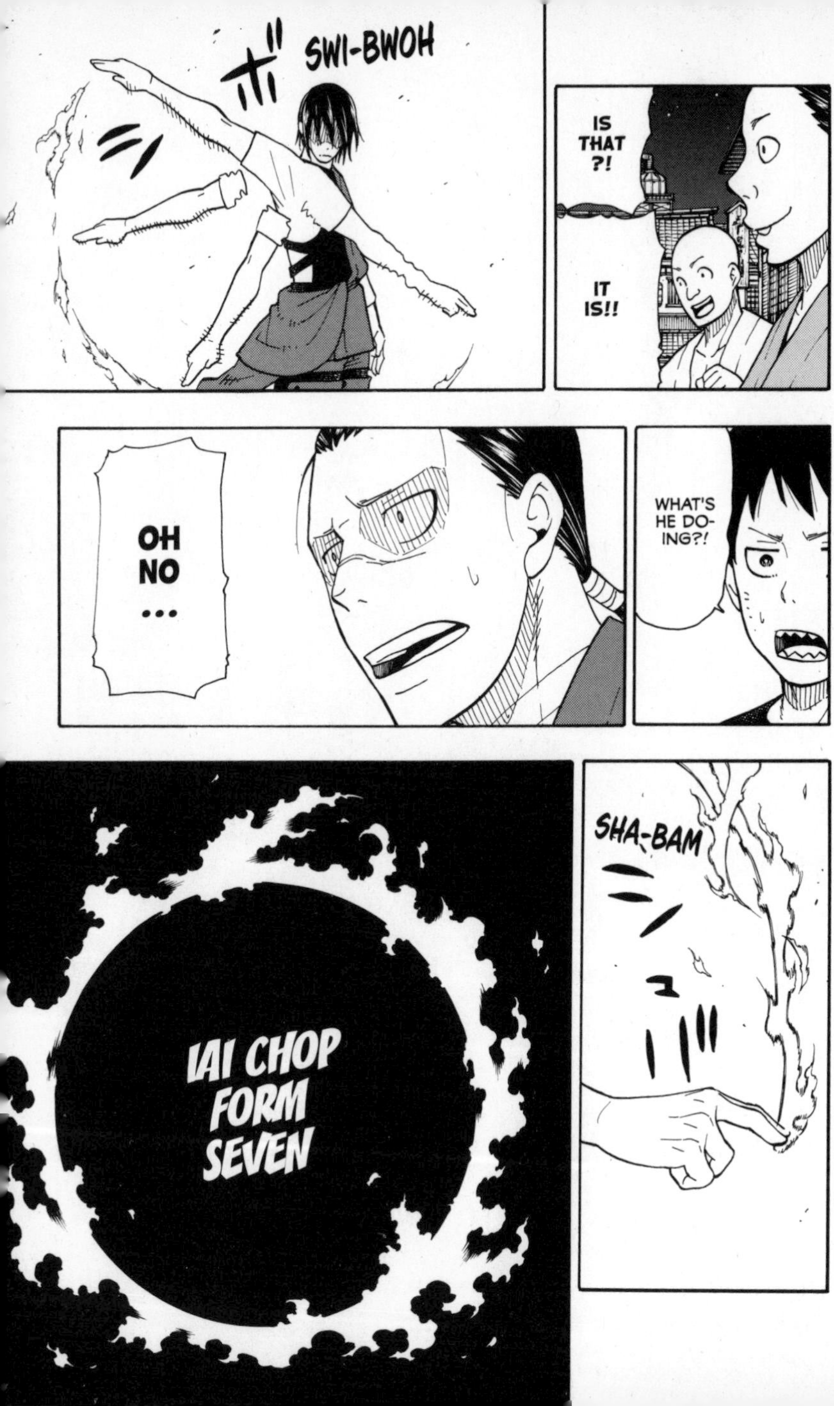
IS THAT?!
IT IS!!
SWI-BWOH
WHAT'S HE DO-ING?!
OH NO ...
SHA-BAM
IAI CHOP FORM SEVEN

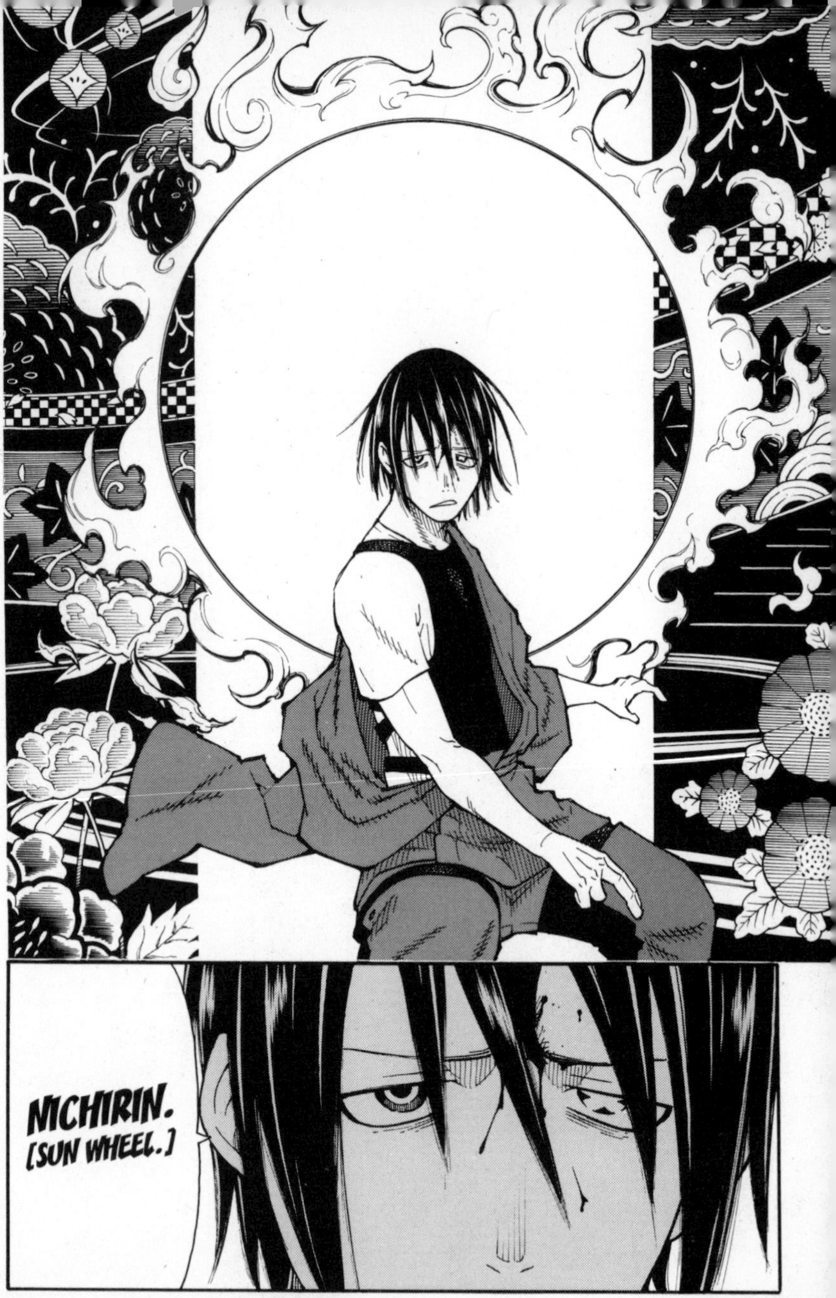
NICHIRIN.
[SUN WHEEL.]

TO BE CONTINUED IN VOLUME 6!!

FIRE FORCE

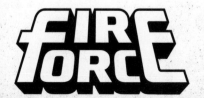

NATSU/SHINRA SCORCHING DOUBLE WHAMMY

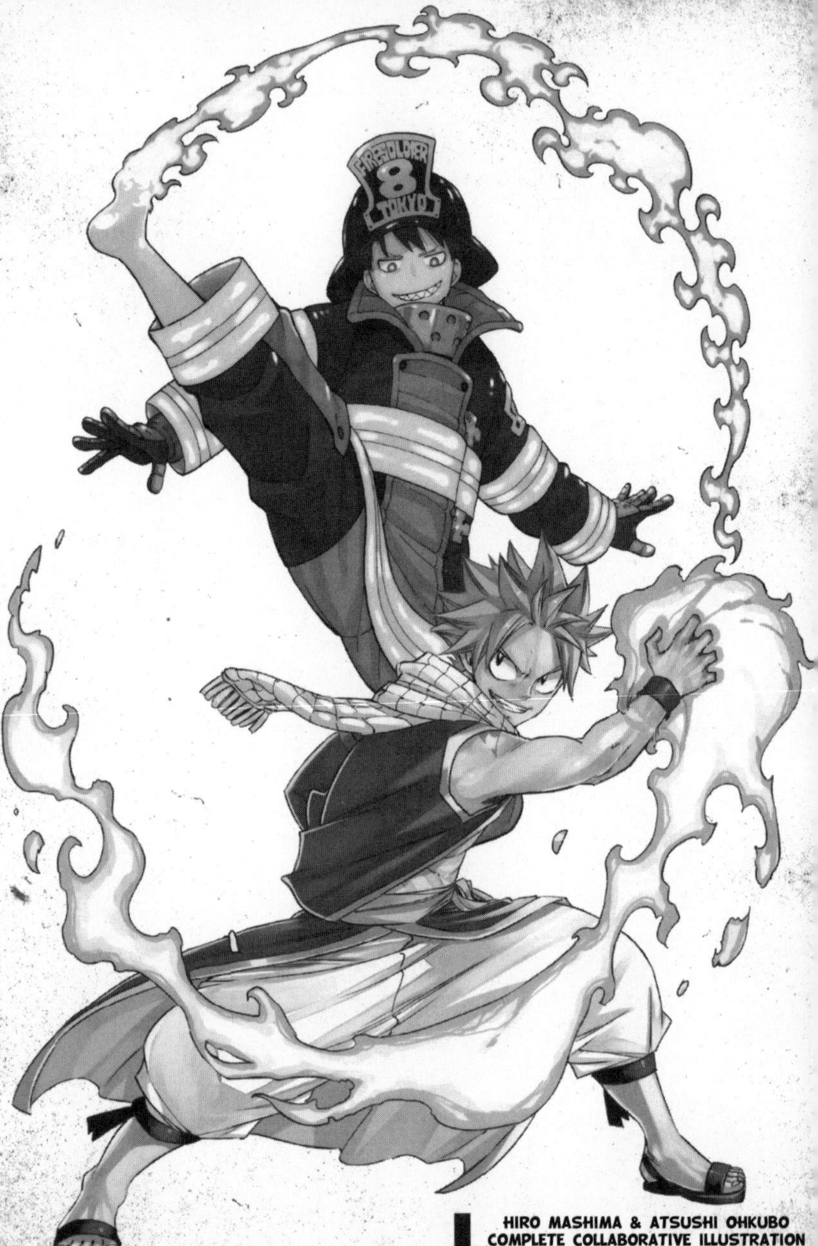
8
TOKYO

HIRO MASHIMA & ATSUSHI OHKUBO COMPLETE COLLABORATIVE ILLUSTRATION & INTERVIEW PUBLISHED IN *WEEKLY SHONEN MAGAZINE* ISSUE 27, 2016 (ON SALE JUNE 1, 2016)

HIRO MASHIMA × ATSUSHI OHKUBO

SEARING WHITE-HOT INTERVIEW!!!!

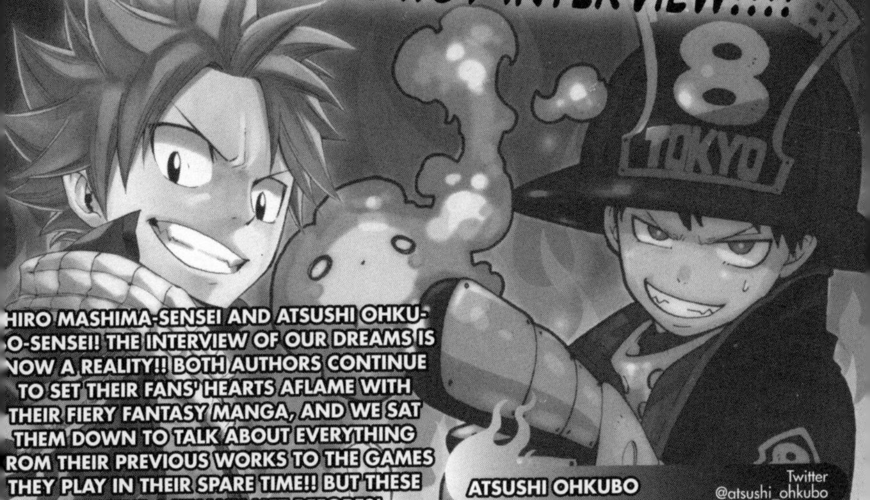

8
TOKYO

HIRO MASHIMA-SENSEI AND ATSUSHI OHKU-O-SENSEI! THE INTERVIEW OF OUR DREAMS IS NOW A REALITY!! BOTH AUTHORS CONTINUE TO SET THEIR FANS' HEARTS AFLAME WITH THEIR FIERY FANTASY MANGA, AND WE SAT THEM DOWN TO TALK ABOUT EVERYTHING ROM THEIR PREVIOUS WORKS TO THE GAMES THEY PLAY IN THEIR SPARE TIME!! BUT THESE TWO HAVE ACTUALLY MET BEFORE?!

HIRO MASHIMA Twitter @hiro_mashima

WINNER OF THE 1998 *SHONEN MAGAZINE* MANGA NEWCOMER AWARD FOR "MAGICIAN." HIS SERIES *RAVE MASTER*, WHICH BEGAN IN *WEEKLY SHONEN MAGAZINE* IN 1999, WAS A BIG HIT, AND WAS EVEN MADE INTO AN ANIME SERIES. HE'S BEEN WRITING BATTLE FANTASY MANGA ABOUT THE BONDS BETWEEN FRIENDS FOR *MAGAZINE* EVER SINCE. CURRENTLY, HE IS WORKING ON THE CLIMAX OF *FAIRY TAIL*! WHEN HE'S NOT WORKING, HE ENJOYS PLAYING GAMES WITH HIS STAFF!

ATSUSHI OHKUBO Twitter @atsushi_ohkubo

WINNER OF THE 3RD ENIX 21ST CENTURY MANGA AWARD IN 2001. THAT SAME YEAR, HE MADE HIS SERIAL DEBUT IN *MONTHLY SHONEN GANGAN* (PUBLISHED BY SQUARE-ENIX) WITH *B. ICHI*. HIS *SOUL EATER* ('04-'13, SAME PUBLISHER) WAS A BIG HIT THAT WAS ADAPTED INTO SEVERAL FORMS OF MEDIA. CURRENTLY, HE IS DRAWING *FIRE FORCE*. HIS UNIQUE CHARACTERS AND WORLD-BUILDING HAVE ATTRACTED MANY FANS. HE AND HIS STAFF DECIDE WHAT TO EAT AT WORK USING ROCK-PAPER-SCISSORS.

THIS ISN'T A FIRST-TIME MEETING ?!

QUESTION: Two artists of battle fantasy manga, with similar age and career histories, now battling it out for the first time! (ha ha)

ATSUSHI OHKUBO-SENSEI (OHKUBO): Yes! Mashima-sensei debuted three years before I did (Mashima-sensei debuted in 1998, Ohkubo-sensei in 2001), so I've been really excited to meet him today!

HIRO MASHIMA-SENSEI (MASHIMA): Actually, this isn't our first meeting. I said hi to Ohkubo-sensei once when he was working as Rando Ayamine-sensei's assistant on *GetBackers*.

Mashima (cont.): We were both about 20 years old. How long did it take you to go from assistant to your debut?

Ohkubo: Exactly two years.

Mashima: That's really fast. And if you don't mind my asking, if you were an assistant for *Magazine*, why did you debut in *Monthly Shonen GanGan* (ha ha)?

GIVING THE READERS SOME *MAGAZINE* FANTASY!!

Ohkubo: The reason I debuted with *Monthly Shonen GanGan* is that Enix (now Square-Enix) was close to my house... (ha ha). So I brought my work to them, and thankfully they said, "Let's publish it." It's the company that did *Dragon Quest*, so I thought I should write fantasy. Did you always know that you wanted to write fantasy, Mashima-sensei?

Mashima: Oh no, not at all. When I was just starting out, I drew modern stories, too. I wanted to draw fantasy, but they didn't really do that at *Magazine* at the time, so it was actually pretty rough.

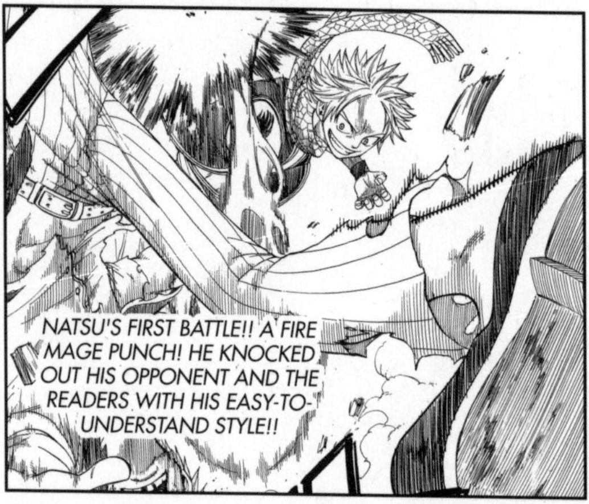
NATSU'S FIRST BATTLE!! A FIRE MAGE PUNCH! HE KNOCKED OUT HIS OPPONENT AND THE READERS WITH HIS EASY-TO-UNDERSTAND STYLE!!

Ohkubo: Right, even *GetBackers* was kind of outside of the norm. *Rave Master* was more of a fantasy, so I guess it kind of paved the way.

Mashima: I talked it over with my editor, and I was told it can't be like a *GanGan* or *Jump* fantasy; it had to be a *Magazine* fantasy.

Ohkubo: So what does that mean, specifically?

Mashima: It means, if nothing else, to make it easy to understand for readers who aren't used to fantasy. I was young at the time, so there were parts where I thought, "They'll understand if they just read it!" but thinking back on it, I'm glad my editor wasn't so lenient.

Ohkubo: I see. Readers who know fantasy will fill in the gaps in their own imaginations, but if they're not used to it, you have to explain the rules of the world clearly, or they might get frustrated and quit before they get to the really good parts. Actually, for *Fire*

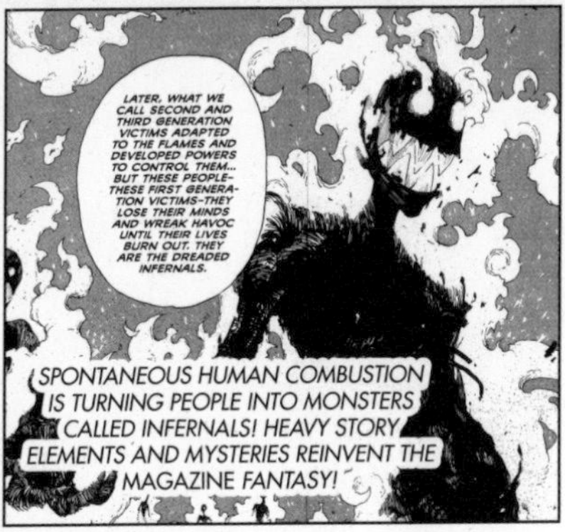
LATER, WHAT WE CALL SECOND AND THIRD GENERATION VICTIMS ADAPTED TO THE FLAMES AND DEVELOPED POWERS TO CONTROL THEM... BUT THESE PEOPLE– THESE FIRST GENERATION VICTIMS–THEY LOSE THEIR MINDS AND WREAK HAVOC UNTIL THEIR LIVES BURN OUT. THEY ARE THE DREADED INFERNALS.
SPONTANEOUS HUMAN COMBUSTION IS TURNING PEOPLE INTO MONSTERS CALLED INFERNALS! HEAVY STORY ELEMENTS AND MYSTERIES REINVENT THE MAGAZINE FANTASY!

Ohkubo (cont.): *Force*, I don't always bother to explain; I just go for it (ha ha). I probably wouldn't be able to do that if you hadn't laid that foundation, and if not for the current readership.
Mashima: Now the way I've been doing it is so firmly ingrained in me that if I do another series, maybe I'll have to borrow some strength from *Fire Force* to leave more things out (ha ha).

WHY MANGA? WHY FANTASY?

Question: Was it the influence of other fantasy works that you've come into contact with that motivated you both?
Mashima: That's right. I like manga, but I loved *Dragon Quest*.
Ohkubo: Yes. RPGs are very popular among our generation. And I had this thought, "Because I can only draw fantasy while I'm young!" But here I am in my 30s, still writing fantasy (ha ha).
Mashima: We'll probably still be doing it when we're 50 (ha ha).
Ohkubo: And maybe there's a lot of, "Only in manga." For example, if you tried to make a live-action *Fairy Tail* or *Fire Force*...
Mashima: Yeah, there are some things that you might not be able to pull off.
Ohkubo: Exactly. So I want to draw a world that works because it's a manga.

YOU LIKE THE GIRLS?! (HA HA) ABOUT THE CHARACTERS

Question: Allow me to ask you about each other's manga. Ohkubo-sensei, do you have a favorite character in *Fairy Tail*?
Ohkubo: Brandish! She's too cute!! Mashima-sensei's series have such cute girls, I look forward to every issue!
Mashima: Thank you very much (ha ha). Speaking of female characters, I like Tamaki. I've never seen a character like that, with a lucky lecher lure.

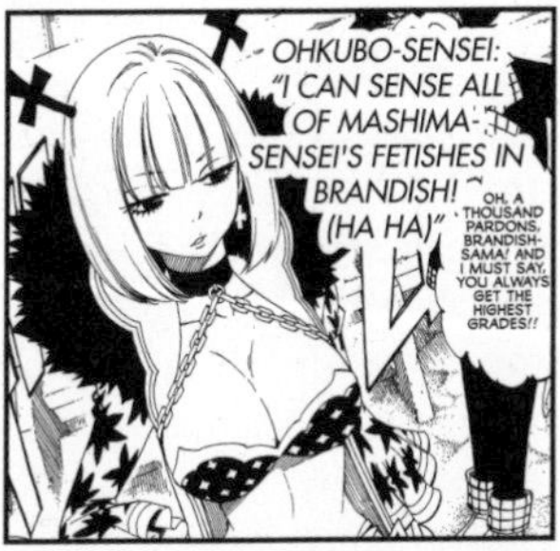
OH, A THOUSAND PARDONS, BRANDISH-SAMA! AND I MUST SAY, YOU ALWAYS GET THE HIGHEST GRADES!!
OHKUBO-SENSEI: "I CAN SENSE ALL OF MASHIMA-SENSEI'S FETISHES IN BRANDISH! (HA HA)"

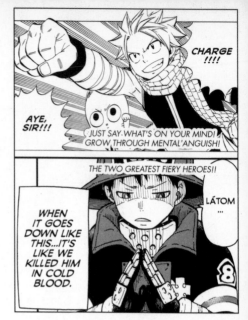

CHARGE !!!!
AYE, SIR!!!
JUST SAY WHAT'S ON YOUR MIND! GROW THROUGH MENTAL ANGUISH!
THE TWO GREATEST FIERY HEROES!!
LÁTOM ...
WHEN IT GOES DOWN LIKE THIS...IT'S LIKE WE KILLED HIM IN COLD BLOOD.

Mashima (cont.): But it's actually funny without getting vulgar.

Ohkubo: Sexy scenes don't get so dirty when you make them comical, so I'm always keeping that in mind.

Mashima: I want you to transfer her to Company 8 so she can be in it more (ha ha).

Ohkubo: Thank you (ha ha).

Mashima: And Shinra's smirk when he gets nervous—that left an impression on me, too. I love drawing faces like that. I read it and thought, "It must be hard to keep going with that."

Ohkubo: He's not smiling out of overconfidence—he's really taking these problems very seriously, but he can't help smiling. But Natsu is a hero with a lot of confidence. I can't draw that type of character myself, so I really admire it when I see it.

Mashima: Yeah, *Rave Master*'s Haru was the angsty hard-working type, so I thought let's just take it easy this time (ha ha).

Ohkubo: I see! In my case, I tried to challenge myself with an upbeat character and failed, so we went in reverse order (ha ha). And I'm dealing in a somewhat serious theme with firefighting, which isn't really a good fit with a character who doesn't think too much, so that was part of it.

Mashima: I really get that from reading it. I feel like there's a lot of entertainment out there right now that doesn't care much about human life, but *Fire Force* takes it very seriously. You're really portraying life and death like a real thing, and I think that's amazing.

Ohkubo: Well, life was treated very casually in *Soul Eater* (ha ha), so it might be the pendulum swinging the other way.

Mashima: And I think it's pretty original that everyone's powers in *Fire Force* are fire-related. Usually you get all different types, right?

Ohkubo: I'm a little twisted, so I was like, "It'd be pretty interesting if everybody had the same power." The lucky lecher lure came from my twisted and kind of perverse nature, too (ha ha).

HARDCORE!! GAME TALK!!

Question: This is your first weekly series, right, Ohkubo-sensei? How is the schedule working out for you?

Ohkubo: I'm surprised at how fast the graphic novels come out, but I do get breaks. When I'm not working, I play video games. Lately, I spend all my time on *Dark Souls 3* (the latest in the action-RPG series from FromSoftware). I've been through it three or four times now.

Mashima: Seriously?!! I've been wanting to play that forever, but I haven't gotten a chance to (ha ha). My staff even tells me, "If you like *Monster Hunter*, you'll wanna own this one!"

Ohkubo: I've been playing *Monster Hunter* since the first game, too, but now I'm taking a break from collecting honey (a standard item used in combinations) (ha ha). You're pretty famous for liking video games, Mashima-sensei. What are you playing lately?

Mashima: I just beat *Far Cry Primal* (the latest in the hit action-adventure series by UbiSoft). I've been playing a lot of western games lately.

Ohkubo: Western games are great. I'm hooked on them, too. You can really become the main character, and get immersed in the world. I like watching the really cool cut scenes, too.

Mashima: I like to play for the stories, too, so I'm the type to just keep watching cut scenes forever (ha ha).
(After this, the two talked at length about first-person shooters, fighting games, and other video games.)

TRICKS OF THE TRADE ?!

Question: You're too hardcore! This isn't going in a game magazine, you know! Talk about your jobs! (ha ha)

Ohkubo: Yes, sir (ha ha). I get a full day off every week. What about you, Mashima-sensei?

Mashima: That's impressive. I think I could get a full day off, but I couldn't spend a day without drawing.

Ohkubo: You're always drawing on Twitter, too.

Mashima: If I don't draw, my art really suffers.

Ohkubo: That's true; I might be a little off my game on my first day of work. Or maybe I just don't want to tackle the manuscript (ha ha).

Mashima: For me, the first day is the most fun, and then I get tired of it as it goes on (ha ha).

MASHIMA-SENSEI'S TWITTER FEED (@HIRO_MASIMA) IS FULL OF FUN DOODLES♪

Mashima (cont.): By the time I get to the finishing touches, I'm already composing my next rough draft in my head (ha ha). Do you draw in order from page one, Ohkubo-sensei?

Ohkubo: Yes. Don't you?

Mashima: I start with the page I want to draw (ha ha). But I've changed my perspective lately, and now I'm trying to save those scenes for later so I don't get bored by the end. Like the pervy scenes...just kidding (ha ha). If there's, like, a scene with Natsu looking really cool, I'll save that for last.

Ohkubo: I know the feeling! It's important to have scenes that get you excited! If you're gonna be a manga artist, you have to have fun with it! (ha ha)

Question: We're almost out of time, so.... One last question: do you have any requests for the kinds of scenes or plot developments you'd like to see?

I WANT TO SEE THIS HAPPEN!!

Mashima: I want to know about all of the Special Fire Force Companies, and have lots more characters, good guys and bad guys. And I'm looking forward to when the world expands past the bounds of the Fire Force. And one more thing—this is very important, so I'm repeating it. Please put Tamaki in Company 8 with Shinra! (ha ha)

Ohkubo: Look forward to it (ha ha). For me, first, I want scenes with cute girls! (ha ha) Also, I'm reading *Fairy Tail*'s climax with bated breath. I want to see lots of Natsu doing big cool things for a long time. Whether it's fighting or drama, I want to see Natsu! I'm sure he's still got some crazy super-powerful techniques up his sleeve!

Mashima: You might see one soon. One thing I can say is that the series has gone on so long, I have to end it in a way that the readers can be happy with. Let's just say there definitely won't be a bad ending.

Ohkubo: Yay! I'm excited! I'll be looking forward to it with the all of the other readers!

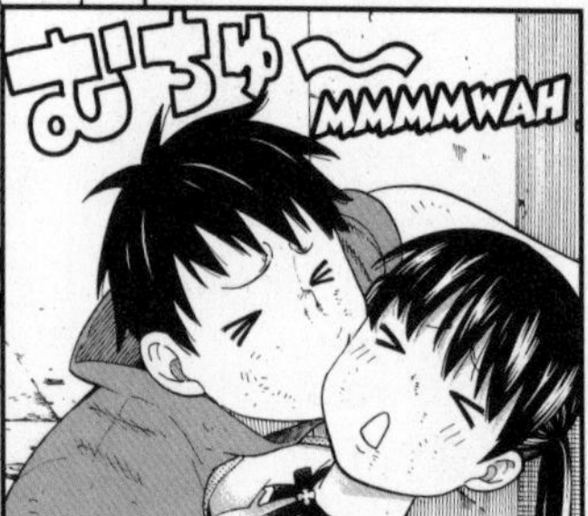
むちゅ〜
MMMMWAH

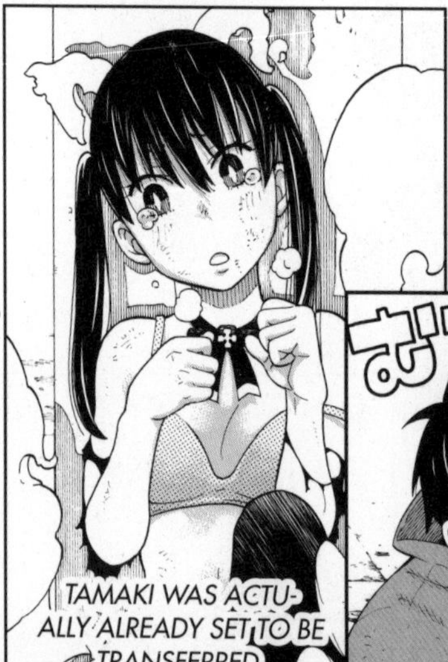
TAMAKI WAS ACTUALLY ALREADY SET TO BE TRANSFERRED.

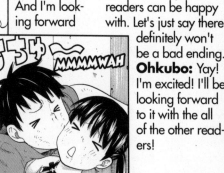

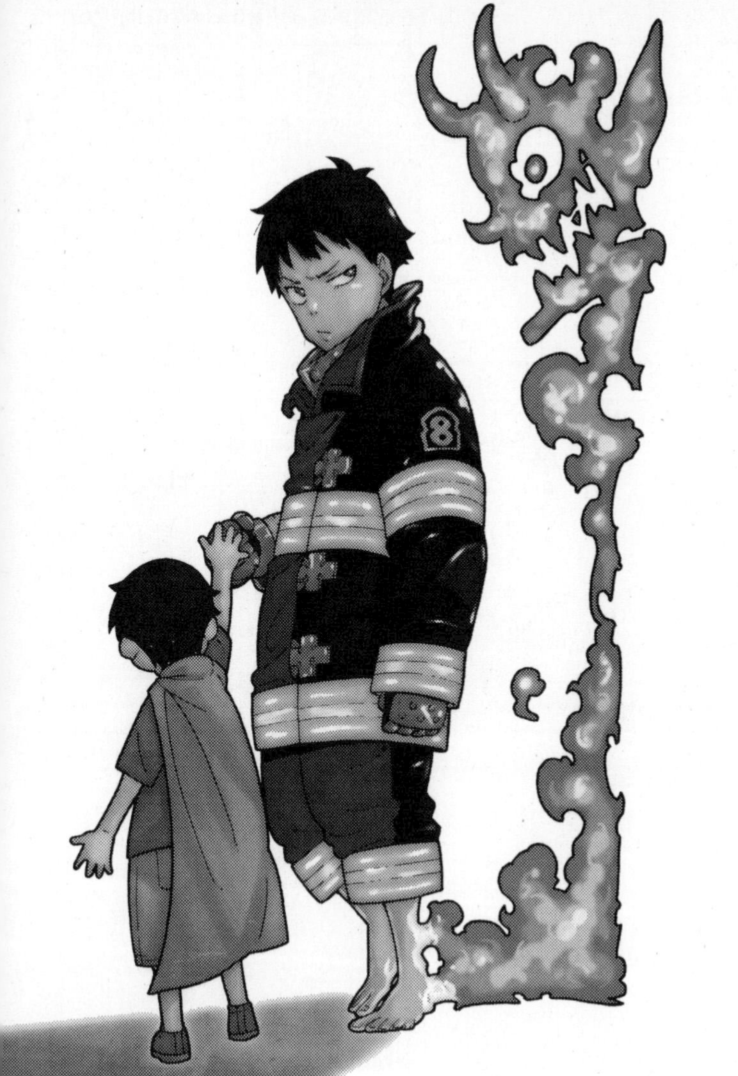

TO BE CONTINUED IN VOLUME 6!!

AFTERWORD MANGA: ATSUSHIYA

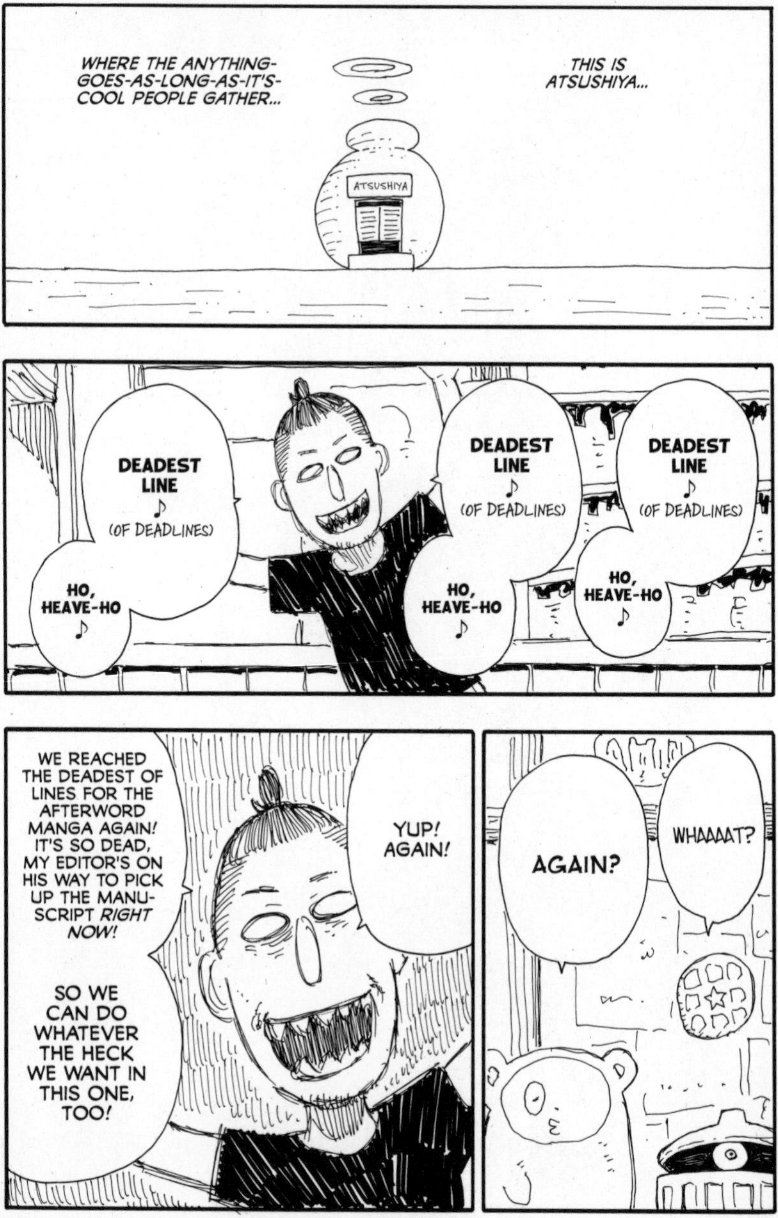

THIS IS ATSUSHIYA...
ATSUSHIYA
WHERE THE ANYTHING-GOES-AS-LONG-AS-IT'S-COOL PEOPLE GATHER...
DEADEST LINE ♪ (OF DEADLINES)
HO, HEAVE-HO ♪
DEADEST LINE ♪ (OF DEADLINES)
HO, HEAVE-HO ♪
DEADEST LINE ♪ (OF DEADLINES)
HO, HEAVE-HO ♪
WHAAAAT?
AGAIN?
YUP! AGAIN!
WE REACHED THE DEADEST OF LINES FOR THE AFTERWORD MANGA AGAIN! IT'S SO DEAD, MY EDITOR'S ON HIS WAY TO PICK UP THE MANU-SCRIPT *RIGHT NOW!*
SO WE CAN DO WHATEVER THE HECK WE WANT IN THIS ONE, TOO!

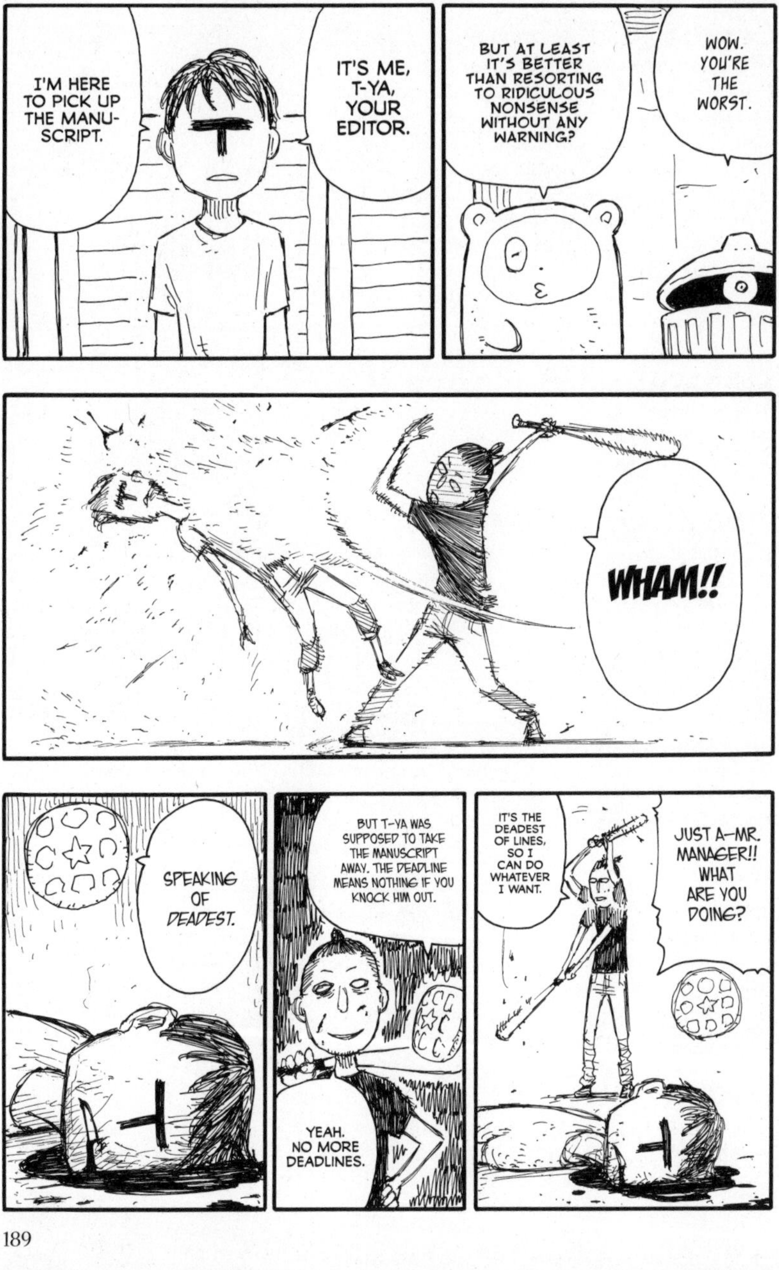
WOW. YOU'RE THE WORST.
BUT AT LEAST IT'S BETTER THAN RESORTING TO RIDICULOUS NONSENSE WITHOUT ANY WARNING?
IT'S ME, T-YA, YOUR EDITOR.
I'M HERE TO PICK UP THE MANU-SCRIPT.
WHAM!!
JUST A—MR. MANAGER!! WHAT ARE YOU DOING?
IT'S THE DEADEST OF LINES, SO I CAN DO WHATEVER I WANT.
BUT T-YA WAS SUPPOSED TO TAKE THE MANUSCRIPT AWAY. THE DEADLINE MEANS NOTHING IF YOU KNOCK HIM OUT.
YEAH. NO MORE DEADLINES.
SPEAKING OF *DEADEST.*

Translation Notes:

Candle in the wind, page 16

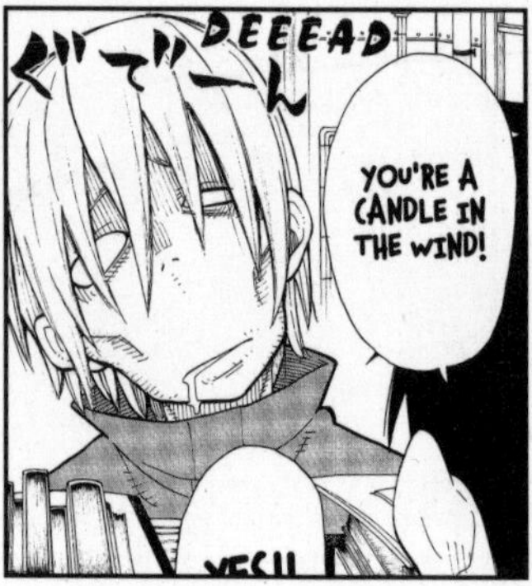
DEEEAD
YOU'RE A CANDLE IN THE WIND!

A Japanese idiom that refers to someone on the brink of death is *fūzen no tomoshibi*, or "light in the wind." Normally the translators might have used a more obvious idiom for this modern era of electricity, but first, fire imagery is always appropriate in this series, and second, while Shinra probably wouldn't use the phrase if he knew this, by calling Arthur "a candle in the wind," he is also making a reference to The Candle in the Wind, the last book in T.H. White's Arthurian fantasy series, *The Once and Future King*.

Signature stamp, page 46

Here, Takehisa is "signing" the paperwork to complete this registration. In Japan it is common practice to use an *inkan*, or signature seal, to stamp one's name on official documents, package delivery forms, etc., in lieu of signing one's name.

Two infernals, page 53

In Japanese, there are many different ways to count things, depending on what those things are. In this scene, Ōbi is describing the infernals using the counter for people, while the officer from Company 3 uses the counter that signifies animals, meaning he sees the infernals as less than human—something that surely contributes to Ōbi's decision!

Kaminarimon, page 86

Despite the steampunk embellishments, this temple is still recognizable as the Thunder Gate of the famous Sensō-ji temple in Asakusa. The big lantern, while being one of the temple's most identifiable features, has a dragon carving on the bottom that is supposed to be a charm to ward off fires.

Hoppy, *motsuyaki*, and *monja*, page 87

Hoppy is a drink that is unique to Tokyo and was made as a substitute for beer, which was considered a luxury back when Hoppy was invented in 1948. It's mostly non-alcoholic, but is intended to be mixed with stronger (and cheaper) spirits. *Motsuyaki* is grilled organ meat (heart, liver, etc.) served on skewers, and *monja* (short for *monjayaki*) is a sort of thin, savory pancake that is cooked with all kinds of chopped ingredients such as vegetables, seafood, or even cheese.

Daifuku, page 90

Daifuku, or *daifukumochi*, is a sweet Japanese treat. It's a mochi glutinous rice cake on the outside and red bean paste filling on the inside.

Fire brigade and the flowers of Edo, page 99

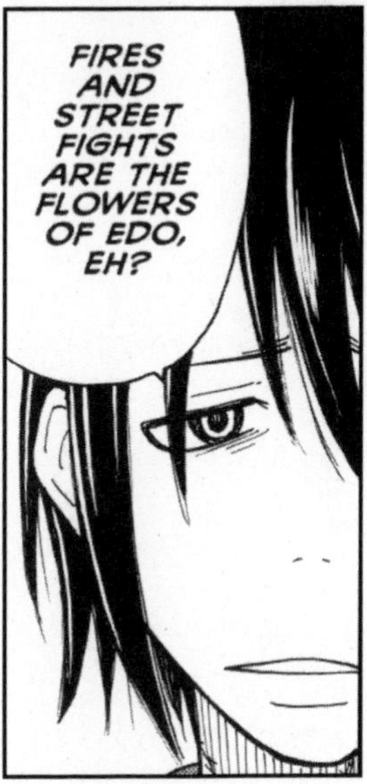
FIRES AND STREET FIGHTS ARE THE FLOWERS OF EDO, EH?

Edo is the old name of Japan's capital, Tokyo. Back when it was called Edo, widespread fires were a common occurrence, and the people themselves were so hot-tempered that fights would break out easily as well, hence the saying that fires and street fights were the flowers of Edo. To fight these fires, a *hikeshi* system was formed. *Hikeshi* literally means "fire extinguisher," and it can refer to the organization, or to a single firefighter—the translators chose to use "fire brigade" for the organization and *hikeshi* for individuals. The *hikeshi*'s main method for putting out fires was to prevent them from spreading by destroying the buildings surrounding the fire. Of course, the system had its own problems, which led to several fights among *hikeshi*, thus increasing the "flowers" of fighting in an attempt to weed out the flowers of fire.

Matoi, page 101

Just as they are being used here, a *matoi* is a kind of banner used by *hikeshi* during the Edo era to signal to the other firefighters which building or area is on fire. The *matoi-mochi*, or standard-bearer, would take the *matoi* to the roof of the building and wave it to catch the attention of the others. Each *hikeshi* brigade had its own *matoi*, and often there would be a race to see who could get to the fire first. This particular *matoi* carries the number seven, for Company 7.

Hey, kites, page 119

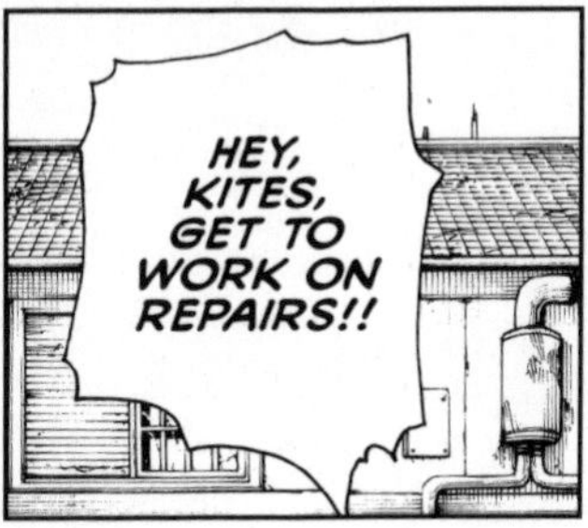
HEY, KITES, GET TO WORK ON REPAIRS!!

Here, Benimaru calls these men *tobi*, which is the Japanese name for the black kite, a type of bird of prey. It's also a slang term for any sort of laborer who works in high places, like a firefighter or construction worker. It originated as a word for firefighter, because they jumped from roof to roof, and because the tool they used for pulling down burning buildings was a *tobiguchi*, or "kite's mouth," probably because of its resemblance to a bird's beak.

Iai Chop, page 153

Iai, or *iaido*, is a Japanese martial art that specializes in techniques that involve drawing a sword and striking an opponent down in a single motion. As the reader can see, Benimaru has no sword, so instead, he uses his hand as a *shuto*, or "hand blade."

A Kodansha Comics Trade Paperback Original.

Fire Force volume 5 copyright © 2016 Atsushi Ohkubo
English translation copyright © 2017 Atsushi Ohkubo

Published in the United States by Kodansha Comics, an imprint of Kodansha USA Publishing, LLC, New York.

Publication rights for this English edition arranged through Kodansha Ltd., Tokyo. First

published in Japan in 2016 by Kodansha Ltd., Tokyo.

ISBN 978-1-63236-432-6

Printed and bound in Germany by GGP Media GmbH, Poessneck.

www.kodansha.us

9 8 7 6

Translation: Alethea Nibley & Athena Nibley
Lettering: AndWorld Design
Editing: Lauren Scanlan
Kodansha Comics edition cover design: Phil Balsman